Microsoft® Exchange Server

Planning, Design, and Implementation

Digital Press Editorial Board

Samuel H. Fuller, Chairman
Richard W. Beane
Donald Z. Harbert
William R. Hawe
Richard J. Hollingsworth
William Laing
Richard F. Lary
Alan G. Nemeth
Pauline Nist
Robert M. Supnik

Microsoft® Exchange Server

Planning, Design, and Implementation

Tony Redmond

Digital Press
Boston • Oxford • Johannesburg • Melbourne • New Delhi • Singapore

Digital Press™ is an imprint of Butterworth–Heinemann

Copyright © 1997 Tony Redmond

∞ A member of the Reed Elsevier group

All rights reserved.

All trademarks found herein are property of their respective owners.

No part of this publication may be reproduced, stored in a retrieval system, or transmitted in any form or by any means, electronic, mechanical, photocopying, recording, or otherwise, without the prior written permission of the publisher.

∞ Recognizing the importance of preserving what has been written, Butterworth–Heinemann prints its books on acid-free paper whenever possible.

Library of Congress Cataloging-in-Publication Data

Redmond, Tony, 1959–
    Microsoft exchange server : planning, design, and implementation / Tony Redmond.
        p.   cm.
    Includes index.
    ISBN 1-55558-162-5 (pbk. : alk. paper)
    1. Microsoft Exchange. 2. Client/server computing. I. Title.
QA76.9.C55R42   1997
005.7'13—dc20
                                          96-32690
                                              CIP

British Library Cataloguing-in-Publication Data

A catalogue record for this book is available from the British Library.

The publisher offers special discounts on bulk orders of this book.
For information, please contact:

    Manager of Special Sales
    Butterworth–Heinemann
    313 Washington Street
    Newton, MA 02158–1626
    Tel: 617-928-2500
    Fax: 617-928-2620

For information on all Digital Press publications available, contact our World Wide Web home page at: **http://www.bh.com/dp**

Order number: EY-U089E-DP

10 9 8 7 6 5 4 3 2 1

Design and composition by ReadyText, Bath, UK
Printed in the United States of America

Dedication

Clearly I couldn't write books about e-mail systems without an enormous amount of support from my wife and children. They continue to provide that support in an uncomplaining manner, although I know that when I write they suffer the pains generated by a concentrated author. They deserve every dedication I can muster.

Microsoft Exchange Server is a hot new technology which, like most new technologies, is evolving rapidly all the time. Exchange will go through many new versions over its lifetime, and Digital Press is committed to keeping you up to date with these new versions of Exchange via this book. As such, there will be frequent new and revised editions of this book. For more information on when new editions will be available, and information they'll contain, please be sure to visit our WWW site at:

http://www.bh.com/dp
or
http://www.butterworth.heinemann.co.uk

Contents

Preface   xi

    A practical approach   xi
    Building towards success   xv
    Acknowledgments   xvi

1 Introducing Microsoft Exchange Server   1

    The Exchange program   1
    The Microsoft BackOffice program   4
    A quick overview of Exchange Server   6
    One-stop system management   14
    MAPI: the rock on which Exchange Server is built   16
    A wide range of Exchange clients   21
    Schedule+   38
    Is Exchange Server a mail system or groupware?   39
    Integration with other Microsoft products   45
    Exchange and the Internet   47
    Challenges for Microsoft Exchange Server   51

2 Establishing the Infrastructure for Exchange Server   55

    Introduction   55
    Organizations, sites, and servers   55
    Windows NT, domains, and security   59
    Connecting sites   75
    Permissions   87

3 Selecting Hardware for Exchange Server — 91

Hardware resources — 91
Sizing an operational system — 92
A growing strain on existing network resources? — 112

4 Managing Exchange Server — 115

Recipients, mailboxes, and people — 115
Managing user mailboxes — 118
Client installations and settings — 130
Replication — 136
Maintaining Exchange Information Stores — 145
Managing the Public Information Store — 171
System backups — 186
Information store maintenance — 198
Keeping messages secret — 201

5 Connecting Exchange Server — 219

Exchange connectors — 219
Maintaining the Message Transfer Agent and connectors — 229
General notes on Exchange connectors — 234
Configuring and operating a site connector — 236
Exchange Server, X.400, and X.500 — 240
The Exchange Internet Mail Connector — 261
Connecting to Microsoft Mail — 276
The Microsoft Exchange Directory Service — 282
Directory synchronization and replication — 291

6 Conducting a Pilot for Exchange Server — 301

Introduction — 301
Approaching a pilot — 302
Training — 305
Was the pilot successful? — 307
Summary — 308

7 Migrating from Other Messaging Systems — 309

Introduction — 309
An end, or a beginning? — 309
Why migrate at all? — 311
When will the migration be over? — 319
Migrating information — 322
Coexisting with other messaging systems — 334

8 Keeping your Exchange Server Healthy — 341

Performance Optimizer — 341
Message tracking — 347
The Exchange Load Simulator — 353
Using the Windows NT Performance Monitor — 360
Logging and viewing Windows NT events — 364
The Exchange Resource Kit — 365

9 Using Electronic Forms with Exchange Server — 371

Introduction — 371
Components of the Exchange Application
   Design Application — 372

What types of e-forms applications can I build? 376
Developing a new e-form application 378

10 Bringing It All Together – How to Proceed 385

10 things you'll enjoy about Exchange Server 385
Some things that aren't so good 386
10 essential points to get right when
   implementing Exchange Server 387

Acronyms **389**
Useful Points of Reference **393**
Appendix **395**
Index **399**

Preface

A practical approach

Microsoft, along with many other attributes, is probably the world's best marketing company when it comes to PC software. It is very easy to fall into the habit of believing everything that comes out of Microsoft HQ in Redmond, Washington (I think the name of the town is so appropriate...), and sometimes I feel that the books written about Microsoft products occasionally (or even frequently) fall into the trap of wearing rose-tinted glasses.

This is not a book lauding the virtues and benefits of the Microsoft Exchange Server. It is, I hope, a hard-nosed and practical look at what the server is good at along with some views on the places where the server, in my view, falls down. All furnished with a pragmatic approach to the business of implementing Exchange Server and its clients within corporate messaging infrastructures.

I have deliberately neglected the opportunity to write in detail about the various clients that can be connected to an Exchange server. Clients are mentioned whenever appropriate and a brief overview of their functionality is included. Overall, I believe the server is much more interesting than the clients, and the successful implementation of multiple Exchange servers distributed across a networked landscape presents enough issues to challenge even experienced electronic messaging specialists. The temptation to recycle the contents of the Microsoft Exchange Server documentation has also been avoided. I should note that the documentation provided with Exchange Server is comprehensive and often illuminating. Much good advice is contained therein, and anyone who wants to work with Exchange Server should invest the necessary time to carefully peruse the documentation.

I work for Digital Equipment Corporation (referred to as Digital from here on), a company which occupies an interesting position when it comes to Microsoft Exchange Server. There have certainly been a wide variety of views within different parts of Digital over the last year or so. As a long-standing Digital employee I'd very much like to see Exchange Server being implemented on Windows NT systems powered by the high-speed Alpha (sometimes called AXP) CPU. On the other hand, as a Digital employee who has been helping customers to install and operate electronic mail systems since 1982, I sometimes find that Exchange Server is in direct competition with some of the Digital products that I've advocated in that time, an issue amplified by the migration utilities packaged with Exchange to enable users of Digital's ALL-IN-1 server to move over if they (or rather, the people charged with operating the messaging system) decide.

But I like to think that I'm a practical kind of person and I believe customers come to Digital looking for clear and unbiased advice about all sorts of products including Microsoft Exchange Server, and expect our consulting staff to deliver. A lot of the content in this book comes from that background – our aim is to help customers evaluate how well Microsoft Exchange Server fits into their plans, with or without an existing messaging system in place, and then proceeding from that point to implement solutions working with Microsoft Exchange Server in one way or another.

I strongly believe that the experience gained through working with many other messaging systems in the last fifteen years will prove valuable during enterprise-scale implementations of Exchange Server. The longer I work with Exchange the more apparent it is that the majority of the lessons learned from the deployments of other corporate messaging system can be taken over and applied to Exchange. There are obvious differences, such as the interaction between Windows NT and Exchange, but establishing a good base for the deployment of any system is a good initial step to take, and using experience to avoid the potholes waiting along the road to trap the unwary is only sensible.

I imagine that some of the views expressed in this book will conflict with those held by others. I'm not always positive about Microsoft Exchange Server, but then again, I'm not always positive about any product (software and others) that I use. You've just got to make the best of what you've got.

The aim of this book

Writing a book about new computer software poses questions about the shape and content of the book to authors. I think it is impossible to attempt to write the definitive book about any software until that software has stood the test of time in the hands of normal users and system administrators. Exchange Server has a couple of years to go before that stage is reached. Above all else, it is the experience of working with software in production environments that generates the interesting parts of many books.

Given that Exchange Server is still so relatively new, I have attempted to document my impressions of the software and the issues and challenges involved in its implementation in product messaging environments. As such, this book is full of ideas and opinions, filled in with background information such as the SMTP versus X.400 debate that I hope will help you decide whether Exchange Server fits into your messaging plans. The target audience is, I think, composed of system administrators and planners, consultants, and anyone else who's interested in making their own assessment of Exchange Server, rather than people who want a set of detailed 'how do I do that' lists covering every aspect of the operation and deployment of Exchange Server.

The subtitle for the book emphasizes corporate messaging environments. This gives you a good guide to my own experience and background which is heavily biased towards large-scale messaging projects involving thousands of clients and tens or even hundreds of servers. I think some very interesting challenges exist in the implementation of client–server based messaging systems in the corporate sector. A lot of this book focuses on those challenges rather than the somewhat easier, in my opinion, task of upgrading a Microsoft Mail Post Office to an Exchange Server. Maybe this attitude reflects a certain arrogance on my part, but thinking about the issues involved in corporate implementations has been a major and compelling reason for me to write this book.

Many topics are covered in a paragraph or two and I cannot and will not pretend that this is always enough information, especially if you are up to your neck in a large implementation project. Treat these topics as placeholders, items to be checked out and included in a project plan, or even calling for more extensive research through the formal documentation and white papers written by Microsoft. The Exchange Server administration guide, concepts and planning guide, and white paper on Windows NT domains are all essential reading for people involved in implementations. The concepts video included in the documentation set is also useful. Microsoft's TechNet CDs are another rich source of information and contain a wide range of articles and tools for Exchange Server. A TechNet subscription is a very useful tool for anyone dealing with Windows NT, Windows 95, Exchange Server or the other BackOffice products.

If you're looking for a book that details the behind-the-scenes stories of how Microsoft Exchange Server was developed don't read on. You won't find grand explanations about the philosophy surrounding

Microsoft Exchange Server, or even the reasons why some design decisions were taken. I simply don't know these things and don't have any direct contact with the engineers who have built Microsoft Exchange Server to pose interesting questions as them. In that respect, I'm like the vast majority of all the people who work with Microsoft Exchange Server, so I'm not exactly uncomfortable with the position. In the same vein this book does not attempt to provide step-by-step instructions for performing system management or other operations with the server. That type of information is best left to the formal documentation provided with Microsoft Exchange Server, and does not need to be duplicated here.

Reading books from different authors will generate a wide spectrum of opinion about any topic and Exchange Server is no different. I like reading books to occasionally stop, think, and reflect on the issues presented by the people who have taken the time to sit down and analyze the product they describe. I suggest that you read the book with an open mind. Feel free to disagree with my views and insert your own. Books covering software topics are static sources of information. They stop growing in content approximately six weeks before publication date, and for this reason information contained in books can age rapidly once they're published. All of the information presented is based on Exchange Server V4.0 plus whatever Service Packs (patches containing bug fixes and enhancements) available up to the date when the book was delivered to the publishers. It is inevitable that new versions of the server, add-ons for Exchange Server or clients, and service packs will appear over time, so keep this point in mind as you read. Use the advice, opinions, and conclusions presented here in conjunction with your own experience and knowledge of the systems, hardware and software, in use in your company as inputs to the creation of your own implementation plan. Those who write in books or magazines know little about what you or your organization actually do, so never accept the written word as final. Make your own mind up.

My own Exchange environment

It's difficult to write a book in a pure vacuum. Day to day experience with any system or product is a great trainer. I work within a Digital consulting group that's focused on large-scale messaging deployments for major corporate customers. Projects involve Exchange Server and Digital's own messaging technologies, including ALL-IN-1, MailWorks for UNIX, TeamLinks, MAILbus 400, and Digital's Alta Vista Directory Services.[1] Our operational environment is therefore hetero-

---

1. *The Alta Vista Directory Service product was previously known as Digital X.500 Directory Services.*

geneous and accommodates all of the technology we implement for customers. The screen shots used for illustrations throughout this book come from our production Exchange servers and connectors to X.400, the Internet, and Microsoft Mail. There are no pilot, test, or prototype servers in use and everything is based on the experience gained of putting Exchange Server to work as a production messaging system.

If you look carefully at the screen shots you'll realize that our production systems are imperfect. In other words, they don't fully reflect the way that we might have liked to bring the systems into production had we the time and luxury of a fully planned and designed implementation. The names given to our Windows NT servers, for instance, follow no naming convention. In acknowledging such imperfections I suspect that our systems are not too far removed from many others in use throughout the world. The important thing is that we have learned from the mistakes we made putting Exchange into production, and most of the mistakes are noted here so that you can avoid the same pitfalls.

Building towards success

There's little doubt in my mind that Exchange Server will be a successful product. Microsoft estimates that there are between seven and nine million users of Microsoft Mail and three million users of the original Schedule+ product. Using these figures, albeit in the knowledge that creating an accurate count of the users of any product is nearly impossible once sales go past the million mark, a quick calculation reveals that if there is an average of 25 clients connected to each Microsoft Mail Post Office, there are some 28,000 post offices ready to be upgraded to Microsoft Exchange Server, and this represents the major initial market. With these numbers in mind it is clear that, while server upgrades will produce a nice revenue stream, the really lucrative income will pour into Microsoft's coffers through client upgrades.

Other initial markets for Exchange include migrations of other PC LAN-based e-mail systems such as Lotus cc:Mail as well as the direct replacement of obsoleted mainframe mail systems like PROFS, Exchange will be successful. Growing into such well-established and lucrative markets is enough to quickly achieve success and establish a healthy installed base, certainly enough to give Microsoft the time to iron out the bugs that inevitably appear in the first release of any complex and feature-rich product (even though Microsoft refers to the first release of Exchange Server as version 4, from a factual perspective it is still a version one product). New versions of Exchange should exhibit increased stability and throughput and establish the server as a more than credible contender to act as the base for distributed corporate messaging infrastructures.

The whole world of electronic mail is going through a boom period right now, and the success generated by Microsoft Exchange Server in the corporate sphere is shared by other messaging systems. The technical community has nearly always been comfortable with electronic mail and the benefits it could bring to businesses. People within the technical community have been using electronic mail to overcome the barriers imposed by distance or time since the late 1970s, and a whole sub-culture built up around mail, but it's taken time for the concept to spread. Prompted by the explosive success of the Internet, everyone outside the IT community now has a basic understanding of electronic mail and are willing to try it out for themselves. Many millions of new mailboxes are added to the Internet every year, and counts of between 32 million and 60 million have been reported in 1995. Of course, no-one can physically count all the mailboxes in active use, so numbers like these have to be treated as estimates that have been arrived at with a great deal of deduction and a fair amount of 'finger in the air' calculation.

Apart from making electronic mail more available to ordinary people, the Internet has also greatly driven down the investment required to get connected. In most cases a simple low monthly payment is sufficient to enable connectivity into the big bad world of electronic communications. All of this makes electronic mail an exciting area to work in right now, and I hope that some of the excitement filters through the pages of this book.

Acknowledgments

My four previous books were all much easier to write than this one. From one perspective it is easier to write about a new product, possibly because the level of knowledge available within the general computing community is lower than after the product has been available for some time. However, because I have tried to discover the potential pitfalls involved in implementation the task of discovery and documentation has been harder, albeit more satisfying and generally a more elucidating experience. I have been greatly helped by many people, all of whom deserve my thanks.

Many people within Digital and Microsoft helped in one way or another as I struggled to come to grips with Exchange Server and assemble the information contained in the book. There's a long list of people to acknowledge and I'm sure that I will miss someone along the line. With this in mind I'd like to thank Frank Clonan, Pierre Bijaoui, Geoff Robb, Bill Rafferty, Kieran McCorry, Kevin Gallagher, John B. Horan, Eric Purcell, Peter McQuillan, Pat Baxter, Pam Wiess, Chris Jordan, Bob Read, Angus Fox, Tina Kinirons, Kieran McDonnell, and Anthony Quigley. In particular I would like to acknowledge the special contribution made by Stan Foster. Stan is one of the internal messaging architects for Digital Equipment Corporation and has been up to his neck in the ins and outs of the implementation of Microsoft Exchange Server within Digital. As such he has accumulated a wide range of practical knowledge about the good and bad in Exchange and has been very willing to share his experience with me. Stan also corrected many of the mistakes I made as the book was written. I'd also like to acknowledge the contributions of my external reviewers, people who are either responsible for the deployment of Exchange Server in large corporate sites or those who advise on electronic mail technology in general. In this category I'd like to thank Chris Blandford, Sohrab Mansourian, and Don Vickers.

Mike Cash, International Publisher of Digital Press, hounded me to write the book and eventually succeeded. Once the decision was made to proceed Mike provided as much encouragement as an author would hope for from a publisher. The task of production was greatly eased by Elizabeth McCarthy, who handled all the complexities of taking a book from Word for Windows files into print.

In closing let me note that all the errors in the book are mine. No-one else can claim responsibility. All I can offer in defense of any error is the simple fact that they are honest mistakes generated during my own experience gained working with Exchange. Exchange is a big product with lots of interesting (and some not so interesting) challenges for people interested in deploying it into a networked, heterogeneous messaging environment. I hope you have as much fun meeting that challenge as I've had. Whatever you do, keep the thought in mind that Exchange is only a software product and life is much more interesting than any one product can be. Let's go forward on that note.

Tony Redmond

Introducing Microsoft Exchange Server

The Exchange program

Microsoft Exchange Server represents a new departure for Microsoft messaging products. Instead of a situation where it is enough to be able to send electronic messages to other users connected to a common system, the promise is held out of 'Information Exchange', defined by Microsoft as the ability for people to share and manage information they need with anyone, anywhere, anytime. Of course, you need to be connected into the program before you can do all this, and, in one way, that's what this book is all about.

'Exchange' is often applied as a general catch-all title for the integrated suite of client and server electronic mail products released by Microsoft. It's important to differentiate between the clients and server because each stands on their own, linked by a common application programming interface (MAPI, Microsoft's Messaging Application Programming Interface). You don't have to use clients created by Microsoft with Exchange Server, and you can connect Microsoft clients to other servers.

Exchange Server is viewed as a very strategic product within Microsoft. Developing a high-capacity robust mail server with client and gateway connections is not an easy task. Providing good migration facilities to accommodate the needs of an installed base (in this case, Microsoft Mail) adds complexity to the task, as does the requirement to build for an international market. To the end of 1995 some 800 man years[1] had been used to develop the many millions of lines of code necessary to build Exchange Server and its clients. As large as it is, the massive Exchange code base does not represent the work done in associated development groups within Microsoft, such as that to develop the MAPI architecture and to make some necessary changes

---

1. *Statistic supplied by Microsoft at the Fall DECUS conference in December 1995.*

to the Windows NT operating system itself. All in all, the whole effort to bring Exchange Server to market has been enormous.

It's fair to say that Exchange Server was just about to ship for quite a long time. Never has a messaging product gone through quite such a long gestation, although I think it fair to say that the delay in the release date allowed both Windows NT and Exchange Server to mature to a point where both exhibit the qualities necessary for deployment in heavy-duty sites. Microsoft first started to reveal its plans for a high-end messaging and information server to the industry in 1993, but the complexities encountered during the development process contributed to the delayed release. Exchange Server was in beta test for two and a half years and through seven different beta versions released to an ever-growing set of customers willing to undergo the trials and tribulations of working with beta software. To complete the trivial pursuit section I'll note in passing that during development Exchange Server had an array of code names including Spitfire, Touchdown, Firefox, and Mercury. The first version of Exchange Server was eventually released in March 1996.

Exchange Server is designed to compete in corporate electronic mail markets. By their very nature corporate implementations tend to be international, so the fact that Exchange Server can run in English, French, German, and Japanese, and support clients running in 24 different languages is important. Any Exchange server can support any Exchange client no matter what language the client operates in, so a single Exchange server running English could, for instance, support the requirements of a Swiss installation where clients might run in English, French, German, and Italian. The internationalization of Exchange is based on the UNICODE base established by Windows NT itself. Later on in this chapter we'll discuss the different components that collectively make up a messaging system based around Microsoft Exchange Server.

The Exchange value proposition

New products coming to market for the first time must create a value proposition before customers will consider a purchase. This fact is as true about software applications as it is in respect of any other product. If it wasn't true, then any new product which appeared would instantly gain market share and acceptability. As we all know, while marketing executives might hope that their products will succeed, not all products do.

The value proposition put forward by Exchange Server can be broken down into a small number of succinct points:

- A strong set of electronic mail functionality for users, system administrators, and programmers;
- Good security;
- Highly integrated system administration;
- A wide range of easily installed and configured connectors (gateways) to other messaging systems;
- A building block approach to messaging infrastructures beginning with individual servers and growing right up to distributed networks of servers accommodating many thousands of users;
- A distributed and largely self-managing directory;
- A distributed document repository (public folders);
- Exploitation of the electronic mail infrastructure through mail-enabled applications and electronic forms.

All provided in a reasonably priced, easy to install package.

The growing influence of Windows NT as a major operating system provides one of the major reasons why the value proposition put forward by Exchange Server is attractive to customers. Windows NT has developed rapidly over the last few years to a stage where it can provide a single-login, location-independent infrastructure onto which enterprises can layer and deploy distributed applications such as Exchange.

The evolution of TCP/IP to become the *de facto* protocol for networking is also an important point because much of the fundamental building blocks for TCP/IP-based distributed computing are included in the base Windows NT operating system. Off-site access for users is also facilitated by in-built standard remote access services (RAS). Microsoft's obvious dedication to the task of making Windows NT the operating system of choice for corporate computing is evident by the speed in which new and important technologies are built into Windows NT. Apart from the growing feature list incorporated into the operating system, a number of trends have emerged in the recent past to support Windows NT. Among the most important of these are:

- The level of technical difficulty of migrating Novell NetWare V3.11 LANs to NetWare V4.0 (or above) has caused installations to review their methods of providing shared file and print services to PC users. Windows NT provides excellent file and print services and quite a number of NetWare V3.11 installations have moved over to Windows NT, figuring that the move to NT is easier than an upgrade to NetWare V4.

- The opportunity exists to replace some large database applications running on mainframe and mini-computers with equivalent applications built around high-end Windows NT servers. Because of the huge disparity in hardware purchase and maintenance costs the financial equation is usually, if not always, highly favorable, even when the cost of migrating the application is factored in.

- Applications designed around the client–server model mean that the power of PC desktops can be leveraged much better than the situation where PCs act as expensive terminal emulators for monolithic centralized application systems.

- Generally, PCs (using the broadest possible definition of the term) have become all-pervasive on the desktop. Video terminals and workstations still exist and there's a good population of low-end older PCs to deal with as well, but steadily dropping hardware costs and escalating performance levels mean that users receive much more 'bang for their buck' than ever before. System management and administration must follow the dispersed PCs to regain control over applications and user environments before they disappear from sight.

The combination of Windows NT, which provides a common software platform for clients and servers, and highly functional applications, such as Exchange Server and the other components of the Microsoft BackOffice program, can deliver great benefits.

The Microsoft BackOffice program

Microsoft Exchange Server forms part of a set of applications that Microsoft calls 'BackOffice'. The original set of office-related applications from Microsoft (Word, Excel, Access, Project, and so on) are user-oriented. The BackOffice applications are server-oriented and can be classified as applications providing network-based services to intelligent clients. The other parts of the BackOffice suite are:

- *Windows NT Server*, the foundation that BackOffice is built on. Windows NT provides the necessary secure and reliable base platform that all the BackOffice services run on. Windows NT supports Windows and Windows 95 clients and a whole range of network protocols to tie them together, including Novell NetWare, LAN Manager, Digital PATHWORKS, Banyan Vines, and TCP/IP.

- *SQL Server* relational database, a 'high-end database platform' for managing and storing data. SQL Server is used as the basis for any application that needs to share distributed TP data to multiple clients.

- *SNA Server*, providing host connectivity to IBM AS/400 and mainframe systems over the Systems Network Architecture protocol.
- *Internet Information Server (IIS)*, Microsoft's server for the World Wide Web.
- *SMS*, the Systems Management Server that allows distributed sites to centralize many aspects of PC management including hardware and software inventory auditing, automated software distribution and installation and network application management. Remote troubleshooting is an attractive feature of SMS, especially in an electronic messaging environment.

BackOffice has always included a messaging component. From BackOffice V2.0 onwards the standard edition of Exchange Server replaces the Microsoft Mail post office.* The BackOffice license requires all of the server products to be installed on a single system. Because the majority of e-mail servers are likely to be dedicated to messaging activities, this restriction may lead people to buy additional Exchange licenses. Running two or more heavy applications such as Exchange, SQL server, and SMS together on a single system is OK in test environments, but not for production systems.

What do I need from the BackOffice suite?

Aside from a Windows NT server, Microsoft Exchange Server does not require any other part of BackOffice. Unless your NT systems need to run applications based on a relational database there's no requirement for SQL server, and it's only sites that need to connect to IBM mini and mainframe systems that will be interested in SNA server.

From a management perspective the most interesting part of BackOffice is SMS and I think it's a good idea to factor this product into your plans for these reasons:

- Maintaining an up-to-date software inventory is a nightmare on many sites. Who's using what version of what applications where? The legal obligation to maintain an accurate count of

---

* *At the time of writing the exact composition of the Exchange components bundled with the BackOffice suite was uncertain. The likely position is that BackOffice V2.0 contains Exchange Server and the site connector, but this position is prone to change. It is possible, for instance, that Microsoft might decide to bundle other connectors (the Internet Mail connector is a potential candidate) with future editions of the BackOffice suite. Check with your local Microsoft office for up-to-date information.*

licenses in use is a good reason to have some sort of inventory control system in operation.

- Automated software distribution is a very attractive method to keep software up to date. Many problems reported to help desks can be traced back to obsolete program files. It's all too easy to have duplicate copies of DLLs (Dynamic Link Libraries) or EXEs (executables) and then have a program attempt to use an obsolete version that occurs earlier in the file search order than the correct file. In fact, the pre-installed software provided by many PC vendors today is just not suitable for a networked environment. It's great to be able to use software immediately a new PC is booted for the first time, but the short-term advantage gained from pre-installed software pales into insignificance once a new software version is released (or even a patched version) and you have several hundred PCs to be upgraded in a short period of time.

Generally speaking the initial cost of software is a minor factor in the lifetime cost-of-ownership equation. There is no doubt that PC-based electronic mail systems are more pleasing for users, but they are also more costly to run and maintain because the systems are more complex. Support costs are normally higher for PCs than older mainframe-based systems, so it pays to attempt to eliminate as many potential causes for support calls as possible. User education and training is certainly one way to help people solve problems themselves, but making sure that software is correctly installed in the first place and is then managed in an intelligent and hopefully automated manner is a potentially bigger win because it stops valuable (and expensive) system management time being absorbed in repetitive and boring tasks, like software upgrades.

A quick overview of Exchange Server

Microsoft Exchange Server is tightly integrated into the Windows NT operating system, taking full advantage of the multitasking and multi-threaded attributes of the operating system. System management and administration is integrated directly into base system components to make life easier all around. You can, for example, create a mailbox for a new or existing user directly from the Windows NT account administration tool. Possibly more important are the facts that Exchange is layered directly on top of the Windows NT network and security models, so clearly if you haven't managed to get these items sorted out you won't be in a position to even think about implementing Exchange Server anytime soon.

We're just a couple of pages into the book but already the most fundamental and important point about any implementation of Exchange Server has been made. That is, of course, the complete and total reliance on the Windows NT operating system. Anyone intending to do anything serious with Exchange Server must understand that Windows NT is the foundation stone the messaging infrastructure is built upon. A quickly put-together or ill-considered implementation of Windows NT will result in a structure like a house built of cards – pretty to look at, but liable to complete, sudden, and catastrophic collapse. Microsoft cannot be blamed for not telling people to create a solid Windows NT infrastructure before attempting to implement Exchange Server. The message is repeated time and time again in very clear terms in all the technical white papers on the subject issued by Microsoft since 1994.[2]

The close working relationship between Windows NT and Exchange Server implies that a certain degree of competence with Windows NT is required from anyone associated with the design or implementation of Exchange Server. This experience is not acquired by running SETUP.EXE, the ubiquitous Windows installation program to perform the 30-minute installation of Exchange Server, followed by a quick client upgrade for a Windows 95 PC. These activities will result in an operational server and client pair, but that's hardly the same as a corporate-standard messaging system. Ideally, in-house staff or external consultants should be certified as Windows NT system engineers through the Microsoft Certified Professional[3] program.

While this book introduces many Windows NT operational concepts, and discusses some of those concepts to a certain degree, more knowledge than contained herein is needed before a full-scale implementation of Exchange Server can be approached with confidence. The Windows NT Resource Kit (an optional extra available from Microsoft) is particularly useful in this respect. Of course, tight integration into the Windows NT operating system is a double-edged sword. The advantages gained (great system management) are only achieved if Windows NT is going to be your preferred platform. If you want to use anything else like OpenVMS or any variant of UNIX then

---

2. *Copies of the white papers are available from* **http://www.microsoft.com/exchange/** *or from the Microsoft Technet (Technical Information Network) CD-ROM. Technet CD-ROMs are issued monthly to subscribers. The subscription fee is not high and the information gained is well worthwhile.*

3. *Classes covering Exchange Server are available from Microsoft ATECs (Authorized Training and Education Centers). A certification exam covering Exchange Server is included in the Microsoft Certified Professional curriculum and exam schedule.*

Exchange Server is not going to be very interesting at all. The major pieces or services that collectively make up an Exchange server are:

- *The Message Transfer Agent (MTA)*, used to route messages to other MTAs, either another Exchange server or what Microsoft charmingly term 'foreign' X.400 (1984 or 1988) MTAs. While its basic role is to interchange messages with other Exchange servers, the MTA also serves as a connectivity engine which can be used to link Exchange Server to other different types of mail systems. The connectivity engine uses a series of 'connectors' that understand the interconnectivity and formatting requirements of other mail systems to bridge between the raw database format used internally by Exchange Server. Out-of-the-box connectors are available for X.400, SMTP, and Microsoft Mail systems, and all are packaged in the Exchange Server 'Enterprise Edition'.

- *The Directory Store*, a collection of all the data (names and connection information) relating to the Exchange organization (a collection of sites and servers, or individual computers running Exchange Server) together with user account information and shared resources such as distribution lists and 'custom recipients'. All Exchange servers in the same organization share a single replicated directory. There is no chaining or referral as would be found in the more traditional model of a distributed directory. All queries are resolved against a local copy of the distributed directory.

- *The Information Store*, a structured repository broken down into two distinct sections. The first stores personal data for users, grouped into folders, while the second holds all the information available in public folders. The repositories are implemented as relational databases, optimized to store the type of non-structured data classically found in messaging or electronic file cabinet systems. The Information Store is not a passive repository. It takes care of public folder replication and delivers any messages addressed to users located on the same server. The database technology used by the Information Store is similar in many respects to that applied to transaction processing applications and provides advanced features such as the capability to automatically recover transactions (messages) from logs should problems occur with the database. On-line backup is also incorporated, allowing users to work while system administrators take care of daily housekeeping. To my knowledge, these features are not found in the file system or database used by any other high-end messaging system, and are, in effect, a significant competitive advantage for Exchange. See the discussion about the database technology used by Exchange beginning on page 147 for more detailed information.

▶ *The Exchange Administrator and System Attendant* programs provide system management facilities for an Exchange server. These can be broadly defined in activities such as creating new user accounts (mailboxes) that require manual intervention, and those that are carried out in the background; for instance the monitoring of connections between different servers. Manual tasks are performed with the Administrator program, but one of Exchange's most impressive features is the level of automated management carried out by the System Administrator.

All of these components run as multithreaded Windows NT services executing their functions independently of each other. All of the services used by Exchange are managed using standard Windows NT utilities, such as the 'Services' option that can be invoked from the Control Panel applet. Other aspects of Exchange, such as the management of the contents of the directory and information stores, are managed through the Exchange administration program. In addition to the base services Exchange can make use of a number of optional components, not all of which will be operational on every server. These include the Directory Synchronizer, a connector to handle messages going out into the Internet, the Key Management server (to control message encryption and decryption), the Microsoft Mail connector, and the Schedule+ Free/Busy connector. Third party gateways (called 'connectors' in Exchange-speak), such as those that link into older IBM mainframe-based e-mail systems like PROFS, SNADS, MEMO, and OfficeVision complete the comprehensive functionality line-up.

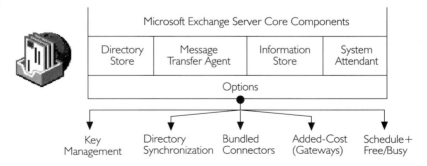

Figure 1.1 *The basic structure of the Microsoft Exchange Server*

Clearly, sites running existing mail systems will have to pay special attention to directory synchronization.

Microsoft provides synchronization tools for Microsoft Mail systems, but it is unlikely that other network directories can be synchronized as easily, at least soon after Exchange is officially available. A special Directory Development Kit is scheduled to be available to allow third parties to build tools to facilitate easier synchronization.

Packaging

Microsoft has adopted a building-block approach for Exchange Server packaging to allow people to purchase only the parts of the server that they really need. The different packages available for Exchange V4.0 are described in Table 1.1. Note that local market conditions may dictate different packaging, and special offers may be made available from time to time. Contact your local Microsoft office or reseller for up-to-date information.

Table 1.1 *The different packages available for Microsoft Exchange Server*

Package	Functionality
Microsoft Exchange Server (standard edition)	Basic server package including all the components necessary to install a single server – public and private information stores, Schedule+, directory service, Exchange MTA, Microsoft Mail connector, electronic forms designer, administration, and the migration wizard. Packs of 5, 10, or 25 client access licenses are also included.
Microsoft Exchange connector	Required to connect multiple Exchange servers into an integrated messaging system. The connector allows an Exchange server to join an existing Exchange site and/or to connect with other sites. Functionality added with this connector includes public folder and directory replication, encryption control through the Key Management server and digital signatures, and the Remote Access Server connector.
Microsoft Exchange Internet mail connector	Required to allow an Exchange server to connect to the Internet, or use the Internet Simple Mail Transport Protocol (SMTP) to send and receive messages from other Exchange servers or other messaging systems. The connector includes support for the MIME protocol for exchanging multi-format files.
Microsoft Exchange X.400 connector	Required to allow an Exchange server to connect to other X.400-compliant messaging systems, or to use an X.400 backbone to link Exchange servers together, including the ability to connect servers within a single site.
Microsoft Exchange Server, enterprise edition	All of the functionality included in the basic server and all the connectors (site, Internet, and X.400) bundled into one package designed for corporate messaging deployments. This package also includes a 25- or 50-pack of client access licenses.

The choice presented by the different packages allows people to start small with a single server and then grow as they need to by adding the different connectors as required by their individual messaging requirements. Those charged with corporate deployments will probably select the enterprise edition straightaway, if only because the enterprise edition is a very convenient way of getting the majority of the functionality required by large-scale deployments in a single package. Corporate deployments always seem to require some special items, so the enterprise edition doesn't hold the solution to all problems, but it's a great start.

Remember that client access licenses are required before any client can connect to an Exchange Server. Some of the packages include a number of client access licenses, but it's unlikely that there will be enough for all the clients you want to operate.

Generally speaking, installations running Microsoft Mail post offices (DOS) covered by the Microsoft Select maintenance program will receive upgrades to Exchange Server on a one-to-one basis. Client licenses maintained under the same program will also be upgraded. Select maintenance was never offered for Microsoft Mail for Macintosh, so Apple fans will have to pay for a new server. Various contractual limitations and different business conditions apply from country to country, so it's wise to check with Microsoft locally to determine exactly what will be upgraded and what additional components you'll need to buy in order to move to Exchange.

Getting Exchange Server up and running

What sort of computer will you need to run Exchange Server? The answer is, of course, that it all depends on the type of user community you tend to support. If you just want to run Exchange Server for a small pilot for 20 to 30 users you shouldn't need much more than a reasonably well-equipped desktop system, preferably one equipped with a fast (66MHz or above) 80486-class processor and at least 32Mb of memory.

The stakes get a little higher once you start to look at a system intended for production use. First you'll need a high-specification system running Windows NT V3.51[4] or V4.0. I wouldn't bother with a system equipped with an Intel 80486-based CPU unless you really

---

4. *Exchange Server V4.0 requires Service Pack 4 for Windows NT V3.51. Essentially a Service Pack is a collection of bug fixes or improvements to system components. Some products, like Exchange server, make specific demands on the operating system which in turn require the bug fixes or improvements included in the Service Pack.*

only want to connect a couple of clients. Go for a high-end Pentium or Alpha-based system and make sure you have plenty of memory. Disk space, although getting cheaper all the time, is still a factor to consider and you'll need 250Mb to get the software up and running. The space used afterwards will depend on the number of messages handled by the system and the type of messages and attachments generated by your user community. Clearly, a system dealing with users specializing in large Word for Windows or PowerPoint attachments will consume disk space quickly. Microsoft recommend that you consider a striped disk set for better performance, but you shouldn't have to go this far to be able to run a pilot. In all cases it's best to have the Exchange software installed on a different drive to Windows NT. More details about hardware configurations and performance can be found in Chapter 3.

In general, Exchange Server is not supported on the workstation edition of Windows NT. ADMIN.EXE, the Exchange administration program can be run on a NT workstation. In this situation the administration program communicates with server processes running on a remote server via RPCs. None of the server processes such as the Internet Mail Connector can function or are supported on a Windows NT workstation. Windows NT server differs from the workstation edition in a number of aspects, including support for features that enable higher resilience – disk striping, for instance. But the level of difference is hardly enough to impose any technical limitation so perhaps some hard-coded restrictions have been inserted. In view of the onerous task involved in supporting, testing, and qualifying software across the wide variety of platforms supported by Windows NT a restriction like this would be very understandable.

Apart from Exchange you may have to install other software components on your Windows NT server before everything hangs together. For example, you require TCP/IP for Windows NT if you want to use TCP/IP as the protocol to tie servers and gateways together. Microsoft Mail sites will need to install the Mail Connector, and anyone dealing with Macintosh clients will need Windows NT Services for Macintosh.

The architecture laid out for Exchange Server and clients is reasonably modular. Well-defined components work together to achieve tasks such as the dispatch of messages or directory look-ups, and because all the components are based on a single architecture (MAPI) there is no restriction on the source of the various components. Essentially, each component provides a service to users, so the common term used for Exchange components is 'service provider'.

Hundreds of independent software vendors and other third parties are working to integrate their own products with Exchange. The nicest integration is to be able to present new functionality, such as voice mail, to Exchange Server as if it is a standard part of Exchange. In short, to create a new service provider.

Apart from adding new functionality to Exchange Server it is also possible to build a client-centric service provider which enables standard Exchange clients to connect to other mail servers. The usual implementation is to install software (some DLLs) on the client to intercept MAPI calls made by clients and redirect them to a different server, translating the functions *en route* into the server's own API if the server doesn't support MAPI. This is the approach taken by third parties who wish to allow clients such as the Windows 95 Universal Inbox to connect to their own servers.

From a user perspective it's all a matter of describing the different service providers you want to use in the form of a *profile*. A profile typically details the type of message transport in use, the directory that can be used to locate addresses in, and the type of message store that's available. For example, a profile might specify that Exchange Server is used for message transport, the Exchange global address book is used for directory, and the Exchange information store is used as the message store. A profile can also detail multiple transports. For instance, it is possible to configure an Exchange client to be able to send messages via Exchange Server, a FAX, and CompuServe mail.

You can have multiple profiles to deal with the different circumstances in which you process mail. A PC used by multiple users will have a different profile for each person, if only to specify that a connection should be made to a different mailbox and/or server for each user.

Communication between clients and servers is carried out by RPCs (Remote Procedure Calls) using named pipes, NetBIOS, or Windows Sockets over a range of network protocols including IPX/SPX, NetBEUI, and TCP/IP (but only TCP/IP implementations that support Windows Sockets). The Exchange designers selected RPC as the mechanism for client–server communication precisely because it supports so many different underlying network protocols. RPC connections between clients and servers enable a high degree of service robustness. You can stop and restart Exchange services on a server, or even the server itself, and clients will not receive any error messages unless they attempt to communicate with the server. When the server reappears or the services are restarted clients reconnect seamlessly, giving the impression to users that a single continuous link has been maintained.

In the 1996–1997 period, as Exchange Servers replace Microsoft Mail Post Offices, the NetBIOS/NetBEUI combination is likely to be the most common network base for Exchange. However, in most corporate situations I've seen over the past few years there has been a steady march towards the combination of Windows Sockets and TCP/IP, and I see no reason why this trend shouldn't continue as Exchange is accepted in corporate installations, especially in light of the fact that people are so excited about Intranet applications which depend on TCP/IP.

One-stop system management

Market analysts have rightly criticized PC LAN-based e-mail systems over the years for the high cost per seat associated with these systems. Once a decision is reached to move towards a client–server model there's not much that can be done about the cost of the PC hardware and software, including network cards and other items required to link a user into the corporate network. All of these costs are based on items that have largely moved into the commodity category and similar expense is incurred no matter which vendor's e-mail system is used.

While hardware and software costs have descended in real terms people costs have risen. Due to the number of parts contributing to the whole system and the complexities involved in connecting all the parts together PC LAN-based e-mail systems require more hands-on maintenance time per user than older mainframe or mini-based systems. A lot of time is spent in fire-fighting mode getting users' mail through rather than proactive preventative maintenance. Where two or three full-time people might administer a large centralized system serving a thousand users it is common to find the same number taking care of a hundred users. Even worse, valuable user time is absorbed doing work that they are not trained for, such as PC software installation or printer maintenance. Overall, it is the human factor that has contributed more than any other to the overall high cost per seat in the PC environment.

Microsoft Exchange Server is designed to permit a single point of contact for system administrators for all components that might require management intervention through the Exchange administration program. All of the servers in a site can be managed from a single workstation, and each individual server can cope with far more users than a single older-style post office. Using a highly graphical, point-and-click interface for system administration is most appropriate when not too many items need to be displayed or manipulated. The

Exchange administration program is wonderful for low-end or medium-sized systems, but information can be slow to find and then displayed in situations where there are, for example, thousands of mailbox entries in a single recipient's container.

In much the same way just occasionally the graphical design limits the information about an item that can be viewed. For instance, when tracking a message it would be nice to be able to view more information about a selected message; but because the graphical interface is designed to show a particular set of data, you can't. These comments are mild criticisms of the administration program which is, in general, a very commendable step forward in messaging administration.

Some of the safeguards built into the graphical interface of the Exchange administration program can be circumvented by running the program in 'raw mode'. Raw mode is invoked by specifying the /R switch when ADMIN.EXE is started. *Using raw mode is like playing around with explosives.* If you know what you're doing and you take care there's a fair chance that you won't do any damage. On the other hand, you've got to remember that raw mode gives you direct control over the directory structures normally safeguarded by the graphical interface, and that if your finger slips when typing a command (or when responding to a prompt) it's entirely possible to wreak havoc. In this context, havoc means causing enough internal damage to necessitate a complete restore of the Exchange directory store. Deleting a container or other important structure in the directory is a pretty good example of what I mean. Raw mode certainly isn't intended for day-to-day use. Because its use carries such a high potential for accidents it cannot be recommended unless you proceed with great care.

Many of the tools you can use to manage a group of distributed Exchange servers is described in Chapter 8, beginning on page 341.

Managing connections to other systems

Because Exchange is able to handle direct connections to the X.400 and SMTP worlds and offers good backwards compatibility with Microsoft Mail there are fewer issues to overcome to link Exchange into corporate messaging environments. Allied with the vastly increased capabilities of the messaging system Windows NT is a far more stable, robust and powerful operating system than the DOS base used by the post offices, so fewer problems are encountered on a day-to-day basis. The net effect of these points is to reduce the overall workload for the people who have to manage the e-mail system, releasing skilled people for more useful activities and delivering a much better degree of service to end users.

Handling software installations and upgrades

Any step that contributes to high system availability and a consistent level of service is good. The advances in one-stop system management delivered in Exchange Server will be welcomed by system administrators. But the nature of software technology and the demands of both users and the market mean that new hardware and software appear on a very regular basis. A system will therefore never be fixed in time and plans must be made to evolve the system in a planned manner in order that advantage can be taken of the advances and new technology offered by faster and more capable hardware, or the newest version of Exchange Server, Exchange clients, and the desktop applications such as word processors and spreadsheets. Over a three-year period you can expect to see at least two new releases of Windows NT, Exchange Server and clients, and the desktop applications. Will this new software feature in your plans? How will the new software be made available to users without undue disruption and while maintaining the advances in system reliability achieved through the deployment of Windows NT and Exchange Server?

Microsoft's System Management Server (SMS) technology can provide an answer to the problem of managing PC desktops. SMS is to desktop application management and distribution what Exchange Server is to PC e-mail systems: a radical step forward in the right direction. SMS allows system administrators to distribute and manage application software out across networked PCs. It's easy to plan for an update of Exchange server software, even if a number of servers have to be updated at the same time within a site, but normally there is a ratio of hundreds of clients per server so the work necessary to update all the clients to the required software revision level is quite a different matter. SMS helps to solve the problem, allowing all the Exchange clients to be updated in a controlled manner precisely when the new software is required.

A full description of SMS and its capabilities lies outside the boundaries of this book. Hopefully, you'll consider the common and very real problem of software distribution posed here and look at the answers available to you. Windows NT, Exchange, and SMS combine well together and enable true one-stop system management and for that reason you should take a serious look at SMS.

MAPI: the rock on which Exchange Server is built

MAPI is Microsoft's Messaging Application Programming Interface. Great attention has been paid by the computer industry to application programming interfaces, mostly because programming to a set of well-documented and understood functions which are supported by multiple products is very much easier than having to create different interfaces for each product.

MAPI is part of a general set of APIs called WOSA, or Windows Open Systems Architecture. Each API within WOSA addresses a specific need. MAPI takes care of messaging, TAPI (the 'T' stands for Telephony) caters for telephone-based applications, and so on. None of these APIs are formally agreed by an industry standards body. It is the sheer market force generated by Microsoft that has moved the WOSA APIs into the lead position for PC development. Other competing interfaces in the messaging area, such as VIM (Vendor Independent Messaging), an interface chiefly espoused by Lotus Development and implemented in their Lotus cc:Mail product, have long been bypassed by MAPI, which is now the *de facto* interface used by PC applications when they want to integrate support for external messaging products.

While it seems that MAPI is yet another example of where Microsoft has imposed a standard on the computer industry, in this case there are many benefits in having a single pre-eminent standard for desktop messaging. The most obvious benefit is reduced cost, achievable because software developers now only have to code to a single standard rather than supporting many. Paradoxically, the single standard could also lead to increased choice for system implementers and users because more products may decide to make themselves 'mail-enabled' through MAPI, figuring that if everyone is including support for messaging functions in their product they should too.

The different faces of MAPI

The first implementations of MAPI were seen in versions of Microsoft Mail released in 1993. These implementations were not complete in that the full power and scope of the interface had not been built. In fact, just enough functions were available to build a basic messaging system such as Microsoft Mail, leading to the implementation being referred to as 'Simple MAPI', 'sMAPI', or 'MAPI-0'. Simple MAPI is composed of a total of thirteen functions including those necessary to log onto a server and then to create, address, send, and read messages. Even the biggest Microsoft fan cannot claim that Microsoft Mail is anything but a simple e-mail client, and indeed this is a strong selling point for the product as users don't tend to need very much training before they become productive. However, it is also a weakness because a lot of functionality available in competing products from other vendors (for example Lotus cc:Mail or Digital TeamLinks) is not supported by the Simple MAPI interface.

Simple MAPI was viewed as an intermediate step necessary to build a base to move towards the full MAPI interface. In fact, MAPI is composed of three separate and distinct interfaces that allow programmers a great deal of flexibility. The three interfaces are:

- The original Simple MAPI interface;
- CMC, or Common Mail Calls;
- OLE Messaging.

Only the last of these interfaces can be regarded an implementation of the full range of MAPI functionality as envisaged by its designers, and this is the interface used by the Microsoft Exchange Server and clients. OLE messaging follows the general trend of Microsoft application programming interfaces towards well-defined object-oriented interfaces, and through OLE messaging Exchange server deals with users, mailboxes, messages, and servers as objects.

As MAPI is an open interface, or at least one that's published into the public domain, doesn't this mean that anyone can write a client and connect it to an Exchange Server? The answer is that it all depends on what you want to do. The interface between Exchange clients and Exchange Server is built on OLE messaging, the most complex and functional interface. The Exchange Server also makes use of a number of MAPI extensions to build functionality like public folders. So where it's true that building a client using MAPI will allow a connection to be made, the degree of integration afterwards depends on much of the MAPI interface and any particular extensions are supported by a specific implementation. Certainly there shouldn't be much difficulty in sending and reading messages, but dealing with public folders or electronic forms requires a lot more work on the client side.

Client applications can use whichever interface they wish to connect to MAPI servers. The decision is normally based on the degree of messaging functionality required by the client application. Applications written using the original Simple MAPI interface can continue to use it, albeit at the expense of not being able to use the greatly expanded range of functions accommodated in full MAPI. Applications connecting via CMC are likely to be those that simply need to send messages from within the application, normally via a 'Send Mail' option inserted into the application's file menu or a command button added to a button bar. The best examples of such applications are those in Microsoft's own Office 95 suite.

MAPI service providers and clients

Applications have very different messaging needs. Most popular desktop applications only want to be able to send copies of documents they produce as attachments to messages created and dispatched without requiring users to leave the application. This is the approach taken by produces such as Word, Excel, and PowerPoint. It's a highly functional approach because it lets users get on with their job without having to start up a separate mail application.

Full-blown e-mail applications such as the Exchange client typically deliver a lot more functionality. They can read, forward, and reply to messages as well as being able to simply generate and send messages. MAPI provides the messaging subsystem for Windows PCs, and facilitates the requirements of desktop and mail applications through the set of interfaces we've just discussed. The different interfaces – Simple MAPI, CMC, and OLE – are all layered on top of MAPI itself. In effect, MAPI is the collection point for all messaging commands issued by applications on a Windows PC.

A set of Service Providers, or SPIs, are arrayed beneath the MAPI layer. Service Providers are the implementations of driver programs which action the commands issued by clients through the MAPI layer. You can think of Service Providers as the glue connecting MAPI clients to services that are, in turn, physically represented by software running on a server computer somewhere in the network. Microsoft and other software vendors may provide a single service, or collect together a number of different services that can be provided to clients by a mail server. Exchange Server delivers all of the services necessary for a high-end messaging system. The most important services are:

- *Message Store:* how messages are organized and accessed in a structured repository. For example, the set of folders in an Exchange mailbox.
- *Message Transport:* how messages are dispatched to their eventual destination.
- *Address Books:* sources of addressing information that can be made available to end users.

On Windows PCs MAPI service providers are built in the form of one or more Dynamic Link Libraries. This implementation allows the code for each service provider to be loaded as required by clients.

When an Exchange client is invoked it consults its 'profile' to discover what set of services it is configured for. The installation procedure for MAPI providers writes details about the capabilities that can be offered to clients into the system registry. Clients are then able to browse through the set of available services when they configure a profile. Figure 1.2 illustrates the set of MAPI services typically configured for an Exchange client. Details of the Dynamic Link Libraries can be gained by viewing a service provider's properties.

The standard Windows 95 kit contains MAPI service providers for Microsoft Mail, FAX, and the Microsoft Network. You can also add an Internet (POP/3) provider from the Windows 95 'Plus!' kit. When you configure an Exchange client in this environment you are able to select one or all of these service providers to use. And when Exchange Server is available you can install the Exchange service provider and use it to connect to the server. Third parties provide MAPI service providers to allow clients to connect to their servers and if these are available you can configure a client for them as well. The resulting profile might well contain entries for four or more providers, all of which will be connected to when the client starts up

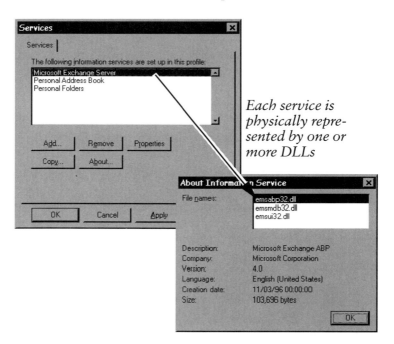

Figure 1.2
MAPI Services and Service Providers

Figure 1.3 illustrates how all of the components in the Windows messaging subsystem work together. At the top clients use calls to messaging functions to create and send messages. The functions are processed by MAPI. Responsibility for processing the messages is handed over by MAPI to the service providers configured in the user's profile, and eventually the messages arrive at a server computer which takes care of delivery. Extended functions such as the address book, Schedule+ meeting requests, or e-forms are handled in the same way, the difference being that the service providers (and the server) must be able to process these type of messages.

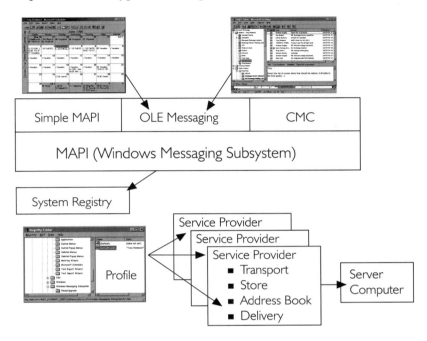

Figure 1.3 *The Windows messaging subsystem*

A wide range of Exchange clients

A wide range of client platforms are available for Exchange Server. Clients[5] shipping with the Exchange Server include Windows for WorkGroups, Windows 95, Windows NT, and good old DOS.

The DOS client is a short-term tactical solution to cater for organizations that have considerable populations of low-end PCs still in place, and is limited by the basic functionality available to DOS. Don't expect to be able to handle embedded OLE objects, for instance. Of course, a purely cynical view of the situation is that providing someone with the DOS client is possibly one good way of convincing them that life could be a lot richer and that they should really start using a more modern platform!

---

5. *Microsoft also refers to the Exchange client as a 'viewer'. This may be in line with the concept of 'Information Exchange' where the server becomes a common receptacle for information arriving from many different sources – interpersonal e-mail, faxes, voice mail, and so on. In this scheme the client can be considered a universal information viewer because it contains all the functionality and features necessary to deal with all the data that arrives at the server.*

Notable for its absence in the clients shown in Figure 1.4 is support for a native UNIX solution, chiefly to address the UNIX workstation market. Primarily due to their understandable focus on Windows, Microsoft has never provided a solution for UNIX workstations. UNIX is a popular and powerful platform for mail servers used by many millions of people, but UNIX workstations, although popular with their users, is a very minor player in terms of the total potential market for client licenses when compared to Windows in all its shapes and forms.

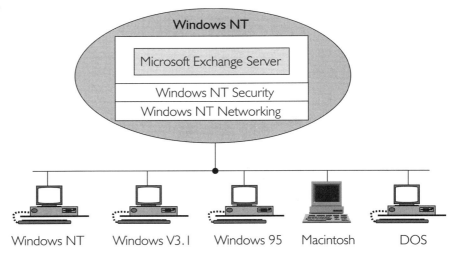

Figure 1.4 *The native client line-up for Microsoft Exchange Server*

With these points in mind the lack of a native UNIX client from Microsoft at this stage is not at all surprising. However, corporate messaging environments demand accommodation for all the different platforms typically found on user desktops, including UNIX workstations. To fill the gap, Microsoft has licensed emulation software developed by Insignia Software. The emulation software basically traps calls made to Windows API functions, translating the calls into UNIX code and allowing the Windows 95 Exchange client to run on a range of UNIX systems, including Sun Solaris. Performance isn't too bad either, especially if the workstation has a fast processor (as most of the latest generation has) and there's plenty of memory available. While emulation might appear to be an ugly kludge it is an effective way of addressing a niche market.

While it's undeniable that Windows has grabbed the lion's share of the desktop market there are considerable and often influential groups of Apple Macintosh users in most major corporations. In comparison to their undoubted success with Microsoft Mail for Windows, Microsoft hasn't had a good record in the Macintosh messaging space over the years. In late 1995 Microsoft transferred Microsoft Mail for Macintosh (and some 750,000 clients) to StarLine Technologies, who were promptly taken over by Quarterdeck (the company made famous by its QEMM memory management product). Quarterdeck plan to develop a new product based on the original Mail for the Macintosh code base,[6] and promise good interoperability between it, Microsoft Mail for the PC and Exchange. Microsoft's new Exchange client for the Macintosh was not released with Exchange Server, eventually arriving some four months after the server and the Windows clients were released.

An important improvement from previous LAN-based mail systems is the provision of out-of-the-box remote (modem-enabled) access. In the previous Microsoft Mail product users had to purchase a separate add-on module to upgrade their client for remote access. The most common way to establish remote connections is via RAS connections to Exchange Server, a good example of how Exchange Server has leveraged off a standard component of the Windows NT operating system.

The facts about the Universal Inbox

While I'm discussing clients, let me take the opportunity to pour a judicious amount of cold water on one of the biggest fables around Exchange, the 'free' Exchange client that first appeared in Windows 95 and then in Windows NT V4.0. Building on the precedent established by the provision of the Microsoft Mail client in Windows for WorkGroups and Windows NT V3.*x*, basic messaging functionality is provided in all Windows 95 and Windows NT systems. In both systems the foundation for electronic mail is referred to as the Universal Inbox. Some fog and confusion is introduced into the picture when the Universal Inbox boldly labels itself 'Microsoft Exchange' when the program starts up, so a quick review of the actual facts of the matter is probably necessary at this point.

The concept behind the Universal Inbox – to provide a single consistent location for all electronic communications to arrive into – is a compelling vision, and Microsoft has done a good job in defining the structure for the single location, especially in Windows 95. As well as acting as a single location for incoming communications (see Figure 1.5) the client is able to act as a fully-fledged message user agent, creating and sending messages via a variety of systems, each of which is defined as a messaging service provider. However, the standard

---

6. *This product is expected to ship sometime in 1996.*

Universal Inbox isn't as comprehensive a mail client as the full-blown Exchange client since it provides only the same degree of send/receive/process messaging capabilities as the older Microsoft Mail clients. The Universal Inbox isn't the same as Microsoft Mail and it would be incorrect to represent it as such, if only because the underlying internal structure follows the same architecture as the full Exchange client.

Figure 1.5
Components of the Windows 95 Universal Inbox

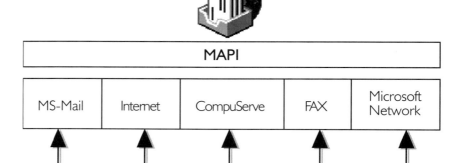

Messages and other electronic communications

Now that you're suitably confused between the Universal Inbox and the 'full' Exchange client, let me reassure you that you're not very different in this respect to many other people. To help address the issue, Microsoft renamed the Universal Inbox and began to refer to it as 'Windows Messaging' from June 1996 on. Now there is a clear differentiation between messaging as incorporated into the desktop operating systems and the full-fledged Exchange client. To back the point Microsoft released an updated version of Windows Messaging at the same time. This client incorporates fixes made during Exchange development and can be downloaded from the Microsoft Web site. However, it will take a while before Windows Messaging becomes the commonly used term so I'll continue to refer to the Universal Inbox for the rest of this book.

So what can you do with the Windows 95 or Windows NT Universal Inbox? First, you can use it as a direct replacement for existing Microsoft Mail clients by configuring the Universal Inbox to connect to a Microsoft Mail Post Office. Then you can expand your horizons by enabling additional messaging service providers. For example, Windows 95 includes the components needed to connect your universal inbox to a FAX service, CompuServe[7] and the Microsoft Network. An additional service provider for Internet mail is available in the Microsoft Plus pack for Windows 95. The Internet service provider is interesting because it allows the Windows 95 client to connect to a large number of UNIX-based mail systems, downloading messages via the POP/3[8] protocol and then acts as an SMTP client when sending messages. Other Internet service providers are available from Netscape and as part of the Microsoft Internet Explorer. Service providers enabled by installing additional software onto a PC bring Plug-and-Play to the world of messaging. The concept is an important part of the way that the Universal Inbox has been built to bring many different forms of electronic communications together in a single consistent place. It's an exciting concept because it means that people can configure their mailbox the way they want to, as long as a service provider exists to connect them to whatever information sources they need.

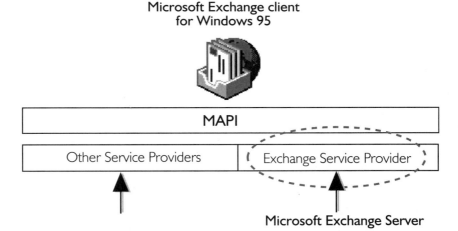

Figure 1.6 *How the Exchange server service provider fits into the Universal Inbox*

The free service providers will meet the needs of many people, but a separate license must be purchased and the Exchange client components upgraded before the Universal Inbox can connect to Exchange, as shown in Figure 1.6. Encountering a requirement to upgrade client software is hardly surprising because Windows 95 shipped some seven

---

7. *The CompuServe service provider is not installed automatically. A service provider for CompuServe is packaged in the Windows 95 kit and can be found in DRIVERS\OTHER\EXCHANGE\COMPSRV. Use the SETUP.EXE in the directory to install the new provider. An updated service provider that addresses some bugs in the original is also available from CompuServe (see the WINCON forum).*

8. *POP=Post Office Protocol, used by mail clients to download messages from a server.*

months before Exchange Server. Most of Windows 95 was finalized in the early summer of 1995, and many of the important internal client-centric features in Exchange changed considerably between the release of Windows 95 through the final builds before eventual product ship in March 1996. Apart from updating the service provider for the universal inbox, the upgrade is necessary to expose server-centric features such as the rules engine and to enable server-based time management via Schedule+. If you're running an earlier version of Schedule+, such as the version provided with Office 95, this software can be updated at the same time. The upgrade is quick and simple, and carried out by connecting to a share-point on a Windows NT server where the client software kit is located. In summary, while it's an attractive notion to have a free mail client on all desktops, there's no such thing as a free lunch and the financial analysis for a general move to an Exchange infrastructure must factor in the costs of client licenses.

No luck for older terminals

'Green screen e-mail' is the term used by a certain Microsoft sales representative of my acquaintance to describe host-based messaging systems. The term accurately describes the green (or other color) glow of the 24 × 80 screen used to log onto mainframe or mini-based computers to access older messaging systems.

Exchange Server offers no method for connecting unintelligent clients like IBM 3270s or the other classic Video Terminals (VTs). If you want to run Exchange Server you have to face the fact that PC clients are the only way forward. Most installations have gone a long way to sorting out their desktop infrastructure over the past few years and there has been a steady decline in the number of VTs in use. However, I know of quite a few sites where VTs are still counted in hundreds, mostly because they are cheap to install and support, and many users only require simple text-based messaging. If you have a substantial VT population you'll either have to remove Exchange from your list of potential messaging solutions or pay the ante and replace VTs with PCs, with all the attendant costs involved.

Basic client functionality

How many features of your word processor or spreadsheet do you actually use? How many have you mastered to a degree where you can use the feature without reaching for a manual or conducting a frantic search through the application's help file? If you're anything like me you'll only ever use about 20% of an application's features, unless it's something that you use every day. Electronic mail is an application accessed by most users every day, so the range of features offered by the application are important and it's more likely that even esoteric features will be discovered and used by quite a few people.

The Exchange clients are highly functional. There are probably more options available on menus, especially if the long versions of the menus are turned on, than most people will ever care about. All of the options are presented in an attractive user interface which is utterly consistent with the rest of the Microsoft office applications. If you're accustomed to using Word, Excel, PowerPoint, and Access you'll be totally at home with an Exchange client, such as the Windows 95 client pictured in Figure 1.7. Even the more esoteric options hidden away on the farther reaches of *Tools.Options*, such as the feature which allows messages to be sent after a certain delay, show evidence of careful research into the finer points of graphical user interfaces.

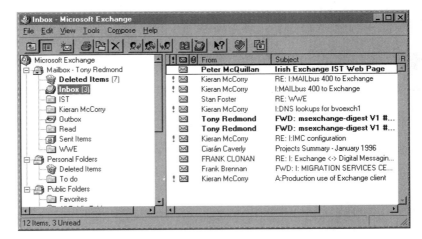

Figure 1.7 *The Exchange client for Windows 95*

Let me give an example to illustrate what I mean. An option to submit a message to a server for delivery later on is common to quite a number of messaging systems, where the feature is sometimes referred to as 'deferred mail'. Most other implementations ask the user to specify a time and date to send the message. There's little wrong in this approach, but the Exchange developers have taken a slightly different view which may make the option more approachable to some users. In Exchange you can ask for a message to be sent after a range of different delays, for instance 1 to 999 minutes, or after 3 days, or 4 weeks, and so on. Instead of requesting an absolutely accurate date and time, which is the correct technical or engineering solution, the emphasis is placed on accommodating humans and the fuzzy logic that humans tend to use. 'When do I want this message to go?'; 'In about two days' time...' You may or may not like the implementation, but it's good to see people trying to do things slightly differently than it's been done before.

Table 1.2 breaks down the most important features of the Exchange clients into four categories. Mailbox maintenance are the features which enable a user to manage their own working environment and organize the information they receive and work with. A user interface is common to all graphical products, but Exchange clients offer a few unique features in their implementation. Cover memo creation is the set of features used for the core activity, creating and sending messages. The features in the Tools category mark the real difference between Exchange and the majority of PC-based electronic messaging clients that have appeared before. While many of the features in all categories have appeared before in other products, the real difference is the breath and depth of the features as a collective whole.

Viewers for different file formats is a feature currently missing from Exchange clients. Viewers typically allow files generated in different formats to be displayed in a Read Message window, avoiding the need to start up a separate application to view file contents.

Table 1.2 *Exchange client features*

Mailbox Maintenance	
Open	Open a set of folders
Move	Move an item from one folder to another
Copy	Copy an item from one folder to another
Delete	Move an item to the 'Deleted Items' folder
Rename	Change the display name for an item
Find	Search a store according to a set of criteria supplied by the user
Properties	Display the properties of an item
New folder	Create a new folder in a selected store
Add to favorites	Mark a folder as one that you refer to frequently
Import	Import messages stored in a mailbox
Send on behalf	Give permission to another user to send messages on your behalf
User Interface	
View…	Turn off/on viewing of folders, toolbar, and the status bar
Sort	Define different sort orders for folder contents
Filters	Apply a filter to folder contents so that only items which pass the filter are displayed

Table 1.2 *Exchange client features (continued)*

	Personal views	Design your own view of a store
Cover Memo Creation		
	Create	Create a new memo
	Send	Send a memo
	Reply	Reply to a memo you've received. Options are reply to sender or reply to everyone who received the note
	Forward	Forward the memo to another user
	Post Note	Post a note to a folder
	Post Form	Post an electronic form to a folder
	Editor	Rich Text Format (RTF) or Word for Windows (V7.0a onwards)
	Spell Check	Spell check the contents of a memo, including automatic check before dispatching a memo to the server
Tools		
	Synchronize	Synchronize local folders with the server
	Remote mail	Access mail over a telephone connection
	Inbox Assistant	Define rules for execution when messages arrive on the server. For example, delete any message with 'For your information' in the title
	Out of Office Assistant	Create informative messages to be sent to correspondents when you aren't able to respond to your messages
	AutoSignature	Apply supplied text to messages before they are sent
	Address Book	Personal repository for e-mail addresses
	Application Design	Design a public folder
	Schedule+	Time management and PIM (Personal Information Manager)
	Customize Toolbar	Customize the client toolbar
	Services	Configure the services you wish to use. For example: Exchange Server, Personal Folders, Personal Address Book, Microsoft FAX, and so on
	Security	Message encryption and digital signatures

Viewers are more important in a heterogeneous messaging environment where different word processors, spreadsheets, and graphic packages tend to be used across the total user population, leading to inevitable difficulties when one user generates a document in a certain format and sends it to others who haven't got the application installed on their PC. A number of third parties are working to address this need. Two of the best are OutSide In and Quick View Plus, each of which are capable of dealing with all the common PC file formats and quite a few of the more esoteric formats that float around a network.

Exchange clients from non-Microsoft sources

We've already discussed how the user configurations for the Windows messaging subsystem are defined in terms of a profile. A profile describes the services the user wishes to access and the MAPI providers which enable such access. A graphic illustrating typical components configured within a MAPI profile is shown in Figure 1.8.

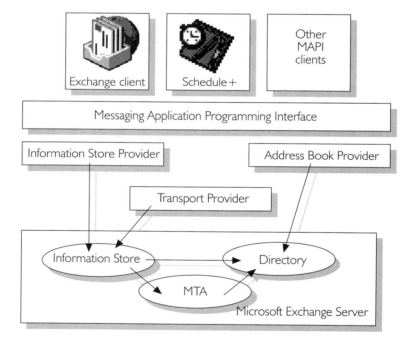

Figure 1.8 *MAPI clients and providers*

If multiple users share a PC a separate profile is quite probably defined for each. It is quite possible for a user to maintain several profiles, each of which describes a totally different environment. For example, one profile might detail a connection to Exchange Server for use when transporting new messages while another specifies that a Microsoft Mail Post Office is to be used instead. Each of the different providers might be capable of making different features available to clients, so these differences can be configured as part of the profile too.

The attractive notion of having a single universal client as the access point to many different messaging services has encouraged many vendors to consider building the necessary software components to link Microsoft Exchange clients (both the full Exchange client and the Universal Inbox) to their own mail servers via MAPI.

Digital has built two separate products (called Digital Drivers for MAPI)[9] to connect Exchange clients to Digital MailWorks for UNIX or ALL-IN-1 (OpenVMS) servers, allowing enterprises to deploy UNIX-based or OpenVMS-based messaging servers while continuing to use the well-integrated desktop functionality available in the Windows 95 clients.

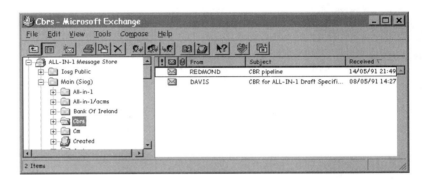

Figure 1.9
Digital's ALL-IN-1 server accessed by the Exchange client for Windows 95

The Digital drivers are full MAPI service providers which define Digital mail servers to the clients in terms of a message store (in Digital terms, a file cabinet), the transport by which messages pass between the client and server, and a directory of mail subscribers to replace or supplement the Exchange Global Address List. Apart from incorporating a huge new range of potential clients, building a MAPI service provider conveys a number of advantages to vendors. For example, changes normally don't have to be made on the server as all the work to translate MAPI functions to server-specific calls can be encapsulated in the service provider DLL that's installed on each client. This alone means that existing servers can continue to operate, in effect gracefully evolving to support new client connections without realizing the fact. While the server side is insulated from change, using MAPI means that a whole client user interface is picked up free of charge, giving the vendor the option of concentrating solely on the server if that makes commercial sense.

---

9. *The first version of the Digital MAPI driver (for MailWorks for UNIX) shipped in November 1995. The ALL-IN-1 driver shipped in summer 1996.*

Figure 1.9 shows the full Exchange client for Windows 95 connected to a Digital ALL-IN-1 server running on an OpenVMS system. As far as the user is concerned all they see is the Exchange user interface. The only hints that it might not be an Exchange server humming in the background are a few discrete mentions of ALL-IN-1. Another good example of how MAPI can be used to build extensions for the Exchange client environment is the provision of an additional directory service. See the discussion beginning on page 298 and the screen shot on page 299.

While a general movement towards a common client for all sorts of electronic communications makes sense in many aspects, especially when client software is bundled with the desktop operating system there will be situations when the Exchange client doesn't fully exploit the capabilities that a third party server can offer. Perhaps the MAPI specification doesn't completely accommodate features of other servers and no amount of magic programming can make the client work with the server. Or maybe the server offers more in terms of features such as workflow or document management. In these cases vendors, such as Digital, will continue to supply their own client software.

Utilizing MAPI to permit enterprises to select clients from one source and servers from another, while all the time presenting users with a seamless service, is a compelling example of the power of the MAPI concept.

In general, I think it's fair to say that mixing different MAPI clients with different MAPI servers is great as long as you're interested in purely messaging functionality. In other words, all you want to do is create, send, and read messages. However, if a particular client or server offers specific functionality you may not be able to access it with all possible combinations. Some testing may be required to establish exactly what's possible with what combination in your particular environment. For example, will public folders be accessible from non-Microsoft clients that connect to an Exchange server? Will Exchange clients be able to utilize the mail delegation functionality as implemented in another vendor's MAPI-enabled server? A purely cynical view of the situation, which is perhaps accurate in many respects, is that open systems work best as long as you buy all the open components from a single vendor. Along this line it may well be inevitable that MAPI components originating from Microsoft will always offer the highest degree of integration and interoperability with the Exchange server. This is somewhat inevitable where client and server components are built by a single vendor. The Microsoft clients will also look and feel exactly like other Microsoft applications, again hardly surprising because all the desktop applications make use of common programming libraries. Vendors selling alternate clients for connection to Exchange servers or servers for Exchange clients have to make a compelling case and provide significant added value before a real case can be made for those alternate solutions to be considered. Better integration with other messaging systems installed within an organization, an integrated set of converters and viewers, or better customization capabilities are all good arguments to go towards another client, especially if you want to establish a situation where a common client (one that's capable of connecting to all servers) is used throughout your organization.

Making a choice for the client platform

Windows NT is the only operating system option for an Exchange server, but as we've just reviewed, there is a reasonably wide choice of DOS or Windows-based clients. Given that all of the Windows-based Exchange clients offer roughly comparable functionality, which desktop operating system offers the best option for large-scale deployment of Exchange clients?

Most large customers I have worked with in the last year or so have reduced the choice for client desktop operating system to two: Windows NT workstation or Windows 95. DOS is seen as a solution only for the rapidly-reducing population of 80386-powered PCs (in corporate computing environments), while Windows 3.1 and Windows for WorkGroups are crippled by the flaws in the old Windows architecture that are so readily exposed if a user attempts to run more than two large applications together at the one time. Moving to Windows NT or Windows 95 on the desktop will cost money for application upgrades and extra hardware, but the costs are somewhat offset by reduced help desk calls generated by frustrated users complaining of depleted system resources.

Windows 95 arrived in a blaze of publicity in August 1995, easily winning the all-time award for hyped-up software. Despite all the talk about the evolution to 32-bit desktop computing, Windows 95 hasn't quite achieved the full status of a 32-bit operating system because its kernel remains a hybrid mixture of 16- and 32-bit code. Microsoft probably would have liked to have more 32-bit code in Windows 95 but time and the need for backwards compatibility for applications dictated that some 16-bit code survived. The resulting mix works well, most of the time. Windows 95 is far more reliable than Windows V3.x, and users can plan for a complete day's work without factoring in the need to reboot to recover leaked system resources. While more memory is needed, far more applications can be run together and Windows 95 will cope with the load. Using Windows 95 as my day-to-day workhorse platform I typically run Word, PowerPoint, Excel, and more multiple mail clients together at the same time without problems.

Windows NT had a slow start but has greatly improved since its early days. The workstation edition of Windows NT V4.0, suitably equipped with the Windows 95 user interface shell, is the top of the range user desktop environment available today. While Windows 95 increased reliability and robustness over the previous version by a user-perceived factor of 10 or more (based on my own personal experience), Windows NT is even more reliable, secure, and network-aware. In addition, Windows NT is hardware-independent and not tied to the Intel $x86$ architecture, allowing screamingly-fast desktop systems to be built around high-end RISC CPUs such as the Digital Alpha chip.

Moving a desktop environment from Windows V3 to Windows NT requires even more memory than Windows 95, but many large organizations are willing to accommodate that cost now in order to create a desktop computing environment that should be able to gracefully evolve into future Microsoft desktop operating systems (such as the object-oriented 'Cairo' release) that are now being discussed and will no doubt be released over the next couple of years. Due to its hybrid nature with its software base split between 16- and 32-bit code, Windows 95 is more of an interim step towards future Microsoft desktop operating systems.

Which desktop operating system should you use? Certainly I would not recommend Windows V3.x. Apart from the restrictions imposed by Windows in its 16-bit implementation Microsoft is not developing Windows V3.x any further. The old saying that 'when the horse is dead, it's time to get off' comes to mind here.

Windows 95 or Windows NT represent the best options for the future, but both require a considerable investment to install across all desktops in any medium to large enterprise. Because it is priced for the home/small office market Windows 95 is the cheaper of the two options. Windows 95 still scores over NT in terms of Plug-and-Play and power management, meaning that if you're interested in using notebook computers Windows 95 is the best choice.

In desktop environments Windows NT is a little more expensive, but it is built on a firm 32-bit code base and is a more robust and secure operating system. Microsoft's direction towards a Windows NT desktop environment is also pretty clear, so if you can afford the extra cost then Windows NT is the option I would go for.

Selecting the desktop operating system is only the start. Apart from a potential requirement to upgrade hardware with additional memory and faster CPUs, if you install a new desktop it's likely that you'll also want to review the application software in use too. Migrating everyone from Microsoft Office V4 to Office 95 costs money, and then all the terminal emulators, databases, programming languages, and other applications might require new versions too if real advantage is to be taken of your new 32-bit desktop. Putting all the costs together that might be incurred in evolving towards a 32-bit desktop it's easy to see how a $60 product[10] could become a major push factor behind a decision to invest between $500 and $2,000 per desktop.

Selecting the right platform to deploy Exchange clients is an important part of your overall computing infrastructure for the next few years. But Exchange clients are only a small, low-cost part of the overall equation. The question therefore needs to be asked whether a $60 client can drive the whole desktop in terms of its evolution and technical environment? Only you can answer that question.

Hardware resources for clients

The rich functionality contained in the Exchange clients is implemented in millions of lines of complex code. Large programs that offer extensive functionality fight a constant battle between the constant demands from users for increased functionality and the need to up the minimum hardware threshold. Complex code, no matter how optimized, has to be loaded into memory sometime, the modules, executables and other data files representing the program must be stored, and all the machine instructions generated by the code will be executed on processors. If there isn't enough memory, disk space, or processing power available to handle the demand generated by the program it will either not be able to execute or will run slowly. Everyone wants programs to run fast, so any slow-down produced through the introduction of new functionality is frowned on by users, no matter how hard they lobbied for the new features. This is the conundrum for all engineering groups.

The minimum specified hardware base for Exchange clients is different from the minimum practical base. The difference is, of course, in that Microsoft certify that Exchange clients will run with a certain hardware configuration, but they don't specify the level of performance, perceived or otherwise, a user will experience with the config-

---

10. *Exchange clients are priced differently depending on the number of clients purchased and the country they are purchased in. I've taken $60 as an average price for the purpose of illustration only. Contact your local Microsoft office to get current price information about Exchange servers and clients.*

uration. This tactic isn't unique to Microsoft as all software vendors seek to qualify products against low hardware configurations in order to increase the total potential user base for their product. While the Exchange client for Windows V3.*x* will run on a 80386-powered PC with 8Mb of memory the performance will be slow and unacceptable.

If you're coming from a Microsoft Mail background expect to have to take a long hard look at current hardware resources on user desktops before migrating to Exchange. Microsoft Mail is a very much simpler product in terms of architecture and implementation and is therefore able to comfortably perform on a PC with a far lower specification. Expect to have to add extra memory to the majority of your PCs and eliminate any low-end PCs that are in use. Don't expect to be able to use 80386-powered systems for anything else but DOS systems.

The situation can be further complicated in terms of overall client hardware configurations if you want to upgrade applications and desktop operating system at the same time, for example to move to a Windows 95/Office 95/Exchange desktop environment. It seems that every desktop application is gently expanding in size and complexity as features are added in each new release, and each addition has to be paid for somewhere. Consider the complex interconnections underpinning a message composed by a user with the Exchange client for Windows 95 using Word for Windows as the cover note editor. Now drag an Excel worksheet from the Windows Explorer and drop it into the memo. Then double-click on the newly embedded icon to start Excel so that the figures in the worksheet can be verified before being sent. Three highly functional applications working smoothly together in a relatively seamless manner under Windows 95. Is it any wonder that PCs need to have faster CPUs today than the largest minicomputers had at the start of the 1990s?

Table 1.3 outlines some sample configurations for desktop computing environments that must support Exchange clients as well as a mix of commonly-used personal productivity applications (Word, Excel, and so on). These configurations are not the minimum specified by Microsoft for any of the operating systems. Instead, they are the minimum configurations I recommend to people who come to me for advice, based on the idea that users generally want a system that works well (all the time) and has scope to grow and accommodate increased demands generated by users, or new versions of operating systems or applications. Any system that appears to be slightly over-configured today will be the smallest usable system in the future, and that future comes closer every day.

Table 1.3 *Sample configurations for desktop clients*

Desktop operating system	CPU	Memory	Basic hard disk requirements
DOS (V5 or above)	Intel 80386 upwards	8Mb upwards	200Mb upwards
Microsoft Windows V3.1 or Windows for WorkGroups	Intel 80486 25MHz upwards	12Mb upwards	300Mb upwards
Microsoft Windows 95	Intel 80486 33MHz upwards	16Mb upwards	400Mb upwards
Microsoft Windows NT workstation V3.51 or V4.0	Intel 80486 50MHz upwards; any Digital Alpha CPU; MIPS RISC	20Mb (Intel); 32Mb (Alpha)	512Mb upwards
Apple Macintosh System 7.5	PowerPC	8Mb	200Mb upwards

'Outlook': the cut-down version of an Exchange client

As previously mentioned, many of the users who upgrade from Microsoft Mail to Exchange will discover that the client platforms they had been using are totally unsuited to the load imposed by all the extra features and functionality bundled in Exchange. The full-feature Exchange client is designed for corporate messaging environments and perhaps contains too much functionality if you're just interested in sending a few quick messages. All the features have to be implemented in code and paid for in system resources, leading to a situation where the clients are too unwieldy and storage-intensive for many installations.

Microsoft reacted to the criticism by announcing plans for 'Outlook', a desktop information manager scheduled to ship with Office 97, the next major release of Microsoft's desktop applications suite. Outlook includes electronic mail functionality along with scheduling and PIM (Personal Information Management) features. Outlook uses Exchange Server for messaging, but apparently doesn't offer nearly as much e-mail functionality on the client side. Microsoft has said that customers who want to deploy Office 97 as their standard desktop applications suite should consider Outlook as the messaging and groupware client, mostly because the Outlook client is designed to integrate with the word processing, spreadsheet, and graphics applications much more tightly than Exchange clients are able to at present. Other Microsoft statements give assurances that there will be seamless interoperability between the Exchange clients we have today and the new clients in the future.

The problem in announcing a new client is, of course, the confusion it causes among system developers and designers. If you're still in a 16-bit world the standard Exchange client is the only one available to you, but if you're planning to implement Windows 95 or Windows NT you can opt to use Outlook or the standard client. Creating the confusion that's obviously in people's minds today is not the effect Microsoft intended when it set out to design an integrated desktop information manager that included e-mail, but that's what they've achieved in some cases. At the time of writing the final shape of Outlook hasn't yet been determined so it's too soon to say where this client scores over the existing clients or vice versa. Suffice to say that anyone who's interested in getting involved in an Exchange deployment should keep their ear close to the ground and make sure they know the trade-offs, if any, that have to be made between one client and another.

Schedule+

Apart from its comprehensive electronic mail functionality, Exchange Server comes complete with a good time management and personal organizer application called Schedule+ (see Figure 1.10). A command button to invoke Schedule+ is included in the Exchange client button bar.

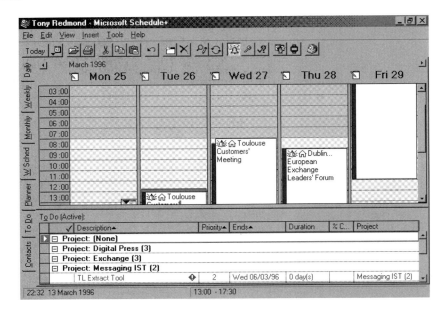

Figure 1.10
Schedule+

A little confusion might arise here because Microsoft also provide a version of Schedule+ with their Office 95 application suite. There are considerable differences between the two versions of Schedule+, the most notable being:

- The Exchange version of Schedule+ operates in a client–server mode which facilitates group scheduling across a distributed network whereas the Office 95 version is primarily designed for standalone operation.
- The Exchange version of Schedule+ stores scheduling information in special folders managed as part of the Information Store.
- The Exchange version of Schedule+ is managed as an integral part of Exchange. This means that you don't have to make any special provision for managing the scheduling information as it's all taken care of for you by normal system management procedures like backup.

If you've been using previous versions of Schedule+ (the versions released with Exchange Server and Office 95 are labeled V7.0) you won't be able to share scheduling information with Exchange. This is because the internal structures are different and the only way to address the issue is to migrate users as quickly as possible to the new release of Schedule+.

Schedule+ is a fine personal calendaring system. Meetings can be set up between different users, and a certain amount of resource scheduling (for example, booking a conference room) can be achieved. Schedule+ includes many items found in low-end project management, personal information systems, and contact managers (all terms I sometimes feel have been generated and then used to help sell software packages). As a user I find little to complain about. Perhaps it would be nice to be able to view an overview of the calendars for a group of different users, subject to permissions, but this is a small point.

Is Exchange Server a mail system or groupware?

'Groupware' is a strange term which means very different things to different people, but it's basically all about helping groups of people to work together in more intelligent ways. In terms of application software groupware is very different to electronic mail because the focus tends to be more on widening information sharing rather than the often purely singular interchange involved in the sending and receipt of an electronic mail message.

Table 1.4 *Exchange groupware capabilities*

Groupware applications		Exchange capabilities
Interpersonal messaging	Used by almost everyone in an organization. Can be thought of as one-to-one communication.	Strong, the basic function of an Exchange server.
Structured document repository (file cabinet)	Location available to applications to store objects. Usually accessible from multiple client applications and often network-enabled, allowing access to documents from points distributed across a WAN.	Medium, based on mixture of public and private folders.
Bulletin boards	Used to make relatively static information from central sources that is available to users on a read-only basis. Can be thought of as one-to-many communication.	Strong, using read-only public folders.
Workflow/electronic forms	Structured form of messaging where "intelligent" items are routed from user to user, following rules which determine the processing steps taken at each stage.	Weak. Electronic forms do not provide the type of comprehensive workflow functionality available in workflow-specific applications. See note on MAPI-Workflow Framework.
Interactive conferencing	Many-to-many communication where users have the ability to post their ideas in electronic forums.	Strong, using writeable public folders.
Time management/ scheduling	Applications that allow users to schedule meetings and appointments with each other. Often includes requests to schedule fixed items such as conference rooms, projectors, or white boards. Electronic mail is commonly used to transport meeting requests between users or across a network.	Strong (Schedule+)

Software vendors have differing definitions of groupware too. Much depends on the aspect of groupware that their products excel in. Microsoft's edge in messaging leads to an assertion that electronic mail is the most important groupware application, with electronic forms and good interpersonal scheduling close afterwards. Lotus, on the other hand, considers information sharing and application development to be at least as important as electronic mail. Both can be right, because each customer situation poses different requirements. I think groupware can be broken down into a number of discrete areas of functionality or user requirements as described in Table 1.4. For each area I've indicated my view on whether Exchange Server provides a solution to the requirement.

Remember that the assessments offered in Table 1.4 are mine, and you will probably have different views on the subject. From the table you can see that Exchange Server offers a great deal of potential in most areas of groupware. The weakest area is probably workflow processing, and this is where competing products will no doubt stress their own capabilities. In rebuttal there are many third-party software developers who are able to provide more sophisticated workflow solutions that can be integrated into Exchange.

Microsoft announced a plan to add workflow capabilities to Exchange in April 1996 with the unveiling of MAPI-Workflow Framework (MAPI-WF), engineered in conjunction with Wang Computers. Documentation and sample code began to appear later on in 1996 but MAPI-WF has not yet been included in shipping releases of Exchange Server at the time of writing.

Given the competitive requirement to include workflow functionality in Exchange Server we can expect to find MAPI-WF functionality in clients and servers sometime in late 1996 or early 1997.

The Exchange application design environment

If Exchange is just a mail server, albeit one that includes notable attributes like an X.400-compliant MTA, would there be any reasons to consider Exchange to be an advance on the previous Microsoft messaging system? Of course, the answer is yes, mostly because Exchange Server is far more reliable and scaleable than any Microsoft Mail post office, but perhaps a more compelling reason is rooted in its groupware capabilities.

In some cases groupware applications are instituted in the form of intelligent document routing functionality enabled by a messaging infrastructure. Others look at collaborative working, functionality enabling people to share information in a more developed and intuitive manner than they can through the simple exchange of mail messages. Lotus Notes has built a huge market around replicated document-oriented databases that allow easy sharing, and its market share has established Lotus Notes as the *de facto* groupware standard in many people's eyes.

Exchange Server approaches groupware from a messaging perspective rather than looking to build applications around document databases. The foundation for Exchange's groupware functionality is provided by public folders. These are repositories whose contents can be automatically replicated to 'replicas' located on other Exchange sites.

Exchange servers sharing a common location (a site in Exchange terminology) share public folders so a user connecting to any server within a site can look at the same set of public folders, access controls permitting, of course.

Public folders can store any type of object. Electronic forms are an intelligent form of object which contain code that can be executed when the forms are accessed by users. A set of sample forms applications are provided with the Exchange server to form a toolkit that can be drawn upon by programmers to develop site-specific applications. The toolkit contains commonly-required applications such as electronic conferences, bulletin boards, and a range of intelligent forms like travel requests. The electronic forms designer component can be used to design forms from scratch, and programmers are able to take the code automatically generated by the forms designer and enhance it with Visual Basic to complete the necessary functionality for production-quality applications. A more comprehensive discussion about the electronic forms designer can be found in Chapter 9.

Application development extensions

The forms designer is able to initiate complex applications, and programmers can complete the application with Visual Basic but this combination does not always deliver a complete application development environment. Exchange server addresses this requirement through the MAPI interface which can be used with Visual C/C++ to build extensions for Microsoft Exchange Server.

Microsoft is busy seeking opportunities to add value to Exchange and create the utmost degree of synergy by weaving Exchange into the fabric of as many applications as possible. One obvious example is to mail-enable the Microsoft desktop 'Office' applications like Word for Windows and Excel. Another is the integration between the Microsoft Internet Explorer (Microsoft's version of a World Wide Web browser) and Exchange. The setup wizard for the Internet Explorer will install 'Internet Mail' as a valid Exchange service provider.

Outside Microsoft a wide range of Independent Software Vendors (ISVs) are engaged in the task of writing extensions for Exchange. Quite logically, most extensions focus on the concept of the Universal Inbox, extending its capabilities to accommodate technologies other than electronic mail. The integration of Delrina's WinFax Pro product to add sophisticated FAX support for the inbox, or the incorporation of voice mail capabilities are good examples of typical third-party extensions to the Universal Inbox.

Exchange Server versus Lotus Notes

Comparisons are invariably made between Exchange Server and Lotus Notes Release 4. On the surface, both appear to have many similar features. Each offers highly functional electronic mail, each uses replication technology to distribute information. Each allows for complex form-based applications to be built and distributed to users. While easy to focus in on specific points of difference, in overall terms it is difficult to compare Lotus Notes and Exchange Server due to the different underlying design philosophies taken by the two products. One bases its strength on great messaging capabilities, the other on applications built around a distributed database.

Selecting one above the other is not simple because it all depends on:

- The situation you are currently in;
- The functionality you expect to use.

In some situations the decision to go with Exchange Server or Lotus Notes doesn't require very much contemplation. For example, if you're running a Microsoft Mail system at the moment then evolving to Exchange Server is very much easier than a migration to Lotus Notes. If you already have Lotus Notes installed and operational it makes sense to continue along that path unless you have compelling reasons to change over.

Exchange is more closely integrated into Windows NT than Lotus Notes. This simple statement marks a fundamental difference between Exchange and Lotus Notes. One depends on a single server platform – Windows NT; the other supports multiple servers.

Achieving the highest possible degree of integration with the base operating system is important, but only if you are happy to base everything around a specific system. Exchange's tremendously close relationship with Windows NT requires your Windows NT infrastructure to be in good shape before an Exchange implementation can begin whereas Lotus Notes uses its own security and management routines that don't explicitly depend on features of Windows NT. A case can therefore be argued that it's easier to deploy Lotus Notes than Exchange, albeit at the cost of losing the close integration of messaging with the operating system. Users suffer a little too. They'll have to log onto Windows NT (or another operating system) and then into Lotus Notes. Providing multiple passwords is very annoying, and keeping track of multiple passwords isn't always easy.

Moving swiftly to the bottom line, I believe that Exchange Server is better in terms of sheer electronic messaging functionality. This assessment is reached not only because of the wide array of client features, but also because of the high degree of integration between the Exchange MTA and the different connectors it supports. Because of the connection engine (the MTA) and the wide range of available connectors for other messaging systems it's easier today to introduce and operate Exchange in a heterogeneous multi-standard messaging world than Lotus Notes. After Lotus release their announced SMTP and X.400 gateways (or MTAs, as they are referred to in Lotus documentation) for Notes the situation may be different, but that assessment must be left until those products are shipping. It's worth noting at this stage that a number of third parties, including the Mesa group and LinkAge software, have products that can connect Exchange with Lotus Notes or even migrate Lotus Notes databases to Exchange.

Leaving messaging aside, if you want to create database-oriented applications which enable users to share information in a structured manner, then Lotus Notes Release 4 offers more flexibility out of the box than Exchange Server. This couldn't have been said about earlier releases of Lotus Notes, but Release 4 has greatly enhanced its development capabilities. The Lotus product has the lead in this area, at least for now. Lotus Notes offers better workflow functionality at present, but this lead might well be cut back after the workflow extension for MAPI makes an appearance.

When looking at systems it's important to ask: "What is the most important function the system is going to fulfill?" If that function is messaging then Exchange Server is better. Even if Exchange doesn't quite have the same degree of flexibility and tools as Lotus Notes it will be able to satisfy most people, albeit with a little extra effort. On the other hand, if the most important function is to help people work together with purpose-built applications that can leverage off the capabilities in the Lotus Notes database structure, then you should probably go for Lotus Notes.

The requirement to extend the infrastructure to reach all interested parties is a common problem in the establishment of groupware applications. In other words, if you're not connected to an electronic mail system that's able to deal with application-specific messages you can't participate in mail-enabled workflow (document routing). A similar point is true if you want to use groupware applications developed around a database. If you can't connect to the database, because you don't have the right software or a network connection is unavailable, then the information contained in the database can be a random collection of bytes for all the use it is to you.

Before you make a decision perhaps it's wise to ponder on two thoughts. First, electronic mail is the predominant groupware application to the majority of users and as such a high degree of importance should be attributed to the capabilities of the electronic mail system. Second, the cost of developing groupware applications is often quite high. A figure of between $50,000 and $60,000 per application has been quoted at Lotus conferences.[11] Either the applications have to be bought in or they must be developed from scratch. In this case internal staff need to be trained or external consultants employed to design, develop, implement, and then support these applications. At this stage the fundamental question is whether a return on investment can be achieved by deploying these purpose-built or bought-in applications? The ads would have you believe that it's easy to achieve the often elusive return on investment, even to an accountant's satisfaction, but do you believe everything that you read in an ad?

Just after the official release of Exchange, a fairly heated debate took place between Lotus and Microsoft regarding the relative merits of Lotus Notes and Exchange (the actual documents can be fetched from the Microsoft and Lotus Web sites). Judging from the comments in the published texts it's clear that Microsoft wants to take the groupware crown away from Lotus and a titanic struggle can be expected in this space over the next few years.

Integration with other Microsoft products

There are several different office product suites available for Windows. If you select Exchange Server as the basis for your messaging system does it matter if you choose a word processing, spreadsheet, or presentation graphics application, or an integrated suite from another vendor?

All the current releases of desktop applications from the major vendors such as Lotus and Novell support the major aspects of Windows integration such as OLE so on the conceptual level there should be no difficulties attaching files generated by applications such as Lotus 1-2-3 or WordPerfect for Windows to messages created by an Exchange client, or storing similar files in public folders for replication throughout an Exchange network.

However, while things may work on a purely practical level it's safe to assume that Microsoft desktop applications will enable a more

---

11. *A considerably higher figure was quoted by an IBM speaker at LotusSphere '96. However, while complex applications need a high level of investment there are many small groupware applications built with Lotus Notes. This fact, along with the better development tools included in Lotus Notes Release 4 will drive down the overall cost per application.*

complete degree of integration. For instance, look at the ability to use Word for Windows as the message creation editor for the Windows 95 Exchange client. You'll need Word for Windows V7 (from Office 95)[12] before 'WordMail' is possible, but it's a nice example of how you can take a standard word processing editor and utilize it for as many tasks as possible, including message composition. The integration isn't perfect at this stage – the ability to insert the text from other messages or add digital signatures to messages is removed once WordMail is used – but I'm sure these small points will be ironed out over time. In a purely practical sense it's more important to consider whether your PC is capable of invoking Word for Windows every time you want to create a new message. Word is, after all, quite a heavy-duty application.

Note that no matter whether Word for Windows or the normal rich text editor is used to create message text the content is always stored and sent in Microsoft Rich Text Format (RTF). This ensures that all clients are able to read messages when they arrive, even if Word for Windows isn't installed.

Other features that can be gained from a purely Microsoft desktop environment include the ability to use the Exchange or Schedule+ address book as the source for mail merge operations carried out by Word for Windows, or the use of MAPI functions to post documents or worksheets directly from an application into a public or private folder. It's difficult to see other applications creating an integration with Exchange that goes to the length of accommodating address books for mail merges, but it should be possible to build code to bridge the gap between an application and Exchange folders. MAPI is, after all, a publicly documented interface.

Exchange server will extract and display OLE properties from objects created by OLE-compliant applications when those objects are imported into Exchange. For instance, the author, title and summary information for an Excel worksheet are stored as OLE properties, so if a worksheet is dragged from the DOS file system and dropped into an Exchange folder, the user is not prompted for a title as it's extracted automatically. Of course, this magic is only viable if users care to fill in the information held as OLE properties. The feature is not restricted to Microsoft applications either as any application is able to support OLE if they desire. However, it's fair to say that the most complete implementation of OLE across a complete suite of applications is found in the Microsoft Office suite.

---

12. *You need a patch for Office 95 to upgrade it to Office 95a before some of the advanced features such as 'Post to Exchange folder' from Word or Excel work properly.*

If you are going to switch to a purely Microsoft desktop environment it may be best to do so in conjunction with a change to the desktop operating system as this will concentrate all the changes in a single operation. Switching to the latest version of Windows and the Microsoft Office suite at the same time is something that many corporate installations are considering today, but remember that such a changeover may have other impacts like hardware upgrades.

At the end of the day the decision about which desktop applications are going to be used depends on many factors, including some historical aspects and how the people who actually use the applications feel about things. An attempt to change someone's word processor or spreadsheet can be taken as a personal insult, especially if people have accumulated personal libraries of useful macros or other shortcuts. The retraining requirement plus the cost of switching applications, no matter how tempting the trade-in offers seem, are other points to bear in mind.

Exchange and the Internet

The Internet has been around for years, but over the past few years there has been an explosive growth in interest from both the computing and non-computing communities in the potential possible from a global information highway. The establishment of the World Wide Web (WWW) and easy availability of Web browsers such as Netscape, Mosaic, and Microsoft's Internet Explorer has brought the power of distributed computing home to many people. The ease by which anyone with an Internet presence can make information available to others by establishing a Web site is stunning when considered against the problems that the same exercise would have met a few short years ago. Look at the number of newspaper and magazine advertisements published today that include URLs[13] for Web sites. If you pick up a magazine from 1995 or before you'd perhaps find one or two examples. Now URLs are everywhere, despite their technical and non-user friendly nature.

Another interesting aspect to consider is the influence that Internet-evolved standards are having within corporate computing networks. Once the focus was on using functionality like the World Wide Web or TCP/IP as a basis for presenting a corporate external face to

---

13. URL = Universal Resource Locator, a network pointer to a page on a Web site. Enterprises commonly publish the URL for their 'home page', the entry point to their Web site. `Http://www.digital.com` is the URL pointing to the home page for Digital Equipment Corporation.

the world, but now there's more and more use of technology from the Internet within internal networks to form the Intranets.[14]

Developments such as secure tunneling (the ability to make a direct connection from the Internet through a firewall to an internal network via an encrypted communication channel) meld the Internet with Intranets to present what's apparently a single seamless network to users. Indeed, the real growth over the next few years are likely not to be in the Internet itself, but rather in the development and deployment of Internet-originated technologies within corporations as people move towards a more distributed way of working.

In terms of electronic mail it's a sobering thought that the number of people equipped with Internet mail accounts may already have passed or will soon pass the number of mail accounts operating in corporate systems.[15] The Internet has truly delivered e-mail to the masses. Metcalfe's Law, part of the lore of the computer industry and named after Bob Metcalfe, the inventor of the Ethernet networking protocol and founder of 3Com Corporation, states that the power of a network increases with the square of the nodes installed in the network. In other words, as PCs are added to a network people have more and more opportunity to share information using those PCs via e-mail, the Web, traditional file and print services, and other mechanisms. All of this means that the available network bandwidth had better increase in line with the extra nodes else the performance delivered to users will steadily degrade over time. This fact is as true for private networks as it is for the Internet.

Some observers of computing trends have pointed to the evolution of Web browsers to include e-mail functionality and asked whether a compelling case exists for enterprises to consider jettisoning their messaging and information distribution infrastructures in favor of a move to an Internet-based solution. Cost is a major reason for such a move even being considered. Comparing the cost of Internet connections together with WWW software versus the costs of installing and operating networks, servers, and clients internally appears to make a great case for a move to do business on the Internet because, generally speaking, everything can be done much more cheaply. Today the degree of functionality available in Internet-centric e-mail systems is lower than a fully-fledged system such as Exchange. These systems will

---

14. *An Intranet is a network built from Internet-type components (World Wide Web, TCP/IP networks, etc.) but which operates purely within the boundaries of a single company or enterprise.*

15. *'Electronic Mail and Message Systems' (April 29, 1996) reports 47,260,000 LAN-based mailboxes and 30,810 host-based mailboxes installed as of March 31, 1996.*

never be as functional as long as they are based on protocols such as POP/3, where clients pull messages down from the server for local processing. This system works, but only as long as you are content to use the same PC all the time and never want to move from PC to PC within an organization.

The promise of low-cost connectivity seems compelling but while the costs involved in connecting a single individual to the Internet are cheap, the costs of achieving consistent, secure, and reliable messaging across the Internet for hundreds or thousands of people aren't necessarily so low, especially if a high value is placed on system availability, data security, and 100% guaranteed message delivery. Internet messaging tools exist, but other applications like scheduling, workflow, and collaborative authoring don't. The Internet already creaks and groans (in an electronic sense) during heavy processing periods, chiefly when the working hours for people on the east and west coasts of the United States overlap, so perhaps moving to a structure that's already having problems handling the load isn't such a wise move for a corporation?

Even if a general move isn't going to be made to use the Internet as a corporate infrastructure the desire still exists within corporations to achieve whatever leverage is possible from the resources available within the Internet. Seeking to create close links between the information held in internal systems and the information available externally (subject always to the installation of a good firewall to prevent unauthorized access) is a good strategy to take. Microsoft has announced their intention of building a high degree of Internet connectivity into their desktop and server products. The Internet Assistant for Word for Windows, which allows users to save documents in HTML (Hypertext Mark-Up Language) format suitable for publication in a Web site is a good example of how a desktop application can be made Internet-sensitive. Products like Front Page (to generate and manage the contents of a Web site) and the Internet Information Server are examples of Microsoft products directed completely at the Internet, and plans have been announced to add to existing products with a firewall for Windows NT and the capability to support secure electronic transactions for Web applications.

Exchange Server delivers Internet-supporting features by:

- Permitting a high degree of access to people using Internet mail through the Exchange Internet Mail Connector. The Internet Mail Connector is described in detail in Chapter 5.
- Supporting URLs placed in messages to be used as a starting point for WWW browsers. If a URL is placed in a message a user can double-click on the URL, and if a WWW browser is avail-

able on the PC it will be launched in order to access the information pointed to by the URL.
- Permitting a high degree of access to Internet information sources by allowing the contents of Internet Newsgroups to flow into public folders held on an Exchange server.
- Allowing information held in Exchange public folders to be accessed by WWW browsers.

Newsgroups are the traditional mechanism on the Internet to allow people to share information with lots of others in the form of electronic discussions. The Microsoft Exchange Internet News Connector (available at the end of 1996) is able to direct the articles placed in a USENET newsfeed to a nominated public folder on an Exchange server. Exchange users are then able to read the articles from the public folder and post replies back to the original newsgroup. A direct TCP/IP connection is made between the Exchange News Connector and the relevant newsfeeds to send and receive data.

Exchange and the World Wide Web

Public folders are also used with the Microsoft Exchange Web Connector (available in late 1996). The combination enables information held in public folders to be shared by anyone who has access to a WWW browser. The Web connector is able to translate the structure and content of public folders and provide it to a WWW browser in HTML format. The public folder hierarchy is converted into a set of hot spots within a page. Clicking on the hot point for a folder forces the messages, documents, and other items in the folder to be listed to the browser, again as hot spots in a page. Clicking on the hot spot for an item instructs Exchange to send the item's content across the network to the Web client, where the only dependency comes into play – no attempt is made to convert the content into a form that any client can read. A viewer or application must be available on the client to enable everything to come together and have the content fully accessible to Web clients.

HTML pages are generated dynamically as users browse through public folders, so new items are available immediately after they have been posted. Dynamic HTML generation avoids the need for complex HTML authoring tools to make general document-oriented information ready for publication on the Web. HTML authoring tools will still be required if you want to generate highly graphical or eye-catching pages, for instance to use as a home page, but using dynamic HTML generation Exchange folders can serve as a largely self-managing repository for the majority of the information you need to publish externally.

The essential point about the Exchange Web Connector is its ability to make data understandable to just about every WWW browser available today. Even if your strategic direction is to move towards the concept of a Universal Inbox for electronic information, not everyone will use Exchange clients and have direct access to public folders, but everyone wants to have free and easy access to information. Because information is everything, the need to share information is becoming more and more business-critical. The Exchange Web Connector makes sure that the electronic mail community within an enterprise doesn't fall into the trap of introducing yet another restricted information repository.

The Exchange Web Connector works in conjunction with the Microsoft Internet Information Server and is built using the Microsoft ISAPI (Internet Services Application Programming Interface). The Internet Information Server allows URLs to be published to point to a public folder which then appears to the WWW browser like any other resource. The beauty of using public folders in this manner is that a single consistent source of information is established for access internally and externally, thus eliminating redundant information storage. The Microsoft Internet Information Server is built into Windows NT V4.0 as part of the base operating system. Because a web server is always going to be available on the same computer as Exchange it can be expected that closer and closer links between the two technologies will develop over the next few years.

Allowing Exchange Server to meld in a fairly seamless fashion into the world of the Internet is good news for system implementers. It means that the advantages of being able to communicate with Internet correspondents and publishing to a world-wide audience via the Web can be attained using the same infrastructure, leading to high degree of synergy. Possibly more important is the merging, from a user perspective, of multiple information sources into a cohesive whole, pointing the way forward to a stage when the desktop explorer paradigm is expanded to accommodate PC resources, mailboxes, and the Web. In summary, the Internet extensions for Exchange are good examples of the 'Universal Inbox' concept reaching fruition in this space.

Challenges for Microsoft Exchange Server

Every new software that arrives on the technology scene faces challenges that must be overcome before the software is deemed to be successful. Some of the challenges are inherited from the environment the software is deployed into; others arise from people who work with the software, or in the links to other products established by APIs or network connections. Microsoft Exchange Server is not built with magic, nor can the server perform tricks. Along with its own set of challenges the eventual success of the Exchange server is influenced by many of the same challenges that face other messaging products. This section outlines, in fairly broad strokes, the most important challenges. Details of how you might face those challenges and how to be successful in your implementation follow in later chapters.

The Microsoft legacy

The obvious first challenge for Exchange Server is the fact that Microsoft has no history in the design and implementation of enterprise-level messaging systems. In fact, Exchange Server can be described as the first family of e-mail products that Microsoft has engineered from scratch. The previous generation of e-mail clients, post offices, and connectors was largely bought in from an external company in the form of a product called Network Courier, and then released as Microsoft Mail. The fundamental principles of LAN-based e-mail systems established in products like Network Courier and Lotus cc:Mail are preserved to this day in Microsoft Mail, and I think it's fair to say that the evolution of Microsoft Mail since its purchase has been in a series of small steps rather than a total redesign.

But it's important to note that the Microsoft Mail clients and its Post Office (server) are far removed from the Exchange program and, apart from the fact that Microsoft Mail clients can be incorporated in an Exchange environment via the Microsoft Mail connector, there is no direct link between the two. It would therefore be unfair to draw any conclusion about Exchange from past experience with Microsoft Mail.

Moving on from a basic e-mail client, Exchange Server is intended to be much more than a 'mail user agent.'[16] Bundled into Exchange server is a messaging server, a messaging backbone, a directory service, and the connections that enable the 'Universal Inbox.' Implementations from other vendors have not attempted to build all this functionality into a single product, preferring instead to spread it across several products that can, if required, be interconnected to form a logical MTA. The fact that Microsoft has little or no background in this type of messaging technology allows a fresh and brand new look at MTA designs, and maybe it's the right way to go! Certainly, the level of integration established within Exchange Server has set a new standard for the electronic mail industry.

---

16. *A very basic definition of a mail user agent is a program that allows users to compose, read, and send messages. Many additional options can be built on top of this basic set of functionality.*

Competing in the corporate messaging market

One fundamental truth of client–server computing is that older methods of piloting system implementations are obsolete and invariably produce inaccurate results. When I started working with mainframe computer systems we used to pilot new software by running test suites against a limited set of users, carefully recording results as we went. Those results were then used as the basis to determine the likely sizing for full-scale implementations of whatever system we had in mind. In simple terms, if the pilot was run for 20 terminals (users) then roughly 5 times the resources were required to support 100 users, and so on.

The 'test then multiply' methodology survived the mainframe era. Suitably modified I have seen it used to size PC LANs. For example, how much disk to attach to a server, and so on. The same methodology just does not work in client–server implementations because it is so hard to accurately predict what will happen when the system goes live.

In working with e-mail systems over the last fifteen years or so I have found that users learn more about the system every day they're connected. People keep on trying to do new things and learn through a process of trial and experiment. Where users might start by sending two messages a day soon they're up to ten, and then on to twenty. Where once someone would limit themselves to a few brief lines in an electronic memo, tomorrow they write their life story. Where two or three addresses are the norm on messages numbers grow to a stage where large (200+) distribution lists become the norm. Where users would never consider rich text attachments they progress to attach anything and everything that can exist on their hard drive, including multi-megabyte files. Overall, the average size of messages is going up and up and some large organizations have experienced a ten-fold increase in average message size (from approximately 4Kb to 40Kb) in the period 1991–1995. This trend can be expected to increase and the average message size may well reach 100Kb in some networks by the year 2000, or even sooner if the artistic side of users finds fulfillment in the increasingly graphic capabilities of today's desktop applications.

What affect will it have on your e-mail system if someone attaches a 20Mb video or multimedia presentation to a message and sends it to all their friends throughout the network? You may think that a 15 or 20Mb file is never going to be circulated via e-mail within your organization, but I have seen larger files than this sent out across a number of customer networks many times already. Large PowerPoint presentations originating from marketing departments are particular culprits.

Most mail servers receiving such large messages don't perform quickly or smoothly, and some collapse under the load.

The increasing volume and size of messages mean that messaging systems are becoming more and more loaded as time goes on. If systems are not monitored and tuned on a continual basis the old adage that all performance always degrades over time (the best performance you ever see is immediately after a new system is switched on for the first time) comes into play and service levels for users degrade.

Running an Exchange server is not the same as running a Post Office on a LAN. There is more to think about, Windows NT is a more complex operating system than DOS, Windows, or Novell NetWare, and connectivity with other messaging environments is more of an issue than ever before. Exchange servers will support larger user communities than any LAN-based Post Office, so more users are affected at one time if anything goes wrong with the server.

There's a whole new skill set to learn to, littered with masses of new acronyms calculated to wear out valuable system management brain cells. Hopefully, the remainder of this book provides some illumination to guide the way.

2

Establishing the Infrastructure for Exchange Server

Introduction

Every computer system or application is built on a set of basic concepts that must be mastered before an implementation can be considered. This chapter is my attempt to explain what I believe are the most important concepts relating to an implementation of Microsoft Exchange Server. We'll look at the basic organization of the Exchange messaging infrastructure, how to connect servers together, and the impact of Exchange Server on a network.

More detailed discussions about some of the points raised in this chapter, such as how to select and deploy the different connectors to link sites and other messaging systems together, are described in detail in Chapter 5.

Exchange Server and its clients are packaged and sold as shrink-wrapped software that you can purchase at many retail computer outlets. Unwrapping the packaging and taking out the CDs is done in a blink of an eye, but it's unwise to continue to rush forward and run the SETUP utility to install the new server. Successful implementations of Exchange Server require a lot of detailed up-front planning and system preparation, especially if you plan to operate a multiserver, multisite, distributed organization. The process of planning begins by understanding how an Exchange Server environment is developed on top of Windows NT.

Organizations, sites, and servers

Anyone considering the implementation of a messaging infrastructure built around Microsoft Exchange Server needs to understand what the terms 'organizations', 'sites', and 'servers' mean within the context of the overall system.

The *organization* you create to implement Exchange Server represents the total messaging enterprise and is layered on top of the Windows NT security model. The organization can be described as the full messaging infrastructure, and is composed of one or more Exchange sites.

A *server* is a computer running the Windows NT Server operating system, with Exchange Server software installed on top of the Windows NT operating system. Note that there is a differentiation between Windows NT Server and Windows NT workstation, the two variants of the operating system. A computer running Windows NT workstation can be an Exchange client, but is not able to act as an Exchange server.

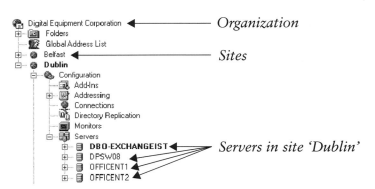

Figure 2.1
Organization, sites, and servers

A *site* is often a single physical or geographical location where one or more Exchange servers are situated. Communications between the different Exchange servers forming a site are carried out with synchronous RPCs so the network links between the servers must be capable of supporting the load generated by client-generated calls in a very responsive manner. It is also important that the network connections within a site are reliable and predictable, and not prone to failure as this will affect the replication of data between the different servers in the site.

Knowing how users communicate with each other is good information to have when planning where servers are located or how they might be formed into sites. Keeping messages on a single server provides the fastest possible delivery service for users, so it's a good idea to locate users who need to communicate on a frequent basis on the same server. Building a site from a collection of user groups who pass information between the groups is a logical progression of the same idea. Clearly it's easiest to build up message patterns when you already operate a mail system, but even if you don't have an existing system to monitor it pays to spend some time on the subject to try and develop some educated guesses. Any data based on reality will result in a much better initial implementation of Exchange Server than would otherwise occur if users are allocated to servers in an unstructured manner.

If you do have an existing system look for opportunities to improve the current message flow. It's a sad fact of life that many systems have evolved through passive management and there is no guarantee that users are allocated in an optimum fashion today. Don't be afraid to move users from server to server (within a site) after the implementation begins, if that seems to make sense.

Network connections are an important influence on the decision whether a location will be a discrete site or join other servers in (usually) close physical proximity to form a site. An office serving many people might, for instance, be deemed to be a site in its own right because its network connections to the rest of the organization cannot sustain the predicted traffic generated by the flow of messages in and out of the server. Unlike other messaging systems, Exchange Server uses a type of specially-encoded message to replicate data, so items like directory updates must be taken into account when predicting network traffic. It is also a reasonable argument for a single server to become a site because of the number of supported users. However, in situations where many users are to be supported, multiple servers will always provide better system availability as you'll eliminate a potential single point of failure.

Once a site is established all of the Exchange servers that collectively form the site share a single collection of data relating to connections (to external systems), and recipients and other directory information. All of the servers in a site can be administered from a single central location. General wisdom is that it's better to limit the total number of sites within an organization if at all possible because this makes everything easier to manage. While there are no real limits to the total number of servers that can form a site, you should restrain yourself to no more than 50 servers in a site. The logic behind this recommendation is simply based on the fact that it's easier to manage less servers than more.

Network connections between Exchange system components

Perhaps it makes things easier to associate the network links that tie things together with the terms that have just been introduced. A range of different types of links are normally used to create the network infrastructure that ties an organization together. Consider a multinational enterprise with offices in Europe, Asia, and the United States. Three separate geographical areas are involved in this scenario, and each is likely to have different characteristics in terms of the connections that are available. Within the United States, for instance, it's easier and cheaper to establish high-speed, high-bandwidth connections between locations than in Europe or Asia. Within the organization therefore you might find satellite intercontinental links, 64Kb landline links between offices in an individual country, and fiber-optic FDDI extended LANs connecting locations in a single metropolitan area.

Within a site the range of network links is much simpler. All the Exchange servers in a site share a common repository of information, but this is impossible unless the connections between the servers is fast enough to accommodate the data that passes around. Consider directory replication. In a site directories are replicated automatically in the form of messages generated, sent, and processed as background operations. An automatically updated directory ensures that messages are not addressed incorrectly and permits users to send messages to new recipients as soon as they are added to the system.

Exchange clients are normally connected to their servers via a LAN so the connection is fast and only limited to the speed of the LAN, for example, 10 Mbit/second for Ethernet. You shouldn't ever encounter problems transferring data between servers and clients unless message contents are huge or the LAN itself is saturated. Abnormal conditions will sometimes occur to interfere with the perceived transfer speed (for users), such as when very large messages are accessed by many users at one time, but in general LAN throughput shouldn't be an issue.

Two or more organizations

As we've seen, the model used by Exchange attempts to encapsulate a complete enterprise in terms of a single self-contained unit called an organization, breaking the enterprise down into sites and eventually servers. The model works well for smaller enterprises where cooperation is easier to achieve but poses some challenges for larger corporations. If the corporate operating model stresses decentralization with each department taking charge of their own computing destiny, then multiple Exchange organizations can easily evolve, perhaps one for each country or one for each operating unit. What can be said about these situations?

Apart from its messaging connectors, Exchange is equipped with no mechanisms to facilitate the transfer of information from one organization to another. According to the rules no form of public folder sharing is possible, encryption will be stripped from messages as they leave one organization for another, and directory entries cannot be replicated automatically. Workarounds must be found to transfer information, either via the messaging service or with some home-grown manual processes.

A little lateral thinking reveals that a certain level of inter-organization data exchange can be accomplished as follows:

- Messaging between the two organizations shouldn't be a problem. If both organizations use a TCP/IP network and can connect to the Internet the easiest way to establish a messaging connection is via the Internet Mail Connector. Using TCP/IP as the base protocol for an X.400 connector is also more than feasible.
- It is possible to create rules for public folders so that when new information is posted it is automatically sent to a recipient, which could be a public folder in the other organization. Deletions cannot be handled by rules, so manual notifications of deletions are necessary if the different sets of public folders are not to become very much out of step with each other. Also, conflicts which occur when public folder contents are changed by multiple users at the same time cannot be detected as would be the case within a single organization.
- Directory information can be exported from each participating organization and imported into whatever other organization is interested in it. Directory exports are in the form of CSV (Comma Separated Value) files which can be mailed to an appropriate recipient. The contents of the export file need to be edited before they are imported as the mailbox recipients from the exporting organization are custom recipients for the importing organization. Editing can be done with a variety of tools, including a spreadsheet, but as it's a repetitive operation following well-defined rules it's best to write a program to do the job.

As Exchange grows in popularity I'm pretty sure that either ISVs will create a toolkit to make interorganization transfers easier or Microsoft will upgrade Exchange to allow superorganizations be created from a group of subsidiaries. After all, not every enterprise has the luxury of being so well coordinated to fit into a single self-contained unit.

Windows NT, domains, and security

Apart from mail encryption and digital signatures, Exchange Server provides no special security features of its own. Instead, Exchange relies on all of the security facilities built into Windows NT operating system. For instance, a user must be able to authenticate themselves to

Windows NT before they can ever connect a client to an Exchange server. A user is authenticated by providing a valid account name and password during the initial log-on from a client to a Windows NT server. The Windows NT NetLogon service validates the account name and password against the Security Account Manager (SAM) database, and if the authentication check is successful a user process is created on the client. After it is created the process is granted the set of rights allocated to the user account in the form of a security access token. The access token contains information about the user and can be used to check whether a user is entitled to access a file or other object, for instance, a Microsoft Exchange mailbox.

Because Exchange is so tightly integrated with Windows NT you must take account of the Windows NT domain and trust models that are already in place, or design a model that will accommodate the needs of the messaging system. No implementation of Exchange will succeed if the underlying Windows NT structure is unstable. It is important to note at this point that restructuring a domain is not a matter of setting a few switches or parameters following a reboot of all the systems in the domain. In most cases, changing anything fundamental in the domain structure requires a complete re-installation of Windows NT on each system in the domain. Given the potential workload generated by reinstallations as well as the impact on users and an organization, this is clearly not something that any reasonable system administrator wants to even consider.

Just to get a formal definition in place, a Windows NT domain is a logical set of workstations and servers that are managed as a single unit. The domain shares a common security policy and user account database, as encapsulated in the SAM. The SAM is stored as part of the Windows NT registry and contains information about global and user accounts, including the user name, password, groups which the account is a member of, any restrictions that might be in place, and the account's SID (Security Identifier). All this data is doubly encrypted.

The minimum requirement for a domain is one system running Windows NT server software, which acts as the Primary Domain Controller (PDC) and holds the copy of the domain's SAM. A domain can also contain many other servers and workstations distributed across a wide area. Because all servers in a domain share a common SAM it is only necessary to create a user account once for each domain. Once equipped with a valid account name and password a user is able to connect to their resources by logging on to any of the server computers within the domain. A domain can contain one or more Windows NT servers and manage a wide array of clients including Windows NT workstations, Windows for WorkGroups, and DOS.

Domain controllers

Within each domain at least one server will be allocated the task of authenticating all the log-on requests from clients. This server stores and maintains the security database for the domain and implements all the changes made by applications throughout the domain. For example, if a user is granted the necessary access rights to be able to manage someone else's mailbox, the fact that the access rights have been granted will be registered in the security database. A small domain will have one server, referred to as the Primary Domain Controller, and there can be only one PDC per domain. However, large domains typically implement one or more backup domain controllers to enable operations to continue should anything happen to the PDC. These servers are called Backup Domain Controllers (BDCs) and they hold copies of the security database. Changes to the security database are automatically replicated between the PDC and the BDCs, normally every five minutes. The copies of the security database therefore should never be more than 5 minutes out of date, although it is possible for some small inconsistencies to arise if replication has not been completed.

PDCs are computers and all computers, no matter how reliable the operating system and reliable the environment, are prone to operating problems. If the PDC experiences a problem such as a system crash or becomes unavailable due to a network outage, one of the BDCs can be promoted to become the PDC on a temporary basis until normal service is resumed. This switch-over arrangement allows the domain to continue to operate while the original PDC is off-line. When the original PDC is available again any changes the backup controller has made to the security database are automatically replicated back and synchronized.

Apart from the possibility of taking over from the PDC in case of failure, BDCs can also be used to balance the load generated by user authentication requests and so provide a degree of fault tolerance in this respect. When this happens the authentication requests are channelled to the BDC for verification in a totally transparent manner. Users are certainly not aware which server is responsible for handling their log-on. In large installations it's wise to avoid PDC saturation at peak times such as the start of the business day by sharing the authentication load across BDCs. The general recommendation is to have a BDC for each physical LAN or site running Microsoft Exchange Server. Up to 2,000 users can be serviced by a BDC.

In any relatively medium to large Windows NT installation the PDC will have to satisfy a reasonable workload of authentication requests and updates to the security database. Whatever the speed in which updates are applied to the security database, it is critical that authentication requests are serviced quickly and users can complete the log-on process quickly. For this reason it is unwise to install Exchange Server on the same Windows NT computer that acts as the PDC. A more practical consideration is the fact that if Exchange Server is running on the same computer as the PDC it is difficult to restore the Exchange information and directory stores from backups to an operational state should a problem occur. We'll discuss this particular issue in Chapter 4 (see page 193).

Types of servers

The retail versions of Windows NT is broken down into server and workstation software. We've now seen that Windows NT supports different kinds of security workload for a server. This leads to a point where we recognize that there are systems running Windows NT server which never participate in security processing (as a PDC or BDC). These servers are dedicated application servers, or sometimes called non-domain servers.

Application servers off-load security processing to a PDC or BDC, allowing all the resources of the server to be dedicated to a specific application or set of applications. Because of the potentially heavy demands made by a messaging system, it is a good tactic to plan to install and operate Microsoft Exchange server on systems acting as application servers.

In a small domain it is possible to have a server that acts as the PDC, provides file and print services to a set of users, and runs Microsoft Exchange Server. However, there is a limit to the number of users that can be supported in this case, depending on the hardware configuration that's installed. When the time comes for expansion the natural option is to install a dedicated application server into the domain and move the majority of Microsoft Exchange processing over to the new server, perhaps leaving workload like directory synchronization with external sources or a specific connector on the original system.

Trust relationships

Windows NT uses trust relationships to link domains in terms of the actions a user can take. If domain A trusts domain B it means that a user from domain B will be able to log onto a server in domain A, and then access resources controlled by domain A. This can occur because the trust relationship between the domains attributes rights and permissions for objects controlled by domain A to any registered user from domain B. Of course, there are some limitations to what a user from a trusted domain is allowed to do or the data they can access, but this simplified explanation will serve for now.

Shared mailboxes provide a good example of the domain trust mechanism in action. Shared mailboxes can serve as common repositories for messages sent to organizational units. For example, inquiries about new products could be sent to a mailbox controlled by the marketing department, and the messages arriving there can be processed by any user who has permission to access the mailbox. If all the accounts that need to process messages in the mailbox connect to the same server or site then the question of trusted access does not arise. However, if you wanted to allow a remote user to access the mailbox that user must belong to a trusted domain as Windows NT will not allow a non-trusted domain to even see the mailbox.

Windows NT domain models

Understanding an existing Windows NT domain and security model or designing an appropriate domain model (if you are starting to use Windows NT) are important pieces of an Exchange implementation plan. In fact, getting the domain model right or understanding how best to leverage off an existing domain model is probably the single most critical item on the path to a successful implementation.

There are four distinct Windows NT domain models that can be implemented within an organization. These are:

- Single domain model
- Single master domain model
- Multiple master domain model
- Complete trust domain model

Obviously if you don't have a Windows NT infrastructure already in place you have total freedom over the type of domain model you select. Lots of enterprises have experimented with Windows NT since it was first released in 1993 but may not be using Windows NT for anything other than a desktop operating system or to provide shared file and print services to other Windows clients.

Windows NT is probably the finest desktop operating system available today and it certainly does an excellent job of providing shared file and print services, but these implementations tend to be carried out in a local or departmental manner and do not pay special heed to the needs of the organization as a whole. In other words, you can very quickly install Windows NT servers and connect clients in to form your own domain, but if everyone does this for their own department the resulting Windows NT infrastructure is fragmented. It's also highly likely that no comprehensive set of trust relationships exist. We'll return to the question of what tactic to take in this instance, but first let's review the options open for domain models.

Single domain model

The single domain model (see Figure 2.2) is by far the simplest domain model that can be implemented for Windows NT. It is also the most common model selected for departmental-style implementations, especially where Windows NT has replaced another network operating system such as Novell NetWare as the base for shared file and print services.

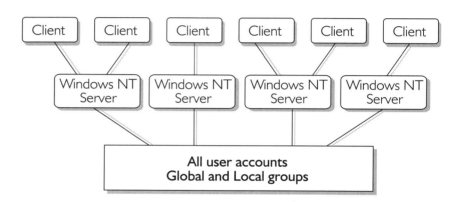

Figure 2.2 *Windows NT single domain model*

Within the single domain model all users are registered in a single security database, but there are practical and technical points that need to be borne in mind.

Windows NT V3.5 increased the upper limit for the number of user accounts that can be registered in a domain from 10,000 to a theoretical limit of 40,000. However, the logistics involved in managing such a large number of user accounts almost always means that another model is considered well before the 'old' limit of 10,000 is attained, unless there are lots of system administrators waiting around for work to be done.

The technical limitation of 40,000 is not actually a simple matter of Windows NT reaching a magic number and then refusing to register any more users. Instead, the upper limit is determined by the size of the SAM database file in conjunction with the amount of physical memory available on the PDC. Microsoft recommend that the size of the SAM is kept below 40Mb. Databases larger than 40Mb have been tested in software laboratories and work, but it's wise to pay attention to the firm recommendations from Microsoft. A quick calculation of 40Mb for 40,000 users appears to indicate that the details of each user account occupies 1Kb in the database and indeed it is possible to create a situation like this, as long as global groups or machine accounts[1] *are not created.*

Within any large user population the normal situation is to operate with a selection of global groups, if only to reduce the level of system administration overhead required to manage access to shared resources, so it's highly unlikely that no groups will be active. Group details occupy varying amounts of space, depending on the number of members within the group. Microsoft suggest using 4Kb as an average for each group, driving down the space available within the SAM for individual user accounts and decreasing the theoretical maximum from 40,000.

Within a single domain model no trust relationships are required because no other domains are known. If you are a small, single-site enterprise with a small number of users (well below 10,000) then the single domain model is a natural choice. This model allows fairly simple and straightforward centralized management of all user accounts and global resources, including those used by Exchange.

The major drawback is that the PDC can become overloaded or slow down other computers if it is a small computer, has too many user accounts to manage (remember each authentication request or log-on is processed by the PDC), or has slow network links to servers and clients located in different parts of the domain. The authentication workload can be somewhat offloaded to BDCs, but the PDC still has a lot of work to do in circulating security information updates to its backup controllers. Concentrating the security workload in a single PDC is the major reason why the single domain model is not recommended for large numbers of users or an enterprise that is distributed across many sites.

Single master domain model

Once a number of different sites are present within an organization you might start to consider expanding away from the single domain model. The natural evolutionary step is the single master domain model, named because a single central domain is established as a point of unification for subsidiary Windows NT servers. User accounts and global groups are registered in the central domain but local resources

---

1. *Machine accounts are automatically created by Windows NT to allow workstations or servers to participate in the security model.*

can be managed from the subsidiary servers. Because of the reliance on the central domain it's essential that systems to act as BDCs are maintained.

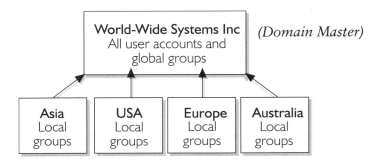

Figure 2.3
Single master domain model

Figure 2.3 illustrates a single master domain created for a company called World-Wide Systems Incorporated. It is possible to create a model where authentication is carried out in one place for log-ons and other security requests originating in Asia, the US, Europe, and Australia, but this would only be practical if extremely fast and dedicated network links are available all the time. Possibly a better and more realistic example would be a single master domain established to serve all users within a large metropolitan area like London or New York, with the individual subsidiary servers distributed to different locations within the area.

Complete trust domain model

Once an organization grows past approximately 10,000 user accounts a single domain often becomes unwieldy. Two options exist, one usually regarded as fairly difficult to set up and administer while the other is fairly simple, albeit less structured. The simple option is the complete trust domain model, a way of distributing the management of all resources to different domains located throughout an enterprise. Each domain creates and manages its own user accounts and groups, for instance. No attempt is made to unify the domains together, but each domain trusts the others so resources such as Exchange public folders can be shared. The model is very flexible because new domains can join at any time, but it can also be somewhat chaotic because no strong central coordination is achieved.

Figure 2.4
Complete trust domain model

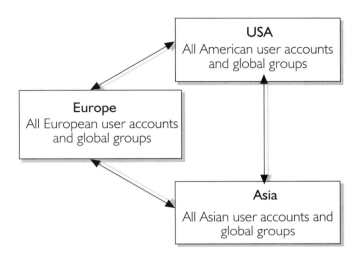

The complete trust domain model (Figure 2.4) removes the upper limit of 10,000 users and can therefore be considered to be scaleable. Connecting two or three domains together in this manner to allow people to share information certainly does the job, and if you are not worried about having a complete trust relationship with the other domains the simplicity of the model has much to recommend it, especially if the major Windows NT application is Exchange Server. However, if you require better coordination, centralized management, or the ability to partition your Windows NT infrastructure in a more controlled manner the complete trust domain model may not be appropriate.

Multiple master domain model

The most scaleable model is provided by a two-tier domain model (Figure 2.5). The first tier contains a set of master domains that maintain two-way trust relationships between each other. User accounts are registered in one of the master domains and the trust relationship between the domains means that all user accounts are known throughout the enterprise.

The second tier is composed of domains serving discrete sections of the overall organization. These sections might be created along departmental, organizational, or, as shown in the figure, geographical divisions. The responsibility for managing resources resides at the second tier. Note that the second-tier domains all maintain one-way trust relationships with the first-tier domains. This means that the second-tier domains trust any information provided by the first-tier whereas the opposite is not true.

Each new domain added at either tier increases the number of trust relationships that must be managed so it's wise not to become too enthusiastic when creating first-tier domains. Try and establish a fairly high-level picture of the overall enterprise at the first-tier, using convenient divisions such as the continental sections as illustrated. Enterprises broken down into operational divisions such as Manufacturing, Sales, Marketing, and so on can consider using these divisions but geographical lines are probably more practical because network links are normally organized like this, with very fast connections within a physical location and slower connections maintained between countries. Once again it's important to have BDCs deployed within each second-tier domain, just in case.

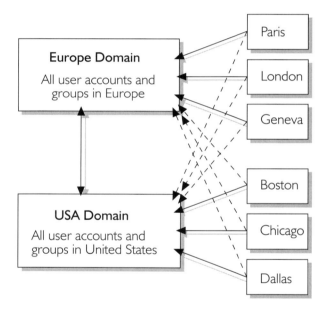

Figure 2.5
Multiple master domain model

Because of its relative ease of management that scales well over thousands of user accounts, most large distributed enterprises, including the internal networks operating by Microsoft and Digital, use either the master domain model or multiple master domain model. This in itself is not necessarily a recommendation that these models are best for you, but if you are running a large-scale implementation the master domain model and the multiple master variant are both leading contenders for deployment.

Getting help – automated tools

The Microsoft TechNet CD-ROM (May 1996 edition onwards) contains two software tools which help to collect information about the essential characteristics of the Windows NT and Exchange organizational structures that are best for your enterprise. These tools are:

1. The Windows NT Domain Planner
2. The Exchange Server Modeling Tool

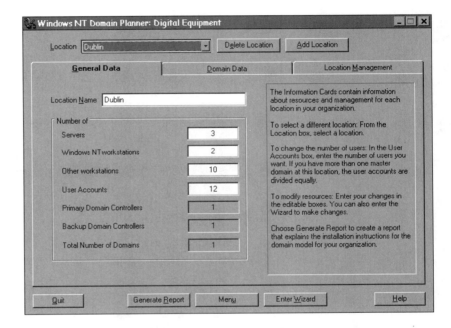

Figure 2.6
Windows NT Domain Planner

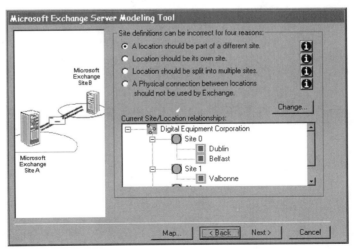

Figure 2.7
Inputting site information into the Exchange Modeling Tool

The basis of both tools is simple. A question and answer session is conducted using 'wizard' technology. In the case of the Domain Planner you answer questions such as the total number of users, whether you want to administer all servers centrally, and so on. After all questions are answered you can generate a report containing the recommendations arrived at by the wizard. If you don't like the recommendations you can go back and modify earlier answers (see Figure 2.6) and see if the recommendations change.

Everything you enter into the domain planner is captured into a configuration file. In turn, the domain information held in the configuration can be fed into the Exchange modeling tool. This reflects the close and intimate relationship between a solid implementation of a Windows NT domain structure and eventual success with the deployment of Exchange on top of that structure.

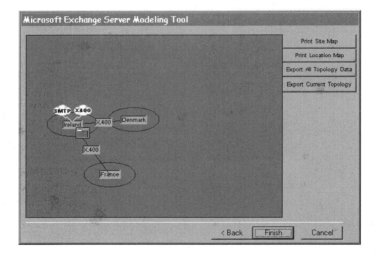

Figure 2.8 *An organizational diagram built by the Exchange Modeling Tool*

The Exchange modeling tool offers similar opportunity to input details about the type of Exchange organization you want to build. The questions cover points such as the different network connections available to link sites, which sites will host public folders, whether messages can flow constantly or if they'll follow a schedule, and so on. The design is arrived at through a process of constant refinement, and the graphical nature of the tool allows you to quickly see the current situation at any time. Figure 2.7 shows how site details are input. As you can see, it's possible to experiment with different scenarios to analyze how a change will affect the overall situation. At the end of the exercise the modeling tool creates an organizational diagram (Figure

2.8). Note the representation of the different external connectors (X.400 and SMTP in this case).

Both tools store the data they record and analyze in Microsoft Access V2.0 databases. It's possible to open either EXSERVER.MDB (for Exchange) or OLPGDATA.MDB (for the NT domain tool) and have a look at the data. If you can figure out all the relationships you'd even be able to create your own extensions. Most people, I imagine, will be quite happy to leave the data to the tools.

I've used quite a number of automated system design tools in my time. Those available for Windows NT and Exchange provide an excellent starting point for the design exercise. Apart from anything else, using tools like this forces you to collect information together in a logical fashion, something that's extremely valuable in itself. If you feel that you lack knowledge or experience with Windows NT or Exchange you can engage in the data collection exercise yourself and then bring the data along for analysis and review by an expert.

Treat the recommendations issued by the tools as an input to the design process, not the final and absolute decision. Automated tools are all very well, but human knowledge and experience often produce insights that have critical influence on the shape of the best possible design.

Installing Exchange on top of an existing Windows NT infrastructure

As discussed previously there are going to be a large number of situations where Windows NT domains are already operational within enterprises. The question now arises of how to incorporate or leverage an existing infrastructure for use with Exchange Server. If the enterprise is small and a single domain is in use then introducing Exchange Server is a straightforward process, providing the network in place is able to handle the volume of additional traffic introduced through Exchange messaging and replication activities.

Planning is more complicated where several different domains are already in use. If possible the different domains should be rationalized to form a more unified Windows NT infrastructure. If these domains have only been used to provide shared file and print services it shouldn't be too hard to connect the desired services to the new domain and then move or even recreate user accounts. Some user accounts may need to be renamed if the same account name has been used in multiple domains.

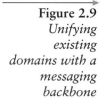

Figure 2.9
Unifying existing domains with a messaging backbone

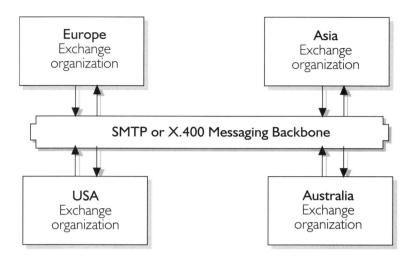

Enterprises distributed across large distances where LAN connections are not possible can use the complete trust domain model to unify domains that are already operational. The complete trust model requires trust relationships to be set up between the different domains, without which public folder access is impossible, but the bulk of this work is a one-time operation. Additional work is required if sites are to span domain boundaries. When a new server is installed the installation program requests details of an existing server in the site and then attempts to retrieve information about the site from that server. A Windows NT trust relationship is enough to allow the two domains to see each other, and this permits the installation program to make the request to the remote server for site information. However, if the account being used to perform the installation does not possess permissions to administer the organization, site, and configuration objects on the target server it won't be able to update the remote server's configuration. Failures to possess the necessary permissions will cause the RPC queries to be rejected by the target server and the installation procedure will not be able to proceed.

A privileged Windows NT account is required to install Exchange Server. The standard Windows NT Administrator account can be used for this purpose, but it's a good idea to create a special account in each domain to use for all aspects of Exchange administration, including installations. Use an account name such as EX-ADMIN, but make sure that the same name is used on all servers where Exchange is installed. If you decide to use a separate account for Exchange make sure it has the same privileges as the standard Administrator account and include it into any Administration user groups that are active. The Exchange installation procedure grants special rights and permissions over

Exchange objects to the account used to perform the installation. If you want to use other accounts to administer Exchange servers afterwards you'll have to grant those accounts the necessary permissions to deal with whatever objects they are interested in. Tracking down all the places where permissions have been granted is a little tricky, so it's best to leave the original account used for installation alone if at all possible.

In situations where multiple Windows NT domains are already operational with many active users it is often difficult to completely redesign the existing domain model(s) and impose a new structure. In these situations the best approach may be to accept the existing domain model and introduce Exchange Server by treating each domain as a separate organization, rather than a site as would be the normal course. The different Exchange organizations can then be connected together with an internal SMTP or X.400-based messaging backbone, as shown in Figure 2.9. This is a practical and pragmatic approach to get Exchange servers up and running quickly without attempting radical surgery on existing systems.

Remember that Exchange sites can map domain models in different ways. Sketching out the basic shape of the Exchange organization to illustrate where sites and servers will be located and the names each site and server will have is a very fundamental and important step in the planning of any Exchange implementation. A site can map a domain on a one-to-one basis and this is the most probable implementation where domains and sites are created to serve different geographical locations (London, Paris, Geneva, and so on). And as we've seen, sites can also be built from servers spanning different Windows NT domains as long as the necessary trust relationships exist.

Integrating standalone Exchange servers into a unified organization

Suddenly being given the job to create a unified messaging environment from an already-installed loose collection of Exchange servers is a variant of the problem created by an existing Windows NT infrastructure. One of the joys of Exchange Server is the ease of installation. Forty minutes or so after the shrink-wrap is removed the server can be up and running with clients happily sending messages to each other. Once you have a Windows NT server you can install Exchange and unfortunately sometimes people get carried away and Exchange servers can proliferate within an organization, perhaps as a result of different organizational units carrying out their own pilots. The net result of all this activity can be a collection of Exchange servers providing a messaging service to small user communities but little or no coordination. Rectifying such a situation to bring all the servers together into a coherent and cooperative whole is not an easy task, largely because of the close interrelationship between Exchange and the base Windows NT operating system.

So what can you do to integrate standalone systems into an Exchange infrastructure which spans the enterprise? There are two basic approaches.

1. Leave the existing servers in place and integrate everyone with a unified messaging backbone to connect all the different servers together. In this scenario each location that operates an Exchange Server retains its existing user accounts, server names, and other attributes and is treated as a separate and distinct Exchange organization (rather than site).

2. Start over by designing the Exchange infrastructure from the base up so that all the servers are connected together into sites within a logical Exchange organization. In this scenario all the existing servers will eventually be assimilated into the new infrastructure. Because of the dependence on Windows NT domains, security, and networking this process will inevitably be more painful for some user communities than others.

Clearly the first approach is faster and easier to implement. It devolves the responsibility for operation away from a central coordinating body to the system managers in individual locations, and this may make the approach attractive to managers of central MIS groups who struggle with shrinking budgets. All the central group has to provide is the messaging backbone and this can be based on SMTP or X.400. A centrally coordinated corporate directory is an optional extra.

Requiring servers which are already up and running to basically stop operations and change to come into line with standards determined for a corporate Exchange infrastructure will clearly impact system managers and users alike. Software may need to be reinstalled to change server names. Servers may have to join different Windows NT domains to facilitate access to public folders. User accounts may need to be renamed to come into line with whatever corporate standard is felt best. If you've just been running pilot systems the best idea may well be to stop and start from scratch again, but clearly this approach is more difficult for all concerned if the system has been operational for any length of time. This is another good reason to pay attention to the overall design for Windows NT and Exchange before attempting a corporate implementation.

Connecting sites

Once you have an Exchange server up and running and some clients happily connected and sending mail to each other the next natural step is to consider how you can connect your server to others. Connecting a new server into an existing site isn't an issue because connectivity is largely transparent and is automatically accomplished when the new server joins the site.

The major options for connecting Exchange sites together are:

- Direct Exchange server to Exchange connections;
- Using an SMTP-based backbone;
- Using X.400 connections between Exchange servers;
- Using an existing X.400 backbone (in other words, a non-Exchange MTA).

These methods are listed in order of convenience. In other words, making a direct connection between two Exchange servers is a quick and easy way to get things going. It is also the lowest cost option and probably the way that most people will use when they start to connect sites together. However, it is an Exchange-specific solution and only suitable where a low to medium volume of messages need to be transported within the boundaries of a single physical WAN. Direct connections between Exchange servers are enabled via RPC (Remote Procedure Calls) and can be made over a LAN, WAN or asynchronously using the Windows NT RAS (Remote Access Server) facility. In turn, RAS can be configured to run over modems, an X.25 network, or ISDN.

Selecting a corporate messaging backbone

Once the requirement arises to connect to other messaging systems, inside or outside your organization, another approach must be taken. At this stage a fundamental decision about the corporate messaging structure may have to be taken. Are you going to use SMTP or X.400 as the basic messaging backbone? This decision is one of the most important that messaging system implementers must make.

X.400 is an internationally-agreed standard designed to enable interoperability between different messaging systems. The standard describes the structure and format of messages, and how they can be exchanged between different systems. It is issued in the form of a set of recommendations that can be used by vendors when they build messaging systems. Microsoft Exchange Server complies with the set of recommendations issued in 1988 and is able to connect to systems that support either the 1984 or 1988 recommendations.

SMTP is the messaging protocol generally used to send messages throughout the Internet and is designed to operate over TCP/IP networks. Exchange Server uses a component called the Internet Mail Connector to allow connections to SMTP-based mail systems. You can use the Internet Mail connector to send messages to other messaging systems, as long as you can connect to the system via TCP/IP and it is able to accept SMTP-type messages either directly or via an SMTP gateway, or you can use the Internet connector to tie Exchange sites together over a TCP/IP network.

Table 2.1 *Comparing X.400 and SMTP*

	X.400	SMTP
Security	✓	
Reliability	✓	
Target population		✓
Cost		✓
Technical complexity	Difficult	Easy
Ease of interoperability		✓
Ease of operation/administration	Difficult	Easy
Ease of use (addressing)		✓

Debates about the best messaging backbone have raged over the years. Over the last decade X.400 has traditionally proved to be more popular in Europe than in the US, possibly because of the high level of support the majority, if not all, of the public telecommunications carriers in Europe have given to establishing X.400-based messaging services. The Internet was slower to spread in Europe and the number of Internet connection points and choice of public providers is still far lower in Europe. A purely cynical view of the X.400/SMTP debate is that X.400 was designed by a committee so it's bound to be overly complex and bureaucratic whereas SMTP has evolved through practical implementation so it's more down-to-earth. The truth lies somewhere in between.

Table 2.1 looks at X.400 and SMTP backbones from a number of perspectives important to system administrators. These are personal opinions and you're quite welcome to agree or disagree. X.400 offers more inherent security features than standard SMTP, but these are largely offset by Exchange Server's ability to encrypt and apply digital signatures to messages before they are transmitted over either backbone (within a single Exchange organization). In some respects an X.400 backbone tends to be more reliable than a SMTP equivalent, if only because of the superior notification options supported by X.400, including nonrepudiation of messages. It should be noted that a draft specification intended to allow SMTP to support delivery and read notifications is currently under active consideration, and this may well erode the current advantage held by X.400. At the end of the day SMTP scores heavily in terms of its target population (the number of people reachable through SMTP), the cost of deployment, and the ease of use when it comes to addressing.

Using the Exchange directory to mask the complexities of addresses necessary to reach remote correspondents makes the point about addressing somewhat academic. However, if an SMTP-type address is exposed to a user it's obvious that:

Tony.Redmond@dbo.mts.dec.com

is a little friendlier and more understandable than:

/C=IE/A=EIRMAIL400/P=DIGITAL/O=DIGITAL/OU=DBO/G=TONY/S=REDMOND

Addresses can change as they move from network to network so an address that starts off being stated in a fairly simple form (as shown above) can become very cluttered and hard to decipher, even for people who are very au fait with messaging standards.

Possibly the most important difference from a user perspective is the way that an SMTP backbone enables easy interoperability for compound messages. These are messages composed of both cover memos and attachments or embedded objects. SMTP backbones use the MIME protocol to encode compound messages, and almost every messaging system available today is able to understand and interpret MIME, making it very much easier for people to send each other messages containing Word documents or Excel spreadsheets via the SMTP/MIME combination than through the sometimes extreme contortions necessary with X.400. The pragmatic approach of user-driven standards as seen in the Internet beats the conformance-driven approach of X.400. Making things easier for users has a bonus for system administrators too because less time has to be spent setting up the connections between servers and the backbone, tuning parameters to enable complex messages to travel from one system to another, and responding to user queries when problems arise.

Ease of use and administration also makes SMTP a more attractive option from the point of cost. Time is money, so the less time spent setting up and managing the backbone the better for all concerned.

Compare the time taken to configure the Exchange Internet Mail Connector and the X.400 Connector to see how more configuration effort X.400 requires. The extra effort also requires more knowledge of X.400 and OSI which implies training and experience on the part of the system administrator, or an additional cost to buy in expertise from external consultants.

Lest it be assumed that I overly favor SMTP over X.400 let me review some of the arguments often used in rebuttal by the proponents of the X.400 recommendations.

The establishment of the X.400 recommendations has enabled bridges to be built between vastly different messaging systems. The recommendations are well understood and supported by many public electronic mail carriers and PTTs (public telephone authorities) throughout the world. Because X.400 is supported by so many organizations it's easy to make connections between different companies. Finally, the construct of X.400 messages follows an agreed scheme which preserves content as messages move from one system to another. All are valid assertions, but the value of the arguments are being eroded all the time by the sheer weight of the SMTP/MIME combination driven forward by the Internet juggernaut.

Factors governing the choice

Both X.400 and SMTP allow you to build and maintain connections between Exchange sites. The decision as to which to use depends on a number of factors including whether an X.400 or SMTP infrastructure is already in place and type of connections you want to make with other people outside your company.

For example, if you are migrating from a situation where a well-established X.400 backbone is in place to connect different messaging systems together and to provide connections to external companies, then it might well be best to leave the existing backbone alone and concentrate on integrating Exchange Server in with the other messaging systems using the X.400 connector. Remember that Exchange isn't limited to a single X.400 connector and two or more might be used, some to connect Exchange sites together and another to link Exchange to the corporate backbone.

If your organization only uses X.400 for external connections or another OSI application, such as Electronic Data Interchange (EDI) transactions with trading partners, the best idea is probably to leave the X.400 backbone in place for its present purposes and establish a single X.400 connector between a designated Exchange server and X.400, otherwise using SMTP as the basis for the internal messaging backbone. In circumstances where sites are upgrading from Microsoft Mail or Lotus cc:Mail to Exchange and no messaging backbone exists the easiest option is to go with SMTP.

My own prediction is that 75–80% of all Exchange implementations that need a messaging backbone will use SMTP, and the rest will use X.400. In most cases there will be a gateway between the two backbones, mostly because the messaging world is still so diverse.

Some system administrators propose to use SMTP to connect Exchange servers together using the Internet as the glue in between. Again, I think this is a reasonable plan to get systems connected quickly, but some of the attributes of the Internet, such as its openness and availability to all, are not conducive to the creation of a reliable, dependable and secure messaging system. For example, do you know what route messages will travel along as they proceed through the Internet? Can you be certain that other people aren't going to be able to intercept your messages and gain access to commercially sensitive information which could potentially damage your company? Also, what guarantee have you that messages will move across the Internet in any guaranteed time, and will the operations of your company be compromised if the message flow is interrupted by network problems within the Internet? A lot of the same issues crop up within internal networks, but at least the network is under your control and can be managed as such.

Knowledge of your existing messaging environment, the systems involved, how they are connected, the external connections in place or required and how you want the overall messaging environment to evolve are important inputs to the SMTP/X.400 backbone decision. Because this decision is so critical and its effects pervade all parts of the messaging infrastructure it's critical that the decision is right, so if you don't have the right level of knowledge and experience it's a good idea to seek help. The details of how to go about connecting into SMTP and X.400 backbones are covered in a later chapter. You may want to read these sections before considering your options.

Naming systems

The name given to a Windows NT system is not only the name that the computer is known as within your network, it's also the name that Exchange Server will use when the software is installed. With this fact in mind it is clearly important to define a well-structured and easily understood naming convention for Windows NT systems intended to run Exchange.

A good naming convention allows system administrators to gain an immediate snapshot of a computer's role in the overall scheme with a quick look. This requirement immediately rules out any name that might be defined as 'cute'. For example, it's a bad idea to name all computers after cartoon characters because there's a reasonably small pool of names to choose from and there's no indication of what a computer might do or where it might be located if it is given a name like 'Goofy', 'Happy', 'Sneezy', and so on.

Exchange is designed to be an organization-wide system so the naming convention must reflect this aim. Any organization is likely to include a number of geographical sites, and each site may have one or more computers that act as mail servers. This three-tier structure can be expressed in the naming convention. For example, let's assume that the XYZ corporation is located in three sites in Asia, Europe, and the United States. The initial servers in the three sites might be named as follows:

```
XYZ-ASIA-001
XYZ-EUROPE-001
XYZ-USA-001
```

As servers are added in the three sites it's easy to see that the numeric value at the end of the name is incremented by one to create a name for the new computer that's unique and conveys some idea of the overall organizational structure. You can take this idea further and incorporate as many different levels as you like. Larger organizations who operate many Windows NT domains might like to include the domain name as the second element in server names. As an example, if the XYZ corporation operated with manufacturing and sales divisions, each of which was represented by a different Windows NT domain, the names for the computers might look like this:

```
XYZ-MAN-ASIA1
XYZ-SALES-MAN-ASIA1
```

Note that this scheme implies that the divisions operate different Exchange sites in addition to the two Windows NT domains. You also have to make sure that the server names don't exceed the 15 character limit imposed by Windows NT. There may be situations, especially with smaller offices, where multiple organizational units are represented in the same place, perhaps a location that has a slow network link back to the rest of the organization. Clearly it would be silly in this situation for the users from each unit to have different Exchange servers, so the server naming scheme might need to have some flexibility built in to allow for such circumstances.

Creating an arbitrary naming convention is an activity that system managers may enjoy, but users sometimes find confusing. Sometimes the need for a structured naming convention is obvious, but in situations where sites span single geographical locations such as Dublin, London, and Paris, the naming scheme for Windows NT domains and Exchange sites could be based on city names or other geographical terms. A naming scheme based on Australian cities is used for illustration purposes in many places in the Exchange administration documentation.

Geographically-based schemes provide the immediate and obvious advantage of creating a very familiar naming convention that is totally obvious to all. Given that sites are named on a geographical location, for example 'Dublin', the servers within a site might be named:

DUBLIN-001, DUBLIN-002, DUBLIN-SALES, DUBLIN-ORDERS

and so on.

If you plan to connect to other X.400 messaging systems it is not recommended that you use the underscore character in any name associated with Exchange (server, site, or organization). Exchange passes information about itself to the receiving X.400 systems and can't handle underscores in system names – leading to undeliverable messages. To avoid problems in the future, use hyphens instead of underscores to separate parts of server and site names as shown above.

Naming the organization and sites

We've just discussed the somewhat esoteric topic of how to name Windows NT servers. Applying a well-designed naming convention to Windows NT servers makes it easier for system administrators to instantly recognize a server's location and purpose, but it's only going to be possible if you're able to install and commission the servers from scratch.

Any installation that's been operating Windows NT for some time won't have this luxury and will have to do with the server names that are in place, as in the case of the installation illustrated in Figure 2.10 where existing servers called DBO-EXCHANGEIST, DPSW08, OFFICENT1 and OFFICENT2 have been used to form the 'Dublin' Exchange site.

Figure 2.10
Different servers in site 'Dublin'

This is a practical real-life example of where Exchange has been installed on four existing Windows NT servers which have been combined to form a site. It would be wonderful if you always had the chance to create and implement a logical naming scheme throughout an organization, but this won't always be possible.

You may not be able to do anything about the names given to Windows NT server, but you do need to plan out names for the Exchange organization and the sites that will comprise it. These are important decisions that shouldn't be taken on the spur of the moment because these names are used as the basis of directory entries and eventually messaging addresses. Directory information is propagated to many places within the Exchange environment so it's impossible to change the name of the organization or a site in a single place. If you need to change the name of the organization you need to reinstall Exchange on every server within the organization while a change to the site name implies a reinstallation for every server in the site. In effect, you will be rebuilding the organization or site from scratch.

Cryptic, heavily coded, or artificially short names are not necessary for site names. All system administration is carried out through the rich graphical interface provided by the Exchange administration program. Use fully spelled-out names which make sense and look good.

How many sites should I have?

When designing the organization for your Exchange implementation will you:

▶ Create a small number of large sites?

▶ Create a large number of small sites?

▶ Create a mixture of large and small sites?

The automated tools mentioned earlier in this chapter (see page 68) can help clarify the best solution to your requirements.

Sometimes the decision will be made for you. If you don't have fast network links between servers that are capable of handling the RPC load generated to synchronize site-wide shared data structures such as the directory then you won't be able to combine the servers together into a site. Anything less than a dedicated 64Kb link (the Microsoft recommendation) provides too little bandwidth for site connectors to operate in a satisfactory manner. Be wary of assuming that just because a network connection is there its total available bandwidth can be used by Exchange. In most instances other applications will want their own slice of the bandwidth, leaving Exchange with whatever's left. Because bandwidth tends to be absorbed in many different ways it is best to plan to use 128Kb links if you want to operate site connectors.

In general the recommendation is to limit the number of sites within an organization. While moving objects within a site is easy, moving users and servers between sites are difficult, manual processes. Putting effort into the organization/site design is important. Ask yourself questions like 'How can we expand without breaking the organization if a large number of new users needs to be added?' or 'What happens if our company sells a building, decentralizes, or otherwise physically changes the shape of the company?' A design should be flexible and able to expand (or contract) as business requirements dictate.

An organization with more than fifty sites is going to be difficult to manage. A site with more than twenty servers in it will also be difficult to manage. Try to restrict the number of points of management, at least at the beginning. It is very easy to add a site or server to your Exchange organization afterwards, if required, but organizations that start off sprawled and scattered don't tend to regain any coherent shape without great effort on the part of system administrators.

Installing a new Exchange server

The process of installing a new Exchange server is straightforward. Two basic scenarios can occur:

1. Installation of a server for a brand new site, including the first site in a new organization;
2. Installation of a new server within an existing site.

In all cases you should know:

- The name of the site you are creating or wish to join;
- The name of the organization (if not already selected).

As normal with Windows applications, installations are performed by running SETUP.EXE. You'll be asked to provide the organizational details noted above, and if you want to join an existing site (and organization) you'll be asked for the name of an active server in that site. The installation process must be able to access the Exchange configuration data for the site before the new server can be introduced.

If you want to join sites across Windows NT domain boundaries you must set up trust relationships between the two domains before attempting the installation. Without a trust relationship in place the installation procedure will not be able to make the necessary contacts between servers in the different domains. Setting up a small number of trust relationships (such as the situation illustrated in Figure 2.11) creates an acceptable level of administrative overhead, but it's easy to lose track of which domain is trusted and which isn't if you allow domains to be created and spread without control.

Removing a system from a site

Removing a system from a site is accomplished by selecting the server from the administration program and then selecting the delete option (or press the delete key). The administration program must be run on another computer holding administration permission for the target server as a server isn't allowed to initiate the process of deleting itself.

Figure 2.11
Trust relationships

Exchange will check that it is safe to proceed (the server is not currently active) and advise on the consequences of the action. For example, mailboxes or connectors will be lost if not moved, public folders may be discarded, and so on. If the server is the only one in a site the result is to remove the site from the Exchange organization. Neither step should be taken without carefully planning the removal. After all, you have planned the construction of the organization in terms of the deployment of sites and servers, why not pay the same attention if you have to adjust the plan by removing something?

Before proceeding to delete a server make sure that:

- You move all user mailboxes to another system in the same site, or to a system in another site. These steps are accomplished using the procedures described on page 128.
- All public folders hosted by the server have been relocated to another server. In other words, make sure that at least one other replica of each public folder exists elsewhere.
- You check all connectors hosted by the server. Sometimes it won't matter if you remove a server that hosts a redundant or excess connector, but it's a pity not to ask a simple question and end up deleting the sole Internet Mail Connector used by everyone in the organization!

After all user mailboxes, public folders, and connectors have been relocated to other servers it's a good idea to wait a couple of hours to allow the details of the changes you've made to replicate around the rest of the organization. Check that everything is working normally after the changes have been replicated. Then shut down the server to see if that affects anything. If this test proves negative you can proceed to reboot the server. After the reboot, proceed to delete the server.

After the server has been removed you can run the setup utility to remove all the installed components.

Server software upgrades

A constant stream of software upgrades and patches appearing from development laboratories is one of the few things you can be sure will happen over the next few years. Even though development effort is reduced and simplified through software development toolsets the resulting software is still so complex and contains so many lines of code that bits, albeit small, are bound to break when they're exposed to the stresses of production use. Bugs arise and need to be fixed, and it's often the smaller bugs that cause the most pain for users.

Just over a month after Microsoft released Exchange Server V4.0 to its manufacturing facility the development team assembled the first service pack, referred to as SP1.[2] A service pack is a collection of bug fixes and minor enhancements that have become available since a product was first released. Service packs are cumulative. The number allocated to a service pack indicates its position in the chain. Thus if you install service pack 4 for Windows NT V3.51 (the version required by Exchange Server V4.0), you also affect the bug fixes in service packs 1, 2, and 3. Remember Exchange's close interrelationship

---

2. *Service packs can be downloaded from Microsoft's Web site (try* **http://www.microsoft.com/exchange** *for Exchange service packs) or obtained from your local Microsoft support center.*

with Windows NT. If a service pack appears for Windows NT you need to be aware of it and know whether the service pack impacts Exchange, or whether Exchange requires the new service pack to be installed.

Judged on their past record, Microsoft follow a fairly aggressive development schedule for most products. Exchange is a new product and you can expect to see several full product releases of Exchange Server appearing during the 1996–1998 period. These releases will add functionality, increase the degree of integration between Exchange and other technologies (such as the Internet), and smooth out any interoperability issues that appear between Exchange and other messaging systems as systems are introduced into production messaging environments. All good news, but another complicating factor for an implementation plan.

Good plans for the deployment of computer systems take software patches and upgrades into account. In most enterprises the exercise to define and plan the implementation of Exchange Server is a new activity, so it's an appropriate time to factor software upgrades into the plan. Consider the questions listed below and see if you have good answers for each question:

- How will service packs be obtained? Who's responsible for monitoring Microsoft for news of service packs for Exchange, Windows NT, or other associated products?
- How will service packs be tested before they are introduced into production? What tests will be performed? Who is responsible for testing and certification?
- What approach will be taken to new product releases for servers (and clients)? How will the new software be tested, especially in relation to communications with older Exchange servers and other messaging systems? Will the new product releases require any changes in the electronic forms you may have developed?
- How can service pack and new product releases be distributed and installed throughout the organization? Who is going to be responsible for the coordination of the organization-wide deployment?
- How will system administrators, programmers, and users be trained or otherwise acquainted with any new features made available in service packs or product releases?

Planning is not an exact science. Knowing about potential pitfalls is a great aid in driving up the degree of accuracy that can be achieved within any plan. Once software upgrades and patch installations can be factored into your plan it's likely that things will proceed smoothly and without undue disruption to the service provided to users.

Permissions

We've just discussed the requirement for trust relationships to exist between two domains that wish to join sites. Trust relationships are only part of the picture as there are two different types of permissions involved in Exchange. Trust relationships correspond to Windows NT permissions, required to access Windows NT itself and then assume the privileges to perform administrative functions. After access is gained to Windows NT there are a number of separate Exchange permissions used to manage and control access to Exchange resources. Exchange permissions are totally different and separate to Windows NT permissions. This fact often causes confusion when people can't understand why they aren't able to 'make' Exchange do something despite having all known Windows NT permissions granted to their account.

Naming contexts

Exchange Server stores configuration data within containers arranged in a hierarchical structure. Four naming contexts are established within the container hierarchy. Windows NT accounts can be allocated permissions within each of these naming contexts. Once a Windows NT account has been granted a set of permissions for a particular naming context within the hierarchy it also automatically inherits the same permissions down through objects arranged beneath the naming context. The four naming contexts are:

Enterprise container (1)
➡
    Site container (2)
    ➡
        Configuration container (3) ➡
        Recipients container ➡
            Schema container (4)

Thus if a Windows NT account is granted a set of permissions over the site container it also inherits the same permissions over the configuration and schema containers. The recipients container is an exception. Permissions for this container are inherited from the site container, but not from the enterprise (organization) container. Permissions are modified or granted by double-clicking on an object and then selecting the permissions property page.

It can take several seconds for Exchange to display the permissions property page within large organizations that span several domains. This is because contact must be made with all the different service accounts in the different domains before their details are listed among the properties.

Many of the problems seen in replicating directory or other information between sites lie in the fact that the Exchange site service accounts do not possess the necessary permissions for containers in remote sites. In summary, to avoid replication difficulties, the site service accounts should be granted the Exchange Admin role (or a role with equal or greater rights) on both the configuration and site containers in both sites.

Defining Exchange roles

Windows NT accounts assume permissions for Exchange Server through a role. A role is a set of rights that define the exact type of access a user has to objects held within a container. A set of default roles are provided with Exchange Server. These are:

- Admin
- Permissions Admin
- Service Account Admin
- View Only Admin
- User
- Send As

The account used to install Exchange Server is allocated the Permissions Admin role. The site service account is granted the Service Account Admin role. The difference between these roles that the Service Account Admin role holds all available rights whereas the Permissions Admin role lacks the replication, mailbox owner, and send as rights (see Table 2.2). The site service account is also granted the Windows NT Logon as a Service and Restore Files and Directories permissions for the local computer. These permissions allow the site service account to start the various Exchange services and to perform essential system backup and restore operations.

If you don't like these roles or believe you need additional roles you can proceed to define a new role by deciding which rights or permissions should be incorporated into the role. An Exchange right defines a specific action that a Windows NT account can perform within an Exchange context. The available rights are listed in Table 2.2.

Table 2.2 *Rights used to define roles*

Right	Meaning
Add Child	Gives the account the ability to create a new object underneath this object. For example, to add a new custom recipient to the recipients container
Modify User Attributes	Modify the user attributes associated with the object
Modify Admin Attributes	Modify the administrative attributes associated with an object
Delete	Delete an object
Send As	Send messages from a mailbox. This permission allows a user to send messages from a mailbox as if the owner of the mailbox has connected to it. It is different from 'Send on Behalf' option because the messages appear to have come from the mailbox's owner and are not marked as having been sent by another user on behalf of the mailbox's owner
Mailbox Owner	Able to log on to a mailbox and use it to send and receive messages
Logon Rights	Log on to any server within a site using ADMIN.EXE (the administrator program)
Replication	Replicate directory information with other servers
Modify permissions	Modify permission to use the object

Bringing everything together, the different Exchange permissions allocated to the set of predefined roles are listed in Table 2.3.

Table 2.3 *Roles and permissions*

Roles ➡ Permissions ⬇	Admin	Permissions Admin	Service Account Admin	View Only Admin	User	Send As
Add Child	✓	✓	✓			
Modify User Attributes	✓	✓	✓		✓	
Modify Admin Attributes	✓	✓	✓			
Delete	✓	✓	✓			

Table 2.3 *Roles and permissions (continued)*

Roles → Permissions ↓	Admin	Permissions Admin	Service Account Admin	View Only Admin	User	Send As
Logon	✓	✓	✓	✓		
Modify Permissions		✓	✓			
Replication			✓			
Mailbox Owner			✓		✓	
Send As			✓		✓	✓

3

Selecting Hardware for Exchange Server

Hardware resources

Hardware resources are an emotive topic. Software engineers want their software to work well and not encounter difficulties imposed by what they see as insufficient system configurations. System administrators want to run with correct configurations too, but are often restricted by operational or financial constraints.

In general, Microsoft Exchange Server requires more hardware resources than the computers used for LAN Post Offices. This reflects the demands of the Windows NT operating system as well as the expensive functionality available within the server, especially in the system management subsystem. Installations upgrading from Microsoft Mail need to reconsider the system configurations they use today to see whether the computers can be used with Exchange Server. Anyone else beginning to use Exchange Server needs to go through the same process of analysis and determination of the right configuration for their needs.

It's foolish to begin any project with 'just enough resources'. Always plan to be successful and expect growth to happen. Electronic mail systems are characterized by rapid growth in user interaction with the system. As people become more familiar with electronic mail they'll send and receive an increasing volume of messages and provoke more demand on the system, and if the system can't handle the demand users will perceive a reduced level of service.

The important elements of any Windows NT computer configured to run Exchange Server are:

- ▶ The power of the CPU
- ▶ The amount of memory (RAM)
- ▶ The number and capacity of the hard disks
- ▶ The speed and capability of the connection to the network

These elements need to be combined together in proportion to each other to form an effective recipe for good performance. Too much of a resource can be as bad as too little. A little extra memory may, for example, help to compensate for a lack of sheer CPU processing power, but it can also disguise the underlying problem. In this case you might overcompensate totally and throw lots of memory where the real problem is the slow CPU. In general it's fairly safe to say that systems configured to run Exchange Server need to have a fast CPU, lots of memory, a fast network connection, and lots of disk space. In terms of disk space remember that it's the number of spindles (physical devices) rather than the sheer amount of storage space that's important.

I am always a little suspicious about vendor-provided system sizing tables. Vendors, through no fault of their own, are forced to measure system performance and throughout in artificial circumstances. No-one can predict how your local user community will interact with the computer on a daily basis, so the workload used in system tests is created to represent the work that 'average' users produce. Now show me an average user!

Sizing data and recommendations derived from that data will inevitably improve in accuracy as Microsoft Exchange Server is implemented in different situations. The reasons for this statement are simple:

- Customers will provide realistic data taken from real-life situations back to Microsoft, and this data will be reflected in the testing scenarios used to produce sizing tables.

- Consultants, Microsoft, and customers will all gain experience from operating Microsoft Exchange Server and will be better able to size systems based on that experience. The way people use the system and the load produced by users are especially important factors in this experience.

- New versions of Microsoft Exchange Server will become available, and the performance characteristics of the new releases should reflect the experience gained from real-life operation.

Nevertheless, if you want to get a server up and running today what can you do to adjust vendor-provided sizing information?

Sizing an operational system

A good first step is to gather information from your current system, if you have one. Clearly an operational electronic mail system can provide a wealth of valuable and up-to-date data about user workload, and this will enable you to create a set of parameters to measure against the vendor tables. For example, you should know how many registered users are allowed to use the system, and also how many of those registered users actually connect at any one time. Some installations have a high ratio of registered to active users, sometimes as high as 10:1. However, in my experience the most common ratio is around 2:1. In other words, if there are 100 registered users, 50 are connected at any one time.

After you know how many users you have to cater for you can proceed to estimate the demand created by that population. Electronic mail is not like transaction processing. The same volume of work is not seen during the entire day. Most installations I have worked with over the years experience a number of 'hot points' during the day when the demand for system resources is at its highest. Typical hot points include just after the start of the working day, usually around 9 am each morning, around lunch time, and again towards the end of day. At these times users want to send or receive mail, perhaps to complete tasks to meet deadlines. Heavy message traffic has the potential to cause bottlenecks as the system struggles to process message queues, so clearly it's important to size the system so that it can cope with the maximum predicted traffic plus a comfortable margin for error.

Tracking the flow of messages in and out of an existing messaging system and understanding where those messages originate from and go to is invaluable data when sizing a new system. If some sort of message log is available, you should be able to determine figures for:

- The total number of messages processed each day. It is useful to determine the average number of messages processed each day over a reasonable period of time, for instance a month. Try to analyze the highs and lows in the traffic pattern so that you can see the peak demand.
- The number of messages sent each day by users in your organization. Users can be categorized in terms of the message traffic they produce, and it is helpful if you know how many of your users fall into each category. I use categories like 'Light,' 'Medium' and 'Heavy'. We'll discuss various numbers that could be used to categorize users later on in this chapter.

Again, expect demand to grow over time. Users will generate more messages as their experience grows. You might not like some of the messages that are generated, especially those that don't have a direct connection to any particular item of business, but I think it's a sign of success when users become so accustomed to electronic mail that they use mail for just about everything!

Knowing what the system will do

Electronic mail is only one potential source of load for a computer system. All the other applications that will run on the system generate load and remove resources from the pool available to Microsoft Exchange Server. Thus, to create an accurate prediction of the resources required to provide good service to users you must be aware of the load likely to be produced by other applications and Windows NT system services.

All computers that run Microsoft Exchange Server software within a site offer the same set of core functions to users. These functions are:

- The Information Store;
- The Directory Store;
- Mail Transfer to other servers.

The other Exchange components that can be distributed across different servers within a site are:

- Connectors (gateways) to other electronic mail systems;
- Public folder hosts;
- Exchange administration;
- Site-to-site connections.

All of the other components are optional and can be distributed across different Exchange servers within a site. For example, in a small site (up to perhaps 100 users) it makes sense to have a single client installation point, and if you already have a server acting as a shared application area, perhaps for the other Microsoft Office applications, it would be logical to make that server the place where clients access the Exchange installation kit. Depending on the speed and saturation of the network a larger site might determine two or more client installation points. After the initial burst of installations an installation point does not normally generate a great deal of day-to-day network traffic, so its overall impact on the network and host computer will probably not be heavy. However, this is not a reason to place an installation point on a server that is already stressed.

Administration is the only constant across all Exchange sites. The load generated by all the other optional components is highly site-dependent. Sites migrating from another mail system are likely to generate a high volume of message traffic through a gateway to the original mail system until all users are migrated over to Exchange. If you don't use public folders at all, or only use them to distribute small files the replication load is not going to be heavy, but if electronic forms are used or large documents are stored in public folders, or there is a high and consistent level of remote access to the public folders then a substantial load can be generated for the server.

When facing the first implementation of Exchange Server within an organization it is difficult to predict what load will be generated by any of the Exchange services. This fact isn't at all surprising because the same is probably true of any moderately complex application. A great deal of intelligent guesswork is needed to come up with a configuration that will last in terms of adequate performance for more than a few months.

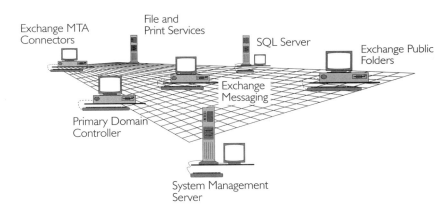

Figure 3.1
Different applications distributed across servers in a Windows NT domain

To complicate the entire sizing equation, the Windows NT systems you might want to use for Exchange Server may already be providing other applications to users. One of the attractive points about Windows NT is its ability to construct a logical domain composed of many different server computers all connected by network links. Building a complete Windows NT environment to use as the base for Exchange Server will inevitably use more applications than just messaging, yet this fact of computing life is often missed by people considering Exchange Server who focus in on Exchange Server and ignore the needs and requirements of all the other applications. Of course, vendors add fuel to the fire of confusion by publishing benchmark results for a particular application, and then detailing the exact hardware specifications of the systems under test. These results are accurate, but often must be adjusted to factor in the demands of more normal application mixes, as well as the load placed by network communications.

Putting everything on a single server

You can opt to try and put all your applications on one server. This is an acceptable course of action as long as you:

- Don't have many users to service
- Don't have a requirement for a resilient system
- Don't have any budget limitations so you can buy the largest and fastest Windows NT system on the market

As these circumstances don't arise very often the more common course of events is to distribute applications across servers. This approach allows system administrators to match available hardware configurations to application demands, so you end up with a situation where hardware is optimally used rather than perhaps being discarded as being of little use. For instance, a computer can be allocated the task of acting as the Primary Domain Controller and nothing else. A low-end 80486-class system could easily act as the Primary Domain Controller for a domain supporting a relatively small user community. The same system might also be used for shared file and print services. Making use of older systems in this way allows newer hardware to be reserved for new applications, like Exchange Server.

Some of the common options for distributing application load across individual servers within a domain are illustrated in Figure 3.1. The need to distribute an application differs from organization to organization and depends on the way that the application is used, if at all. For instance, if you run an Exchange-pure messaging system then there is no need for SMTP or X.400 connectors to other messaging backbones, so apart from the network connection overhead you remove the need to translate messages from internal Exchange format to the formats supported by the backbones in question. Because of all the different factors in the equation it is difficult for anyone to give hard guidelines for system sizing and load distribution without a detailed examination of current configurations in conjunction with some fairly accurate estimates of future demand.

The worst situation to be in is where Exchange Server and another application constantly contend for system resources. It is easy to see where some areas of contention might arise. A system acting as a Primary Domain Controller, or even as a Backup Domain Controller, for a large domain needs to provide fast responses back to authentication requests generated across the domain, so placing an Exchange server which acts as a gateway to a heavily-traveled public X.400 connection on the same system is not wise. In the same way, a system acting as a database server is hardly likely to be a good host for Exchange Server.

In these situations it is usually wise to leave the existing system alone and install a new computer for Exchange. This stops any prospect of application contention and creates a degree of resilience because applications are better distributed. You'll also be able to configure one or more systems especially for Exchange Server and won't have to compromise because of existing hardware. The configuration you install is also more likely to last longer, require less administration, and provide better service to users. Overall, initially it's a more expensive approach but better over the long term.

Where system load comes from

So far we have discussed the load created by Exchange services and some additional Windows NT applications. However, the system load generated by Exchange and Windows NT represent only two parts of the overall equation as so far we haven't discussed the load imposed by user activities, such as reading and sending messages. User load can be generated unwittingly, even by supposedly skilled and experienced people. For example, people connected to a server I manage complained bitterly about its performance, yet everything worked smoothly whenever I looked at the system performance monitor, or was working with the system itself. The answer lay in an OpenGL screen saver which I had turned on for the server in a fit of security consciousness. The screen saver worked, but whenever it was active it generated a huge load on the server (taking up to 100% of the CPU) to create all the pretty and intricate graphic images displayed on screen. This was a small, but telling point!

Table 3.1 attempts to summarize the different loads that might be placed on a server. Not all potential loads are listed here and the load will differ from environment to environment. Use the table to create an idea of the work you expect your servers to handle.

Table 3.1 *Different loads placed on a server*

Users	Exchange Services	Windows NT applications
Reading messages	MTA activity	Primary or Backup domain controller
Creating and sending messages	Connectors	DNS/WINS/DHCP
Searching folders	Replication	Web Server
Updating the contents of public folders	Executing rules	SQL Server
	Monitoring links and servers	System Management Server
	Key Management Server	SNA Server

The total load imposed by user activity tends to increase proportionally as the user population grows. However, unlike other elements in the load that maintain a consistent and constant demand on system resources, the user load arrives in peaks and furrows and is not distributed evenly over time. The classic view of messaging systems is that three peaks occur during a working day – first thing in the morning as users arrive and want to read mail; at midday as users send a couple of messages before lunch; and at the end of the day when users strive to clear their desks. Exchange Server is hardly likely to be different to other messaging systems in this respect.

Given that peaks will occur it is wise to configure systems that can accommodate peak demands without too much stress. Any system that runs at 90% load (for memory, disk, or CPU) is unlikely to be able to deal with sudden increases in demands. In reflecting on this point it should be understood that the additional demand will not come from Exchange or Windows NT services. Rather it will be generated by users, and users will experience bad service times from the system if it cannot react or respond to the demand as quickly as it should. Systems also tend to degrade in performance over time, reflecting the eternal struggle between fragmenting disks, user demands, and system tuning and maintenance activities and the efforts of the system administrator to keep things running. With all these factors in mind it is clear that an attempt to operate an under-configured system close to the edge of its performance envelope generates a potential for horrible performance.

Categorizing users

Should you attempt to categorize users? In other words, should you attempt to analyze the demands made on Exchange Server by the different people who use the system?

I think it's always good to know what's happening on the servers you're responsible for. Each user is different, but it is possible to place users in a number of broad categories, and then use that information to predict the likely demand those users will place on system and application resources. Going through this exercise before system implementation is good, but repeating the exercise on a regular basis is even better as the information gained will allow you to more accurately predict the time when additional system resources need to be introduced. Proactive system management is harder than reactive system management, but it provides a much higher degree of service to users because system performance and response will be more predictable and less prone to sudden interruptions.

Table 3.2 details one set of categories that could be used to analyze users. The decision process used to determine the boundaries for each category wasn't very scientific, but the categories serve as a starting point for the discussion. For instance, if you follow the categories precisely no user who sends messages would ever be responsible for managing a public folder. This isn't likely to happen in reality, so you should try and adjust the criteria laid down for each category to match your own view of the situation.

Table 3.2 *Categorizing user types*

	Type of user					
	Very heavy messaging	Heavy messaging	Public folder maintainer	Medium messaging	Light messaging	Intermittent access
Number of items in private folders	2,500 to 5,000+	1,000 to 2,500	circa 100	500–1,500	200–750	Under 100
Number of private folders	50 to 300+	50-200	10	40–100	20–50	5–10
Total size of data held in the private information store	50–300Mb	30–60Mb	1–5Mb	20–40Mb	10–25Mb	1–5Mb
Number of outbound messages generated daily	50–100	35–75	1–5	10–40	3–10	1–2
Number of inbound messages received daily	75–200	25–50	1–10	15–40	5–20	2–5
Number of public folders owned/maintained	0	0	5–10	0	0	0
Load factor	10	6	4	3	2	1

In the model laid out in Table 3.2 a user in a category is defined as capable of placing a certain load on a server, and this is expressed as a multiple of the load generated by a user who makes intermittent access, or someone who reads a couple of new messages every day. Thus, a user in the very heavy messaging category generates roughly ten times as much load as an intermittent user. Think of a user in the heavy messaging category as someone who is logged on all day and seems, at times, to do little else but create, send, and read messages.

Clearly a system supporting users in the first two categories will exhibit significantly different characteristics than one supporting users in the last two categories. One obvious difference is the amount of disk space that will be required to support the volume of message traffic generated by the users, and in turn probably lead to further requirements to optimize disk performance through RAID-5 arrays or disk mirroring.

The next chapter contains a discussion on how users occupy space with messages in the Exchange server information store. For now, let's consider a simple example of how the different types of users impact the information store. As illustrated by the categories described above, users generate different loads and traffic patterns, resulting in varying demands on the information store.

The Exchange architecture imposes a 16Gb limit for the private information store where user messages are held. This creates an absolute upper boundary for the size of the user community that can be supported on a single server. A quick calculation shows that you can allocate 32Mb each to 500 users, seemingly a nice comfortable amount to work in, but only enough for users placed in the 'medium' category described in Table 3.2.

When calculating the amount of users that can be supported by any one system it's unwise to allocate up to the limit. Users of messaging systems tend to fill any space they're allowed and leave you with no room to maneuver. Try allocating 20–25Mb to each user as a start, but remember that a theoretical allocation is useless unless there's physical disk space available to meet user demand. If every user is going to occupy 60Mb within the private information store you'll end up with a maximum user population of approximately 266, whereas if the users are at the other end of the scale occupying only 5Mb each the potential user population soars to 3,200 – a very considerable difference. The potential user population per server can therefore be limited by the load generated by users, and it is definite that you'll need more servers around if your users tend to fall into the heavy use categories.

Keep the view you've formed about your own user community in mind when the information store is discussed in order to arrive at a conclusion about the size of store (and hence disk space on the server) you'll need to operate.

Selecting the right hardware platform

Unlike its lower-end desktop cousins, Windows NT is designed to be hardware independent. The Hardware Abstraction Layer (HAL) masks the complexities of different computer hardware architectures (Intel, Digital Alpha, RISC, and PowerPC) from Windows NT system software and the applications built on top of Windows NT, including Microsoft Exchange Server.

Simply put the function of HAL is to intercept instructions issued by applications or the operating system and translate them into the hardware-dependent code required by whatever specific processor type is in use at the time. HAL supplies the magic that allows Windows NT to work across different platforms, but its existence does not assure availability of any particular application. Just because an application is available for the Intel platform does not imply that the application can run on the PowerPC. An application must be compiled for each target platform to create a suitable binary executable, and this is the reason why the Exchange CD-ROM includes separate installation kits for each of the supported platforms – at the time of writing computers built around the Intel x86, MIPS, and Digital Alpha architectures.

Apart from Intel and Alpha, Exchange Server is able to run on systems equipped with MIPS or PowerPC processors. With so much freedom of choice in mind the important thing is not to become focused on one particular platform unless absolutely necessary, perhaps because a strategic buying decision has been made to go with one platform or another. Use the flexibility of the Windows NT HAL implementation to select the right computer for the task in hand.

Typical hardware configurations

The content of any publication ages over time. Whether or not the value of the content decreases with age is another matter, but one thing's for sure – the pace of hardware development makes it impossible to offer guidelines for configuring systems that last for any length of time.

CPU speeds increase all the time. Alpha processors have moved from 150MHz to 333MHz in just over two years. The first Alpha Windows NT system (the AXP150) is now well down the power scale. The same is true of Intel-powered systems where the first 60MHz Pentiums have now reached 150MHz, new versions of Pentium CPUs are heading towards 200MHz with development continuing. The successor to the Pentium, the Pentium Pro, is optimized for 32-bit operation, which is good for Windows NT, and is faster again than its Pentium counterparts. And so the race to develop faster and faster CPUs goes on.

While processors get faster memory gets cheaper, at least in relative terms, and disk storage has reached the stage where the megabyte/$1 plateau has been achieved in many world markets. The combination of increasing processor power, affordable memory and cheap large disks means that even very large and powerful Windows NT systems are well within the reach of restrained budgets. If falling prices help free money from your budget and a little extra to spend it's probably best to put it into peripherals that make systems easier to manage such as uninterruptible power supplies (UPS), automated tape loaders and RAID-5 disk arrays.

Vendors commonly publish suggested configurations for systems to support specified workloads. For example, you'll need a Pentium-powered system equipped with 64Mb of memory and 4Gb of disk to support a 200-strong Exchange user community. Guidelines like these are a useful starting point, but they should not be treated as the sum of all knowledge. The problem is that each operating environment is different, so the results obtained in your installation will be different to those seen by Microsoft when they measure the performance and throughput of Exchange Server. Users behave differently and some will do very strange things that are never factored into simulated system workloads. Network overhead is also different across installations, and of course, system performance tends to degrade over time due to factors such as disk fragmentation. All of these things contribute to differences between performance results achieved in software laboratory conditions and those seen in real life.

Table 3.3   *Comparing processors for Exchange*

Hardware family	Pros	Cons	Suitable for:
Intel 80486	Cheap!	Old	Dedicated servers such as Primary Domain Controllers, File and Print servers, or small Exchange servers.
Intel Pentium	Performance at lowest cost	None really	Most Windows NT-based systems.
Intel Pentium Pro	Optimized for 32-bit	Relatively expensive	High end servers
Digital Alpha and MIPS systems	Sheer power	Requires more memory than Intel-based systems	High end servers and messaging connectors

Table 3.3 summarizes the hardware situation at the time of writing. As I've said above, the situation is likely to change over time. I haven't had an opportunity of testing Windows NT or Exchange on the PowerPC platform.

To try and put a more practical slant on the matter let's take the suggested categories from Table 3.3 and build a system configuration to meet a set of requirements. With the high pace of change in CPU performance a chart like this is only able to offer some generic recommendations, so no attempt has been made to list all possible combinations. Remember that MIPS or PowerPC-powered computers are also able to act as platforms for Exchange Server.

Sizing an operational system

Table 3.4 *Sample server configurations*

Requirement	CPU	Memory	Disk	Extras
Primary Domain Controller or File and Print server	Intel 80486 50MHz or above	32Mb	600Mb	
Exchange messaging server for testing or to serve small (10–100) user community	Intel Pentium 100MHz	64Mb	2Gb	
Exchange messaging/public folders server for small user community	Intel Pentium 120MHz	64Mb	8Gb	RAID-5
Exchange messaging/public folders server for medium (100–400) user community	Dual Intel Pentium 133MHz or Digital Alpha 200MHz	128Mb	16Gb	RAID-5 array, UPS
Exchange messaging/public folders server for large (400–800) user community	Quad Intel Pentium Pro or Digital Alpha 300MHz	256Mb	24Gb	RAID-5 array, UPS
Dedicated Internet Mail Connector	Dual Intel Pentium 100MHz	128Mb	4Gb	UPS

Note the configuration for the system dedicated to the Internet Mail Connector, an example of how to deploy an Exchange server that does nothing else except concentrate on a single task. The growing volume of corporate connections to the Internet and the amount of messages flowing through those links means that many organizations need to consider a scenario that includes a system dedicated to the Internet Mail Connector. Depending on traffic patterns you may need one system dedicated to outgoing messages and another dedicated to incoming.

Performance tests carried out by Microsoft reveal that Exchange Server is sensitive to disk configuration changes at the high end of the performance spectrum. This means that if you want to build large servers you must be prepared to add lots of disk capacity. Large disks provide lots of capacity, but having multiple spindles available to spread the load and support disk striping is better still. If in doubt, use the Performance Optimizer utility (see page 341) to check your current configuration and make suggestions to possibly improve the distribution of files across the available spindles.

During the discussion on the information store (from page 145 onwards) a suggestion is offered to use a FAT-formatted drive for Exchange transaction logs rather than an NTFS-formatted drive. There is a significant penalty to pay in terms of wasted space allocated to small files in FAT-formatted drives once they go beyond 512Mb in size. However, the transaction logs are large (5Mb) and it shouldn't be a problem to have a large FAT drive in situ.

Remember that the Performance Optimizer cannot distinguish the difference between partitioned drives created on a single physical disk. Each drive on a system is measured in exactly the same way, so the suggestions made to redistribute files across partitioned drives may not be optimum and require reassessment once the Performance Optimizer offers its suggestions. As referred to above, more physical disk spindles are generally always better from a performance perspective than a single large disk. In other words, given the choice of a single 4Gb disk or 4 × 1Gb disks you'll get better performance from the latter option. The way the Performance Optimizer analyzes disks proves that you should never place too much trust in automated utilities. They're a great starting point and a guide towards better performance, but they are not infallible.

Pentium-based servers are likely to be the general workhorse system chosen for Exchange deployment in 1996–1997. New processors tend to fall in price after they have been available for a while and competitors have started to appear, so the Pentium Pro will start out as a more expensive option which should become the baseline system for Exchange server from 1997 onwards. If the pace of development seen over the last three years is maintained the Digital Alpha processor will maintain its lead in terms of sheer speed. Unlike its competitors Alpha is a 64-bit processor and the net effect of this is an increase in the amount of memory required on Alpha-powered systems in comparison to others.

A heavily loaded Exchange server demands a lot of a CPU. The sheer speed of the Alpha processor makes it an excellent choice for systems supporting large user populations or those that handle a high message interchange workload. Systems that act as X.400 or SMTP connectors must translate messages from internal Exchange format to the formats used within X.400 or SMTP backbones, and this work can generate a lot of processing especially with large messages or those addressed to big distribution lists. Similar workloads are generated by incoming messages arriving from the X.400 or SMTP worlds.

If you're unsure about the potential of any particular configuration to support Exchange, perhaps that of a system which you have on hand ready to go, you can run the Exchange Load Simulator (LoadSim). The load simulator program creates a workload for the system and measures how it responds. A full description of the program begins on page 353.

Preparing for success

I think it best to over-configure a system rather than attempt to get it just right. In order words, to expect the system to be successful and grow over time. The 'just right' state lasts about one week after a system goes into operation and after that it's a constant battle between system administrators (who want to preserve as much resources as possible) and users (who have quite the opposite viewpoint). Apart from the general contest between users and administrators a number of other factors may have an impact on system performance after they go into production. Common factors include:

- New applications are added. For example, Web service based on the Microsoft Internet Information Server is started. Some of these applications may have the capability to be 'mail-enabled' through MAPI, and if enabled will use Exchange to create and send messages.
- The characteristics of user workload change as they become more familiar with the system. Instead of small, simple messages large complex, multi-attachment messages are generated and sent. Heavier use is made of Schedule+. Electronic forms applications are created and put into use. Users begin to move away from using messages to share information to the more powerful, but also more demanding, paradigm enabled by public folders.
- Heavier use is made of Internet or X.400 connectors. For instance, because the Internet Mail Connector provides very easy access to Internet messaging resources users start subscribing to news groups and other mailing lists, resulting in a new source of external messages arriving into the system.
- New features are incorporated into the overall messaging service. For example, Electronic Data Interchange (EDI) communications with trading partners, voice mail, a FAX gateway, a paging service, and so on.

For these reasons it's better to fight the battle to get the necessary budget to build a really well-configured system from the start. Building redundancy and growth into systems from the start avoids the situation of having to continually patch in new hardware or other resources and play catch-up with user demands. Having additional memory, disk space, and CPU power from day one gives an element of assurance that the system will last a reasonable amount of time before it begins to creak at the edges.

Large versus small servers

As far as I am aware no prize has yet been made available for building the largest Exchange server in the world. In general, it is unwise to put too many users on a single server. Try to balance your user community across the set of available servers, keeping no more than 500 or so on any individual server. More than 500 users on a single server makes administration unwieldy and extends the time necessary to perform regular housekeeping or maintenance operations.

The Exchange Load Simulator (LoadSim) application (see the discussion starting on page 353) allows you to conduct automated tests on selected hardware configurations. Microsoft and hardware vendors use LoadSim to determine how many users can be supported on different CPUs. The results of these tests indicate that many computers (albeit sometimes equipped with multiple CPUs) are capable of supporting over 1,000 users. The upper limit (as tested) is set by 8-CPU Alpha systems tested at up to 20,000 users. Treat such figures cautiously. They are fine in theory but not in practice, not least because the 16Gb limit for a server's information store places a practical limit on the number of users that can be comfortably supported on a server. There's no point in configuring a system to support 2,000 if they aren't able to create and send messages because there's no disk space available.

Although Exchange is clearly capable of supporting many more users on an individual server, the Microsoft group responsible for co-ordinating the internal implementation of Exchange Server determined that there should be no more than 315 user mailboxes on an Exchange server. This reflects a pragmatic solution to the need of e-mail users within Microsoft where they are allowed 50Mb of disk space each in the information store. Sizing systems for user communities of similar size allows consideration of a wide range of hardware configurations. You can configure for the bare minimum, allow room for growth, or expect success and over-configure initially in order to deal with an expected growth for computer resources as users become more familiar with the system or as new facilities are introduced.

Many experienced administrators of high-end messaging systems advocate mixing different types of users on each server so as to spread the workload generated by user activities evenly across all servers in a site. Spreading users across a set of smaller servers avoids a single point of failure and increases the amount of space within the private information store that you can allocate to each user. Smaller systems are cheaper to buy and you have a wider range of hardware to choose from. You may even be able to use existing hardware after applying disk and memory upgrades rather than buying expensive new high-end computers. However, there are disadvantages. Lots of different servers in a site increase the overall complexity of the installation and drive up the time required to accomplish day-to-day housekeeping tasks, such as backups. You may have to spend time moving user mailboxes from server to server in an attempt to balance the load, and the range of hardware installed within a site may make maintenance harder, especially for older hardware.

For instance, there is no point in grouping all the really heavy messaging users together on a single server unless you want to equip that server with the resources needed to handle their demands. Another tactic worth bearing in mind is to try and have as high a degree of message locality as possible on each server. In other words, try and allocate users who need to send messages to each other on the same server so that the processing by Exchange's various connectors is reduced to a minimum. The same tactic can be taken with public folders, placing them close to the users who need to access the data held in the folders most often.

Resilience through clustering

In simplistic terms clustering is the ability for a group of computers to transparently share common information while allowing computers to join or leave the group without interfering with the service provided to users. People who use a clustered computer system see a single identity for the cluster and are not normally aware of the complex interaction that takes place behind the scenes to make all the component systems work together.

Clustering is important for messaging systems because it allows you to build highly-available resilient systems. Messaging, for many enterprises, rapidly becomes a mission-critical application, and whenever a problem occurs to interrupt the messaging service, howls of pain can be heard throughout the organization. For example, it's easy to see why a marketing department would be annoyed if the server hosting the public folder where all the latest pricing information is located goes down. Or how people who communicate with external organizations might have their plans interfered with if the server where the X.400 or SMTP connector is located goes off the air. A personal observation of mine is that there is less tolerance for interruptions the higher up users are within an organizational structure, leading to situations where it is imperative that the messaging system is available for as close to 100% as possible.

The first production-quality clustered systems were delivered in the middle 1980s when VAXclusters were developed by Digital Equipment Corporation. VAXclusters originally required a very tight hardware-based connection between the individual systems within the cluster, but were evolved to allow looser coupling over network-based connections. A later development expanded clustering to accommodate different computer families and allowed the 32-bit VAX family of systems to be clustered with 64-bit Alpha systems, all using the single OpenVMS operating system.

Microsoft is currently working on its own implementation of clustering for Windows NT systems. The Microsoft implementation isn't the first, as products are already available from Digital (mid 1996) and AT&T[1] (early 1996), and Compaq. Other clustering vendors may have come to market in the time between the date of publication and when you read this book. Digital have licensed their clustering technology to Microsoft where it is being used as the basis for the development of Microsoft clustering software, so it's fair to say that the Digital implementation provides a glimpse into the future in this respect.

The features of the Digital clustering solution include:

- Works across Intel and Alpha processors, and supports the shrink-wrapped version of Windows NT
- Requires no hot (or cold) standby system, so you don't need to keep a system hanging around doing nothing until a problem occurs
- Is not a port of clustering technology from another platform (such as OpenVMS or UNIX), and is optimized for Windows NT
- Requires no special hardware or interconnection devices.

The Digital cluster software connects systems together with SCSI adapters on a shared SCSI bus, allowing systems to share disk devices (standalone or RAID arrays). Fail-over capability is included, so that if a problem occurs cluster services (such as the Exchange Information store) or a shared resource (like the install point for Exchange client software) are maintained. From a client perspective, an alias is given to the cluster as a whole to use when addressing cluster resources, so users don't have to know how many systems actually form the cluster and what their individual server names are.

One way of looking at clustering is to draw an analogy between it and the way Exchange Server allows a site to seamlessly expand itself across a number of individual servers, all of which share common data

---

1. *AT&T's clustering product is called LifeKeeper for Windows NT.*

structures. When you want to add users from a new department all you need to do is to install a new Exchange server and have it join the existing site. Once data has been replicated the new server is up and running as full and participating member of the site. A clustered system works at a lower level, but also allows you to expand the overall power and resources available to users by allowing you to introduce new hardware when required without affecting the hardware that's already installed.

Do you need to cluster the systems you use for Exchange Server? Clustering helps high-end Windows NT servers to attain a higher degree of overall system availability, but the current implementations of Windows NT clustering is based on NT file sharing and doesn't accommodate the type of database application that Exchange Server basically is. More resilience is therefore gained through a RAID-5 array (discussed further on in this chapter) than through clustering.

The decision as to deploy clustering or not depends on the role Windows NT servers play within your organization. In circumstances where a lot of small sites supporting single servers are in use there probably isn't much call for clustering. The exception to this rule is for sensitive servers or those that require the highest possible degree of resilience. On the other hand, if you have a number of large servers, each of which supports several hundred users you'd be wise to consider some sort of clustering to drive down the probability that an unforeseen problem will deprive users of the services (that can take advantage of clustering) for any length of time.

Protection through fault tolerance

Most high-end Windows NT servers have multiple disk drives and applications are carefully distributed across all available drives in order to maximize the disk I/O capability of the system as well as minimize the effect of a failure. I believe that the majority of systems used to run Exchange Server in production mode will automatically have configurations that mark them as high-end systems. In circumstances where reasonable hardware configurations are available, keeping everything on a single drive is similar to keeping all your eggs in one basket – tidy, but prone to leave an awful mess should anything go wrong.

RAID, or Redundant Array of Inexpensive Disks, is a method of combining several inexpensive disks into what appears to be a single large physical device, largely replacing older methods implemented mainly for mini- or mainframe computers. The fault tolerant features enabled by RAID technology makes it an item to consider when configuring medium to large systems for use by Exchange Server.

It is possible to implement RAID in hardware or software, and indeed Windows NT facilitates both approaches. Hardware implementations are normally preferred, largely because the hardware can be optimized to provide a much higher level of overall disk performance than is possible with a software implementation. RAID comes in different levels, from 0 to 5, and each level offers an increased degree of fault tolerance at higher expense. Windows NT servers support RAID levels 0, 1, and 5 in software, but all six levels can be supported by hardware implementations. Apart from fault tolerance RAID can also achieve higher disk throughput through disk striping, a technique that creates a logical disk from a set of physical disks.

Disk striping increases performance by spreading the read and write I/O operations across the physical disks in the set. In the case of an Exchange server that has large public and private information stores concurrently accessed by many clients, far better performance will be seen if the stores are placed on a striped disk rather than large physical devices. A simple step towards better performance is to place the public and private information stores on separate physical disks.

Any server deemed to be critical, such as those supplying messaging services to large user communities, should be equipped with some degree of fault-tolerance for disks that store essential information. The choice for Windows NT servers are mirrored disks, duplexed disks, or stripe sets with parity. When a disk is mirrored it means that a perfect duplicate copy of the contents of a disk partition is kept on a second partition, so that when a write operation is made to the primary partition the same data is written to the mirrored partition at the same time. Disk mirroring provides the same level of fault tolerance as RAID-1. It provides a reasonable degree of protection against faults as long as errors are confined to a single partition and do not afflict the physical disk where the partitions are located or the disk controller that the disk is attached to.

Disk duplexing expands the concept of disk mirroring by removing the mirrored partition to a second disk controller. The technique used to assure data protection is similar to mirroring. Extra protection and resilience is afforded by spreading the two write operations across two separate disk controllers. A further advantage is achieved because the I/O load generated by the write operations is split, so there is less danger that an individual drive will become saturated by the I/O operations generated by applications or even Windows NT itself. Windows NT always attempts to read from the drive that it regards as the fastest path to the required data, so a slight potential increase in read access to data can also be considered an advantage gained by splitting activity across two controllers.

Striped disks with parity provides RAID-5 fault tolerance. In a RAID-5 array the equivalent of one disk is dedicated to the storage of backup information, but the actual backup data is spread across the entire array.[2] RAID-5 permits multiple read and write operations to proceed simultaneously.

If RAID is operational and a drive fails the array should continue to operate. In these situations the array will mark the failed drive as bad (the correct term is orphaned drive) and continue to use the good drives that remain. However, at this point in time fault tolerance disappears and the bad drive must be replaced as soon as possible.

In a RAID-1 (disk mirroring) environment it is normally sufficient to replace the faulty disk with a new one and then take steps to break up the mirror set and then introduce the new volume to the set. All of this is done with the Windows NT Disk Administrator utility, and when the new volume has been successfully added Windows NT will copy the data from the other volume in the set. After the copy is completed and both drives mirror each other fault tolerance is resumed.

Roughly the same concept applies with striped arrays, the difference being that a new physical disk is added to the set. At this stage the backup data from the rest of the array is restored to the new drive and the full array becomes active again.

Hardware implementations of RAID use 'hot-swapping' when drives become faulty. This means that as soon as a fault is detected in a disk it can be removed from the array and substituted with a new disk while the system is active. Digital StorageWorks controllers take this a little further by allowing a hot spare, or a disk that remains inactive until a problem occurs at which time the controller automatically switches the faulty disk out of the array and brings in the hot spare.

Fault-tolerant disk technology evolves all the time and you should pay attention to new developments as they arise. The detail provided here is hopefully enough to inform you about some of the options available to help create a high-availability Windows NT system and form a solid base for Exchange Server. A messaging system that continually breaks down is good to noone and it's normally very visible within an organization. For that reason alone (job preservation for system managers), make sure that all important systems in your installation are satisfactorily protected against disk faults.

---

2. *Striped disks with parity demands a minimum of three disks in the array.*

A growing strain on existing network resources?

Does your LAN and WAN operate in a satisfactory manner today? Of course you'll say 'yes', and why wouldn't you? But the facts are that many LANs are tied together with so much string and good wishes and just about manage to limp along on a wing and a prayer. If you're in this type of situation then you need to consider whether you can even attempt to implement Exchange Server in such a flimsy network environment. Even if your network is in good shape Exchange Server is going to impose some extra demands. If you replace several LAN Post Offices with one or more Exchange servers you may find that people will start to use the system more because message delivery is more reliable. They'll also like the additional functionality that Exchange provides. Clearly with such a range of network capabilities it is important to plan how information is exchanged between the different systems.

All Exchange servers should be equipped with the best and most capable network adapter you can afford. Don't try and limp by with an old or low-throughput adapter because its flaws will be revealed once the pressure goes on. Given that client–server systems place a huge emphasis on network stability and throughput it's important that you provide a solid base for your clients to connect to servers and for the servers to service the clients. Servers designed to support large numbers of clients should be equipped with multiple LAN adapters and caching controllers on disks to ensure that network and disk I/O demands generated by clients can be met. Equipping the servers with fast CPUs, fast disks, and lots of memory will be wasted investments if the server can't pump data down to clients as quickly as it would like to because of an old or underpowered network adapter.

Sources of network demand

What are the potential sources of additional network demand? First, there is a general increase in the average message size being seen within messaging networks. In the old text-based environments an average one-page message, complete with all its header information and whatever other data was necessary to transmit the message from originator to recipient could comfortably fit into the 4Kb–6Kb range. The advent of rich text messages complete with all the huge attachments regularly generated by the current suites of desktop office products has driven the average message size up dramatically. As we've already discussed in Chapter 1, some installations report an average message size of 40Kb, some see higher, and all expect the average message size to grow. The features and functionality of desktop applications encourage users to incorporate highly graphical items in their documents, and all the 'glitz' must be paid for in size.

Users gain in confidence all the time. Electronic mail was once an application to be approached with care, but not any more. The electronic age makes e-mail just another way to communicate and users create more and more messages all the time. Added to the increased comfort zone there are more ways to create messages through mail-enabled applications. Almost every application today can add a 'Send Message' option to its menus. External message feeds from other organizations and the Internet drive up the number of messages within the system. If just a few users subscribe to some Internet news groups you can expect to see many hundreds of messages coming in from that source on a daily basis.

You can help users to work with Exchange in an intelligent manner and restrict their use of system resources. Most of this is done through good habits instilled into individuals through training (a good reason not to skimp on user training during any implementation). An example of a good habit is using public folders to share documents rather than mailing large documents around to multiple recipients during a review cycle. Training allows you to divert people away from using neat client features which, although attractive, impose a real strain on the network.

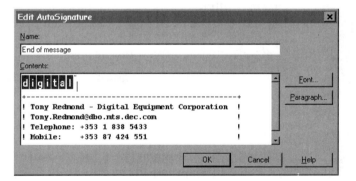

Figure 3.2 *A really bad user habit – inserting a logo into auto signature*

Including a bitmap image of the corporate logo in an Auto Signature is a good example of how a feature can be misused, the reason being that several kilobytes of bitmap data will be appended to every outgoing message. Figure 3.2 illustrates how easy it is to include a logo into the auto-signature feature. In this case the overhead is relatively low at 2Kb per message, but only because the bitmap was available in 16-color format. It is entirely possible for users to insert a complicated graphic that's only available in 256 colors! As long as you can use the standard Windows cut and paste facility to move a graphic around it can be slotted neatly into an Exchange auto signature. And of course, users aren't necessarily going to insert the corporate logo. All manner of smiling faces, cute cats, or other icons can be pasted into an auto-signature. Those interested in discovering where the contents of your auto-signature are held should look for a file called AUTOSIGN.SIG in your Windows directory. The file's stored in Rich Text Format and can be edited with NotePad or WordPad (if you want to see the native RTF formatting commands), or Word for Windows to see the auto-signature in all its glory.

You can also help to enforce good user habits by placing restrictions on some of the available gateways or connectors. Not allowing users to send messages larger than 1Mb seems like an intelligent step in the right direction – if a user really has a good business need to transmit a message larger than this they should really find out if there's a better (faster or more functional) method to accomplish the same task before possibly clogging up a vital e-mail link. Directives (or 'Tips on how to use the system better') can easily be brought to users' attention by distributing easy-to-reference hint sheets.

The enhanced functionality available in Exchange Server imposes some additional demands of its own. It's great to be able to distribute public folders throughout the organization, but there's an overhead incurred by the messages sent to get data from one place to another. The automatically synchronized Exchange directory is great, but again more messages are generated and exchanged between systems to keep the directory synchronized. And if you turn on advanced security there will be authentication requests generated too.

Finally, just to make the situation even more complicated network planners must take account of the impact of the World Wide Web, whether it's used in an Intranet or out on the Internet. Users love being able to browse remote locations to discover new information, and that information is generally presented in a very graphical and attractive manner. But again, the network must be able to handle the load generated by shipping all the data from one place to another. System administrators and network planners in quite a few corporations that I work with are now discovering that Web traffic is taking more and more network capacity. I think this trend will continue over the next few years, and the net effect will be a continuing and growing demand for more and more network bandwidth.

These are just some of the potential sources for growth in network demand. Implementing a new messaging system often focuses minds on the infrastructure required by the new system, so this is a good time to perform a health check on the underlying network and take steps to ensure it is able to cope. Without a good network you have little chance of a good implementation of Exchange Server.

4

Managing Exchange Server

Recipients, mailboxes, and people

Users are the most important part of any system, and perhaps especially so in the case of systems that automate common office tasks and enable better human interaction. Without users there's simply no point to an electronic messaging server. In this chapter we'll look at the challenges involved in day to day operation of an Exchange server, covering topics like setting up and managing the user community, backup, system monitoring, tuning, and so on.

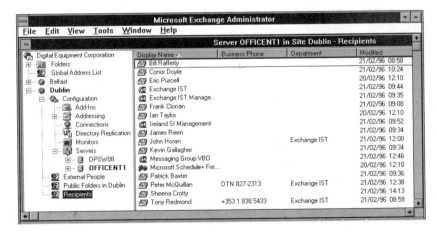

Figure 4.1
Contents of the recipients container from a small Exchange server

Anyone who has ever faced the task of managing a mail server knows that people have to be registered before they can use the system. Exchange Server is no different in this respect. Users have to be registered and allocated space to hold their messages, but Exchange is a little different because a wide range of valid mail destinations, including people, are registered together in a single directory. Some or all of the recipient types are supported by other servers, but possibly not in as complete a fashion as Exchange. Valid types are:

- *Mailboxes.* This is the most common type of recipient. Everyone who wants to use Exchange Server to send and receive interpersonal messages must be able to access a mailbox. Several users can share a mailbox, and it is possible for someone to delegate access to their mailbox to other users (see section on mailbox surrogacy starting on page 126).
- *Distribution lists.* A distribution list is a collection of recipients of any valid types. When messages are sent to distribution lists copies are dispatched to every recipient that appears in the list.
- *Custom recipient.* Someone who uses any other messaging system. For example, an Internet user who receives mail via SMTP, or a someone who receives messages sent via an X.400 link between Exchange and another X.400-compliant messaging system such as AT&T Mail.
- *Public folders.* A folder is a sub-section of the information store, used to arrange information in a logical order. Unlike folders in the personal message store, information placed in public folders becomes available to anyone who has access to the folder.

By default, details of user mailboxes and distribution lists are stored in the Recipients container in the Exchange directory (see Figure 4.1). Two interesting aspects of mailbox entries in the Exchange directory are:

- You don't have to reveal all mailboxes by adding them to the Global Address List. The 'Hide from Address Book' checkbox on a mailbox's Advanced property page controls whether a mailbox is included in the Global Address List. Senior management or other individuals occupying sensitive posts are often excluded from directory listings, the e-mail equivalent of an ex-directory telephone number.
- The Directory Restrictions property page controls the addresses a mailbox can send messages to as well as the people the mailbox will accept messages from. You can use these properties to restrict users to a subset of total possible recipients, or to stop messages arriving into a mailbox from people you'd rather not receive mail from. Contract workers who join an organization for a short time and need e-mail connectivity are candidates for restricted send options. Senior management might also like to be protected from a flood of messages, so they are candidates for restricted delivery options. Controlling a large exclusion list for send or delivery restrictions can be quite time-consuming, but you can cut down on the work by using distribution lists instead of specifying individual mailboxes, as shown in Figure 4.2.

Recipients, mailboxes, and people   117

Figure 4.2
Using a distribution list for delivery restrictions

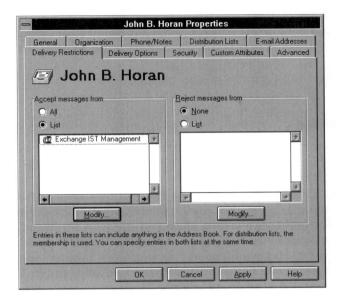

Breaking up the directory

Multiple containers can be defined to hold recipients, allowing you to break up large user communities into more manageable chunks. Apart from anything else, dividing recipients up into different containers makes it easier for users to select from a set of particular addresses when they add recipients to mail messages.

Figure 4.3
Selecting a custom recipient from a special container

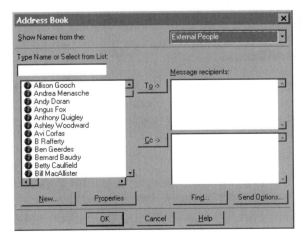

Figure 4.3 shows addresses for a new message being selected from a special container called 'External People.' This container holds all the custom recipients defined system-wide. It's easier for someone to

look through a small container holding all the addresses of a specific type, in this case, everyone external to the company, than it is to wade through a potentially very large global address list.

Public folders are fairly special entities. As such they deserve a separate discussion removed from the topic of how to set up and name the accounts used by people to access Exchange Server.

Distribution lists

In Exchange V4.0 a maximum of 5,000 objects can be specified in a distribution list. Note the word 'objects.' An object can be an Exchange mailbox or a custom recipient, but it can also be another distribution list, leading to a situation where distribution lists can contain nested distribution lists, greatly expanding the total possible user population that can be addressed through a single list. However, while it's nice to know that it's technically possible to create a mega-distribution list to address thousands of users at a single keystroke, once a list contains more than 100 users or so perhaps public folders offer a much better way of distributing information to wide interest groups?

Because they are treated by Exchange Server like any other recipient distribution lists are useful when setting permissions on folders, much along the same lines as delivery restrictions. When permission is given to a distribution list all members of the list inherit the permission. The advantage lies in the fact that it's very much easier to grant permission to a single entity, the list, than it is to manage separate permissions for each individual on the list. And better still, when people join a distribution list they'll inherit permissions granted to the list, and when they are removed from the list the permissions are revoked.

Managing user mailboxes

We've already discussed the topic of well-designed server names. If you've been running an electronic mail system, including PC LAN-based systems, you're also aware that each user must be uniquely identified to allow proper control of access to the system and also, possibly more important from the user perspective, to make sure that messages are delivered correctly. To accomplish this each person wishing to use the Exchange Server messaging system is allocated a unique identifier, otherwise known as an account or user name.

Successful operation of Exchange Server requires management of user accounts and mailbox names. Plunging forward to create accounts and mailboxes without considering the long term ramifications of what you're doing may work for a 20-user operation but you're bound to run into problems when the system expands and has to accommodate more accounts or mailboxes, so it pays to consider your options before starting.

All messaging systems impose their own requirements in terms of the number of characters that can be used in an account name, and which characters may legally appear in the name. Some installations have well-defined guidelines as to how account names are made up, although some of these ideas are a little obscure. For example, if your organization allocates numbers to staff members it may seem sensible to use the same staff numbers as the basis for allocating e-mail account names. In reality however such a scheme falls down badly as the resulting addressing scheme is very unuser-friendly. I hold badge number 150847 in Digital's personnel system, but I'd hate to be thought of as a mere number, or to have other people forced to address messages to me as 150847. National social security numbers are unique and are sometimes proposed as the basis for an even more unuser-friendly account naming convention. Thankfully it's illegal to use social security numbers in this way in many countries. But, strange as it may seem, there are organizations who think it's a good idea to use cryptic, esoteric naming schemes.

The most sensible principles to remember when considering what type of account naming scheme is appropriate for your organization are:

- *Logical.* Users shouldn't have to go through mental contortions to remember the account name for the people they want to send mail to.
- *Friendly.* Some logical schemes are well, too logical. Look for a compromise between logic and user-friendliness.
- *Straightforward.* Avoid complexity at all costs.

Surnames are often considered to be the first and most obvious basis for planning a naming scheme, and it's often possible to use surnames in small e-mail systems. However, the statistical fact is that the more users a system supports the more chance there will be that common surnames exist. In a small system supporting 50 users you might only have one 'SMITH' (or the equivalent most common name in a country or language), but I'll guarantee that in a system supporting more than a hundred or so users there will be more than one surname clash to contend with.

Accessing your mailbox

Everyone who wishes to use Microsoft Exchange Server to send and receive messages must have access to a Windows NT account. Normally, a Windows NT account is associated with a single Exchange

Server mailbox, although a privileged account is able to use its elevated permissions to access a mailbox apparently reserved for another account. You could, for instance, log into the computer's privileged Administrator account, run the Exchange client program, and define a profile to connect to a mailbox allocated to another account. This is quite legal and understandable, if not altogether desirable from a user perspective. All that's happening is that standard permissions are being used to override the protections on a mailbox. Being able to log-into a user's account in this way is a useful feature for an administrator, but it can be disconcerting for users to discover that their mailbox can be accessed in this manner, especially as no permanent trace or audit record is left that a mailbox has been accessed from a different account.[1]

Exchange Server is little different from many other messaging systems that permit privileged administrators to 'take over' user mailboxes for debugging or maintenance purposes. System administrators (and sometimes operators) basically have access to any data held on a computer unless special steps are taken to restrict their access to specific information. This fact is something to think about when appointing people to fill positions with access to such a range of sensitive information. The advanced security features of Exchange Server (discussed later on in this chapter) help by preventing unauthorized access to encrypted messages. Even if someone else is privileged enough on the Windows NT level to be able to access your mailbox they shouldn't be able to read encrypted messages unless you hand over your security password.

The implications of privileged user access to electronic mail should be factored into your security policy and the consequences of unauthorized access to messages clearly spelled out. A wide variety of views are present in the computer industry on the nature of information held in electronic messages. I believe the majority of companies treat the contents of electronic messages as private to the sender and recipients and take steps to ensure that no unauthorized access is tolerated.

---

1. *The log-ons property page for the Private Information Store lists the mailboxes which access the Private Information Store together with the Windows NT account last used to access each mailbox. This information provides the only obvious sign of instances where a privileged account was used to access a user mailbox. However, the information is transient and is over-written each time a mailbox is logged on to. It is possible to log the use of privileges to access user mailboxes by turning diagnostic logging on for the logon category for the MSExchangeIS Private service through the Diagnostics Logging property page for a selected server. When logon diagnostics are enabled privileged access to user mailboxes is recorded in the Windows NT event log. You can see these events by viewing the log (look for events 1011, 1016, or 1009).*

However, the increased incidence of 'discovery' actions taken by lawyers in attempts to uncover potentially damaging revelations about incidents or business dealings is causing companies to review the data contained in electronic mail systems with an aim of protecting themselves if the time comes to defend such an action.

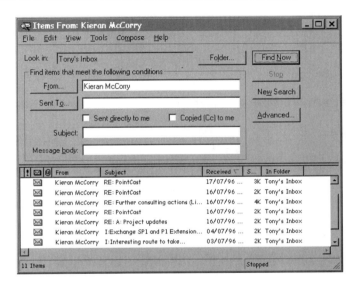

Figure 4.4
Searching for a message

How would you deal with a request to search your system to identify and recover all messages relating to a specific topic? Would it make things harder if the request focused in on a particular range of dates? I've been involved in a couple of discovery cases where lawyers requested copies of all messages sent by a particular group of users over the period of a month two years back from the time of asking. Fulfilling such a request is an expensive and time-consuming exercise. Exchange Server does not offer any text search and retrieval functionality capable of meeting such a request, so the only option in this case is to check the mailbox of each user on the list to see what it contained during the particular period. In fact, the standard find option provided in the Exchange clients (see Figure 4.4) is only capable of searching the cover memo text of messages and won't, for instance, search through a Word document or a PowerPoint presentation.

Note that the 'search subfolders' option is disabled automatically whenever a search involves folders that may span multiple servers. While it is reasonable to expect a search to be able to conduct a fast scan through all the folders in a specific folder tree when the folders are stored locally, it's quite another matter to attempt to do the same thing when the folders may be scattered throughout the network.

Executing live, distributed queries would take a long time to complete. It's a problem that database vendors have been looking at for quite a time, but so far no good answers have arrived.

In a discovery situation before any check can be made, the system must be restored back to the exact state it was at the time in question. This point raises the question of just how long you need to keep system backups around in today's legally-charged atmosphere. Is two years enough? Probably not. If you take full system backups at regular intervals you should plan to keep the backup tapes around for at least five years, just in case.

Mailboxes and Windows NT accounts

Mailboxes can be created when new Windows NT user accounts are set up or by using the Exchange Administrator program to create a new mailbox for an existing Windows NT account. In most situations there will be a one-to-one mapping between users and mailboxes, but it is also possible for several users to have access to a shared mailbox, such as in the case where a group of users need to monitor messages arriving at a mailbox set up as a generic recipient. For example, a mailbox created to receive requests to register for training events.

Windows NT account names tend to be rather terse and pretty un-user-friendly, and are limited to 20 characters. For instance, my account names on the two servers I connect to regularly are T_REDMOND and TONYR. Exchange treats everything associated with the server as an object in one form or another, and the Windows NT account name is an attribute of a user object, albeit one that's pretty important. However, you're not limited to account names as Exchange Server also allows for a more complete name as another user attribute, so I can be referred to as 'Tony Redmond'. A complete user name is sometimes referred to by users as a 'pretty name', probably because it's nicer to look at on-screen or in printed format than the shorter computer account names. While it's by no means essential to have two names for an account, from the human interface point of view it's also possibly true that people feel better addressing messages to 'Tony Redmond' than 'TONYR'.

Using surnames as the basis for Windows NT account names meets the criteria of being logical, friendly, and straightforward. So it makes sense to persist and try and use a variation of pure surnames as the basis for a naming scheme. How about adding an initial to the surname so that I, for instance, become 'TREDMOND'. This is more unique but incurs the disadvantage of throwing all our account names out of synchronization, mostly because it's easier and more logical to view a user directory when it is ordered in the same way as the telephone directory – in surname order.

It's therefore better to use initials as a suffix rather than a prefix, giving us 'REDMONDT'. Now all the names are sorted according to the same order you'd expect, making it easier for users to follow. If Tony Redmond and Tom Redmond are on the same system we can add another initial to create a difference. For example, 'REDMONDTY' and 'REDMONDTO'.

Some installations separate the surname from the initials with a character such as ',' (comma), or '.' (period). Underscores ('_') should be avoided in electronic mail addresses because some mail systems are unable to deal with addresses that contain underscores. My preference is to use a period as a separator, but only because this has been successfully used within Digital for many years and has therefore withstood the test of time. Thus, the preferred Windows NT account name is a choice between 'REDMOND.T' or 'REDMOND.TONY'. Remember that 20 character restriction. It may limit your options in situations where you have to cater for very long names, so be prepared to be flexible.

Account names and Exchange Server

After you've successfully managed to log onto your Windows NT system you can proceed to connect to Exchange Server. Mailboxes have a number of user name attributes that link Windows NT accounts with the correct Exchange Server mailboxes. These are:

- *Display Name*. The name that appears in the Administrator window (and used to select mailboxes when their details are changed or otherwise worked with by an administrator). This name can be up to 256 characters long, so even the longest name in the universe should fit. The display name is sometimes referred to as the 'pretty name' because it is seen when addressing messages, as part of a distribution list, or in the header information when a message is viewed or printed. Because the information from Global Address List cannot be customized when recipient information is viewed by users large organizations often include some additional data in recipients' display names to allow users to distinguish between common names. For example:

  John Smith (Sales)

  John Smith (Training)

If department names aren't enough consider using locations or other hints. For example:

John Smith (Sales – London)

John Smith (Training – Geneva)

The display name is also shown when the contents of a recipients container is viewed using the administration program.

- *Alias Name*. An alias can be up to 64 characters and is used to associate other mail addresses with an Exchange mailbox. As such, the mailbox alias must be unique on a server. Exchange will stop you if you attempt to allocate an existing alias to a mailbox. Apart from its use within the directory the alias is used as the 'account name' portion of an SMTP address. Many experienced system administrators like to set the Exchange mailbox alias to be the same as the Windows NT account name.

- *First Name, Initials, and Last Name* are all optional naming attributes that can be up to 32, 2, and 64 characters long respectively. While you don't have to enter this information it is useful to do so, especially in an X.400 environment where these attributes form part of fully qualified X.400 originator/recipient addresses.

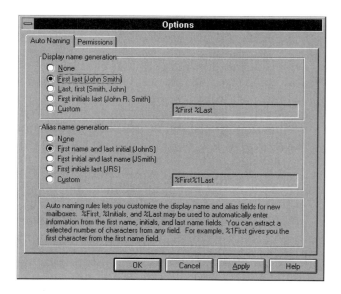

Figure 4.5
Automatic name generation options

The auto-name generation feature of Exchange Server, as shown in Figure 4.5, is able to generate a display and alias name for a new recipient when you enter details of the first name, initials, and last name. If you don't like the names generated by Exchange feel free to override the defaults and create your own versions. For example, you might decide to generate aliases based on the new recipient's surname and the first letter from their first name. To do this, select the Options menu from the Administration utility, select the 'Custom' radio button for Alias name generation, and type %Last%1First into the provided field. If you change the scheme used for automatic name generation midway through adding mailboxes or custom recipients some newly-generated aliases may clash with entries already in the directory when you attempt to add them. Fixing this problem is easy – all you need to do is create a custom alias for the affected recipient or mailbox.

When addressing messages Exchange clients allow you to enter the full display name, a mailbox's alias, or a user's surname in the TO:, CC:, or BCC: controls. Names are always checked before messages are sent from the client to the server. Names that are successfully validated against the global address list (server or off-line) or the personal address book are underlined in the control to show that Exchange Server has recognized the address and knows how to route the message to it. Names that are not underlined have not been validated but Exchange Server will validate the names when the message is sent and before it is actually passed on to the MTA for onward dispatch. If a name cannot be found in the global address list by reference to the full display name, a mailbox alias, or a surname, Exchange Server signals this to the client and refuses to accept the message. At this stage the user must 'fix' the address, possibly by perusing the global address list to select the address they actually want, before resubmitting the message to the server.

Maintaining mailbox details

Exchange Server allows system administrators to enter lots of information about user mailboxes, possibly more details than you would ever want to know about users, including who their manager is and who their direct reports (if they have any) are.

One possible flaw in the implementation is the fact that only system administrators, or rather people who hold the privilege to run the Exchange administration program, are able to amend user mailbox details. The logic behind this stance is easy to understand. User mailbox details are used as the basis of the directory and are replicated to other sites within the organization. It is therefore important to have a certain level of quality control and consistency imposed on the information entered into the directory.

To achieve quality in the directory users are not able to change even the most non-sensitive fields, such as their telephone numbers. Everything has to be done by system administrators, and I can foresee many help desk requests from users to change small details about the information that's been entered into the directory.

Other implementations of corporate messaging systems allow users to update their own details in the directory, so is this a competitive disadvantage for Exchange? Not really, those same implementations have discovered to their pain that user-initiated directory updates produce a lot of potentially unnecessary network traffic to propagate user-initiated changes throughout the organization. Restricting users from endless fiddling with their own details stops this traffic and helps to maintain the quality of directory information.

Mailbox surrogacy

Mail surrogacy or delegation is where users are authorized to take control of other users' mailboxes for specific purposes. The classical example of this functionality in action is where a secretary or administrative assistant controls a senior manager's mailbox. Even today, a minority of very senior executives actually process their own electronic mail and some are still at the stage where they demand that their messages are printed down each day for their perusal. They then mark the printed copies of the messages with their comments or replies and leave the marked-up messages with their secretary who takes care of generating an appropriate response.

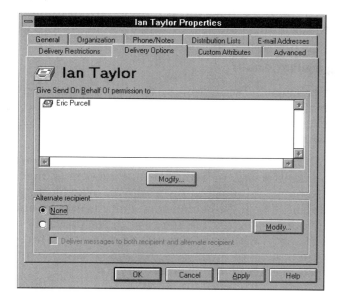

Figure 4.6
Delegating access to a mailbox

Managing user mailboxes

In the early days of electronic mail systems tended to be unsophisticated when compared to the systems in use today. Delegation was accomplished in an easy to work but totally insecure manner when users would give their system password to whoever was going to process messages on their behalf. System administrators hated this method because it totally compromised system security, but users found it easy to understand, especially when passwords were handed over on scraps of paper that could be conveniently posted on their bulletin board or securely stored in their desk drawer!

As electronic mail systems evolved attention was paid to eliminating the security hole caused by such a general interchange of passwords. Facilities to allow other users to connect to all or specific parts of mailboxes began to appear in the early 1990s, but even so many users persist in their old habits and continue to exchange passwords today. Exchange Server takes a comprehensive approach to the problem by:

▶ Not restricting users to only allowing one other account to access their mailbox. Any number of users can be granted the permission to send on behalf of a particular mailbox.

▶ Allowing system administrators to control the permission centrally by using the Administration utility (see Figure 4.6) to edit details of user mailboxes while also permitting users to issue their own permission using the client *Tools.Options* menu choice (Figure 4.7).

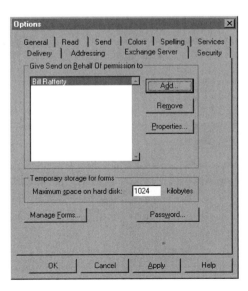

Figure 4.7 *Mail delegation from the client*

A newly delegated mailbox does not automatically appear after permission has been granted. Users must reconfigure their profiles to access additional mailboxes and then reconnect to the server after permission is received. Exchange Server does not break any new ground in mail delegation. However, it does build on the lessons learned in other messaging systems and has made the whole process a little easier.

Transferring users

It's hard to achieve perfection when the time comes to allocate users to servers, unless of course you only have a single server to work with. In any large system the time will come when you have to redistribute user accounts across servers, to balance the user-generated messaging load on each server or perhaps to keep users who communicate together on the same server in order to reduce off-server message traffic.

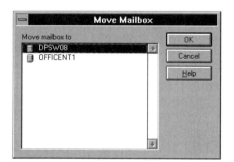

Figure 4.8
Moving a user's mailbox

Moving a user's mailbox from one server to another within a site is child's play. Select the 'Move mailbox' option from the Tools menu in the Administration program (Figure 4.8), select the user to move and the server they are to be moved to, and leave Exchange to do the work.

Because Exchange servers in the same site share the same directory and configuration information and are normally connected by high-speed links it's feasible to allow the software to take total control of:

▶ Locking the user's mailbox so that new messages are not delivered while the move is in progress. Messages are queued and delivered to the relocated mailbox once the move is complete.

▶ Moving all the folders and messages from the private information store on one server to the private information store on another.

▶ Updating the directory to indicate that the user's mailbox is now hosted on a new server. Apart from ensuring correct delivery from external sources this step ensures that other servers within the same site copy new messages to the correct private information store.

The process of moving all the information in a user's mailbox may take time to complete, especially if the user has managed to build up a large mailbox or the servers involved are busy. It's best to perform all moves during off-peak server times and after the user has been 'encouraged' to delete any unwanted messages from their mailbox. If the user won't cooperate with the request to clean their mailbox out, you may have to convince them by threatening to use the 'Clean Mailbox' option (see discussion starting on page 161). Because of the obvious potential difficulties that might occur it makes sense not to attempt to move a mailbox when the user is logged in. This is yet another good reason to move mailboxes when everyone's gone home and the systems are quiet.

Moving someone from one site to another or from one organization to another is not so straightforward. No options exist to do the job for you, so it's pretty much a manual task which requires coordination between the system administrators for the source and target systems. The basic steps are:

1. Have the system administrator on the target site create a new mailbox for the user. After this is done, hide the user's original mailbox from the global address list using the 'Hide from Address Book' option when editing mailbox details. This prevents two mailboxes for the one user appearing in the global address list. You should also modify any distribution lists that the user's old mailbox featured in by changing each list to include the new mailbox.

2. Set a redirect address for the old mailbox on the source server to transfer all newly arriving messages to the new mailbox on the target system. All newly arriving messages should now be delivered to the new mailbox.

3. To speed up the transfer process ask the user to delete all unwanted messages held on the server or do the job for them with the 'Clean Mailbox' option.

4. Create an auto-reply message stating that the user has moved to a new server. This step is optional and is really only important if the user is physically transferring location and won't be able to answer messages for a few days.

5. Move the contents of the user's server-based mailbox to a personal information store (.PST file). This is a manual process that

requires the user (or the administrator) to log on and move the messages with drag and drop operations.

6. For any reasonably sized mailbox the PST file will be quite large. You will need to make arrangements to transfer the PST file to the target system, possibly through a simple FTP copy.

7. Disable the Windows NT account for the user on the source server to prevent them logging on once the transfer process is complete.

8. On the host system users can import their messages from the PST file into their new mailbox. Or, better still, they can use the PST file as an archive for messages processed before their move.

9. After you are happy that the new mailbox is operational you can delete the old mailbox, erase the directory entry, and generally clean up any trace of the user on the source system. This will also remove the redirect address and the auto-reply message, if set.

These steps take no account of items like distribution lists where the old mailbox is included. Distribution list memberships must be updated manually.

If you're using advanced security no special steps have to be taken for intra-site transfers. However, moving users with secure messages from one site to another requires care if they are to be able to access their messages afterwards. The Exchange Resource Kit (see page 365) contains a tool to help with this task. It would be nice if a utility was provided by Microsoft to address the need to move users extra-site. Until such a utility is provided we'll have to do things manually, as described above.

Client installations and settings

The Windows registry holds details of user profiles. A profile consists of information about a user's working environment including the mailbox and server they connect to as well as the services they have configured. The normal set of services includes Microsoft Exchange Server and the Personal Address Book, and traveling users will probably configure Personal Folders as well. Optional services such as Microsoft Mail or Internet Mail can be configured as required, and all the details written into the registry. Figure 4.9 shows the Windows registry editor, REGEDIT.EXE, being used to view details of a user's profile on a Windows 95 client. The registry key in this case is:

HKEY_CURRENT_USER\Software\Microsoft\Windows Messaging Subsystem\Profiles

The system registry is also used to store user-specific settings for Exchange on Windows NT. On a Windows V3.*x* the settings are held in a standard application initialization file in the Windows directory. For example:

```
C:\WINDOWS\EXCHANGE.INI
```

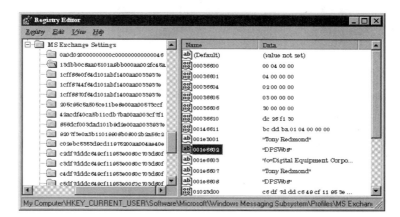

Figure 4.9
Exchange profile settings held in the Windows 95 system registry

Application initialization files group settings into a series of sections, each of which holds values applicable to a specific part of the application. An initialization file can be edited with any ASCII editor, such as the Windows Notepad editor, but care should be taken when editing as it's all too easy to slip and make an inadvertent change which doesn't quite have the intended effect. Always make a copy of an initialization file before making changes. Just to be complete let me note that the settings for DOS clients are stored in a file called EXCHANGE.PRO.

Setting default client options

From a support perspective it's a lot easier if everyone uses the same client options. By defining a default set of client options you also have an opportunity to enforce good housekeeping habits, such as erasing the contents of the Deleted Items folder when a client logs off.[2] This simple option prevents large amounts of unwanted objects accumulating, probably unnoticed, in the Deleted Items folder and frees up space in the private Information Store. Many users are reluctant to change settings at all on the basis that if the client works it's a bad idea to attempt to fix or make things better by changing options, so

---

2. *Always emptying the contents of the Deleted Items folder when exiting is good housekeeping but it has a potential side-effect too. See the discussion on restoring deleted documents on page 197.*

establishing a good default set of options is something that should be considered early on in a deployment. After all, it's much easier to have the system make a change when a client is installed than it is to travel around and visit multiple PCs afterwards.

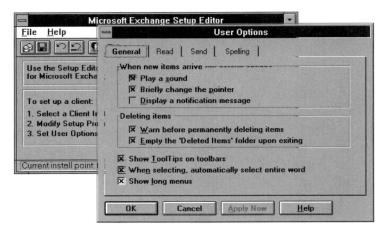

Figure 4.10
Exchange Setup editor

Exchange Server provides a Setup Editor to enable administrators to change options for kits installed in a shared installation point. A shared installation point is a location on a server where clients can connect to when they wish to install software. Installation points for all the clients you wish to support can be created automatically when you install the Exchange client software on a Windows NT server. Use the following steps to alter user settings with the Setup Editor.

1. Review the options available to each client you support (DOS, Windows NT, Windows 95, Windows V3.1) and decide which default settings you would like to change. The best way to conduct a review is to actually use a client for a period of time.

2. Start the Setup Editor from the Microsoft Exchange Administrator program group.

3. Select the installation point for the client you wish to change.

4. Make the changes as shown in Figure 4.10.

5. Close the Setup Editor.

Changes made with the Setup Editor are written into the EXCHNG.STF files in the selected installation point.

All clients installed after you make changes with the Setup Editor will pick up the new default values. Note that you can revert to the default set of options shipped with Exchange by clicking the 'Default' button on the Setup Editor form. Clients that were installed before you make the changes will not be affected.

'Hot' PCs and roaming users

A 'hot' PC is one that isn't always used by the same person. It might be a PC used in a multi-user shift environment, or just one that's available for visitors to use when they arrive at an office. User mailboxes, public folders and directory information are all maintained by Exchange servers, so users can connect to the information held in these containers from all PCs. There are some files and other information that can cause concern to those who move around. These include:

- Personal Information Stores (see page 166)
- Off-line folders (see page 168)
- Advanced Security Encrypted Password Files (see page 215)
- Personal Address Book (PAB)
- Profile Information

Personal Information Stores can be located on any disk. In the normal course of events users create personal stores on local hard drives, although I know of some cases where stores have been successfully used on floppy diskettes. If a store is held on a floppy it's easy to move from PC to PC, but there are some disadvantages including the high potential for media corruption (in comparison to hard drives) and the relative lack of space. Floppy diskettes are really only suitable for moving stores containing simple messages, not large amounts of complex documents. In most cases it's more realistic and useable to place personal information stores in personal directories on a networked file server. The only problem then occurs when people want to work in a location where they can't access the file server.

Off-line folders are snapshots of server-based folders that allow users to work with the folder contents when they are disconnected from the server. People who move from PC to PC and are able to connect to their server won't need off-line folders. Problems only occur when server connections aren't possible and off-line folder files aren't available. Exchange requires users to make an initial connection to the server before they can use off-line folder files, probably to ensure that the folder hierarchy is correctly synchronized between the server and client. This means that you can't just take an off-line folder file from one PC and move it to another and expect it to work. First you'll have to create a profile (or update an existing profile) and indicate that off-line working is required, and then make a connection. Catch-22 if the network's unavailable!

Encrypted password files are only necessary when advanced security is enabled. A user who wishes to encrypt or decrypt messages, or apply digital signatures to messages, must be able to access their password file. It's easy to move the password file from PC to PC, but it's embarrassing and frustrating to find yourself in a remote location after forgetting to copy your password file before you left home base.

The PAB is typically stored in a location such as:

`\EXCHANGE\MAILBOX.PAB`

Losing access to your PAB becomes a minor annoyance if you wish to use another PC, especially if the PAB contains the addresses for many external correspondents who don't have an Exchange mailbox. The 'Briefcase' feature of Windows 95 can be used to move a PAB from one PC to another (along with many other files), and then synchronize any changes that may have occurred when you return to the original PC. However, using the briefcase in this manner requires a discipline that lots of people just don't have so some frustration is likely. It's also important that you don't overwrite a PAB belonging to someone else when you move your PAB onto a PC, so it's good to recommend to users that they give a more appropriate name to their PAB, such as REDMOND.PAB.

Exchange profiles contain details of user working environments. On a shared PC it's quite possible to find many different profiles set up, one for each person who's passed by and used the PC. When you move to a PC you've never used before you'll need to either create a new profile or change an existing one to reflect items like

- The name of the server you want to connect to
- The name of your mailbox
- Whether you want to work with off-line folders
- The name of your PAB

Later on, after you've started the Exchange client you'll need to decide whether you want to work with a personal information store. If you do, you'll have to configure Exchange by adding 'Personal Folders' to the list of services and specifying where the personal information store is located.

While the steps necessary to move a complete working environment from one PC to another seems complex and full of potential error it's important to say that roaming users who use shared PCs normally only want to access a basic messaging service. They want to quickly use a PC to see whether any important messages have arrived, or have the chance to send a few messages of their own. Given that this is the case system administrators can accommodate the requirement of roaming users by ensuring that it's possible to connect PCs to all the servers in an organization. Users who require more advanced facilities, such as security or access to a personal information store, can be coached or instructed how to make their own arrangements.

Remote mail

Roaming users want to be able to get to their mail anytime, anyplace, anywhere. Exchange facilitates remote access by delivering its own 'Remote Mail' functionality or leveraging the functionality delivered by Windows NT Remote Access Server. Remote Mail allows you to make a quick dial-up connection, check your inbox, and decide what messages you really want to download for processing. Once the download is complete the connection is broken. A full RAS connection (Windows 95 Dial-Up Networking makes this operation very easy) enables you to use the Exchange client in exactly the same way as if you were connected to a LAN. All folders, including public folders, are available. Unfortunately, there's a small side effect of the way the Inbox Assistant works that can slow down working on a dial-up link.

The majority of the rules handled by the Inbox Assistant can be actioned when a client is not connected to the server. This is different from the rules services implemented by other e-mail clients, which require a server connection before any rules are processed. A rule requiring messages to be moved to a folder that's not in your mailbox is a notable exception. People commonly use rules like this to move incoming messages from specific individuals to different folders – some of which may be public, or others in a personal information store – but these rules are only processed when a server connection is made. If, like me, you subscribe to a number of Internet mailing lists that generate a fair amount of message traffic daily you can arrive at a situation where you log on, find that the Inbox is cluttered up with messages from all the different mailing lists, and then find that the Inbox Assistant busily goes to work to move messages out of the Inbox to their predetermined locations. The only problem is that while the Inbox Assistant is busy, a great deal of traffic is generated on the asynchronous telephone link and you won't be able to do much work while all this is going on. Even with a 28,800 bps modem, processing 50 or so messages can take a few moments, so prepare by having a good cup of coffee on-hand.

I'm pretty sure Microsoft will do something about this in the future but for now the way the Inbox Assistant processes 'move to other folder' requests leaves a little to be desired.

Client auto-upgrades

During the beta tests of Exchange server Microsoft provided an auto-upgrade feature for Windows V3.1, Windows NT, and Windows 95 clients. Auto-upgrade means that Exchange clients can check the local installation points each time they start, and if the client version held there is later than the version running on the PC a dialog is invoked to inform the user that a new version is available. The user can then make the decision whether to install the new version or not. Clearly this is a very interesting and potentially invaluable utility for system administrators, but it's totally unsupported. Details of the auto-upgrade procedure can be found in the appendix. Be aware that because the utility is not supported by Microsoft you are unlikely to receive any sympathy if you use it and it doesn't work.

Replication

Most system administrators who work with messaging systems are familiar with the concept of individual interpersonal arriving at and being dispatched from the system. This is the basic currency of any messaging system and there is nothing particularly new in the way that Exchange Server deals with interpersonal messages. Replication, on the other hand, is a somewhat more uncommon technique when applied to messaging systems. The major proponent of replication to this point in time has been Lotus Notes, where replication is used as the basic method to distribute information to servers throughout a network.

Replication means that data is copied from an originating computer to other computers according to some predefined rules. In a Microsoft Exchange Server environment replication occurs in two main areas:

1. Directory entries are replicated to servers that share a common directory. Entries are made, amended or deleted by the server responsible for user accounts or other entries held in the directory. Once the entry is made the 'owning' server communicates with the other servers in the network to update them with the new information. Replication is performed with a special type of encoded messages, and it can take anything from five minutes to several hours before the process of replicating an update to all servers in an Exchange network is accomplished. Latency in data updates is an inherent fact of life when replication is concerned. The speed that replication takes place depends on how many servers are in the network, the connections between those computers, and the other traffic that flows between the servers.

Directory entries do not impose a great strain on the network because the size of the messages containing replication data are quite small.

2. Objects placed in public folders can be replicated to copies of the folders held on other Exchange servers so that users connecting to those servers can access the information held in the folders as quickly as possible. Like directory entries public folders are associated with an originating server, the location where objects contained in the folder are managed. When a decision is made to share the contents of a public folder with another Exchange Server, a replica of the public folder is created on the 'foreign' server. Thereafter, whenever a change is made to the original public folder the amendments will be automatically replicated to the replica folders on all the servers that maintain an interest in the folder. Replication is performed by a background process and does not happen immediately.

Updates can also be applied to objects via replica folders. In this case the changed data is replicated back to the original source folder and the update applied there. However, the distributed nature of Exchange Server which underpins the ability for updates to be applied in this manner opens up the question of what happens when updates arrive concurrently for the same object from two different replicas. We'll discuss what actually happens when multiple users make changes to a replicated document later on in this chapter.

Directory entries are all pretty similar in size, so the traffic pattern and network load generated by directory replication is predictable and should not change dramatically over time. Occasionally there may be major changes in the directory, for example, when a large group of people using a new server join the network, but in most organizations the volume of directory changes is low, ranging from 1% to 5% of the user population per week.

Replication of public folders and directory entries is only possible when servers are connected together; thus, each system participating in replication must be licensed to run either Exchange Server (standard edition) and the Exchange Connector, or Exchange Server enterprise edition.

Public folder replicas and affinities

Generally speaking there are two ways to distribute information in a networked environment. One method is to place multiple copies of the information at different points throughout the network, basically in an effort to keep information close to users in terms of the network resources required to access the information. The second approach is to establish a single point of reference to hold the definitive copy of the information, perhaps supplementing the definitive copy with a number of distributed read-only copies. Microsoft Exchange Server supports both models. Support for multiple distributed copies of information is gained through public folder replicas. Support for a single definitive point of contact is achieved through public folder affinity. Public folder affinities are local pointers to remote folders.

The argument for folder replicas, or multiple synchronized copies of folders established at different locations distributed around a network is based on three points.

- Synchronized copies of public folders distribute the processing load generated by user access to folder contents. This improves response time for users because they will generally be accessing content from a location close to them rather than from some remote network location.

- Synchronized copies of public folders established at strategic locations within a network can dramatically reduce the amount of long-distance or wide area network traffic generated by users attempting to access folder contents.

- Synchronized copies of folders maintained on multiple servers mean that users will always be able to have access to the information, often mission-critical, held in replicated public folders. If one server becomes inoperative users are automatically and transparently switched to another location holding a synchronized copy to access information.

As shown in the top portion of Figure 4.11, public folder replication is accomplished by servers exchanging mail messages with each other. The messages, of course, contain the data being replicated. You can limit the size of the messages used during replication operations to prevent the replication of very large objects interfering with the smooth operation of the MTA. Getting interpersonal messages through quickly is much more important than delaying system-generated background messages a little.

Users are completely unaware that public folder replication occurs because Exchange Server hides everything from them. As far as users are concerned they are able to see a public folder and access its content, and they don't really care that substantial programming and network magic has been performed to enable them to view a document, form, or other object with such ease. Because users retrieve information directly from a copy held on their own server access to information is as fast as it can possibly be. With such strong arguments for replication why would anyone choose to incur the potentially long delays in accessing a single definitive copy of information held on a remote server?

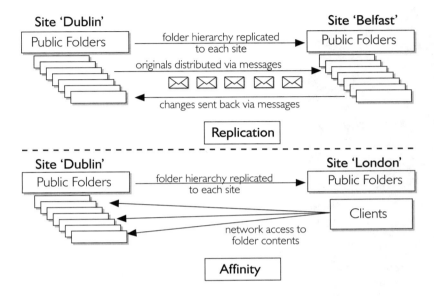

Figure 4.11 *Replication and affinity*

Replication is, by far, the mechanism which receives most attention in documentation and marketing material. Some of the reason for its high profile can be assigned to competitive pressure, but perhaps replication is viewed as a more high-tech option.

All the Exchange servers in a site automatically share the same directory and set of public folders. Thus, no replication is performed to update the servers within a site. Replication is only necessary when you want to share information between Exchange servers in multiple sites connected together by a network, but even still you can force another site to connect to remote public folders through 'affinity', a facility managed by the system administrator on the sites that wish to connect to public folders stored on other sites. Affinity is only possible when the two sites share a high-speed connection capable of handling the traffic generated by users accessing the contents of the folders.

The concept of public folder affinity (see the bottom part of Figure 4.11), a scheme where a single copy of a public folder is maintained in a set location and accessed there by clients from all points of the network, offers a number of potential advantages over replication that are attractive in concept:

- No network overhead is incurred to replicate new objects and changes to different sites throughout the organization
- No latency is experienced between the time when changes are made and the same data is available to everyone throughout the network
- There is no need for conflict handling, and finally, information is not duplicated in different locations.

In all instances, whether public folders are distributed via replication or accessed via affinity, Exchange always sends a copy of the public folder hierarchy from each site to all the other sites in the organization. This is a logical step to take otherwise the system administrators in remote sites wouldn't know about the existence of any of the interesting folders they might otherwise connect to. There is no requirement to replicate any or all folders to all sites. System administrators have a great deal of control over folder replication and are able to select particular folders for distribution to one or more servers (see Figure 4.12).

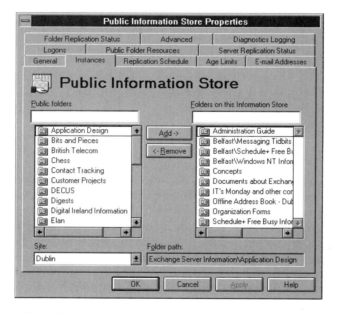

Figure 4.12
Selecting Public Folders for replication

All of these points are valid and should be considered before taking the replication option. In the example illustrated in the bottom part of Figure 4.11, whenever a user in the London site wishes to access an object stored in a public folder serviced by a system in the Dublin site, Exchange makes a transparent network connection between the two sites to retrieve the object's content. When this happens a copy of the object's content is moved into the Windows temporary directory and is operated upon there.

The case for affinity is harder to argue in terms of user convenience. However, because a single copy of information exists within a network it can be regarded as definitive. This can't be said of a replicated folder because the possibility always exists that a change to the content has been made somewhere in the network and hasn't yet arrived on the local server. Lots of organizations will be attracted by the concept of a single definitive source of information, especially when that information is critical corporate information, but you have to make a decision whether your network is able to facilitate fast (or at least acceptable) access times to the information. If there are many slow links in the network replication is possibly a better solution.

Network traffic generated by public folder replication

Objects stored in public folders are highly unpredictable in terms of size and content and no assessment can be given as to the traffic and network load generated by the replication of a public folder until its content and usage pattern are analyzed within a specific production environment. Instead, some broad guidelines can be given and taken into account when designating the owning server for public folders. For example:

- Public folders used as document repositories may not have many updates, but the size of the objects held in the repository can span an enormous range. PowerPoint presentations equipped with highly graphic pictures, OLE-enabled worksheets and documents, and perhaps even a set of speaker notes can quickly occupy 10Mb. Word for Windows files, such as those used to hold the content for this book, are normally smaller, unless screen captures and other bitmap images are featured. Excel worksheets tend to be smaller again, but can swiftly grow when some graphs are included. Remember too that the basic unit of replication is the item or document, and not a page, section or field where a change was made. For these reasons it's a good idea to make smaller subsets of objects available whenever possible. Store chapters of a document rather than putting everything into a single file.

Replicating a large object can saturate a network link for several minutes and hold up more urgent message traffic. With this in mind I think that it's important not to make too many changes to documents if you want to use a public folder as a point for revision control.

- Public folders used as points for interactive information dissemination, such as electronic conferences or bulletin boards have a higher volume of changes made to folder contents but the data involved in the changes is typically smaller. Public folders that use electronic forms produce similar network loads.

- Exchange treats all replicas equally (see discussion later on in this chapter). Thus, no difference is perceived (by the Exchange replication technology) between a replica created on a server running on a low-end 80486 CPU connected by a 56Kb circuit and another running on a high-end server equipped with 4 Alpha CPUs that's on an ATM circuit. Look at the network link to a server before deciding to place a replica there.

- Rules defining when replication occurs can be defined for each server. If the information contained in a public folder is not time critical you can place the folder on a server which only performs replication outside normal business hours. Of course, business hours are different throughout the world because of work conventions and time zones, so don't assume that replicating large documents at 6pm each evening will not interfere with other, more important network traffic.

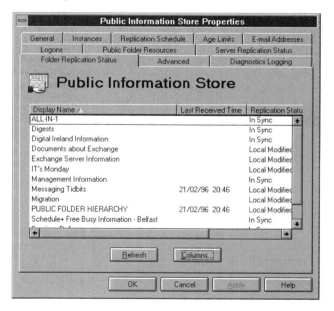

Figure 4.13
Displaying the replication status

The status of the replication activity on a server can be viewed in a number of different ways. A quick way to check that everything's in order is to look at the replication status via the properties of the Public Information Store (Figure 4.13). As you can see, each folder is listed with its current synchronization status. Another easy way to check is to look at the MTA queues. If there are large numbers of messages generated from the Public Information Store queued for transfer to the bridgehead server[3] in any other site there may be a problem with the connector to that site. Using a continually active server or link monitor (see Chapter 8) to check the connections to the bridgehead server in each site is a good proactive way to avoid unpleasant surprises.

Replication philosophy

The design philosophy behind public folders means that everyone's view of a public folder is the same no matter where the folder is physically located. No one instance of a public folder is the master copy. All instances of a public folder enjoy the same standing within the organization. Users are automatically directed to the replica with the lowest connection cost. Even within a site it can make sense to distribute replicas of heavily-used folders to each server so that user requests don't have to travel off the local server.

Locating data close to users is the major advantage delivered by a system of distributed, replicated public folders. However, there are some disadvantages. For example, it is possible to put a copy of a public folder on a laptop's hard disk for use in off-line mode. Changes in folder contents are replicated down to the copy on the PC when it is connected to the network using the normal folder synchronization process. Exchange Server's logical behavior in treating every copy of a folder in exactly the same peer-to-peer manner can lead to an interesting side-effect if the laptop's owner deletes objects from the folder, thinking of course that the copy of the folder on their PC is totally under their control. Eventually the deletions made in a copy of a public folder are enforced in every location where the folder has been replicated to, potentially becoming a rather unpleasant surprise for the other readers of the folder. The lesson here is to be careful in allocating delete permission to public folders. Unless people really need to have delete permission they shouldn't receive it, just in case, following the old system administration principle that sometimes users need to be protected from themselves.

The way you must approach balancing public folders across servers is another interesting side-effect of how public folders have been implemented. It's common to find that public folders begin life on one server just because the folder's owner happens to have its mailbox on that server. An assessment of whether that server is the most appropri-

---

3. *See the discussion on bridgehead servers starting on page 235.*

ate location for the folder is not performed, so you can end up with an array of popular, high-traffic folders on a server that's already struggling to keep up with the demands of normal messaging or other applications.

To move a public folder from a server you must first create a new folder replica on the target server and then wait until the contents of the folder are replicated to the target server. Replication may take some time to complete, especially over slow links or when the folder contains many megabytes of information. Once replication is complete you can remove the original public folder by removing it from local public Information Store. Use the 'Instances' property page for the Public Information Store to remove a public folder from a store (see Figure 4.12). You will not be able to remove a folder in this manner if only one instance of the folder is available. Use an appropriately-permissioned client to delete a single instance of a public folder.

After an instance is marked for removal Exchange Server will delete the contents of the folder from the information store and direct any future client connect requests for the folder to whatever replica is currently available at the lowest (network) cost.

Hiding public folders

The public folder hierarchy is replicated automatically from site to site within an organization. This is a nice feature if you want to publish the names of your site's public folders to everyone else, but sometimes it's nice to be a little more private.

Let's assume that you want to set up a public folder for use by a restricted group of users. You can, of course, protect the folder's contents through suitable permissions, but let's assume that you don't even want people to see the folder's name within the folder hierarchy. In short, you want to create a hidden public folder.

Hidden public folders cannot be created in the top level of the folder hierarchy. There is no mechanism to indicate that a top level folder should be hidden. But sub-folders can be hidden and protected as follows:

- Create a top-level folder and give it a suitable name. For example, 'Executive Information'.
- Set the default permission on the new folder to 'None'.
- Create a sub-folder under 'Executive Information'. For example, 'Secret Information'.
- Set permissions on the 'Secret Information' sub-folder to allow the users you want to have access to its content. If you are grant-

ing access to more than a couple of users you may want to create a distribution list and grant permissions to it. Users in the distribution list will then inherit the access permissions for the folder.

Users without the necessary permissions will be able to see the top-level folder, but any attempt to open the folder will display nothing. Only users with permissions will be able to see the sub-folders and other objects placed into the 'Executive Information' folder.

Maintaining Exchange Information Stores

In Exchange V4.0 the maximum size of an information store or database is 16Gb. The limit is architectural and (based on comments from Microsoft sources) is more than likely to be lifted in future versions of Exchange to allow it to manage information stores many times the current size.

By default, each server has two stores – the private and public information stores, so a maximum of 32Gb of data can be managed by an Exchange server in these stores on a single computer. Within a single Exchange site there can be many servers so the maximum available storage for a site is dictated by the number of servers you care to operate. Users store messages in the private information store of their host server. You can balance disk space usage across the servers in a site by moving user mailboxes from server to server. As this can be a tiresome activity that must be accomplished when people are not using their mailboxes it pays to carefully plan the allocation of users across available servers.

A computer running Exchange Server does not necessarily require the presence of both public and private information stores. It is possible to configure a server to be 'messaging-only' in which case only a private information store is operated. The converse case is to have a server dedicated to public folder access only, in which case only a public information store is present. Smaller sites are not likely to operate servers with only one type of store, but in larger sites a good case can be made to exploit Exchange's flexibility in this manner by deploying servers configured for particular tasks. For example, one large server with a fast CPU and large disk arrays might manage all the public folders for the site, leaving general messaging activity to a set of smaller servers.

When you create a site it is important to consider whether all servers will host both types of store or if different servers will take on different tasks. The 'General' property page for the Private Information Store (see Figure 4.14) is used to define the server location for the associated Public Information Store. When a user creates a new public folder it is normally created on the same server that hosts the user's mailbox, but if the location of the Public Information Store is redefined the new folder is created on the other server.

Figure 4.14
General properties of the Private Information Store

If you decide to configure servers as dedicated systems for public folders make sure that you delete the Private Information Store from each of the dedicated servers as this will prevent user mailboxes being accidentally allocated to these servers. To delete a Private Information Store from a server:

1. Start the Administration utility.

2. Select 'Servers' and then choose the server that you want to make a dedicated public folder server.

3. Select the Private Information Store from the server's configuration.

4. Select the 'Delete' option from the Edit menu.

5. Run the Performance Optimizer utility afterwards on the dedicated server in make sure that the configuration is optimized for dedicated public folder access.

A dedicated public folder server can be reconfigured to support a private information store with the 'New Other' option in the Administration utility and then selecting 'Information Store' from the list of options. Exchange Server will then check the configuration of information stores within the site and allow you to select servers that do not support a private information store. Select the server you want to reconfigure and click the OK button. If the site has both types of store configured on all servers Exchange Server will indicate this fact as shown in Figure 4.15. Remember to run the Performance Optimizer afterwards.

Figure 4.15
Creating a new store

The type of database used by Exchange Server

Exchange server uses a variant of Microsoft's 'Jet'[4] database technology called 'Jet Blue', an object store which is roughly similar to a traditional relational database. A lot of myths and rumors have built up around the database used by Exchange Server. One popular story alleges that Exchange uses SQL Server for all database access, while another says that Exchange uses the same database engine as the popular desktop Access product, probably because Access is also based on Jet database technology (but not the same development as Exchange). As mentioned above, there are some similarities to a relational database such as those implemented in SQL Server and Access, but the two implementations are very different beasts. Both SQL Server and Access deal in rows, tables, and joins like other database applications while Exchange is very much focused on the definition of a MAPI message store.

Based on 'Jet Blue', the Exchange developers have designed the information store to be optimized for the type of activity produced by users creating and sending messages, or the traffic generated by directory and public folder replication. Remember that a large amount of messages are generated, sent, and deleted to carry out behind the

---

4. *JET stands for 'Joint Engine Technology', an internal Microsoft database project.*

scenes database synchronization. Public folder replication, system attendant updates for configurations, and directory updates are all examples of messages which go through the database without too much notice being taken (unless things go wrong). When added to interpersonal messages the traffic generated by background messages was enough to require the Exchange architects to pay special attention to database efficiency in terms of message throughput, leading in turn to the decision reached to use Jet Blue.

Apart from its high-volume message processing capacity the chosen database confers other advantages. In addition to having a smaller 'footprint' (amount of memory that the code occupies) than an SQL-based equivalent the Jet technology allows for a number of unique features such as record level locking and 'on the fly' indexing. 'On the fly' indexing means that Exchange Server automatically indexes the values contained in object properties as objects are added to the database. Good indexes are a critical factor in allowing users to execute very fast searches despite specifying complex criteria. For instance, looking through a large information store for all instances of documents authored by 'Tony Redmond' which mention 'Exchange Server' in the title would take a long time unless the author and title attributes (or rather, MAPI properties) are indexed in some way.

The closest thing a MAPI message store has to the concept of a join across tables is a 'multi-valued property'. If a document stored in a public folder has multiple authors (properties) there is no need to create separate document and author tables and join them just to see who the different authors are. This is another example of a major difference between Exchange Server and other Microsoft database implementations.

Even if Exchange does not use a relational database that's no good reason not to learn from the lessons learned from many years of relational database use in high-availability production environments. The best example of this in practice is the transaction roll-back and roll-forward capabilities built into the Exchange information store, plus the elimination of the requirement to halt the server to perform backup operations. Using the correct tools (those that know about the capabilities of the information store) backups can be taken while users are accessing the information store, a characteristic of high-end transaction systems. Over the long term the plan of record for Exchange is to move from its own database to Microsoft's strategic object store, or OFS. Microsoft people are careful to emphasize that the transition to OFS will follow a conservative approach and should be seamless to end users and administrators alike.

The single message storage model

Unlike PC LAN-based electronic mail systems, which typically create copies of messages for each recipient, Exchange Server uses a shared message model. In other words, a single copy of a message is stored on a server and all of the users who have access to the message hold a database pointer to the single copy within their folders. The shared message model is well tried and tested and has been in use with other messaging systems, such as Digital's ALL-IN-1 server, since the early 1980s. There are a number of obvious advantages in a shared message model. For instance:

- Disk activity is reduced because the system doesn't have to create, delete and otherwise manage multiple physical copies of messages. This is especially important when message content is large and the average size of messages is increasing. Think of the disk activity required to create 100 copies of a 100Kb message. Now scale it up for 250 copies of a message (perhaps one circulated to everyone in a site) that has a very large attachment.
- Disk space required for message data is much reduced because no redundant copies are created.
- Because of the two previous points the shared message model is the most scaleable type of electronic file cabinet or message container.

While it is very scaleable and uses the least disk space a shared message model imposes some additional load on the mechanism used to register messages. The database used in the Exchange server information store is responsible for tracking user access to messages through pointers, and must make sure that 'hanging' pointers, or pointers belonging to messages no longer wanted by any user on the system, are removed. The actual message contents are removed from the system once all the relevant users have deleted their pointers, in effect reducing the count of interested parties to zero. The database must also track the movement of messages from location to location within the overall filing system, and all this must be done quickly and without being obvious to users.

Note that the single message model only extends to the confines of a single server and does not span a site. A message sent to several users in the same site will be delivered to the private information store on each server connected to by the recipients of the message. It is therefore possible to have several copies of a message within a single site, albeit only on the servers whose users have an interest in the message.

Exchange databases

The two most important data structures requiring regular and consistent backups are the Information Store and the Directory Store. The Information Store, containing public and private folders and other system-wide objects, is split between two separate database files called PRIV.EDB and PUB.EDB whose default location is the \MDBDATA directory. The Directory Store, holding information about recipients, other servers, and connectors, is held in the DIR.EDB file located in the \DSADATA directory. Table 4.1 summarizes the major databases and associated files used by Exchange Server's Information and Directory Stores.

Table 4.1 *Exchange databases*

Database/File	Purpose	Default location
PRIV.EDB	Private Information Store. Location for all private folders.	\EXCHANGE\MDBDATA
PUB.EDB	Public Information Store. Location for all public folders.	\EXCHANGE\MDBDATA
DIR.EDB	Directory Store	\EXCHANGE\DSADATA
EDB.LOG	Current log file for Information Store transactions	\EXCHANGE\MDBDATA
EDBn.LOG	Backup transaction log file	\EXCHANGE\MDBDATA
EDB.CHK	Database checkpoint file	\EXCHANGE\MDBDATA
RES1.LOG	Reservation log file used to hold transactions if disk space is exhausted.	\EXCHANGE\MDBDATA
RES2.LOG	Reservation log file used to hold transactions if disk space is exhausted.	\EXCHANGE\MDBDATA

While the \MDBDATA directory is the default location for the information stores there is no requirement for you to keep the stores together in the one directory. Keeping everything together is neat and tidy but it concentrates disk activity to a single place, a situation that will eventually lead to the disk being swamped with I/O requests generated by database activity. If you want to optimize disk performance it's best to keep the two stores apart on separate drives, and also to move the log files (more on log files shortly) to another drive.

On all but the smallest or disk-starved servers the Performance Optimizer will recommend that the various files used by the Information Stores and Directory are spread across all available disks. It is logical to spread the I/O load generated by any application across all available disk spindles, and the approach taken by the Performance

Maintaining Exchange Information Stores

Optimizer is in line with well-established system management practices. Keeping everything on one or two disks will deliver satisfactory performance for small user populations, but performance will steadily degenerate as the number of users grow or the demands created by the users increase. You can amend the location of any of the files through the 'Database Paths' property page (see Figure 4.16). Note that Exchange Server V4.0 does not support the placing of its database files on a networked drive. All databases must stored on local disks.

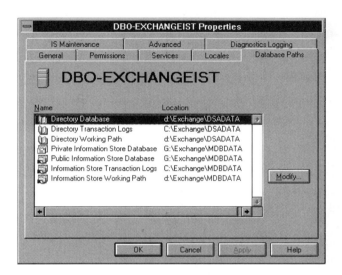

Figure 4.16
Amending database paths

Interaction between transaction log files and the information store

Exchange Server uses a series of log and other files to ensure that the information stores are kept up to date. Each transaction (a new message, for example) directed to an information store is recorded into a transaction log file called EDB.LOG as well as an area in memory (see Figure 4.17).

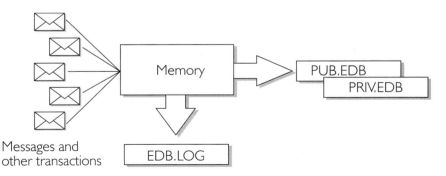

Figure 4.17
Transactions for the information stores

Chapter 4

This avoids the need to constantly write information directly into the information store databases, generating large amounts of I/O for the system to process. Updates are deferred, gathered together into efficient 'chunks', and then committed from memory to the information store when time and system demand allows.

Because transactions are written to a log file and then into the information store it follows that the database can never be considered to be totally up to date until the transactions in the log file are taken into consideration. If no users are using the system for more than five minutes it is fairly safe to assume that all the transactions in memory will have been written into the database. You can 'force' transactions to be written in two ways. First, by using a backup utility to create a backup of the Exchange databases. We'll discuss this operation in more detail later on. The second way is to close down Exchange Server. In both cases it's important to check the system event log to ensure that no error messages have been recorded to indicate problems occurred when the database was updated.

Because transactions are preserved in log files a physical record of the processing that has been performed for the database is always available. The transaction log files can be used in the event of a problem with the information store when transactions can be rolled back from the logs into a recovered copy of the information store to bring it up to date. For this reason it is dangerous to delete transaction logs without first knowing that their contents will no longer be required.

EDB.LOG is the name of the 'active' log file. In other words, EDB.LOG is the file that details of new message transactions are written into. A new log file is created after approximately 5Mb of transactions (message operations) have been recorded. When this happens EDB.LOG is renamed and a new version of EDB.LOG created. On a very busy server lots of transactions flow through the log files and it's not uncommon to see very many separate files created over the working day. You can force log file creation by importing large amounts of data into the information store, notably when the migration wizard is running.

Each log file is allocated its full 5Mb size immediately after it is created. This step ensures that all transactions can be written without running the risk of suddenly exhausting disk space. If File Manager reports that a transaction log is anything other than 5Mb (5,242,880 bytes) it is likely that the log is corrupt. In this case you should check the event log for errors, stop Exchange, take a backup, and then restart Exchange services. All the log files should have been erased and the database brought fully up to date. Check too that the disk where the log files are stored hasn't encountered any hardware problems.

Log files are numbered sequentially using a file naming scheme of EDB*xxxxx*.LOG, where *xxxxx* is a hexadecimal number from 0 to F). After a few days of moderate messaging activity you end up with EDB00001.LOG, EDB00002.LOG, and so on. Depending on the number of messages generated on your system and the frequency that backups are taken it's common to find that the \MDBDATA directory stores ten or more log files.

Systems that engage in heavy replication activity turn over transaction log files quickly. Replication (see page 136) occurs when servers update each other about the contents of public folders or directory information. Servers can be very 'chatty' if allowed to do so. For example, servers will send each other frequent snapshots of the public folder hierarchy, just to make sure that everyone knows where all the different public folders are located. The snapshot information is circulated in the form of messages, and these must be logged in exactly the same manner as interpersonal mail. Systems handling large numbers of directory changes, either in the startup period when many additions are being made or if they act as the point for directory information dissemination to other servers (see page 295), also generate lots of work for transaction logs. You can cut down on the number of messages being produced by replication activities by scheduling replication to occur only at particular times of the day rather than whenever Exchange feels the need. Scheduling in this manner also reduces traffic through whatever connectors used to link sites together, thus preventing any potential delays for interpersonal mail that might otherwise creep in.

The \MDBDATA directory is the default location for both the transaction logs and the information store (see Figure 4.18). It's more efficient to move the transaction logs away onto a separate physical disk so that the disk I/O activity generated by message traffic is divided across multiple spindles. From a performance perspective it's best to place transaction logs on a FAT-formatted drive because:

1. less overhead is incurred by the system when writing files to FAT drives than NTFS.

2. transactions are written in a sequential manner to the end of the logs. Thus, no sophisticated indexing or file structure management is required.

In all cases make sure that the disk where the transaction logs are created has plenty of disk space.

Figure 4.18
Files in the \MDBDATA directory

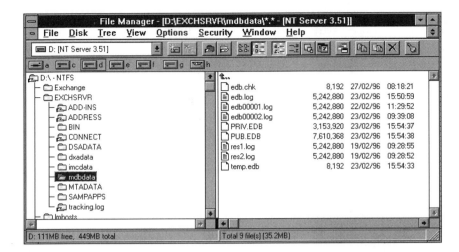

The EDB.CHK file acts as a database checkpoint. Its function is to track the transaction log files and make sure that they are synchronized with the databases. When the Exchange database engine starts up it checks EDB.CHK to determine the current status of the database and takes whatever action is required to enable the database to commence operations in a stable state. At this stage any transactions in the log file that have not been recorded are applied. If you are ever unfortunate enough to suffer a major corruption of the database you may be able to get up and running fast by restoring a recent backup and starting the server. If possible, all of the transactions that occurred since the backup was taken will be applied and the database restored to full working order. Of course, this type of restoration depends on good quality backups being taken at regular intervals.

When backups are taken the transaction log files are automatically purged by the backup utility. The process of purging basically zeroizes EDB.LOG, to ready the log to accept new transactions. All other log files (EDB00001.LOG and so on) are deleted and the disk space returned to the system. Cleaning up log files in this manner is logical because the database has been written to backup media in a consistent state with all outstanding transactions applied before the backup is allowed to begin, so there is no longer any need for the log files to be retained. As the log files can take up quite a bit of disk space the automatic deletion is welcome, but if you want to be cautious you can always back the log files up before commencing the database backup.

Two special log files, called RES1.LOG and RES2.LOG (the reservation logs) are used by the system to ensure that there's enough disk space available for Exchange to complete operations in a controlled manner should the computer run out of disk space. In other words, if disk space is exhausted, Exchange can use the space allocated to RES1.LOG and RES2.LOG to complete whatever it needs to do before halting.

In any case where Exchange discovers that there isn't enough space available on a disk to create a new transaction log an error condition is generated that causes the information store to shut down, hopefully in a graceful manner. When a shutdown occurs it is possible that transactions are waiting in memory to be written to a transaction log and of course this isn't possible because there's no disk space. The current log files are also full, which is the reason why the error condition has occurred in the first place. Exchange resolves the immediate problem, what to do with the in-memory transactions, by writing them first to RES1.LOG and then, if necessary, to continue writing on into RES2.LOG. It's not clear what happens if there is more than 10Mb of transactions waiting in memory, but it's perhaps fair to assume that such a volume and quantity of transaction data would never be held in memory. After all transactions are flushed into the reservation logs Exchange will shut down.

Transactions for the Public Information Store

Transactions applied to PUB.EDB, the database used by the public information store are also written into log files. However, there is a slight difference in behavior in the way that the database expands in size as new objects are added to the store. If you watch PRIV.EDB for a while, even on a fairly heavily used system, it won't expand very often. But if you watch PUB.EDB as new items are added to public folders you'll see that the file appears to grow dynamically. The difference in behavior is logical because the additions, deletions, and modifications of objects held in the public information store occur at a very much lower rate of activity than the often frenetic throughput of messages arriving and departing the private information store. Applying updates to PRIV.EDB in bulk from memory is a more efficient way of writing information while preserving a high level of performance.

Both the private and public information store databases can be compacted with the EDBUTIL utility to reduce their size by optimizing internal structures and eliminating redundant data. Details on EDBUTIL are presented later on in this chapter.

Exhausting available disk space

As a general rule for all messaging servers you can never have too much disk space, just in case. I have seen instances where the Information Store exhausts the space available on a disk. In most cases the problem occurred on systems that have been on the threshold of available disk space for some time, meaning that it was always a struggle to find available disk space for any application let alone one that has to manage shared files on behalf of many users. Failure to pay attention to system administration compounds this particular problem as all systems tend to accumulate files over time, albeit perhaps files that should be automatically cleaned up by the application that produced them. The reality of mail systems is that the amount of disk space used for messages can quickly mount up, so it's important that all system configurations are sized with a reasonable degree of seemingly excess disk space to allow for unplanned growth.

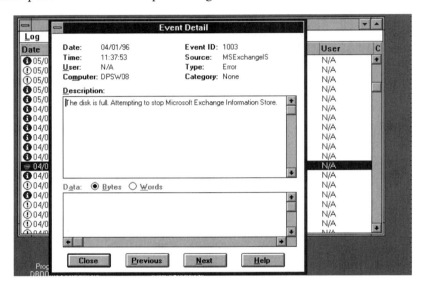

Figure 4.19
Windows NT Event Viewer showing that we've run out of disk space

The most common cause for space exhaustion is where one or more users create large messages with many attachments. When the message is sent its content is moved from the client to the server and Exchange attempts to add it to the Information Store. If space is unavailable or becomes exhausted at this point the Information Store will not be able to extend itself to store the new message. This causes the Information Store to automatically shut itself down as manual intervention is required from the system administrator. A warning message will be sent to the Windows NT system log (see Figure 4.19) and can be viewed through the system event viewer (see above). Users will immediately know that a problem exists because they will be unable to complete a full log-on to the server from clients, in essence because the server will not be able to send details of the folders in the user's mailbox to the client because the Information Store is unavailable. Possible solutions to the problem are:

Maintaining Exchange Information Stores

- Increasing the available space on the disk where the Information Store is located by deleting unwanted or unnecessary files.
- Moving the Information Store to another disk. Files belonging to Exchange Server or other applications might also be moved at the same time.
- Replacing the original disk with a larger disk. You'll need to restore a full backup of the original disk to the new disk before operations can begin again.

In most instances the first solution is both the most immediate and pragmatic, although I would take immediate steps to consider the other two solutions over the long term. If the disk where the Information Store is located runs out of space on one occasion it is likely to do so again in the future.

Circular logging

If desired, you can instruct Exchange Server to implement a scheme of circular logging. In other words, the logs will be used in a circular fashion rather than new logs being created all the time. The logs will still be created, but they are automatically overwritten and reused after the data contained in the logs have been committed to the information store database. Circular logging is supported for the public information store and the directory. To implement the circular logging scheme click the check box on the 'Advanced' page of a server's properties, as shown in Figure 4.20.

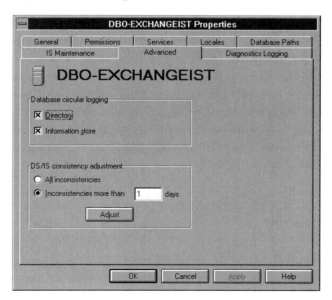

Figure 4.20
Enabling circular logging

If you prefer to avoid taking the easy route to effect the change for circular logging you can display your deep knowledge of Exchange by starting the registry editor (REGEDT32.EXE) to make the same change (see Figure 4.21). All of the parameters affecting the behavior of Exchange Server are stored in the system registry, and a great deal of interesting information can be gleaned by browsing through the registry.

To implement circular logging use the root \HKEY\LOCAL MACHINE and change the key:

\System\CurrentControlSet\Services\MsExchangeIS\ParametersSystem\CircularLogging

from its default value of 0 (meaning create a new file each time) to 1. Circular logging can also be applied to the log files generated for the Directory Store database by editing the key:

\System\CurrentControlSet\Services\MsExchangeDS\ParametersSystem\CircularLogging

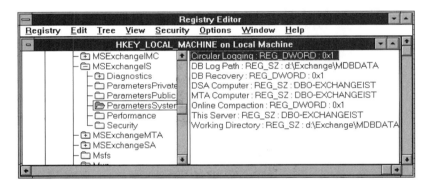

Figure 4.21
Using the registry editor to alter Exchange settings

Remember to restart Exchange Server after you make the change to the system registry. Because mistakes made when changing the system registry can have unpredictable effects, always make a backup before you start.

If you implement circular logging it's important to note that incremental and differential backups of the Exchange databases are not possible. When circular logging is enabled full backups must be taken with all Exchange services halted. If not, no guarantee can be given as to the integrity of the information written into the backup.

The public information store is designed to be used in a situation where regular and frequent backups are taken. Good system management practices dictate that any system supporting important data should be backed up, and in view of these points it is hard to make a case to use circular logging instead of the system of creating and erasing multiple log files. After all, provided you take backups you shouldn't run into situations where the disk space occupied by the transaction log files is excessive and causes problems for the system.

Limiting user disk space

You can limit the amount of space a user can occupy within a store, and if you have the opportunity to set limits and so encourage good habits within users by forcing respect for disk space from the start, you should seize your chance quickly. Users who are allowed free range will run rampant and occupy as much space as they can, a good proportion of which is unlikely to store messages and other data of great strategic importance.

Limits (defined in kilobytes) are set on an individual user mailbox (see Figure 4.22) or on the private information store as a whole, in which case the same limits are set for all user mailboxes. As you can see from Figure 4.22, two different limits can be specified. The limit set by checking the first box determines the point at which a user will start to receive warning messages generated by the system attendant.

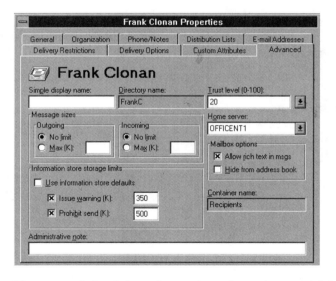

Figure 4.22
Limiting space for a user mailbox

The second check box determines the point at which users won't be allowed to send any more messages. If 'Never' is checked for the information store limits users or particular users will be allowed to continue occupying space until the disk fills up and reaches its physical storage limit or (more unlikely) the information store reaches its 16Gb design limit. Users who have exceeded their quota will not be able to create new messages, but they'll still be able to receive messages that arrive for them. It is therefore possible for a user to grow the space they occupy within the private information store after restrictions have been placed on them.

Interestingly, if a user exceeds their quota in the private information store Exchange Server will also stop them putting anything into a public folder. No doubt this restriction is in place to stop 'smart' users getting around quotas by moving messages and other objects out of their private space into the public area. The only way a user can resolve the problem of an exceeded quota is to delete messages (and make sure that the Deleted Items folder is emptied) until they go under their quota or to have the system administrator give them a temporary increase in quota. Temporary increases in user quotas usually become permanent unless the system administrator is vigilant!

While encouraging you to impose limitations on the space within the database allocated to individual users, make sure that reasonable amounts are allocated. There is nothing so boring or time-consuming for a system administrator as having to answer a continuous stream of requests for increases in allocations. Apart from taking up time to respond to each request, the requirement to ask for more space just to send a few more messages (for this is what it will appear in the mind of users) will cause irritation and reduce overall satisfaction levels with the system.

A proactive approach to system management dictates that every step should be taken to ensure that unpleasant surprises don't occur. Running out of disk space counts as one of the surprises no system manager wants to have, so you should perform manual or automated checks each morning to ensure that:

- The disk(s) where the information stores are located have sufficient free disk space. Start to get worried when less than 150Mb is available on a system serving less than 100 users, or 300Mb on a system serving more than 100 users. Systems serving very heavy mail users may want to increase the warning threshold for free disk space. Remember that a single large message can chew up several megabytes very easily.
- Backups have been taken and the log files for the information store (for example, EDB00001.LOG, EDB00002.LOG, and so on) have been deleted.
- No users have exceeded their disk space allocation. If anyone has they may be unaware of the fact so take steps to contact them and then help the user free up some space.

Maintaining Exchange Information Stores

Every night the Exchange System Attendant checks for people who have exceeded disk quota each night (Figure 4.23). If someone is discovered to be approaching their quota a message is sent to the offending user to indicate that they may not be able to send any more messages. You can instruct the System Attendant to perform checks and send warning messages many times each day, if you think this is necessary.

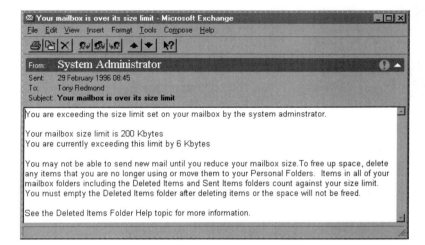

Figure 4.23
Message from the System Attendant to tell a user their disk space is exhausted

Once the System Attendant determines that someone has actually exceeded the quota a stop is placed on any further send operations. Users will be able to create new messages, and save them to their local disk, but they won't be able to send them until they free some of their allocated quota within the information store.

Freeing up some space

Once space within the information store is occupied by messages and their attachments there is no automatic way for a system administrator to free space by deleting obsolete messages from the public information store. Space is returned to the information store when messages are deleted. Deletion is a two stage process as the messages are first moved into the 'Deleted Items' folder, and then only permanently removed from the store when the contents of this folder are purged. Users can set their working conditions from Exchange clients to purge the contents of the 'Deleted Items' folder automatically when they exit. This is one of the choices available from the dialog displayed from the Options entry on the Tools menu. Purging the 'Deleted Items' folder is not default behavior for the client, so users must change the setting manually. As pointed out before, setting default values for options like this is a very good reason to use the Exchange Setup Editor utility before client installations start.

It's somewhat surprising to find that there are no system housekeeping facilities to produce reports of the number of messages each user has in their mailbox and the amount of space these messages occupy. This is a pity, because reports of space utilization taken on a regular basis (for example, every month) provide invaluable data for use when planning the growth of a messaging system. You can, of course, use the Exchange Administration utility to view the contents of the private information store, and note the data presented there (see Figure 4.24), but it would be nice to be able to export this information in the form of a spreadsheet or other formatted data, as this would make the data much easier to work with. The STORSTAT utility from the Exchange Resource Kit (see page 365) provides another option to analyze the contents of a user's mailbox.

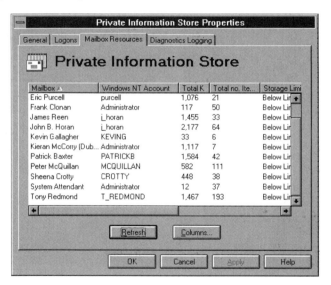

Figure 4.24
Viewing space used in the Private Information Store

Reports on various aspects of Exchange Server can be obtained if you buy third-party add-on products. The best reporting utility for Exchange Server I have seen to date being Crystal Reports for Exchange. A copy of Crystal Reports for Exchange is included in the Exchange Resource Kit.

Unlike the public information store where administrators can set expiry limits on folders, messages held in the private information store never expire (they remain in the mailbox as long as the user wishes to keep them there). Administrators can intervene and clean up a user's mailbox without their permission by using the 'Clean Mailbox' option on the Tools menu (see Figure 4.25), but the sudden disappearance of a whole pile of messages from their mailbox is not likely to make a user very happy. It's probably better to reserve the clean mailbox option for the most intransigent users and restrain yourself to warnings for the others, unless of course you follow the 'I know best' school of thought for system administration. It's not immediately obvious from the user interface or documentation, but you can select multiple mailboxes for the 'Clean Mailbox' option to process with the CTRL/Click and SHIFT/Click key combinations to either select a range of mailboxes or a set of individually chosen mailboxes.

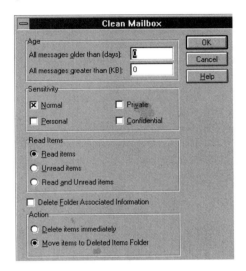

Figure 4.25
The Clean Mailbox option

Along the same line as information store reporting, it would be nice if Microsoft could provide a fully supported and integrated system housekeeping procedure to clean up user mailboxes on a regular basis, perhaps removing all messages over 30 days old from specified folders such as 'Sent Items' as well as deleting the messages waiting to be removed from the 'Deleted Items' folder. A mailbox cleanup agent is part of the Exchange Resource Kit (see the section beginning on page 365), and this add-on provides the missing functionality, albeit at an added cost.

If limits are not in place and mailboxes are left to take care of themselves it is quite a normal state of affairs to find that the private information store grows gradually over time as messages accumulate. When people hit storage limits they are forced to exercise a form of triage over the contents of their mailbox, deciding what should be kept and what can go. Once they've cleaned up their mailbox users can proceed to create and send some more messages.

The space used to store messages

How much space within the information store is required for each message? The answer depends on the size of the cover note, the number of message attributes (addressees and so on), and the attachments. I conducted some very unscientific experiments with a selection of sample messages to see what type of storage requirements were reported for each message type. The results of my experiments are shown in Table 4.2. Be aware that your mileage will vary depending on the types of sample messages you create and the size of attachments you include, but the basic results should be pretty well the same.

Table 4.2 *Storage requirements for different types of messages*

Message type and contents	Size of message reported by client
Simple text message containing 65 words sent to 1 mailbox	610 bytes
Simple text message with 1 page cover note sent to 8 mailboxes	3Kb
Compound message sent to 5 mailboxes with 1 page cover note, 79Kb Word attachment, and 18Kb Excel attachment	100Kb
Compound message sent to 10 mailboxes composed of 5-page cover note and 1.004Mb PowerPoint attachment	1,104Kb

Exchange Server uses a shared message model so all mailboxes on a server share a common copy of a message and its contents. The mailbox resources data reported by Exchange only indicate how much space within the information store is occupied by messages that individual users have a pointer to within their mailbox. This is quite a different figure to the amount of space within the information store that the messages for an individual user solely occupy. In other words, if a user sends a 1Mb message to 10 other users the next time you look at mailbox resources you should see that all of the users associated with the message, including the originator, have had an apparent increase of 1Mb in the resources they occupy within the store. This isn't actually the case as just a single 1Mb chunk is used to store the message. The commonality within the store achieved by sharing the single 1Mb message with 10 other users just contributes to a form of optical illusion.

Any individual user will have a mixture of these message types within their mailbox, and it's probable that the average user will have more small messages than large. If you assume that the space reported by the Exchange client provides the more accurate of the two sets of figures, we can use them to create a rough forecast of the space likely to be occupied by any particular type of user. For example, let's take a user with a mixed set of messages:

Number and type of message	Average size	Total space required
300 simple messages	600 bytes	180Kb
100 multi-addressee 1 page messages	3Kb	300Kb
75 compound messages	100Kb	7,500Kb
25 large messages	1000Kb	25,000Kb

In this instance the total requirement is calculated as 34,980Kb or almost 35Mb. This figure contains a considerable safety margin as a good proportion of the messages are likely to be shared with other users on the same server, unless the predominant communications pattern is off-server to other sites or messaging systems. Even the simplest messages described in our model (those sent to a single addressee) start off by being shared, so the 35Mb of apparent storage might well be less than 20 or 25 in reality. This figure is in line with other shared-model messaging systems that support PC clients where reasonable planning rates for 'average' users dictate 20–30Mb for personal messages. Heavy mail users, of course, are quite another matter and I have known some capable of easily occupying entire disks (over an extended period of one or two years) with the volume of messages they generate.

Commonality, or the degree of sharing for messages within the shared database, is another factor to take into consideration when looking at disk space usage patterns. The level of commonality in shared message systems decreases as messages age. In other words, if a message starts out being shared by ten users over time some of those users will delete their pointer to the message, eventually reaching a point where a single user 'owns' the space occupied by the message. On large systems (more than a couple of hundred users) the degree of commonality is higher than on smaller systems because there are more people to share information, leading to a reduced chance that a message needs to be sent off the server to reach its final destination. For this reason it's wise to encourage users to gain the good habit of automatically filing or deleting messages as they are read and not letting messages pile up aimlessly in a cluttered mess.

In summary, the maximum 16Gb space available in the private information store is enough to allocate 50Mb to over 300 users, a figure higher than the average user population for all but the very largest Exchange servers. The 16Gb physical limit for an information store is very much a theoretical limit because the apparent or logical total size of messages held in the store is increased by the commonality imposed by the single message model. In other words, if a single 100Kb message is accessed by ten users the store logically allocates and shares a megabyte between the users. The physical increase in the store is just 100Kb, give or take the additional bytes used to store message attributes. Thus, on a system with a high degree of message commonality the information store can apparently hold more than you might think.

The maximum size of 16Gb for an information store restrains the number of clients that can be supported by an individual server in a very practical sense. Administrators have to decide whether they want to support hundreds of clients with small space allocations, or to provide a larger allocation to a smaller number of clients. The very practical nature of this trade-off makes some of the claims for massive numbers of supported clients for specific server configurations only valuable in a theoretical sense. There's no point in being able to connect 600–800 clients to a high-end server if they're only allowed to store 50 messages each, unless of course this is precisely the type of system you really want to operate!

Another way of looking at the number of clients that can be supported by a system is to consider the assertion that the majority of computers running Windows NT today have far less than 16Gb of disk storage in total, let alone 16Gb to give over to the Information Store. If this is true, and I have seen no evidence to the contrary, then available hardware resources is the first limit. Another factor that must be considered is that after a server has been in use for some time a set of power users might each occupy a gigabyte or more of disk space, considerably limiting the user population that can be supported by that server. There's a common answer to all these issues: install another server in the Exchange site and transfer some of the users to the new server.

Effective use of personal information stores

Personal Information Stores are files that reside on users' local drives, either those on a PC or space allocated to users on a network device. You can even create a personal information store on a floppy disk, a feature that allows stores and their contents to be quickly transferred from one PC to another. Personal information stores are commonly referred to as PST files and are used to hold personal folders, a term that differentiates the content from that held in private or public folders, both of which are server-based. These files can be encrypted and compressed to enhance security and minimize disk space storage. The encryption depends on a user-supplied password, but there is no mechanism to recover data from an encrypted PST if a user forgets their password.

PST files allow users to create and manage their own private document archive. As we've seen it's obvious that any server is going to have some storage limitations in terms of either the total available physical disk space installed on drives connected to the server or the space allocated to individual users within the private information store. It's easy to run out of space, especially if you're in the habit of creating or circulating messages with large document or worksheet attachments. In these situations space can be freed within the private information store by moving files to a PST. Moving messages into PST files effectively 'unshares' the message in private information store insofar as a separate copy of a message is created and moved to the PST.

Encouraging users to work with personal folders is fine as long as individuals use the same PC all the time. But if people move from one PC to another they'll leave information behind them. In these situations it's best to concentrate on server-based storage (which can be accessed from any PC) and leave personal folders to those who can use the same PC all the time. One way to accommodate roaming users (those who move from PC to PC) is to place their PST in their directory on a file server. If you do this remember to tell users to always fully log-out from each PC they use, otherwise they won't be able to connect to their PST when they move to another PC.

If the same person uses the same PC all the time then personal folders can provide an additional advantage in that Exchange can be instructed to deliver messages to an inbox in a PST. In this scenario messages are held on the server until a user connects and then they are transferred down to an Inbox folder in the PST. Using a PST for mail delivery means that only users with physical access to the PC will ever be able to read messages sent to the PC's owner, eliminating the potential problem of unauthorized but privileged users reading other people's mail. Adopting this solution is a double-edged sword and a price is paid for privacy. Responsibility for backing up and securing the messages in the PST passes from the system administrator to the user once messages are redirected into a PST.

Many installations try and encourage users to view the private information store on the server as a repository for working documents, or those that must be available no matter which PC is used to connect to the server. In this model users are supposed to move files to a PST once the files are no longer current or perhaps become less important. The model assumes a fair amount of discipline on the part of users, something that's not always easy to find, and also devolves responsibility for data security to users once files have been moved away from a server-based store. One of the undoubted advantages of server-based storage is the assurance that someone else will take care of backing up all your important data. People aren't so good when the time comes to create backups or copies of local data on a PC.

Users moving to Exchange from Microsoft Mail will find personal information stores a very natural extension of the mode of working they had become accustomed to. In a Microsoft Mail environment it is normal to pull messages from a post office server down to a mailbox file held on the PC. In an Exchange environment the situation is somewhat reversed as the normal way of working is to leave messages on the server rather than moving them to the PC, but users can move messages down to a PST if they wish, albeit through a drag and drop operation rather than having the mail system do it automatically. Installations moving from Microsoft Mail should carefully consider whether they want to migrate the many megabytes of user messages into the private, server-based, information store. In my opinion it is best to leave messages where they are – on the PC by converting the Microsoft Mail format mailbox to a personal information store. Apart from reducing the demand for server resources, this approach means that users can be migrated to Exchange much more quickly than otherwise possible. Training sessions clearly offer an opportunity to encourage good work habits such as the effective use of PSTs in people. Hint or cheat sheets can also be used to get your point across and so relieve some pressure on server-based resources.

Off-line storage

Microsoft Exchange clients can use off-line folders to store and access information without being connected to the server. In one way the concept behind off-line folders can be thought of as snapshots of server-based folders. In another they can be thought of as a more intelligent version of personal folders. Off-line folders are stored in special files with .OST extensions. You can find out the name of your off-line folder file by looking at the advanced properties of the Microsoft Exchange Server from the *Tools.Services* command. Off-line folder files are created when you configure a user profile and indicate that you want to be able to work in off-line mode. Thereafter the off-line folders are made available when you elect to work in off-line mode rather than connecting to a server.

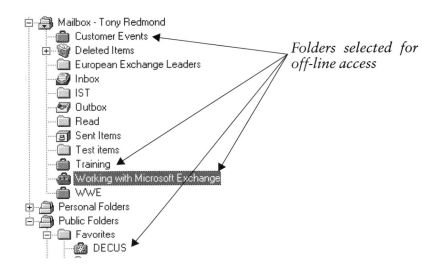

Figure 4.26
Off-line folders

An .OST file can be created anywhere, including network drives, but the usual location is somewhere like:

`C:\WIN95\REDMOND.OST`

Creating an off-line folder on a network drive may seem pointless, but it does mean that off-line folders will be available if you log in from different PCs.

The set of special mail folders – Inbox, OutBox, Sent Items, and Deleted Items are automatically added to off-line folders if off-line folder use has been configured in the user profile. These folders allow you to process messages while disconnected from the server. For example, you can create and send messages to anyone you want. In this case Exchange holds the messages in the OutBox folder and automatically sends them the next time you connect to the server. Sending messages in this way is done by synchronizing the contents of the OutBox off-line folder with the OutBox folder on the server.

All of your personal server-based folders allow you to set properties to determine whether the folder is available off-line. Public folders can also be made available off-line, but only if you first add them to your set of favorites (see the discussion later on in this chapter). Use the synchronization page in a folder's properties to mark a folder for off-line access. Once a folder's properties have been set to enable its use off-line the fact is indicated by marking it with a briefcase rather than the normal folder icon (see Figure 4.26). This is in line with the briefcase paradigm established in Windows 95 to enable users to synchronize files between two PCs.

The contents of folders marked for off-line access can be synchronized with the server using the client *Tools.Synchronize* option. You can elect to synchronize a single selected folder or all folders at one time. Of course, only the special mail folders plus any other folder marked for off-line access are synchronized when the 'all folders' option is selected. Unless you really must have everything available to you when you work off-line it's a good idea to restrict the number of marked folders plus the number of items stored in these folders. Even when synchronizing a single folder the whole process can take several minutes to complete if there are several hundred messages to deal with. Inbox and Sent Items folders tend to accumulate messages so give these folders a good clean out every so often to save yourself some time.

Automatic synchronization of the OutBox folder is performed when a client connects to a server to make sure that any message generated by the user when working in off-line mode is sent to its final destination. After all synchronization operations you can see exactly what happened during the synchronization process by viewing a log that ends up in the Deleted Items folder. As you can see from the sample log illustrated in Figure 4.27, the synchronization process updates new and deleted folders in the folder hierarchy as well as the actual folder contents.

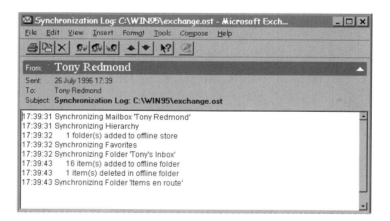

Figure 4.27
Off-line folder synchronization log

Apart from their obvious use in processing messages off-line folders are very useful for anyone who travels. You might, for instance, want to take a copy of all documents relating to a particular project before going on a trip. During the trip changes might be made to some or all of the documents, and when you get back to base you can synchronize the changes back with the data held in the server-based folder. Conflicts can occur when synchronization is attempted. If this happens you'll have to resolve the conflicts manually as there are no intelligent agents available to help out.

Managing the Public Information Store

The Public Information Store, the repository for public folders, is controlled by users who have been granted permission to create, write to or edit information held in public folders. The public information store shares the same 16Gb physical limit per server as the private information store, but again this is more than enough space for all but the most demanding or retentive installation. Indeed, the available disk space installed on a server is likely to be exhausted before you ever approach the theoretical limit for the store. Public folders are always created in the public information store on the home server of the user mailbox who creates the new folder.

Issues to consider in planning public folders

Among the issues to consider when planning the implementation of the Public Information Store you should:

- Pay attention to the information that's being placed into public folders. Public folders should not be used as a dumping ground for all and sundry.
- Restrict the permission to create top level folders in the public folder hierarchy to a limited group of users. It's a recipe for confused storage if everyone is allowed to create folders at the top of the hierarchy. Top level folders represent the entry point to the public folder hierarchy so it's essential that a well designed structure is instituted at this point. Users who have the permission to create top level folders are able to allocate permissions on the folders they create. In this respect, users with permissions to create top level folders can be regarded as guardians or administrators of the Public Information Store.
- Ensure that data is removed from public folders as soon as it is no longer valuable. You can arrange for data in public folders to expire after a set period, and this is a convenient feature where data held in certain folders has a regular and predictable life. However, it would be difficult to impose expiration times on public folders used by people as a point of reference. For instance, it is inappropriate to store documents describing a company's personnel policies and procedures in a public folder with a 60 day expiry. It is very appropriate to set a 60 day expiration limit on a public folder that stores bulletins relating to

training courses or other events with a readily determinable lifespan.

If you have lots of information that must be made available in public folders you might consider:

- Establishing a server to use as host for a set of 'archive' public folders. Data can be transferred from the 'live' set of folders to the archive server after a set period, for instance, every month, perhaps using some automated rules. The traffic to a set of archive public folders should be lighter than its live counterpart so you can factor this into network traffic planning.

- Splitting public folders over a set of servers rather than one specific server. Remember to ensure that everyone who needs access to the public folders has good network links. If you are moving public folders from one server to another you should also make sure that any affinities are transferred as well.

Public folder favorites

From a user perspective having hundreds, perhaps thousands, of public folders to choose from represents a rich vein of knowledge whose contents may hold the answers to many questions. But so much data is hard to track and it's easy to miss important items that are added to a public folder used for particular purposes, such as a folder used for project reports or new sales opportunities. The designers of Exchange Server have helped to get around the potential information overload by establishing the concept of 'Favorite' public folders.

Figure 4.28
Public folder favorites

Each user maintains their own list of favorite public folders. A public folder is included in a user's list by marking it with the clients 'File.Add to Favorites' option. When a public folder is marked in this way Exchange Server knows that it must monitor the contents of the public folder for any new items that are added. New items are indicated by the maintenance of a folder unread count displayed in the same way as the presence of new messages are indicated for the Inbox folder (see Figure 4.28). A quick visual scan of the Favorites section shows any folder where something new is stored.

Setting time expiration limits

Public folders experience different usage characteristics to private folders. Consider the following points:

- Folders are often created for a specific purpose and receive considerable activity for a period of time. For example, a folder might be created to hold documents relating to a particular project. While the project is active the folder is in daily use, but once the project finishes a danger exists that the folder loses relevance but remains in situ, clogging the store up with unwanted material.

- Larger items tend to be stored in public folders. Messages flow in and out of private folders, and messages are usually quite small in comparison to the documents and other items placed in public folders. Thus, a small number of items can occupy a considerable amount of space within the store.

- Public folders may be maintained by a number of different people. Not all of the maintainers will be efficient when it comes to controlling the content of 'their' folders. Some folders will be dynamic and only contain up-to-date information. Others will be stagnant and hold data that was valuable some time ago but is totally unnecessary today.

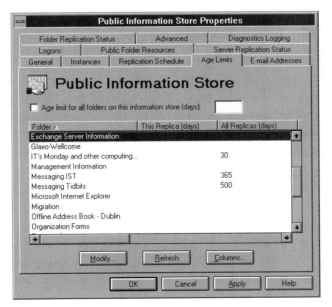

Figure 4.29 *Age limits imposed on specific public folders*

Apart from a steadily growing demand for disk space, the larger the public information store, the slower maintenance operations like backups will be. You should therefore consider whether age limits should be placed on any or all public folders (see Figure 4.29). Age limits dictate how long material will be retained in a public folder. Once an item exceeds the age limit it is automatically removed by the system attendant process, normally once a day.

By default there is no age limit applied for public folders. You can create an age limit which applies to all folders created in a public information store or set specific age limits on certain folders. For example, if you have a public folder used to distribute training announcements it's probable that you won't want to keep announcements that are more than sixty days old. Age limits can also be set on replicas of foreign public folders maintained in a store. The precedence rule is as follows:

1. If set, the limit on a folder is complied with.

2. If a general age limit is set for all public folders in a public information store it is applied to remaining folders.

3. If no limits are in place within a public information store but an age limit applies for all replicas of a public folder, that limit will be applied but only for the folder in question.

Setting a general age limit for new public folders is a good idea. Try 90 or 120 days as a starting point. If no one complains then this limit can remain as a default value. It will take some time before the default limit can take effect so in the interim you can analyze the public folders that are actually in use to try and determine what content is actually stored and how long it needs to be kept. The next stage is then to decide whether specific age limits need to be set on certain folders. Before you set any limits you should consult with the folder's owners as they may understand the effect of the limit on the folder's contents better than you.

Displaying the space allocated to public folders

A quick glance at the \MDBDATA directory reveals the physical size of the Public Information Store, but knowing what's actually occupying the space is more important. It's a good idea therefore to browse through the display generated by the Public Folder Resources property page (Figure 4.30) to see just where all the space is being used.

If you've set time expiration limits on some or all public folders the resources used will change all the time. The folders you need to pay attention to are those that consistently increase in terms of number of items and the space occupied. You should try and determine why the folder keeps on growing and see whether you can restrict the growth

Managing the Public Information Store

in any way. Sometimes the answer is simple. For example, the folder is used as a repository for documentation belonging to an ongoing project. You'd expect that this folder will grow as the project progresses and then can be cleaned out after the project finishes. Folders assigned to hold information about products can be expected to occupy a lot of space (graphics occupy much more space than plain text), but perhaps only hold a relatively few items.

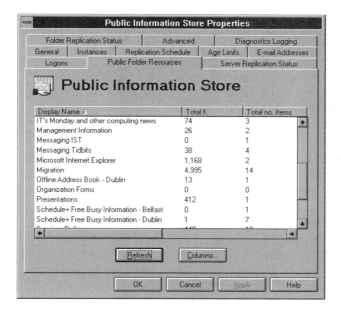

Figure 4.30
Displaying resources used by public folders

It is good system management practice to know what's going on in a server. Reviewing the number of items in public folders and the space they occupy gives you essential system management data and helps you tune your system more effectively. Once you know more about public folders than just the raw size of the information store you can make decisions at the folder level. For instance, public folders experiencing lots of activity should be located on servers capable of handling the traffic whereas folders storing very large items should be allocated to servers with lots of free disk space.

Virus checking

Any Exchange message can include an embedded object. Embedded executables are an obvious source of potential contamination from viruses, whether included in messages received from outside the organization or those perhaps unwittingly passed on by people working inside. Most users are now aware of the problems posed by executable-based viruses and system administrators have taken steps to address the problem. For example, some sites disable floppy drives while most have implemented some sort of automatic virus checking for system memory and .EXE and .DLL files whenever PCs are booted.

The first document-transmitted virus appeared in the Word for Windows 'Prank' macro in 1995. Recognizable by the presence of the 'Payload' macro, the virus worked by inserting itself into NORMAL.DOT, the default Word for Windows document template. The virus is activated and infects a PC whenever a document containing its macros was opened. The virus is irritating but harmless, and easy to clean up. All it ever did was display a dialog box, but so much more damage could have been wreaked if the virus's author had included some more malevolent instructions. Word for Windows' macro language, WordBasic, is capable of including calls to Windows API functions and file operations which can, in turn, inflict grave damage on user files. For instance, it's easy to write a macro that will automatically delete all sorts of important system files whenever the macro is invoked.

Many Windows products have their own macro language, and the majority of these languages are already pretty capable of making the same type of damaging system calls. Exactly the same effect as the 'Prank' macro could be created with an Excel macro written in Visual Basic for Applications, or in a WordPerfect for Windows macro. Macro languages are being improved all the time. They're also being made easier so vicious macros can be written without too much programming expertise. These developments make system administrators nervous because users don't seem to exercise the same level of care and attention when they deal with documents or spreadsheets. The lack of care when opening documents is perhaps natural because so many documents flow around a messaging system, but it means that viruses created as document macros spread rapidly once they've been introduced into an installation. As such document viruses are a major challenge for messaging system administrators, especially so in the case of systems like Exchange Server which place a high degree of importance in information sharing through distributed document repositories such as public folders.

What can you do to defeat the best efforts of document virus creators? There are two basic approaches:

1. *PC-centric*. Most of the commercial virus checking packages now available have been updated to include checks for known document viruses. In general, checking is performed whenever a document is opened. This approach is effective providing the virus

checker is installed and used on every PC. It's essential that the virus checker is kept up to date to ensure that new viruses can be detected soon after they are generally encountered, and arrangements must be made to distribute new releases of the virus checker to all PCs, including notebooks.

2. *Server-centric.* Some virus checkers can be run on a server to scan all the documents held in a file system or electronic file cabinet. In the case of Exchange Server you need a virus checker that understands the internals of the public and private information stores as otherwise it won't be able to check documents stored therein. Checking documents held in user directories is fine, but the real danger exists from documents that are stored and distributed via the messaging system. Given the potential popularity of Exchange Server it's likely that all the major commercial virus checking vendors will create a version that supports Exchange.

One mistake with a virus can be very expensive. Disinfecting a system, especially a large networked system, will take a lot of time and effort and it's probable that the system will be unavailable to users while the viruses are being eliminated. Be proactive and ensure that your system is protected!

Access rights for public folders

Roles, a collection of permissions defining the actions a user may perform on a folder and its contents, are used to control personal access to a public folder. Apart from 'Owner', the role automatically given to the user who actually creates a new public folder, the default role is called 'Author'. A user holding the 'Author' role is allowed to place new items in the public folder and edit items that they have put into the folder. Exchange Server comes with a number of predefined roles to enable you to get up and running with minimum effort and not worry about having to sit down and define out roles and what each role can and cannot do. The default roles are shown in Table 4.3.

Table 4.3 *Default Roles for Public Folders*

Role Name	Allocated to	Rights
Owner	User who creates a public folder	All, including control over permissions allocated to other users.
Author	Default role allocated to other users	Add new items to the folder and edit items they have provided

Table 4.3 *Default Roles for Public Folders (continued)*

Role Name	Allocated to	Rights
Publishing Author	People who will provide information to the folder and use the folder as a work area	Able to process own work and create sub folders
Editor	User who will work on information posted into the folder by others.	Edit, read, and delete all information.
Publishing Editor	Second highest level (after user) of control over the folder.	Edit, read, and delete all contributions. Able to create sub folders.
Reviewer	People who you want to read but not interact with folder contents.	Read only access.
Contributor	People who you want to provide content to folders and forget about it afterwards. On the surface, a rather strange role.	Write only access.

If you don't like the rights defined in the default roles you can create your own. Roles are changed or allocated to users by selecting a public folder and viewing its properties. The Permissions tab allows you to add or remove users to the list of people who have rights over the folder (see Figure 4.31).

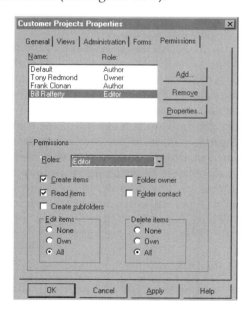

Figure 4.31
Setting permissions on a folder

Roles can be allocated to individual mailboxes or distribution lists. Using a distribution list is a convenient way of allocating the same role to a large group of people in a single operation. It's important to understand that roles allocated to individuals supersede roles gained through membership of a distribution list. The same dialog allows you to define a new role, should the need exist.

Owners of public folders assume certain responsibilities. Apart from being able to control the access and permissions other users enjoy on a public folder owners are the only people who are entitled to create rules via the Folder Assistant. Just like the Inbox Assistant, the Folder Assistant is a rules-based agent which monitors objects placed in folders. If the objects meet the criteria stated in a rule the Folder Assistant will swing into action and execute whatever action is required. For instance, a public folder is created to accept a feed from an Internet Newsgroup. A rule might be created to monitor new objects as they arrive and reject anything that does not originate from the Newsgroup.

Remember our discussion about moving users from one server to another within a site? When a user is moved all their private folders held within the Private Information Store are automatically moved from the source to the target server. However, any public folders that were created by the user before they are moved are retained on the original server. Any new public folders created after the move is complete will be created on the new server, but if a sub-folder is created for one of the public folders on the original server it too will be stored on that server. This is quite logical when you think about it, but some people expect that all public folders are transferred along with a user's private folders.

Using public folders to reduce messaging activity

People will always have the temptation to circulate large files by attaching them to messages. Good examples of what I mean are documents under review by a committee, when a document might go through several review cycles before eventually being approved. Attaching the file to a message is quick and easy and makes sure that everyone the sender wants to see the particular file receives a copy. Whether or not the recipient ever looks at their copy is quite another matter.

While undeniably easy to use, sending large files as attachments does not make the most effective use of the functionality available to users. It is much more efficient and reduces the chance of redundant information being stored in many places throughout the network to place a copy of whatever file needs to be circulated in a public folder. A short message can then be sent to act as a reminder to the circulation list that the file awaits their attention.

Public folders are an obvious source of shared information, but they're not the only one. If your Windows NT environment is designed in such a way as to allow general access to files no matter where they are located within the network you can even include a shortcut to a file, or even a program or installation kit within a message. And of course, Exchange supports embedded URLs to allow speedy access to specific Web pages. After receiving messages containing pointers to public folders, shortcuts or Web pages people can then go and retrieve the information as they wish. In the case of public folders if the folder allows write access they can even make their contributions by directly annotating the document in place so that everyone can see the comments as they are made. Beware of clashes occurring if two or more users attempt to update the document in the shared folder at the same time.

Using a public folder to replace large attachments won't always be possible, and it requires people to make decisions about the method to be used to distribute information to others. Users coming from other mail systems where public folders or similar mechanisms weren't available may not take kindly to the idea at all, but even if you can convince some groups within the user community to pay attention to the way they distribute and share information it will be a contribution towards increased system effectiveness. Users learn from each other (perhaps by a process of osmosis), and if one group sees that there's a better way to do something the new method will spread, slowly at first, but soon to become common practice.

Using public folder for collaborative authoring

Public folders make it easy to distribute any type of information among Exchange servers. Collaborative authoring, the collective creation of objects, chiefly documents, depends on easy access to the item being created by all contributing authors. Systems designed to facilitate and control the steps involved in the collaborative authoring process are sold under the label 'Document Management Systems'. Can Exchange Server fill this role? The answer is a qualified 'yes'. Exchange Server certainly scores highly on its abilities to

- ▶ Organize information in a structured manner within the public folder hierarchy.
- ▶ Control access to information held in public folders through permissions, and to allow different people fulfill different roles during the creation and editing of documents.
- ▶ Distribute initial documents and changes applied thereafter to interested parties in a seamless manner through folder replication.

Problems lie in the way Exchange Server allows multiple users with write or edit permission to concurrently change documents stored in public folders. The underlying reason why the problem exists is that Exchange Server has not implemented any system of document check-in or check-out. In other words, a user cannot reserve a document for exclusive write access while they make changes to the content, and then automatically release or cancel their reservation once the edit is complete.

Consider the following scenario:

1. User1 selects a document in a public folder and begins an edit session.

2. User2 logged into the same server, selects the same document and also starts an edit session.

3. User1 completes the changes they wish to make and exits the editor. Exchange Server saves the changes back into the public folder.

4. User2 completes their changes and exits the editor. Exchange Server flags that the document was changed since User2 began working with it and so cannot be changed again (see Figure 4.32). User2's changes are then discarded and cannot be applied to the item. The work is not actually removed from the system as User2 can save the item as a file and then import it back into the public folder. However, this is a two stage manual process.

Figure 4.32
Error saving a document

Clearly no user will be happy with such a situation. Three separate problems have been encountered. First, no warning was given to User2 that User1 was already working on the same document. Second, no indication is ever given as to which user actually has a document open or was responsible for making the last changes applied to the document. The original author's name is always shown and it cannot be changed by manipulating the document's properties.

Given that these problems exist is there any way that they can be avoided to enable Exchange Server be used as a collaborative document authoring system? The answer again is a qualified 'yes', but achieving a satisfactory status requires users to be disciplined about how changes are applied to documents in public folders because a manual system for change control needs to be established and implemented. Two methods come to mind:

1. All changes to documents are made after a copy is made through a drag and drop operation to a DOS directory. Changed documents are inserted as new objects when they are ready. The advantages of this method are that the last author name can be seen and that changes are never discarded.

2. All changes to documents are made after they are moved to a special 'Work' sub-folder. The same properties will be retained for documents, but it's immediately obvious that someone is working on a document if it is in the 'Work' folder.

Given a little thought many variations on these themes can be constructed. As no document change history is made available by Exchange Server you might like to consider creating a note in each folder that can be updated by users as they make changes.

Conflicts arising from distributed updates

All manner of conflicts can potentially arise when multiple users scattered around a network attempt to change a document. The only real way to avoid conflicts is to lock documents against changes by not allowing anyone except a specified group of users to have permission to edit objects held in a public folder. Others can read and comment, but nothing can be changed. This enforces a simple rule that the author (or their nominees) is the only person permitted to make changes to a document. In this scenario people who want to suggest changes have to mail them back to the author who then takes charge of assessing the proposed change and eventually integrating it into the document. This is a reasonable way of working in many cases, but not always.

Exchange Server recognizes that instances will occur when multiple concurrent changes are made to distributed objects. A mechanism is in place to intercept changes made to objects held in public folders before changes are finally applied. The mechanism operates on the home server for the folder.

Let's go through a fairly common scenario. Two users located in two different sites begin an edit on a document stored in a public folder. It doesn't matter which user starts first, just that both are engaged in edits at the same time. When both are finished they exit from the editor, and all appears to be successful as the edited object is applied to the local copy of the public folder. Thus, if each user was to immediately start another edit they'd see the changes they made last time around. Problems only appear once the replication engine has had time to kick into gear and communicate with the home server for the folder.

Changes to objects stored in public folders are posted back to the home server according to the replication schedule for the folder. In most instances replication occurs every fifteen minutes, although the actual elapsed time before the effect of replication is seen can be longer than this if the home server is unavailable for some reason or a long message queue needs to be serviced before the replication message is processed.

As soon as the home folder server detects that multiple changes have been made it begins a consultation process with the contributing authors to attempt to resolve the conflict. In effect the computer is throwing up its hands at the illogical behavior of humans and sending the problem back to the humans to have them sort it out. Computers, of course, are extremely logical and would never be guilty of attempting to make multiple concurrent updates to a single object. At least, not to something like a Word for Windows document which was never designed to support multiple concurrent updates!

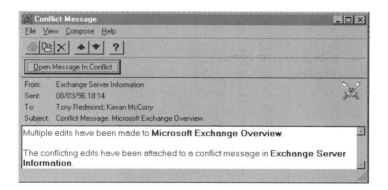

Figure 4.33
Message notifying that a conflict exists

Special messages are generated and dispatched to all of the users who have attempted to make a change to the object. Figure 4.33 is an illustration of an example message sent to two users (Tony Redmond and Kieran McCorry) who attempted to make a change to a document called 'Microsoft Exchange Overview' in the 'Exchange Server Information' folder. The crossed swords icon is used to provide a visual indicator for conflict messages when viewed in the Inbox folder.

When a user receives a conflict message the natural reaction is to go to the relevant public folder and see what's happened. If the user double-clicks on the object in conflict, Exchange Server displays a dialog giving details of the conflicting changes and offering the user a choice of what to do next (Figure 4.34).

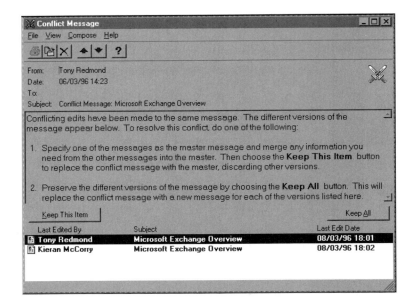

Figure 4.34
Instructions given to resolve a conflict

The options are:

- *Keep this item.* This means that the user has selected one of the changed objects that have provoked the conflict and now wishes to treat this object as the definitive version. All other changes are discarded. The authors who contributed the other versions should be contacted and their changes, if available, merged manually into the new definitive version.

- *Keep all items.* This is the more author-friendly version. It means that all of the versions offered for consideration are kept, each as a separate object stored in the public folder. Later on, if desired, the separate items can be reviewed and their content drawn together into a single version.

If you allow distributed users to contribute to documents in a replicated environment you must set ground rules to cater for instances when conflicts occur, or better still, establish a method for working which avoids conflicts. Computers can resolve problems that are stated in a logical sense, but they have no chance in the resolution of different thoughts and ideas arriving in from multiple users.

Using Exchange Server as a document management system

Given the issues around conflicts and the problems associated with multiple concurrent edits can Exchange Server be used as a document management system?

The characteristics of a document management system include:

- A structured document repository
- Access controls to define who can do what with the objects stored in the repository
- Object check-in and check-out facilities
- Object audit trails
- A flexible high-speed search engine capable of scanning large quantities of information to identify objects meeting user-specified criteria.

Exchange Server exhibits the first two characteristics in a very positive manner. The last three points are not currently met by the standard Exchange software, although a combination of third party offerings may be enough to establish the basis for a document management system.

As we've discussed, an object check-in and check-out facility can be emulated through permissions and user discipline. It's harder to implement audit controls, something to track who did what to a document, for what reason, and when. You could implement a log in each folder and require users to complete it, but this depends on users complying with the request.

High-end document management or text retrieval features can be incorporated into Exchange through third party products such as Fulcrum, KeyFile, PC DOCS, or Verity.[5] In terms of text retrieval the usual approach is not to ever search through the physical contents of public folders. Instead, background processes periodically scan public folders and construct an index which can then be searched against. Much greater flexibility and power is gained when searching, but at a cost of an additional load on the server (to build the indexes and run the search engine). There is also a danger that a relevant object might not be located because it has not been indexed since it was added to the public information store.

---

5. *Check the latest third party product list as new products are added all the time.*

System backups

A very wise person once said that an important difference between electronic mail and word processing applications was that when a word processor stopped working its effect was normally confined to a single user and perhaps a small quantity of documents, but when an electronic mail system collapses everyone is affected and normally it's the people at the top who notice fastest (and complain quickest).

Electronic mail systems depend on many different hardware and software components to keep everything going. If any element fails to operate in the required manner data corruption can occur. If the hardware suffers a catastrophic failure, or the site where the computers are located is afflicted by some disaster, you'll need to know the steps necessary to get your users back on-line as quickly as possible. In all these instances system backups are a prerequisite.

Backups, in their purest sense, are snapshots of a system's state at a certain point in time. All of the data available to the system should exist in the backup and should be restorable to exactly the same state if required. Backups can be written out to many different forms of magnetic or other media, although the most common type is some form of high-density magnetic tape.

The normal backup utility (NTBACKUP.EXE) provided with Windows NT V3.51 is not suitable for taking backups of an Exchange server due to the nature of the complex connections between the information stores and the transaction logs (see the discussion starting on page 150). When Exchange Server is installed the standard Windows NT backup utility is replaced with an enhanced version. The enhancements made to NTBACKUP.EXE are:

- Support for the transactional nature of the Exchange databases.
- Ability to perform on-line backups. In other words, to copy the information and directory stores to tape without having to shut down Exchange services. Users continue to work during backups.
- Extension of the NTBACKUP.EXE user interface to allow system administrators to select which sites and servers they wish to backup or restore.

Figure 4.35 shows an Exchange organization displayed in the Backup utility's window. The system administrator can select the server or servers they wish to backup, and whether or not the directory or information store, or both, should be processed. The concept of single seat administration means that it is possible to conduct all backups and restore operations from a single server. However, the practical network limitations encountered when shipping many gigabytes of information over the network to a single server during backup operations means that you'll probably want to run backup from a server in each site, or even on each server.

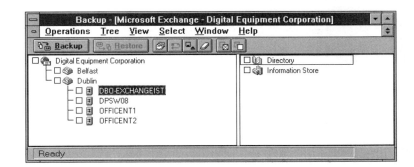

Figure 4.35
Windows NT Backup utility for Exchange Server

On-line backups can only be taken if circular logging (see discussion earlier in this chapter) is not enabled. On-line backups make a huge contribution to high system availability and are an essential part of Exchange Server's design. Moving to use circular logging is therefore a step that should not be taken without thinking through all the consequences.

Don't make the mistake of introducing a third-party extension to your system that conflicts with the requirements of Exchange Server, and don't fall into the trap of retro-fitting older software, such as a Windows NT service pack (patch kit), which might over-write the change to enable the Windows NT Backup utility to support on-line backups of the Exchange information and directory stores.

Third party backup utilities

It must be stressed that, in order to ensure that the backups are capable of being restored, they must be taken with the standard Windows NT or with another specialized utility provided by a third party, such as Arcada's Backup Exec for Windows NT. Arcada's product adds value by allowing (amongst other features) system administrators to create backup selections of disks and/or directories to specifically back up or restore. Backup Exec also provides a graphical backup scheduler which greatly makes scheduling backup procedures a pleasure and probably contributes to making sure that the job gets done.

It's always difficult to justify the additional expense of buying in a package to replace a standard utility, but backups are a system manager's parachute and if they don't work when they are needed then anyone involved may soon be looking for a new job. Apart from anything else, a specialized package often provides very useful features that are missing in the standard utility. One example is the ability to restore a single user account from a backup rather than being required to restore the entire database. Apart from the sheer convenience of being able to process just one user's messages, the time taken to complete the operation is a lot less than if you have to process everyone's messages.

Creating a backup strategy

Although Exchange Server does an excellent and almost automatic job of keeping its databases in shape, contributing to a high system availability level for users, hardware failures can and will occur. And when it's your turn to experience a hardware failure on the server you'll be glad that backups exist.

System failures come in two broad categories.

- Disk failure.
- Other non-critical system component failure. For example, the monitor for the server develops a fault.
- Critical system component failure. For example, the motherboard or other associated component experiences a fault that cannot be quickly rectified.

Any failure situation requires some fast but calm thinking in order to make the correct decisions to get everything up on line again. If the system cannot be brought back up, can you substitute another similar system and restore application data? If it's a particular system component can it be replaced or can the system configuration be altered to work around the problem? Having backups around won't replace making the right decision, but they're a great safety net.

The MTBF (Mean Time Between Failure) rate for hard disks is improving all the time. This doesn't mean that you will never experience a hard disk failure, but it does mean that you are less likely to have one over any particular period of time. A high MTBF is no guarantee that the disk won't fail tomorrow, so the challenge for system administrators is to have a plan to handle the problem when it arises.

Without RAID-compliant disks, if something does go wrong with a disk you'll have to stop operations and fix the problem or swap in a new drive. Once the hardware problem is fixed you'll have to restore the data, and of course this simple statement assumes that you have copies of all the application files that were stored on the faulty drive, and possess the capability to move the data onto the new drive. Backups come into their own here!

Having the capability to take on-line backups is one thing. Making the backups is quite another and there is a temptation to leave backups to the side and concentrate on more interesting work. This is a short-term and dangerous attitude. Nightly backups of the information and directory stores taken in tandem with full weekly backups of the server taken as a whole (in other words, including Windows NT, all the other applications, as well as the Exchange Server files) must be taken if any guarantee as to the integrity of the messaging system is to be given to users.

The database-centric nature of Exchange poses a particular challenge for restore operations. There is no getting away from the fact that if a restore is necessary it's going to take much longer than you may realize. The length of time required to backup and restore the information stores from a production Exchange server may come as a surprise to some. It's easy to forget just how long it takes to move data to backup media. The private and public information stores both have the capacity to expand quickly, so your backup times will grow in proportion. After a server has been in production for a number of months you might find that it's time to consider looking for faster or higher capacity media to help reduce backup times. Remember too that it's not just Exchange data which must be backed up. Windows NT, user files, and other application data all contribute to the amount of data and length of backup operations. These factors must be accounted for in the operational procedures you employ at your installation.

Consider this question: how long will it take to restore one gigabyte of data from your backup media using the backup software you employ? Now, how long will it take to restore three gigabytes, or maybe ten gigabytes, or how about a full-blown sixteen-gigabyte private information store? And what about the public information store? And the directory store? And all the other applications you may want to run?

In most circumstances, even when suitable hardware is waiting to be hot-swapped into your production environment the answer is counted in hours. Even when the restore is complete you may have other work to do before Exchange is available for use again. For instance, messages and other items waiting in the transaction logs may have to be written into the private and public information stores. Exchange does this automatically, but applying masses of transactions at one time delays the startup operation. Users will be yelling at you to get the system back on-line as quickly as possible, so it's going to be a time when stress levels are rising, which just adds to the piquant nature of the task.

I'm not trying to scare you about restores. Instead, I'm trying to point out an essential fact of system management life. You must be prepared and able to conduct a well-planned restore of essential data in order to be successful. No one wants to explain to a CIO why the messaging system was unavailable for one or two days while staff fumbled their way through a restore. We'll discuss restores a little more later on in this chapter, but remember to ensure your job security by being prepared ahead of time.

Knowing how to properly use and safeguard backup media is an important part of a backup strategy. Think of the following questions: After the backups are performed how will the media be moved to a secure location? Is the secure location somewhere local or remote? When will the tapes or other media be used for backup purposes again? How can the backups be recovered quickly if needed?

Taking backups

The simplest way to perform a backup is to double-click on the NTBACKUP icon and start things off, as illustrated in Figure 4.36. Easy as this is to do it's often inconvenient to take backups interactively. Backups should be taken on a regular basis and you're not always going to be around to start things off.

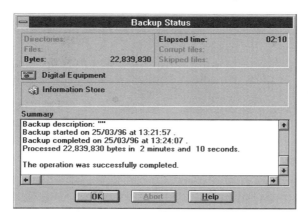

Figure 4.36 *A successful backup of the information store*

WINAT.EXE (see Figure 4.37) is one of the utilities available on the Windows NT Resource Kit.

System backups

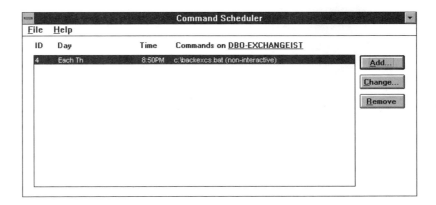

Figure 4.37
Scheduling a daily backup with the WINAT utility

WINAT provides a GUI for the standard Windows NT AT.EXE (command line scheduler) utility and allows you to schedule tasks for execution in the background without human intervention. WINAT is similar to many other third party scheduling programs that are available. These programs often have extended feature sets which ease the scheduling process, but WINAT provides enough functionality to get the job done in many cases.

WINAT schedules batch files (.BAT files) to execute at specified times. Before you can use WINAT you'll need to write a simple batch file and create the commands to tell NTBACKUP.EXE what components should be backed up. You can take both on-line and off-line backups. On-line backups are those taken with all Exchange services active. Off-line backups are taken after all Exchange services have been stopped. Exchange Server has been designed to fully support on-line backups, so there's no reason why you shouldn't plan to take on-line backups all the time. Off-line backups permit system registry data relating to the Exchange configuration to be included in the backup. As such, an off-line backup is a more accurate and complete picture of an Exchange server, albeit one taken at the expense of stopping all services beforehand.

The complete set of parameters for NTBACKUP are described in Chapter 15 of the Exchange Administrator's Guide. A two-line batch file to take a backup of the information and directory stores on the DBO-EXCHANGEIST server is shown below:

```
NTBACKUP backup DS \\DBO-EXCHANGEIST IS \\DBO-EXCHANGEIST /v /d 'On-line backup of
DBO-EXCHANGEIST' /t normal /l
exit
```

Coding-up the commands to stop and start Exchange services before and after an off-line backup is easy. You need to include a NET

STOP command for each Exchange service before NTBACKUP is invoked, and a matching NET START command for each service afterwards. For example:

```
REM Stop the Internet Mail Connector
NET STOP MsExchangeIMC
REM Stop the Information Store
NET STOP MsExchangeIS
NTBACKUP backup C:\ D:\ E:\ /v/d 'Off-line backup for DBO-EXCHANGEIST' /b
REM Start things up again
NET START MsExchangeIS
```

As you can see, there are differences in the NTBACKUP commands used for on-line and off-line backups. On-line backups specify whether the information or directory store, or both, should be backed up whereas off-line backups ignore the stores and concentrate on backing up the files contained on specified disks (C:, D:, and E: in the example shown above).

How on-line backups process Exchange databases

The Jet database engine used by Exchange Server allows on-line backup with users connected and actively using the information and directory stores. It follows that transactions can take place during the backup process, for example when users create and send messages. During on-line backup processes a number of special-purpose files known as patch files are used by Exchange Server to track these transactions.

A separate patch file can be created for each store. The files are called:

- PRIV.PAT – Private Information Store Patch File
- PUB.PAT – Public Information Store Patch File
- DIR.PAT – Directory Store Patch File

The process of backing up an Exchange database follows these steps:

1. A patch file is created for the database. For example, PUB.PAT.
2. The current transaction log is disabled and prevented from accepting new transactions (this only happens with the private and public information stores).

3. The database and log files are written to the backup media. During this time any transactions written from memory are directed to the patch file.

4. The block on the current transaction log is removed to allow it to accept transactions from memory again.

5. The contents of the patch file are written to the current transaction log.

6. The patch file is written to the backup save set.

7. The patch file is deleted.

8. The next database to be backed up is selected.

9. After all databases have been backed up all the transaction logs containing data now fully written and checkpointed in the database are deleted.

Patch files are created in the \MDBDATA directory. You will only be able to see them during a backup process.

Restoring an Exchange server

Having backup tapes taken on a regular basis and then carefully stored away is clearly a great step towards assuring data security, but having the ability to restore data from the backup tapes is an equally important part of the overall equation.

Some sort of hardware failure is the most common reason why a restore is required. It's also possible for the information or directory stores to be corrupted in some manner, perhaps as a side effect of an intermittent hardware fault. In this case the ISINTEG or EDBUTIL utilities (see page 198) may be able to rectify the problem and allow normal processing to continue. If not, a restore is required. In all cases where database corruption has occurred it's a good idea to have the hardware checked out to eliminate it as a potential underlying cause. There is no point in restoring a backup onto a server where a problem lurks deep in the hardware.

Let's assume that a hardware failure has happened. You can't use the server where the failure occurred. What steps need to be taken to get a substitute server up and running? Here's an outline checklist:

1. Create a new server with a hardware configuration as close as possible to the original computer. This includes disks, tape drive, memory, and any special devices.

2. Make sure that the correct version of Windows NT (V3.51 with Service Pack 4 or V4.0) is installed.

3. Connect the new server into the domain structure. The substitute system should have the same name as the failed system. The substitute should assume the same role in the domain structure. In other words, if the failed system was a Backup Domain Controller (BDC) the substitute should become a BDC. If it was a simple server with no role in user authentication that's fine too. The most complex situation is where the failed system was the PDC (see below).

4. Install Exchange Server on the substitute. Use the same site and organization name as the failed system. Use the same Exchange service account. If joining an existing site use SETUP \R to install Exchange. The \R switch tells Exchange that configuration information for the newly installed server should not be replicated to the rest of the organization.

5. You should also install the Exchange client software so that you can test the effectiveness of the restore once it's completed.

6. Run NTBACKUP.EXE and restore the directory and information stores from the backup.

7. Use the Exchange client to check accounts and make sure that messages can be sent and read. Use the administration program to check that the correct correlation exists between Exchange mailboxes and Windows NT accounts.

8. Make sure that all connectors are operating properly. Check directory replication connections if the system being restored should act as a directory replication bridgehead for the site.

9. Use the Directory Consistency checker to adjust any inconsistencies that may have crept in during the restore.

10. Run the Exchange Performance Optimizer utility (see page 341) to optimize the Exchange configuration.

A strong recommendation has already been made not to run Exchange Server on the same Windows NT computer that acts as the Primary Domain Controller, or PDC (see page 61). The link between the Windows NT security database (SAM) and how authentication for access to directory objects is performed is the major reason behind the recommendation. When you only have one server to do everything it's impossible to avoid having Exchange and the PDC on the same system, but in all cases where multiple servers are in use you should definitely separate the two.

If you rebuild a system that acts as a PDC a new SAM is created. When the time comes to restore the Exchange directory any attempt to authenticate against the new SAM will fail, the net effect being that no Exchange service will be able to start and you won't even be able to log onto the Administration program. The information store can be restored and you can use a brand new directory to create mailboxes to access data in the store, but it's obvious that a lot of work is needed to recreate mailboxes and other directory information, and then propagate it to the rest of the organization. Apart from anything else there's lots of potential for error and confusion.

On the other hand, if the system being restored is a BDC a copy SAM will be retrieved from the PDC when the system is rebuilt. Note that you'll need to use the Windows NT Server Manager to demote the system from BDC status and then promote it again after Windows NT has been reinstalled on the computer. This step is necessary to ensure that the SAM data is copied correctly from the PDC to the new BDC.

The simplest case to handle is where the Exchange server being rebuilt takes no part in user authentication. In these cases it is sufficient to rebuild Windows NT and Exchange on the server as outlined above. User authentication will be accomplished by reference to the PDC and/or BDC in the domain that the server joins during the rebuilding process.

Processing single mailboxes

One specific item of functionality not provided by the standard Windows NT Backup utility is the ability to save or restore a single mailbox. The standard Backup utility operates on the information or directory stores as whole entities, so if you want to restore a single user's mailbox (sometimes referred to as a 'brick' or 'bricked' restore) you have to restore the entire information store.

Restoring a user's mailbox is a task that system administrators probably won't welcome with open arms. Experience with other messaging systems indicates that over the course of a server's productive life there is more than a 50% chance that you'll encounter a situation where a user mailbox is deleted in error, or a user deletes some important files in error and only realizes their mistake some time later. Given the capacity for humans to err the latter situation is more likely to arise. It's difficult to restore the complete information store onto a production server. You could do this, but only through a set of complicated steps involving:

1. Shut down the production server.
2. Take a backup of the information store.

3. Restore the backup of the information store which contains the mailbox you wish to restore or otherwise recover.
4. Start up the Exchange information store, but don't allow users to log on and make sure that no external connectors are active.
5. Log onto the mailbox and move all the messages you wish to recover from the mailbox to a personal information store (PST file). You can drag and drop individual messages or select all the messages in the mailbox and copy them in one operation to the PST.
6. Shut down Exchange.
7. Restore the backup taken in step 2.
8. Restart Exchange Server and allow users to resume work. Make sure all connectors and directory replicators are restarted successfully.
9. Provide the user with the PST and instruct them how to access the recovered messages from the PST.

Executing this complicated set of actions will take at least four hours on any reasonably sized server. Shutting down a production system for four hours and depriving users of their e-mail is not a recipe for generating popularity, so another tactic needs to be considered.

The obvious solution is to restore the information store onto another Windows NT computer and use that as the basis to retrieve the necessary messages. To do this you'll need:

- A Windows NT server with the same version of Windows NT and Exchange Server installed as on the production server. We'll call this system the 'recovery host'.
- A tape drive on the recovery host capable of reading the backups created on the production server.
- Exchange Server (on the recovery host) must be configured with the same organization and site name as the production server where the backup originates. If the organization and site name do not match you won't be able to restore the backup taken from the production server.

Equipped with a suitable recovery host you can proceed to restore the backup tape, log into the user's mailbox and extract the necessary messages to a PST. The pressure to do all of this is much less than when you've had to take a production server off-line, so you can take your time and make sure that everything's done correctly.

Lacking the capability to restore a single mailbox from a backup is an obvious flaw in the current Windows NT backup utility. It remains to be seen whether the flaw will be addressed in a future release of Windows NT or Exchange Server, but until that time this feature is high on the list of desirable items to look for if you consider buying a different backup utility from a third party.

Restoring single documents

Users delete documents and messages that they really want to keep all the time. It's easy to hit the delete key when an important message is highlighted, sending the message off to the Deleted Items folder. If you realize the error in time the message can be retrieved from Deleted Items, but it's a different matter if the user logs off from Exchange and the Deleted Items folder is emptied.

Unlike other messaging systems the messages managed by the Exchange information store never exist as individual files. Messages, documents, and other objects added to the information store reside in the database as binary objects, or BLOBS in database terminology. In other words, within the database messages are stored as collections of binary information which make little sense to anything else except the information store. As we've seen there are many advantages in this scheme, but there's a dark side too.

Documents or messages deleted in error can only be recovered by restoring a user's entire mailbox. The restore is only going to be possible if the document or message existed in the mailbox at the time when the backup was taken. Nothing can be done to recover the missing item if it was created and deleted since the last backup.

Restoring the contents of public folders

Accidents can happen to user mailboxes, and users are more than capable of deleting objects from their mailboxes in error, and much the same type of accidents can happen to the contents of public folders. What can be done to recover an important document that's been deleted from a public folder?

The first thing to do is to check whether a copy of the document exists in a replica folder elsewhere in the organization. Changes, including deletions, have to be replicated before they are effective throughout an organization. It is therefore possible to go to a public folder replica on another server and recover a copy of the desired document before the deletion command is replicated. However, it must be acknowledged that such a recovery depends on realizing that the document shouldn't have been deleted as soon as the action is performed, quick access to a remote server hosting a replica (directly via the network or perhaps through a phone call to the local system administrator), and a large slice of luck.

If your luck runs out and you don't manage to get to a replica in time there is no alternative but to refer back to a backup. Much the same problems exist for the restore. You don't want to stop the production server to recover the document if at all possible, so using a separate recovery host is the best approach. After the document is recovered to a PST you can move the document from the PST back into the public folder.

Key Management backups

If you are operating the Key Management Server you should arrange for the security information to be backed up on a daily basis. This information is stored in the SECURITY\MGRENT directory on the central Key Management Server system. Losing security data through hardware failure without having a backup available can have catastrophic implications. All of the users who have been enabled for advanced security will not be able to encrypt messages because their security credentials will have disappeared. Even worse, they won't be able to decrypt messages they received previously.

Information store maintenance

Exchange Server performs maintenance operations against the information store in two distinct manners:

1. On-line maintenance performed as the server is operating
2. Off-line maintenance procedures activated when something goes wrong.

On-line maintenance

Like most databases, the internal structures within the information store become less efficient over time. Data is not stored in an effective manner and becomes fragmented throughout the database. Taking Exchange off-line to compact the databases creates a severe impact for users, so an on-line maintenance facility is included to keep things in order and defragment or re-order data within the private and public information stores. On-line maintenance is scheduled by first selecting a server and then the 'IS Maintenance' property page. The schedule, if active, is then displayed and can be changed if desired (see Figure 4.38). On-line maintenance is also possible for the directory, in which case it's controlled by setting the 'Garbage collection interval' on the general property page of the DS Site Configuration object.

Figure 4.38
Schedule for on-line Information Store maintenance

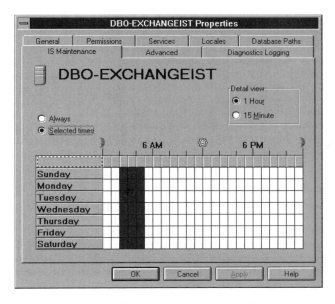

The effect of on-line maintenance is slight on most servers. Unless you are running close to the limits of your hardware's capabilities users shouldn't notice a significant degradation of server responsiveness as the information store is verified and any internal inconsistencies corrected. You can avoid any potential conflicts between the demands of users and the system maintenance processes by scheduling the maintenance to occur when a reduced number of users are active. As you can see from Figure 4.38, I like maintenance to occur when everyone is safely tucked up in bed or otherwise engaged in activities that don't require electronic mail.

Off-line maintenance

Two off-line maintenance utilities for the information store are provided with Microsoft Exchange Server. These are:

- ISINTEG: Information Store Integrity Checker
- EDBUTIL: Exchange database utility

ISINTEG is designed to find and remove errors from public and private information stores. The utility is able to run in two modes; test and patch. In test mode a scan is performed against an information store to determine whether any errors exist. Potential errors include incorrect reference counts for an object, table errors, or the discovery of objects that are not referenced anywhere within the store. Optionally, errors found in test mode can be fixed as they are discovered. All errors are reported to a log file. ISINTEG is used in patch mode to repair an information store if it will not start up after being restored, for example, after a disk failure. Patch mode rectifies any inconsistencies that exist in an information store to ensure that data is not overwritten and that all data within the store is available to users. The most common reason why ISINTEG might be required occurs when the backup used to restore an information store was originally performed by a backup utility that doesn't support the on-line nature of the Exchange Information Store. This is a good reason to always use the Windows NT Backup utility, which is patched by the installation of Exchange Server to be able to deal with on-line information stores, or a third-party replacement utility that is guaranteed to support Exchange correctly.

While ISINTEG could be described as operating on the content of an information store, EDBUTIL operates at a higher level, concentrating on the internal database structures which underpin an information store. EDBUTIL is able to defragment an information store, compacting the database and returning unused space to the disk system; it is able to scan the database and verify its consistency, and to recover transactions from a log file and write them to a database. EDBUTIL is also able to deal with fairly mundane but important items such as ensuring that the count of messages in a folder is correct, and that unread items are displayed by clients in bold face rather than normal.

The private information store gets a lot of message activity. New messages arrive, are read, deleted or filed away, all resulting in database activity, potentially leading to a database that becomes fragmented very quickly. The exact time when an unacceptable level of fragmentation occurs depends on how many people use the system and how many messages they send and receive. I run EDBUTIL every few months on my production server to defragment the private information store and return some valuable disk space. As an example of what you might expect, the last time I ran the utility it converted a 500Mb store to 284Mb. Apart from improving internal efficiency, reducing the time necessary for backup and restore operations is an excellent reason to defragment information stores on a regular basis.

Another good example of when EDBUTIL might be used is after a large number of mailboxes have been moved from one server to another within a site. The space originally occupied by the moved mailboxes can be recovered by running EDBUTIL to compact the private information store. The last use of EDBUTIL is to upgrade a database's internal structures or provide information about those structures. This option is only ever taken upon advice from Microsoft.

ISINTEG and EDBUTIL can be found in the EXCHANGE\BIN directory. All Exchange services must be stopped before the utilities are run. Further details of how to use the utilities can be found in Chapter 17 of the *Exchange Administrator's Guide*.

Keeping messages secret

No-one likes to think that their messages might be read, either en route to a recipient or by someone other than the recipient after messages have reached their final destination. Exchange Server encrypts all messages by default to ensure that message contents are secure as they are transferred between servers and clients. Users aren't aware of this encryption and no client or server options are available to disable it.

Optional functionality is available to allow you to encrypt and decrypt messages and their attachments as they pass from sender to recipient. Messages can also have electronic signatures applied to them to prove that the content was generated by a specific individual. User-driven encryption is not something that you introduce into your messaging environment on a whim as it requires some detailed up-front planning and introduces at least some, and potentially substantial, additional work for system administrators. Such a sweeping statement is true even of a messaging system that has worked hard to integrate encryption as seamlessly as possible, which is the case of Exchange Server where encryption/decryption and electronic signatures are collectively referred to as 'Advanced Security'.

The Advanced Security features of Exchange Server are available to anyone who buys either the Exchange Server Enterprise Edition or who adds the Exchange Connector to an Exchange Server Standard Edition. Advanced Security is controlled by a component called the Key Management Server (KMS). Encryption and decryption are carried out by Exchange clients. Nothing is done on the server. In passing it's worth noting that the DOS client supports Advanced Security.

Different types of encryption

Exchange Server uses the RSA security system and supports both the DES and CAST encryption algorithms. RSA is a public-key encryption system that can be used for both encryption and certification and is probably the most widely used public-key encryption system in use today. RSA was originally developed in 1977 by Ron Rivest, Adi Shamir, and Leonard Adleman at the Massachusetts Institute of Technology. The initials of the authors' surnames make up RSA.

DES (Data Encryption Standard) is a complicated algorithm for the encryption of data designed by the US National Bureau of Standards. The intention behind DES was to create an algorithm that is extremely difficult to break, certainly well beyond the capabilities of anyone equipped with copious time and anything else than a supercomputer or a networked array of workstations. Even with such powerful hardware resources the 56-bit key used by DES[6] to create a binary encryption key with 72 quadrillion possible combinations is enough to make any attempt to break the code a relatively fruitless activity.

CAST is a proprietary encryption method developed by Northern Telecom (who sold a license for their 'Entrust' technology to Microsoft for inclusion into Exchange Server). CAST was originally developed as a more flexible encryption scheme than DES, mostly because it allows for a variable input key of between 40 and 128 bits.

The exact nature of the algorithm used by your particular server depends whether you are in the United States or not. The 56-bit (DES) or 64-bit (CAST-64) encryption algorithms are treated by the United States government as militarily-sensitive items and is therefore only provided with Exchange servers shipped in the United States and Canada. Other countries are restricted to the lowest available form of the CAST algorithm based on a 40 bit key. The real difference between the US and anywhere else is therefore the size of the input key used for encryption (64-bit or 56-bit versus 40-bit). It's obvious that the size of the input key determines the amount of computing effort required to break an encryption code, so the encryption used in the United States and Canada is much more secure than elsewhere.

In a practical sense the presence of different encryption algorithms in use within a single Exchange organization doesn't affect matters in the least because non-US servers are able to decrypt messages originating from the US, and vice versa. The difference lies in how messages are encrypted in the first place rather than in how they are eventually decrypted.

For comparison's sake it's interesting to note that Lotus Notes Release 4 also uses 64-bit keys in its international version. However, the last 24 bits of each key are registered in escrow with the US government, reducing the amount of key-cracking to 40 bits.[7] Of course, giving the US government a head start when the time comes to crack a

---

6. *The specification for DES is contained in the Federal Information Processing Standard Publication 46 of January 15, 1977.*

7. *See 'Using Lotus Notes 4,' Que Books, 1996, page 738.*

key is done just in case someone wants to officially read your mail at some point in the future.

Governments generally like to know what people are up to, and steps are often taken to put obstacles in place to stop people protecting their privacy. The US government, for example, was really upset when Phil Zimmerman, the author of the PGP (Pretty Good Privacy) encryption algorithm, placed his code into the public domain through the Internet. Following much the same line the French government do not permit the import of any encryption software into France, so any Microsoft Exchange Server used in France cannot include the encryption functionality. Even if a server located in France cannot generate encrypted messages people using the server will still be able to read encrypted messages originating from elsewhere. Microsoft cannot be criticized for shipping different encryption technology to different countries. As a US company they are limited by law to the software they can provide, and the implementation in Exchange Server is similar in many respects to the approach taken by other products, most notably the Lotus Notes server which supports a mixture of United States and 'international' keys to encrypt messages.

I'm not sure that it really makes a lot of difference to the average user whether their messages are encrypted with 40, 56 or 64 bits. Huge amounts of computing horsepower are necessary to decrypt even a single message encrypted with a 40-bit key. The resources required are sizable enough to prevent anyone but national security agencies and other government bodies from even attempting to browse or intercept the volume of messages generated on an average server. And anyway, the content of the majority of messages is hardly earth-shattering and is of little commercial or other importance. If you're really interested in probing the outer edges of message encryption perhaps you should investigate messaging systems that support the US Defense Messaging System (DMS) standard. A variant of Microsoft Exchange Server is currently being engineered to support DMS.

The security component of Exchange Server dictates which algorithm is used when a message is encrypted. Thus, if a message is addressed to someone outside your organization (a custom recipient, in other words) Exchange will not allow encryption to occur and messages will be sent in clear text. This approach is reasonable as it's clearly folly to send an encrypted message out across an SMTP or X.400 link to a recipient who potentially uses another mail system that knows little or nothing about Exchange-style encryption. Intelligence is also applied when encrypting messages circulating within an organization. If a recipient is connected to a server located outside the

United States or Canada a 40-bit key and algorithm is used automatically.

If you use the Internet Mail Connector to connect two or more sites it is possible to send encrypted messages and electronic signatures across the Internet (or Intranet, a private SMTP backbone) if Advanced Security features are used everywhere throughout your organization. This means that all users are registered with the key management server so that the flag to this effect can be located in the directory when an attempt is made to send an encrypted message via SMTP, resulting in an inevitable rise in the amount of day-to-day administration. Microsoft has indicated, in a number of public electronic forums, that it is interested in building in features to permit easier encryption for people using SMTP backbones to link sites within their own organizations or when sending secure messages to partners. These features may well appear in a future version of Exchange Server, but no dates have yet been committed to.

Basic points about encryption

Before plunging into the inner details of how advanced security works we need to create a broad sketch of the security implementation. The basic points regarding message encryption, or message sealing, as implemented in Microsoft Exchange Server are as follows:

► Encryption is accomplished through a mixture of public and private keys allocated and controlled by a single nominated Exchange server within your organization. This server runs an optional component known as the Key Management Server. It is obvious that this computer must be located in a secure environment as if it is physically accessible or becomes unavailable the entire encryption scheme is compromised. Because of its need to be as secure as possible the files for the Key Management Server must be located on a disk using the Windows NT NTFS file system. The server must be capable of providing as high a degree of available service (ideally 24 × 365) as a hardware configuration can make possible.

► 512-bit RSA public/private key pairs are used to verify a sender's authenticity. The RSA MD5 message digest algorithm is used for calculating the unique hash used to check message integrity. These techniques are similar to those employed by other encryption products available today. Microsoft didn't build this technology from scratch. It is licensed from Northern Telecom, who sell the base encryption functionality as 'Entrust™ Security Technology'.

- Each user who will encrypt messages must be individually identified to the server to allow a temporary token to be generated. The temporary token is then used to allocate public and private keys for an individual.
- Messages are encrypted with a one-time 'bulk' encryption key generated by the server. After the message is encrypted the bulk key is in turn encrypted using the public key for each recipient. Thus, if a message is addressed to ten different users, the bulk key for the message is encrypted ten times using ten different public keys. When an encrypted message is received it is decrypted by fetching the bulk key using a recipient's private key, and then the retrieved bulk key is used in turn to decrypt the content of the message.

Keys and certificates

The concept of keys is clearly very important when attempting to understand how advanced security works. Signing and sealing of messages is controlled by a scheme of private and public keys in line with the ITU X.509 set of recommendations for authentication information. Each mailbox enabled for advanced security receives a key pair composed of a public and private key. Public keys are provided as fixed-length strings that are published and made known to any process which needs to encrypt information destined for that user. Two public keys are used, one to encrypt messages before they are sent, and one to read electronic signatures on received messages.

Private keys are also stored as fixed length strings. However, their values are kept private to the user and never revealed. The private keys are stored in an encrypted file (with an extension of .EPF) stored on the user's computer. As in the case of public keys, two separate private keys are used within the Exchange security scheme, one for message decryption and one to apply electronic signatures. Table 4.4 summarizes the key types and when they are used.

Table 4.4 *Private and Public Key usage*

	Encryption/Decryption	Electronic Signatures
Sending messages	Public key used to encrypt message contents	Private signing key used to apply signature
Reading messages	Private key used to decrypt message contents	Public signing key used to interpret applied signature

Like passwords, it's easy for human beings to forget their private keys. With Exchange advanced security losing a key isn't a total disaster so there's no need for users to write their keys down on a piece of paper that can be kept in a convenient location. If users forget their private key a new key can be allocated by the key server.

Key pairs are managed by Exchange Server through X.509-compliant special security certificates created and managed by the Key Management Server. When fulfilling the role of certificate manager the Key Management Server is known as the Certification Authority, or 'CA' because it is responsible for creating and maintaining the security key pairs and special certificates.

Certificates are an authentication mechanism used by many security schemes. In Exchange Server certificates are used to transport users' public keys throughout the organization so that they are available to any process which needs them. They are replicated via the Directory Service and contain:

- A unique serial number for each certificate which is generated by the Key Management Server.
- The encrypted password of the Certification Authority. This is sometimes known as the CA signature.
- The directory name of the Certification Authority. This allows clients to send messages back to the Certification Authority via the mail system.
- The directory name for the user who holds the certificate.
- The user's public key for either signing or message encryption.
- The expiry date of the certificate, if set by the Certification Authority.

Two certificates are issued to each user who is enabled for advanced security. One certificate holds the public signing key, the other the public encryption key. A copy of the CA's own certificate is also distributed to each user. This certificate is stored in the user's .EPF file along with the user's personal certificates.

A wax blob impressed with the seal of office of a mayor or other public official and affixed to a formal document is a reasonable analogy for a special certificate, which fulfills the same role in attesting that the item it is associated with has been authorized by a specific individual (or public body).

Electronic signatures

Much of our discussion so far has been focused on message encryption. Exchange Server also allows messages to be 'signed' by users to enable nonrepudiation and message integrity. These features utilize additional keys, known as signing keys, that are quite separate from those used to encrypt and decrypt message content.

Nonrepudiation means that a message can be associated with a specific individual who cannot deny that they sent a message (because it has been electronically signed by them). Of course, just like passwords, nonrepudiation only works if individuals do not reveal their signing keys to others. It is also very unwise to keep copies of signing keys taped to the bottom of a keyboard.

Message integrity can be assured by creating a 'hash' value, an algorithmically derived value calculated by passing the contents of a message through a complex set of computations. The end result of taking such an electronically mixed snapshot of a message's contents is a unique numeric value, the hash value. Before sending the message the hash value is encrypted with the sender's private signing key. When the message is received its contents can be verified by creating another hash of the contents using the same algorithm and comparing it against the original hash which is fetched from the message using the originator's public signing key. Any difference in the two hashed values indicates that the message has been changed since the originator signed it.

Installing advanced security

The installation of the Key Management Server is easy and accomplished by running the SETUP.EXE in the \EXCHKM directory from the Exchange Server CD. After the installation is complete the Key Management service starts up and functions in the same manner as any of the other Exchange services, such as the System Attendant.

The installation of the Key Management Server involves the creation of two passwords, both used to decrypt, or unlock, the 'lockbox' which protects the Master Encryption Key for the Key Management Server. All keys held within the security database are protected by the master encryption key.

The first password is written to file called KMSPWD.INI on a floppy diskette that you'll be asked to provide during the installation. If you want to you can avoid writing the information to the floppy, but this decision can lead to future inconvenience because the password will then have to be manually input each time the Key Management Server is started. If the floppy disk containing the password is not available whenever the Key Management Server is started you'll be asked to insert it, and failing this, the server will not start up because the master encryption key cannot be accessed. Remember, without access to the master encryption key the server cannot even begin to process security requests, so make sure that the floppy containing the master encryption password is always available. Don't leave the floppy in the computer's floppy drive because the computer will attempt to use its contents to boot an operating system the next time it is restarted. Floppy disks are very prone to error, especially when they are used over a long period of time. It's therefore a good idea to copy the diskette containing the password and store the copy in a safe place.

The second password is created for use by the system administrator every time they attempt to carry out any management operation that involves the Key Management Server. For example, if you select a recipient and attempt to enable them for advanced security you'll be asked to enter the password. As it can get quite tiresome to continually be prompted for a password Exchange Server allows you to decide whether the password should be 'remembered' for up to five minutes at a time. This allows you to get on with the task in hand such as enabling a whole group of users for advanced security.

A default value for the security administrator password is provided (the password, strangely enough, is set to 'password') and you should change it as soon as possible after the installation is complete. Remember to share the password with anyone who will participate in any security management operations. At first glance it may seem that the management of the Key Management Server involves lots of passwords being demanded. It's logical when you think of the attitude that should really be adopted when you approach the implementation of a secure messaging system. Either you want to have a secure system or you don't. There really isn't a halfway point in this respect.

As noted previously, a single central Key Management Server is allocated the role of creating and managing all security keys allocated to users within an Exchange organization. In all advanced security implementations the central Key Management Server is installed first. You can switch and change the Key Management Server across different systems, but only within the same site. This process is accomplished by simply copying the security database, security DLL, and service to the target server. If you make a mistake and want to move the Key Management Server to a system in another site you'll have to withdraw all the existing keys and issue new ones, adding up to a lot of work that's easily avoided by making the right decision in the first place.

The effect of the initial Key Management Server installation is to create the 'CA' object in Exchange Server's configuration container. Once created, details of the CA object are replicated to all the other servers in the organization in the same manner as other configuration data. Using the CA object as a marker prevents another server becoming the central Key Management Server for an organization, but only after replication has occurred. It is technically possible for two system administrators to install the Key Management Server in two different sites at the one time, with the resulting chaos afterwards if both servers attempt to allocate and manage security keys. This is one reason why the introduction of the Key Management Server into an organization must be managed and coordinated between all sites.

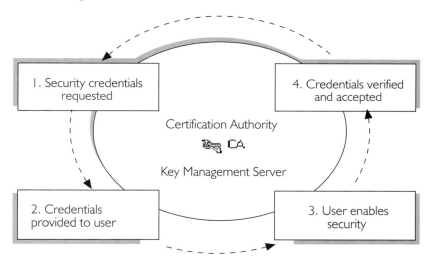

Figure 4.39
Stages in implementing advanced security for a user

Although the central Key Management Server is the sole definitive source of security keys within an organization the Key Management Server software should be installed on a server in each site. These installations can be thought of as secondary Key Management Servers. They don't allocate or control security keys, but allow local recipients to be enabled for advanced security by routing any security-related messages back to the primary Key Management Server for actioning.

All security-related operations such as credential generation and verification are channeled back to the central system where the central Key Management Server is running, so clearly it's important to carefully select the right server to take on this role. The central Key Management Server should be located on a system that has good network links and is able to undertake the load generated by security processes. In small organizations it's not normally a problem to determine which server should be nominated to act as the host for the central Key Management Server, but larger organizations need to look at how advanced security is going to be used in the organization before making the choice. Once the decision is made to implement advanced security and a suitable server nominated you should take steps to ensure some level of physical security for the server (see Figure 4.39). This implies that the server should not be easily accessible to users and that as few people as possible should be able to log-on to the system in a privileged mode.

Enabling advanced security

Before anyone can use the advanced security features of Exchange Server the system administrator must authorize or enable the user for these features. This process can be performed individually, or for a whole group of users at one time. Authorization can only be accomplished after the Key Management Server component is installed and running. Before examining the details of the steps taken to enable a user for advanced security, it's important to know how all the different security components fit together. Security components are divided between Exchange clients and the Key Management Server and are shown in Table 4.5.

Table 4.5 *Security components*

Location	Component	Use	Filename
Client	Security DLL	Contains code to sign/verify or encrypt and decrypt messages.	ETEXCH.DLL (16 bit) ETEXCH32.DLL (32 bit)
Server	System Attendant	Interacts with clients when advanced security is enabled. The System Attendant works with the Security DLL to store and manage key pairs as required by the system.	
	Key Management Server	Allows the System Administrator to use the Security property page to enable advanced security for users.	SECADMIN.DLL
	Key Management service	Accepts and actions requests from the Administrator program and the functions contained in the Key Management Security DLL.	
	Key Management database	A collection of files managed by the Key Management service. These files contain security information about clients.	\SECURITY\MGRENT directory
	Security DLL	Functions to enable the server to respond to security requests generated by clients.	SECKM.DLL

Once everything is installed you can begin to enable individuals or groups of users. As shown in Figure 4.40, enabling a user is a 4 stage process.

1. Temporary security credentials are requested for the user.
2. The credentials are provided to the user.
3. The credentials are used to enable advanced security from a client.
4. The security server recognizes that the credentials have been properly used by a client and allows the user to begin using advanced security.

Figure 4.40
Temporary security credentials

With the exception of mass generation of temporary security credentials using the SIMPORT.EXE program, the same process is repeated when users are enabled en masse. Let's look at each stage in a little more detail. Temporary credentials (sometimes called a token) are generated by selecting the security property page for a recipient from the administrator program and clicking on the 'Enable Advanced Security' button. The Key Management Server then proceeds to create temporary security credentials for the user and displays them to the system administrator, who should note the credentials down exactly as they are displayed. The credentials can be thought of as a password for the users to identify themselves to the security server during the later phases of enabling (see Figure 4.41). At the same time the public and private encryption keys are generated and stored in the security database on the server.

After the temporary credentials have been noted they must be passed by the system administrator to the relevant user. This should be done in a reasonably secure manner, preferably not by writing the password down on a slip of paper or yelling it across a crowded room. In small sites it's probably best for the administrator to visit the user and coach them through the remainder of the process. This isn't practical for large installations where the issuing of keys and their provision to users might fully occupy a system administrator for quite some time. Assuming that it takes an average of fifteen minutes to create the temporary credentials, note them down, visit the user, and enable security from the user's client, only four users can be processed in an hour, or 32 in an eight-hour day. Chasing users to enable security isn't a good use of a system administrator's time, so in this situation it is best for the administrator to concentrate on the task of generating the temporary credentials and noting them down before passing the credentials to one or more others, possibly users who have been nominated to help with this task, who will then visit users to pass on the credentials and help complete the whole process as quickly as possible.

Administrators in remote sites must make arrangements for credentials to be first generated and then passed over by an administrator in the site where the central Key Management Server is running. Credentials can then be passed out locally, again in as secure a manner as possible.

Figure 4.41
Enabling security

After receiving their temporary credentials each user then enables advanced security from a client by selecting the 'Security' property page from the *Tools.Options* menu option (Figure 4.41). The user must now type in the temporary security credential and provide a password of their own (which must be at least six characters long). This step generates the public and private key pair to be used for electronic signatures.

As mentioned earlier, the special security certificates generated for the user and the copy of the CA's own special certificate are written into a file with an .EPF[8] extension. This file is normally stored in the

---

8.   *EPF = Encrypted Password File*

Windows directory, for example: C:\WIN95\TONYREDM.EPF. The security file is encrypted using a CAST-64 algorithm to prevent unauthorized access. The security file must be available before encrypted messages can be read or sent.

Local availability of the .EPF file has implications for users who roam from workstation to workstation to read their mail. It is possible to copy the .EPF file to a floppy and point the client to the floppy when it attempts any security operations, and this is possibly the best way for roaming users to cope. Indeed, keeping the .EPF file on a floppy disk guarantees maximum security at the expense of relying on relatively fragile media. If people opt to use floppy disks to hold EPF files make sure they know that they need to have a copy available just in case problems occur.

After the user enables security from a client an encrypted message is automatically generated and sent back to the Key Management Server to indicate that the user has provided their credentials and a satisfactory password and wishes to begin using advanced security. This message contains the public signing key, which is in turn stored by the Key Management Server.

The Key Management Server checks the credentials and, if they are satisfactory, generates a message back to the user to inform them that they can now begin to use advanced security. The user receives the message from the 'Security Authority', the name that the Key Management Server represents itself by to users. This message includes some hidden data containing the encryption key pair that was earlier generated by the Key Management Server as well as the pair of X.509 certificates to use later on for signing and encrypting messages. A copy of the CA's X.509 certificate is also enclosed. Before the message can be read the user must provide the password they originally specified when they received the original enabling message. This step ensures that the same user is involved at all stages of the enabling procedure. If the password matches the encryption key pair is written into the .EPF file and once it is present the user can begin to encrypt and sign messages.

By default security certificates are valid for one year from the date of issue. As a user approaches the end of a certificate's validity the Key Management Server sends them a message to request whether the certificate should be updated for another year. This process continues from year to year unless the security administrator issues a certificate that is valid for a specific period.

Security keys can be recovered anytime after they have been issued. This would be in cases where users lose (or forget) their password or corrupt the security file on the PC. Another reason is because the users suspect, for one reason or another, that their password is compromised, possibly because they shared it with someone else on a temporary basis.

Along the same theme, security keys can be revoked by the administrator if any reason arises to believe that a user should not be able to use the features of advanced security. Revocation works by the server writing the number of a user's certificate into a revocation list maintained in the directory. Once a certificate has been added to the list no other user can encrypt a message for that user.

Using advanced security

After users are enabled for advanced security they can proceed to encrypt messages and attachments and apply digital signatures. Users can select to encrypt or sign every message by default, or elect to encrypt or sign a specific message. Encryption isn't much good if no one else is able to decrypt the message, so Exchange Server checks any message before attempting to encrypt it to determine whether the recipients will be able to decrypt the message. This process occurs just before the message is sent. If Exchange believes that even one recipient on a message will not be able to decrypt the message it will stop sending the message and notify the user, as shown in Figure 4.42. Digital signatures can be applied to messages sent to users who have not been enabled for advanced security.

Figure 4.42
Nonsecure recipients

Because recipients are checked to ensure that they will be able to decrypt messages you cannot encrypt messages when working off-line. You can create messages, set their security properties so that a message will be encrypted or digitally signed, and then save messages in an off-line folder. Whenever you next connect to Exchange Server the message recipients can be checked as normal and encryption applied.

Common reasons why Exchange will determine a user cannot receive encrypted messages include:

▶ They have not been enabled for advanced security
▶ The message must pass through a gateway before it can be delivered to the recipient. In general any attempt to get encrypted information through a gateway fails.

Encrypted messages or those bearing digital signatures are indicated by using a different icon when messages are shown in a folder (Figure 4.43). The lock icon indicates that a message is encrypted, while the pen icon means that it has been digitally signed.

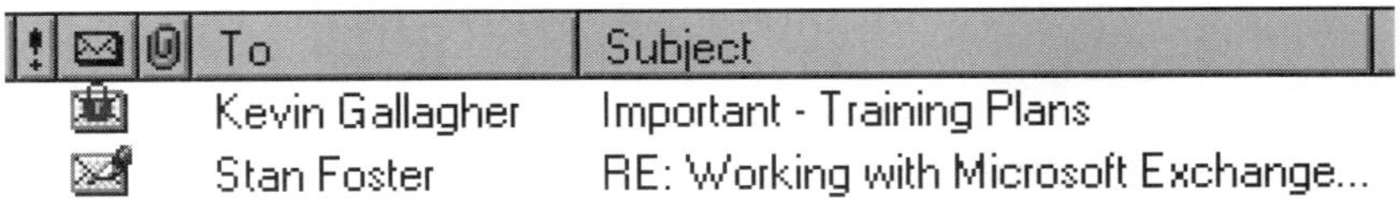

Figure 4.43 *Icons for signed and encrypted messages*

!	✉	📎	To	Subject
			Kevin Gallagher	Important - Training Plans
			Stan Foster	RE: Working with Microsoft Exchange...

Location of security objects

We've been through a lot of fairly complicated and interlinked structures that work together to allow someone to encrypt or sign messages. Table 4.6 describes the location of each security object after advanced security has been enabled for a user. As you can see, there are four main locations.

Table 4.6 *Location of security objects*

	X.509 certificate	Key Management Security database	User's personal EPF file	Exchange Directory Store
User's directory name (mail address)	✓			
Signing certificate			✓	
Encryption certificate			✓	✓
Private encryption key		✓	✓	
Private signing key			✓	
Public encryption key	✓			
Public signing key	✓	✓		
Certificate expiration date	✓			
Unique certificate number	✓			
CA signature	✓			
CA directory name (mail address)	✓			

Making a decision about advanced security

Advanced security is one of those features that seems awfully attractive on the surface, so why won't it be immediately implemented in all organizations that operate Exchange Server? Table 4.7 lists some of the advantages and disadvantages of advanced security.

Table 4.7 *Advantages and disadvantages of advanced security*

Advantages	Disadvantages
Users can apply digital signatures to messages so that the messages cannot be repudiated.	A lot of work is imposed on system administrators to generate, distribute, and manage security credentials.
Users can encrypt messages before they are sent, and decrypt messages received from other users.	Encrypted messages can only be sent to other recipients who are 'security enabled'.
Encrypted messages can only be accessed when a user's personal security password is provided, even if another user's mailbox is accessed by a privileged user.	The .EPF file must be physically available before messages can be decrypted.

System administration workload is the biggest issue influencing the decision whether to implement advanced security. Small organizations or those able to dedicate a person to fill the role of security administrator won't experience too many problems handling the work, but the same cannot be said for larger sites or organizations. Before making a decision consider:

- Who is going to act as the security administrator?
- Who is going to be the back-up to the security administrator to handle their work when they are on vacation or sick?
- What is the maximum number for users in the organization that are going to be security enabled?
- Where are these users located? How and when are they going to be enabled for advanced security? How are the initial credentials going to be provided to users, especially users remote from the security administrator?
- How will roaming users access their .EPF files as they move from workstation to workstation?
- What server is best to act as the Key Management Server? Has it an appropriate hardware configuration to handle the expected load? Is it capable of providing a highly available service to users?

- How physically secure is the chosen Key Management Server? Where is it located and who has access to it?
- When will the security data used by Key Management Server be backed up? Is this operation included in regular system maintenance activities?

Do not attempt to enable advanced security unless you are happy with the answers to these questions. Cleaning up a bad security implementation and starting over again will require a lot of work and co-operation from users, especially when new credentials have to be issued or a new, different Key Management Server installed. In the latter case users won't be able to read any messages encrypted with credentials issued by the original Key Management Server, proving the point that it's very important to get your security implementation right first time.

If you decide that you can't implement advanced security it is still possible to protect sensitive information. For example, it is possible to use application-specific password protection for documents and spreadsheets. Users can set their own passwords to protect items stored in their private folders and shared passwords can be determined and used by groups who want an extra layer of protection for confidential information in public folders. I know of quite a number of installations who have opted to protect information in this manner. It's certainly not an infallible scheme, but it is simple to operate and is enough to stop casual unauthorized browsing through data.

5

Connecting Exchange Server

Exchange connectors

A messaging system that's only able to communicate internally or with other systems of the same kind isn't much use in today's heterogeneous world. This chapter reviews the methods an Exchange server can use to connect to other electronic messaging systems.

Connectors are the components that provide links between the Exchange MTA and other messaging systems, normally over an intermediate network connection. Two types of connectors exist – site connectors and external connectors. Remember that the basic Exchange server only includes the Microsoft Mail connector and you need to either purchase the Enterprise edition of Exchange or individual copies of the Internet, X.400, or site connectors as required by your installation.

As the name implies, site connectors are used to send messages between one Exchange site and another within a single organization. In fact, four different connectors can be used to link sites together:

- Direct site connector
- X.400 connector
- Internet Mail connector
- Dynamic Remote Access (RAS) connector

Direct site connectors operate through Remote Procedure Calls (RPCs) between the connected sites. This is the preferred connection in a LAN environment or when a permanent high-speed connection exists between two sites. The dynamic connector depends on Windows NT Remote Access Server and it is used when a dial-up connection is made between two sites to send mail to each other. The connection between small branch offices where a single server is located for a small group of users and a larger central department is a good example of the type of situation where a RAS connector might be used.

Naturally you'll need to ensure that RAS is configured on the servers involved in the transactions, and provide telephone lines and modems to make the physical connections.

In addition to standard asynchronous connections made over the telephone RAS can also be used over X.25 links. X.25 is a little more complex because you have to install an X.25 card and software in the computers that will talk together. Currently the only X.25 card and software supported by Windows NT are provided by Eicon Technologies. Eicon have one- and four-port X.25 cards available. These cards work with version 3 (release 2 or 3) of the Eicon X.25 software.

Apart from the options available to connect sites, Exchange servers are able to send messages to each other over X.400 and SMTP connectors, even when the systems are in the same Exchange organization. Conceptually the primary function for X.400 and SMTP connectors can be viewed as to exchange messages with non-Exchange mail systems. In reality these connectors are going to get far more use in linking Exchange servers together. They are also a useful fall-back option for situations where it may be more convenient to piggy-back onto an existing corporate messaging infrastructure than to establish one especially for Exchange. For example, if an SMTP messaging backbone is already operational and used to tie together all the different systems used within an enterprise, the best course of action might be to use the Internet mail connector to send messages across the SMTP backbone instead of site connectors.

Reaching outside the organization, the major external connectors provided with the enterprise edition of Exchange Server are:

- Microsoft Mail
- X.400
- Internet (SMTP)

The Microsoft Mail connector facilitates backwards connectivity with the messaging system that's replaced by Exchange. This is important not only because the installed base of Microsoft Mail systems are a rich vein of opportunity for the initial deployments of Exchange, but also because the migration period from one messaging system to another often covers quite a long time, especially in larger organizations. The Microsoft Mail connector also allows installations to continue using Microsoft Mail gateways to other mail systems that might previously have been installed.

The other two basic connectors are also important, but in a slightly different way. Unlike Microsoft Mail, whose development was totally under the control of Microsoft, X.400 and SMTP offer the promise of openness in the electronic messaging world, and most international or large-scale organizations will use one or the other, or even both methods to tie different organizational units or sites together. Without easy and out-of-the-box connectivity to X.400 and SMTP Exchange would face a much harder struggle for general acceptance in corporate environments. Equipped with the ability to connect over both X.400 and SMTP Exchange is in a much stronger position, if only because of the fact that many other messaging systems require you to purchase additional components or gateways before they can connect in a similar manner.

While SMTP and X.400 now represent the generally accepted methods for widespread electronic mail, this hasn't always been the case. Corporations have been deploying electronic mail since the start of the 1980s, and there's an often bewildering array of systems in operation today. Whereas many of the older systems might be tagged with the 'legacy' label and they might be scheduled for replacement by a newer system like Exchange in the long term a connectivity need still exists. A set of add-on connectors are therefore available and must be purchased and installed separately.

Optional connectors

The Exchange MTA is responsible for delivering all messages sent to recipients who do not reside on the originating server. This task includes communication with other Exchange servers over all types of site connectors, X.400 MTAs, and gateways to other messaging systems. As illustrated in Figure 5.1, the MTA does an excellent job as a single point of contact or message switch for messages arriving into the server from many different sources. The clearly defined nature of the connection engine allows third parties to build new connectors and then introduce them to the MTA in a very clean manner. Once installed a connector takes care of accepting messages from a particular source before providing them to the MTA for eventual delivery to user mailboxes. The process of acceptance may involve format translation before messages can be given to the MTA. For example, the Internet Mail Connector converts newly arrived messages from SMTP/MIME format to the internal format used by Exchange. In much the same way outgoing messages may also require conversion by a connector before they are handed over to an external messaging system.

The list of optional add-on connectors is expanding all the time. Check with your local Microsoft office or Microsoft Solution Provider for the current list. At the time of writing the set includes connectors for:

- AT&T Mail

- IBM SNADS (System Network Architecture Distribution System)
- IBM PROFS and OfficeVision
- MCI Mail
- MHS (Message Handling System)

Some of the connectors are very specific both in terms of geographic relevance and mail systems that are supported. AT&T Mail and MCI Mail are, for instance, not generally available or used outside the United States, so European and Asian sites probably won't be interested in them.

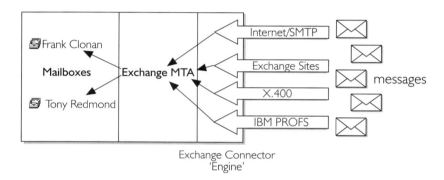

Figure 5.1 *The Exchange MTA acting as a message switch or connection engine*

Some connectors are designed to help in the transition from certain messaging systems to Exchange. The connectors for IBM PROFS, OfficeVision, and SNADS are good examples of this type. PROFS and SNADS were both popular mainframe-based electronic mail systems that were deployed in many 'true blue' sites in the 1980s, but their popularity waned as minicomputer and then PC LAN-based mail systems took over as mainframe computers were downsized. PROFS is often used as a sort of lowest common denominator for connecting different mail systems together. For example, you can connect Lotus Notes mail into a Soft*Switch gateway and connect via the gateway to other systems. In this example the Lotus Notes messages, and the users who generate the messages, appear to be PROFS messages and users. PROFS and SNADS are no longer sold or supported by IBM so corporations using these systems need to consider their migration path. Microsoft would very much like that migration path to lead to Exchange Server, whereas I suspect IBM might prefer to move people to OfficeVision (based on AS/400 computers rather than mainframes) or even Lotus Notes. The availability of connectors for PROFS and SNADS 'helps' people to consider Exchange Server as a more than viable migration option.

MHS-type electronic mail systems represent the other end of the spectrum to the large corporation PROFS deployments. MHS is quite a simple system which is based on file sharing, much like Microsoft Mail. As such it suffers from the same type of architectural and scaleability weaknesses that afflict Microsoft Mail and is therefore a prime candidate to evolve towards Exchange Server. Again there's an element of competition here and I assume that Microsoft has quite deliberately chosen to make the MHS connector available to place pressure on users of Novell NetWare systems, the major proponent of MHS mail. Apart from the argument about what electronic mail system to use, there's an underlying battle between Windows NT and Novell NetWare, a battle that Windows NT appears to be slowly winning in the marketplace. The logic of 'if you're going to move to a better mail system, why not upgrade your shared file and print services as well?' plays to the strengths of the Exchange/Windows NT combination very well.

Apart from the connectors focused purely on the messaging arena, many connectors are available for FAX, but alas, not for its telematics counterpart, telex. It's undeniable that FAX has largely taken over from telex in most situations, but telex is still important in certain circumstances. Directives to airlines to carry out preventative aircraft maintenance operations are usually, if not always, sent by telex because of its unique status as a type of document accepted in legal disputes.

What gets sent, where, and how?

When Exchange sees that a message has been sent to external recipients it passes the message to the MTA to begin a process called message routing, or the determination of how that message is going to be delivered to its recipients. Message routing requires the MTA to check what connectors are capable of getting the message to a recipient as well at what cost, no matter how many connectors the message must pass through en route to its final destination(s). The calculation of cost is based on figures entered by system administrators when connectors are added to an Exchange server.

The final calculation is a cumulative figure composed of the cost required to navigate from connector to connector on different Exchange servers. The simplest cost to determine is, of course, when a direct connection is made from one site to another.

Connectors are configured using the Exchange Administration program. The two most important items specified when a connector is configured are:

- *Address Space:* literally, the types of mail addresses that can be handled by the connector. Directory replication ensures that all servers within an organization know about all the connectors installed on other servers. Thus, the MTA is able to consider all connectors for potential message dispatch. The process of reviewing all possible connectors for message delivery is known as selection.
- *Connected Sites:* the list of sites to which mail can be sent through the connector

After a connector is configured the remote routing table for the server is rebuilt in order to make the new connector active. In effect this includes the new connector in the site address space so that the connector can be assessed and possibly used whenever the MTA reviews the addresses on an outgoing or incoming message. An address for the new connector is also added to each user record in the directory so that messages arriving via the connector can be delivered correctly. For example, the SMTP type address is used to indicate user addresses that the Internet Mail Connector should handle. The set of sites serviced by the connector can be defined by the administrator when the connector is configured.

The information relating to connectors is stored in the configuration container and is replicated by the directory service to adjacent sites. The system attendant and MTA work together to create a routing table known as the Gateway Address Routing Table (GWART) to use when routing messages. Each server maintains its own GWART. You can think of the GWART as a set of address information relating to all possible routes that can be used to deliver messages.

The GWART is stored in the directory and can be viewed through the Routing property page of the Site Addressing object (see Figure 5.2). The routing table is also available as a simple text file in the \EXCHANGE\MTADATA directory. Two copies are kept:

- GWART0.MTA – the current routing table
- GWART1.MTA – the routing table prior to the last change

These text files are created each time a change is made to the routing table. You can force Exchange to recreate the routing table by pressing the 'Recalculate Routing' command button (Figure 5.2); otherwise the routing table is rebuilt automatically at scheduled times. Connectors are installed on specific servers, but every server in a site needs to know how to route messages as a whole rather than individual cases. Normally one server in each site takes care of the task of rebuilding the routing table.

In large sites supporting multiple connectors a rebuild can be a fairly intensive exercise, certainly not one to allocate to a server supporting many hundreds of users, or one that's scheduled to occur at 9 a.m., just as all the users log-on and begin reading their mail. Rebuilding the routing table involves a scan through the address spaces from each server within the site and the connectors installed on all servers. The resulting routing table is then distributed throughout the site via the directory, the same mechanism used to update other sites within the organization. Depending on how directory entries are replicated throughout your organization it may take some time before all servers are made aware that a new connector has been added or a change (such as an update for the routing cost of a connector) been made.

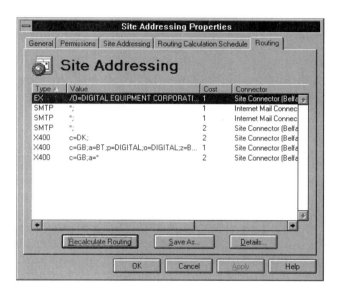

Figure 5.2 *Site Address Space*

As you can see from the Site Addressing properties illustrated in Figure 5.2, the routing table contains a subset of complete addresses. In other words, the table contains only the necessary elements to identify the route that a message should take. The table is divided into three major types of addresses:

1. Type 'EX': These entries refer to native format Exchange Server addresses (distinguished names) and relate to site connectors. The illustration shows a single 'EX' entry corresponding to a single site connector.

2. Type 'DDA' (Domain Defined Attribute): These entries refer to the gateways and connectors used to send messages to custom

recipients. The most common examples are 'MS' (Microsoft Mail Connector) and 'SMTP' (Internet Mail Connector).

3. Type: 'X400' (X.400 Originator/Recipient): These entries relate to X.400 connections to either other Exchange servers (site X.400 connectors) or to foreign X.400 MTAs. As you can see from the screen shot, three X.400 O/R addresses are specified for two different countries (DK = Denmark, GB = Great Britain).

Each line in the routing table corresponds to a route that the MTA can take to deliver a message.

Expanding distribution lists

Before we get to the details of how a message is routed by the MTA to its ultimate destination it's important to understand that the MTA must first expand the contents of any distribution lists in the message recipients. An Exchange distribution list may not be a simple object. It can contain addresses for mailboxes, custom recipients, public folders, and other distribution lists. The process of expansion must be performed recursively until all lists, including those nested within any original distribution lists, are conclusively resolved.

Distribution lists are not resolved when a message is sent by a client. At this stage the message is passed, without interference, from the client to the private information store. It is after the MTA receives the message from the private information store that any distribution list expansion occurs. The rule therefore is if a message contains a distribution list it is always sent to the MTA for resolution, even if the distribution list only contains local mailboxes. For this reason the MTA service must always be active, even on servers that aren't connected to anything else.

Message routing algorithm

The following algorithm is used by the MTA to decide how a message can be delivered to an external recipient.

- According to the contents of the GWART, what connectors are available? Which of the active connectors on this system can handle the message?
- The retry count should not have exceeded for any connector being considered. A check is performed to ensure that the maximum number of retries for a message has not been exceeded. This ensures that a message is returned with an 'undeliverable' status to a user within a reasonable time after sending. Note that retry counts cannot be specified for site connectors, so it's

Exchange connectors

possible for messages to stay in a site connector queue being retried constantly until they expire after a few days, at which time they'll be returned to the originator as undeliverable.

- Scan for active connectors. Which of the connectors that are able to process the message are active on the system right now? Dynamic RAS or X.400 connectors often operate only at specific times during the day. If two routes are available and only one is active (albeit even apparently at a higher cost), then it's logical to dispatch messages via the active route. The valid states for connectors are listed in Table 5.1:

Table 5.1 *Connector states*

Connector status	Meaning
Active now	The connector is currently active and is available to process messages. Active connectors are always selected first by the MTA. Standard site connectors, the Internet Mail Connector, and the Microsoft Mail Connector do not have activation schedules. Thus, they are always 'Active Now'.
Will become active in the future	The connector is scheduled to become available sometime in the future. If several connectors are suitable and in this state the MTA selects the one scheduled to become active first.
Never	The connector is unable to make connections at present. This state might arise when a connector is temporarily disabled.
Remote initiated	The connector cannot be started locally. Instead, its use is always initiated by a remote MTA.

- Lowest retry count. Which of the active connectors have the lowest retry count? In other words, which connector is most likely to be able to dispatch the message first time around? The initial check was to ensure that the message retry count had not reached its maximum value; this check is to determine which connector has been attempted the least number of times.
- Not currently trying. A check is performed to ensure that the message isn't currently being processed by an active connector.
- Lowest cost. Given all else, if two or more connectors are available, which connector can transmit the message at lowest cost? We'll discuss how costs are allocated to connectors later on in this chapter.
- Local over remote. If a local connector is available to handle the message, send it locally rather than attempting to use a remote connector.

Hopefully a suitable connector is determined at the conclusion of these steps and the message can be sent on its way. It may well be that several connectors present themselves as willing and able to dispatch the message, and if so, the MTA attempts to balance the connection load by making a random selection from the set of suitable connectors.

After all that, if a message is returned immediately or very soon after it is sent it's a good indication that the message is either badly addressed or the address space for the target connector is misdefined. The MTA always tries to reroute a message immediately if it encounters a failure on its first attempt. If the message cannot be rerouted it will remain in the MTA queue for the relevant connector and have its retry count incremented by one. The properties of the Site MTA object define the default retry interval (normally 600 seconds – 10 minutes), and the maximum number of retries. These properties are known as the 'Open Interval' and 'Max Open Retries' respectively.

If the message exceeds the maximum number of retries it will be returned to its originator wrapped in a nondelivery notification. The user can then, if he or she wishes, click on the 'Send Again' command button to see whether the message can get through. It may well be, for instance, that a connector which depends on a specific network link is unavailable because of hardware or other problems. In this case lots of nondelivery notifications can be generated, causing considerable frustration to users and lots of calls for the help desk. The sole silver lining in this particular cloud is that the useful 'Send Again' command button on the nondelivery notification gives users a chance to send the message again with little difficulty.

Connector licensing

From a management perspective it's important to realize that you don't need to install and configure connectors on every server or even within every site. As long as the connector is configured properly and appears in the address space the MTA will be able to route messages to the connector. For example, if you have ten Exchange servers in three sites and you want to send messages via X.400 and SMTP you could install the following:

- One server to handle all external messages. This server is configured with the Internet Mail Connector and X.400 connector.
- Three servers configured with site connectors. These servers act as the bridgehead servers for the three sites within the organization and are responsible for passing messages between the different sites. We'll discuss what 'bridgehead' means in a little while.
- Six servers which act as pure messaging or public folder servers.

In this instance all messages for X.400 and SMTP recipients are routed to the server where these connectors are configured and operational. No other servers are able to directly send messages to X.400 or SMTP recipients, but all servers are aware that the X.400 and IMC connectors are available and are able to route messages via these connectors. Because Microsoft license connectors on a per server basis it therefore follows that all 10 servers must be licensed to use the connectors installed within the organization. You could create a mix and match license patchwork from 10 licenses for Exchange Server along with 10 licenses for each connector, but it's easier and more convenient (and possibly cheaper, depending on the prices pertaining in your country) to purchase 10 copies of the Exchange Enterprise Edition because it contains everything you need.

Maintaining the Message Transfer Agent and connectors

While the Exchange MTA and its associated connectors are usually very reliable and self-maintaining it is necessary to keep a watchful eye on them just to make sure that messages are flowing at a regular and predictable rate. The easiest way to check message flow is to select the queues property page for the Message Transfer Agent and then view the list of queues and the number of messages in each queue as shown in Figure 5.3.

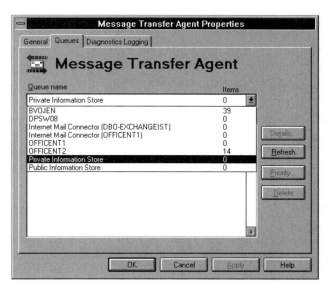

Figure 5.3
Viewing MTA queues

Your own knowledge of a connector and its normal traffic pattern will tell you whether an abnormal number of messages are in the queue. Clearly the best case is to have zero or very few messages in each queue because this indicates that no delay is being experienced in transmission. If you see that a number of messages have built up for a connector consider whether any unusual activity has recently taken place on your server which might have generated a large number of messages. For example, these activities can generate many messages for a connector:

- Moving public folders from one server to another.
- Adding or amending a large amount of information stored in public folders.
- Modifying the contents of the directory by adding, changing, or deleting recipients.
- Importing or synchronizing directory entries from another messaging system.
- Unblocking a connection to another messaging system which results in a large number of messages being delivered to a bridgehead server.

Taking the screenshot in Figure 5.3 as an example, we can see that 39 messages are queued for BVOJEN and 14 for OFFICENT2. Both of these are servers, one located in a remote site (BVOJEN), the other in the local site (OFFICENT2). You should know what's happening with all local servers so it's the first and easiest problem to investigate. In this case the answer was easy – the server was off-line for hardware maintenance, but there can be more problematic situations to resolve such as a server failing due to hardware or power problems. Monitoring queues helps to identify these situations by forcing system administrators to ask questions as to why queues should be building up for a local server.

The BVOJEN situation is a little harder to resolve because the server is remote. First we must know the type of connector used to link our site with BVOJEN. Knowledge of the Exchange environment (sites and servers) should provide the answer. In this case BVOJEN acts as the bridgehead server for the Belfast site and it is connected with a site connector.

The next step is to determine whether the server is operational and whether the necessary Exchange services are running. Link and server monitors (see Chapter 8) help by revealing whether a network connection can be made to a server (link monitor) as well as the Exchange and other Windows NT services that are currently running (server monitor). If you haven't already created and implemented some monitors you should do so now and review the results as soon as they are obtained. Assuming that the server in question is running and the MTA is active on the server you should then review the contents of the queue to see if you can determine why so many messages are there.

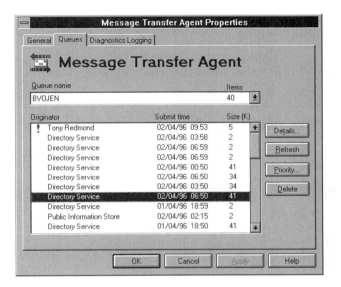

Figure 5.4
Viewing the queue contents for a connector

Figure 5.4 illustrates the beginning of the BVOJEN queue. The contents are ordered in message priority (High/Medium/Low) sequence with interpersonal messages scattered among the messages generated by background system activities. You'll find messages from the Directory Service, the Public Information Store and the System Attendant, reflecting the messages sent to replicate information between servers. The order of messages in the queue shown in Figure 5.4 looks a little strange at first glance. Why, for instance, is there a message generated by the Directory Service at 18:50 on April 1 right at the bottom of the list when messages generated by the same service throughout April 2 are at the top? The reason is simple: messages move up and down within the queue as attempts are made to send them. As problems have clearly occurred sending messages to the BVOJEN server over a period of days the messages from different days have become intermingled. You can manually intervene if you like by giving messages different priorities, but in most cases it is easier to let the Exchange MTA deal with the messages in the order they are presented.

I prefer to give interpersonal messages most importance, so the first step I take when dealing with a blocked queue is to immediately increase the priority of all interpersonal messages to 'High'. This action forces interpersonal messages to the top of the queue and makes sure that they will be sent first when the block is released. The logic behind this attitude is simple. Users complain when they receive nondelivery notifications, but the system components are much more patient and are content to wait for their messages to get through eventually.

The internal ordering of the queues also appears to give large messages a slightly higher priority than small messages. Once I've bumped all the interpersonal messages to the top of the queue I then like to move the small messages forward, the only reason being to clear the queue faster (at least on the surface). If the queue doesn't start to go down after all of this it's time to stop and restart the MTA on the target server, or perhaps restart the MTA on your server if lots of different queues are backing up. Restarting an MTA forces an internal reset and may clear out a problem that you can't see through the GUI. In this instance the problem wasn't connected to Exchange Server at all. The network link between the two sites had become saturated because some large software kits were being copied from one computer to another. This goes to prove that all potential reasons must be considered when problem solving.

The MTA sliding window

A 'sliding window' protocol is used by the MTA to transfer messages to other MTAs or gateways. This means that the MTA sends a certain amount of data, waits for an acknowledgment that the data has been received correctly, and then proceeds to send more data, continuing the process until the whole message is transferred. For comparison, many other messaging systems attempt to send complete messages as single entities, an approach that delivers satisfactory results with small to medium messages. Problems can occur when larger messages are sent, especially with network links that aren't very reliable. Given that the average message size continues to grow due to the influence of large and complex attachments the sliding window protocol is a reasonable solution for a messaging system that is designed to cope easily with large messages.

System administrators can influence the sliding window by setting a number of properties for the Site MTA (using the Advanced page). The important properties are:

- *Checkpoint size* – the amount of message data to send before the MTA inserts a checkpoint. The default is 30Kb.
- *Recovery time-out* – the amount of time after an error occurs before the MTA will wait for a reconnection. If the connection cannot be reestablished the message fails and is returned to the queue. The default is 60 seconds.

Maintaining the Message Transfer Agent and connectors

▶ *Window size* – the number of checkpoints that can remain unacknowledged before the MTA will suspend data transfer. The default is 5.

In most instances the default values are appropriate and should only be changed if you suspect that the MTA is unable to process messages in a satisfactory manner. For example, if you suspect that the network is experiencing some problems that are causing messages to fail (evidence of this would be provided by a queue building up for a connector that doesn't normally have a queue of more than a few messages), then you might reduce the window size from 5 to 2 in order to force the MTA to send less data before an acknowledgment is received. Reducing the checkpoint size from 30Kb to 10Kb is another step that could be taken in a situation where network problems are being experienced.

MTA data files

If you browse through the \EXCHANGE\MTADATA directory you'll come across some data files named DB000001.DAT, DB000002.DAT, and so on. These files are used by the MTA for items such as message queues, internal indexes used by the MTA, and temporary storage of mail messages en route through the MTA.

The installation process creates an initial set of 35 data files which are required to initiate MTA processing. As processing proceeds the set of files changes with the demand placed on the MTA. The number of files is influenced by the number of messages in the queues or other work in progress, but you shouldn't ever see more than 50 files or so in the directory.

The MTA creates additional data files as required. Because the files are all used for internal processing no one can be sure as to the exact contents or use of any particular data file. It is therefore very unwise to take the chance of deleting any of the data files. You might be deleting a message, or a connector queue, or something else needed by the MTA. In much the same way as the information store transaction logs, leave these files alone and let Exchange take care of them.

The MTACHECK utility

Corrupt data files or messages can cause the MTA to stop processing or simply refuse to start. The \EXCHANGE\BIN\MTACHECK utility is provided to help rectify the situation by reviewing the internal structures used by the MTA and make any changes required.

The MTACHECK utility:

▶ Checks the consistency of the MTA queues.

- Checks the integrity of all of the objects used by the MTA.
- Deletes any objects MTACHECK believes to be corrupt. Hopefully it is the removal of these objects that allows the MTA to restart.

Two command line switches are provided:

- /v instructs MTACHECK to run in verbose mode. Lots of detailed information is output as each object is processed.
- /f allows you to specify a file into which details of all of the actions performed by the utility will be logged.

The normal course is to run MTACHECK only in situations when problems occur with the MTA. You can run MTACHECK at any time, just to see what it does. Before running MTACHECK remember to shut the MTA service down so as to prevent any possible contention between normal processing and the potential fixes made by MTACHECK.

General notes on Exchange connectors

All external connectors run as multithreaded processes on a Windows NT computer. You can decide to run all of the connectors on a single computer within your organization, but you must consider the fact that each connector imposes a certain processing load on the system and attempting to push too much work through a single place may create potential messaging bottlenecks. All of the connectors are registered as entries within the Exchange directory, so once a connector is installed and active it becomes available to any user within the organization. This poses some interesting questions, especially with systems distributed internationally.

Do you, for example, want to have everyone sending messages to external bodies worldwide through a single SMTP or X.400 connector? Given the volume of messages that might be sent to recipients in the Internet this might not be a smart idea. Allowing users based in England to send faxes generated by a connector in Germany may not be convenient and might generate higher telecommunications charges. On the other hand, you might decide to take advantage of lower telecommunications charges in a certain country and route all fax traffic out through that country, but would this be legal? Interesting questions, and of course you can configure the different connectors to take account of these issues, but it's amazing how many people never even pause to think.

An implementation plan will ideally clearly identify the set of external communications required by an organization and propose how those connections can be made by Exchange. If you are running an electronic mail system now you'll be able to extract much useful information from whatever connections are already operational, including the volume of messages that are sent and received over a set period. It's better if you have statistics for message traffic over an extended period, ideally taken at a regular interval such as weekly or monthly as these statistics will allow you to see whether volume is growing or declining, and the rate at which the increase or decrease is occurring.

Once you know what connections are needed and the volume that each connection will support (plus a suitable percentage increase to accommodate growth for the first year of operation) you can proceed to plan where the connectors will be installed. Remember to take the network overhead necessary to transport messages to connectors when you look for the correct system to host connectors. The connector software is relatively low-cost so don't try to save too much on expenditure if you're going to impact the service delivered to users.

The bridgehead concept

When you read the Exchange documentation you may come across the term 'bridgehead' and wonder what it means. A bridgehead server is a system within a site that is nominated to operate as a point of connectivity between that site and either another site or a foreign mail system. The bridgehead server acts as a target for other sites or gateways to transmit messages to.

For example, if you had a site with three servers and wanted to establish a connection to the Internet it wouldn't make sense to install and configure the IMC on all three servers. Apart from anything else, an extra cost is incurred for each copy of the IMC. In this situation the best idea is to nominate one of the servers to act as the bridgehead between the site and the Internet and install the IMC on that server. Because of the extra processing performed to send and receive messages to and from another system it is normal to select the system with the best configuration to act as the bridgehead.

Avoiding bottlenecks

Another fact to take into account is that anywhere that connections or gateways exist between one system and another represents a potential bottleneck. Exchange is designed to handle many thousands of messages per hour, but achieving a high rate of throughput relies on optimal transmission paths and a low or nil requirement to convert messages from one format to another. No gateway between systems can be regarded as optimal because electronic mail systems can differ in so many ways, leading to a situation where it is inevitable that some 'fix-up' processing has to be performed before a message can be transmitted from or to Exchange Server. Even the Microsoft Mail connector has to convert messages from MS-Mail format to MAPI and vice versa.

If the network link used by a connector is slow and the messages volume passing through the connector is large you run the risk that queues of messages will build up waiting to get through the connector. Installing a heavily used connector on a server that has good network links but is overloaded by other processing is also a good recipe for bottlenecks. Even with properly configured systems fast connections can be overwhelmed by heavy message volume, and a particular danger time is during a migration from one system to another when connections are used to bridge the gap between the old electronic mail system and Exchange. During migration periods you may have to install and operate several different connectors until the bulk of users have made the transition to Exchange, at which time the message volume should decrease.

Configuring and operating a site connector

Before engaging in the discussion as to how to select and configure a connector between two sites in the same Exchange organization it's important to know the type of data that will flow through the connector. It's also good to know which Exchange components are responsible for the generation and transmission of the data. Figure 5.5 illustrates a site connection. As you can see, the MTA in the bridgehead server in each site communicates with its partner MTA to exchange data in the form of messages.

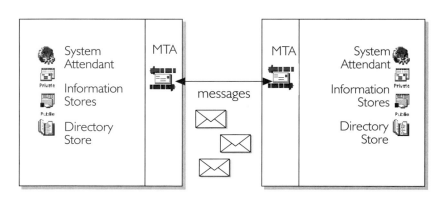

Figure 5.5
Messages sent between Exchange sites

Configuring and operating a site connector

It's easy to see that interpersonal messages flow from the private information store to the MTA for onward transmission. You might also recall that public folder and directory replication is accomplished via messages too. Table 5.2 lists the major types of messages that flow across a link between sites. If you use Directory Synchronization (DX) then messages will also be generated through this service.

Table 5.2 *Messages exchanged between sites*

Type of data	Component generating the messages
Mail messages generated by users	Private Information Store
Replication of changes and additions to objects placed into public folders	Public Information Store
Replication of the public folder hierarchy	Public Information Store
Replication of changes and additions to the Exchange directory store	Exchange Directory Service
Link Monitor test messages	System Attendant (via the Private Information Store)

Note that within a single standalone site composed of a number of different servers the MTA does not handle messages for the directory store. The directory service processes its own messages in this case.

The options to connect sites

The full list of connectors capable of linking sites together has already been discussed – starting on page 219. To recall, you can select from the site connector itself, the X.400 connector, IMC, and dynamic RAS. Which of these should you use? Table 5.3 lists some common requirements along with an appropriate solution.

The standard site connector is generally the fastest in transmitting information, as long as the network link between the servers in each site is capable of handling RPCs in a reliable manner. The connector is relatively simple in comparison to the X.400 connector, so there is less overhead when messages are processed, and the connector performs at anything up to 20% faster than an X.400 or IMC equivalent, both of which require messages to be converted into a different format before transmission.

The standard site connector is also able to transmit to several servers within a site whereas the X.400 connector is restricted to a single named server. On the other hand, the X.400 or IMC connectors are more resilient when it comes to dealing with network connections that are unreliable from time to time. Another advantage that can be gained from the X.400 or IMC connectors is that you're able to schedule the times when messages are transferred, something that's just not possible with the standard connector. Because the functionality of the two connectors is so close (apart from delivery and read receipt notifications) selecting the IMC or X.400 for a site connector often comes down to the question of which messaging standard do you prefer?

Table 5.3 *Selecting a connector to link sites*

Situation	Select
▪ Very reliable network links between the sites connected by networks capable of supporting RPCs (named pipes, NetBIOS, Windows Sockets)	Site connector
▪ TCP/IP, TP4 or X.25 connectivity available between bridgehead servers. ▪ Requirement to schedule message exchange at particular times ▪ Best ability to utilize low bandwidth. ▪ Requirement to restrict message size	X.400 connector or IMC
▪ Dial-up connectivity when no permanent LAN/WAN connection is available	Dynamic RAS

The dynamic RAS connector comes into its own and beats everything else when a telephone connection is all that's available and is the most appropriate connection in cases such as small or distant offices or when you don't want to invest in a network just for messaging.

It is possible to configure multiple connectors for each site. A cost is allocated to each connector to tell Exchange which connector should be used as the default link. Let's assume that you have a site connector and an X.400 connector established to link the Dublin and Belfast sites. The site connector has a cost value of 1 whereas the X.400 connector has a cost of 50. In the normal course of events messages will always be sent via the site connector, but if any problems occur with the site connector messages can be rerouted via X.400. If you give the two connectors the same cost Exchange will attempt to balance the load of messages transmitted across each connector. Load balancing through multiple connectors enables a degree of fault tolerance within the messaging network. If one connector fails the other will continue transmitting messages until its companion resumes.

A connector can be given a maximum cost of 100, but this has a special meaning in that Exchange will only use it as a very last resort when no other connector is available.

Remember that the replication of organizational information means that sites know about the connections existing between other sites. You may have no control over the connectors established by other system administrators or the cost allocated to these connectors. It's possible to get into strange situations with cost values because they are cumulative. In other words, if messages have to pass through one site to get to another the cost of each link is added to form a cost for the overall route. It may well be that a direct route between two sites is created with a cost of 10, but Exchange 'discovers' that it is possible to route messages via an intermediate site using a connector with cost 5 and another (from the intermediate site to the target site) of cost 4, resulting in an overall cost of 9, lower than the direct and preferred route. Clearly this points to a need to understand the connections that exist within an organization and not to introduce new connections without being aware of the potential impact on other sites. Hopefully if you look after the interest of other sites, their administrators will look after yours!

It is possible to attribute different costs to different servers within a site when using the site connector. The normal course of events is to transmit messages to a bridgehead server in each site, but it's also possible to seek to balance the load across multiple servers in the same way that you'd try to balance the connectivity load across multiple connectors.

Making the connection

When a server transfers messages to a remote server in another site, the MTA must bind to the remote MTA using the Exchange service account. It is possible to use different service accounts in both sites, as long as the accounts in each site possess the necessary permissions to bind to the remote MTA, but it's much easier and convenient to use the same service account in both sites.

As described in Chapter 2, you must establish a Windows NT trust relationship between the communicating domains if the sites being connected reside in different Windows NT domains. The rule here is that the domain for the site being connected to must trust the site making the connection. If different accounts have been set up for Exchange in the two Windows NT domains it is necessary to use the property pages of the site connector to instruct Exchange that a specific service account should be used to connect to the remote site. You'll have to provide a password for the account in most cases.

In effect you're telling the Exchange MTA to connect to the remote site using a different account than that used for normal day to day administrative operations. Think of this as similar functionality to the

Connect Network Drive (Connect As) option used by the File Manager when connecting to a file server.

Figure 5.6 illustrates a standard RPC-based site connector being configured. In this case we're configuring the connector in the Dublin site to talk to the Belfast site. Note that the server OFFICENT1 is specified as the server to act as a bridgehead for the local site. The Target Servers property page allows you to specify one or more servers to connect to in the remote site.

Figure 5.6
Configuring a site connector

Configuring a site connector is a relatively straightforward operation which can be accomplished in a few minutes. Once the connector is established it will take a little while for the configuration information for the remote site to be replicated across the link and appear in the organizational tree displayed by the administration utility. As long as the data transmitted by the RPCs can pass without hindrance from one server to another you should see little problem with the site connector.

Exchange Server, X.400, and X.500

Compliance with international messaging standards is a good thing. Without standards it is very difficult to communicate from one messaging system to another, a fact that all too many corporate telecommunications technicians are unpleasantly aware of. It is easy enough to send a text message from one system to another, but sending compound messages, those composed of several different body parts, requires a good deal of understanding on both sides before successful transmission is accomplished.

X.400 and X.500 are two important sets of recommendations for the exchange of electronic mail messages and directory services defined through the efforts of the CCITT (the International Consultative Committee on Telephony and Telegraphy), a division of the United Nations now called the International Telegraph Union (ITU) and based in Geneva, Switzerland. The CCITT bases its recommendations on the Open Systems Interconnection (OSI) model, taking into account the needs and requirements of many different bodies before the final shape of a standard is issued. Although X.400 and X.500 are sets of recommendations which are only mandatory when organizations decide to make them so, a set of recommendations is often referred to as a 'standard'.

The primary goal of any standard is to make things easy. Standard screw sizes make screwdrivers easier to manufacture and sell. The X.400 standard seeks to establish ground rules to allow users of different messaging systems, perhaps in the same organization, to exchange messages with each other as easily as if they were connected to the same system. Three separate sets of X.400 recommendations have been issued to date in 1984, 1988, and 1992. The recommendations continually evolve to better define the internal structure of an interpersonal message and its components (such as attachments), the basic structure of the message handling system, and how messages are transported from one point to another within the system.

Using X.400 with Exchange Server

The X.400 connector is the most generic of the range. It can be used to connect Exchange sites together as well as connecting to any other X.400-compliant MTA. The generic nature of the X.400 connector means that it is slower than the standard site connector. Apart from the range of systems it can connect to the X.400 connector delivers a number of significant features that may well be of interest to administrators when deciding what type of site connector should be used. Among these are:

- Message transmission can be set to occur at scheduled times. This optimizes the traffic that goes across potentially expensive network links by ensuring that data is passed in a long continuous stream rather than in small pieces throughout the day.
- A limit on the size of messages accepted by the connector can be set. This stops people sending very large messages and potentially blocking a slow connection to all other traffic.

- Limits can also be set on the set of users authorized to use the connector. Due largely to deployments in corporate messaging environments it is common practice in X.400 implementations not to let everyone communicate with external parties via X.400. Apart from the obvious risk that confidential information is transmitted to unauthorized individuals, restricting the set of users reduces the risk of virus-laden binary files arriving through the mail. Remember that for many years X.400 was the only way to transmit binary information through the mail with some assurance that files could be read by a suitable application when it reached its destination. SMTP/MIME offer this capability too, but MIME has only been readily available in the recent past.

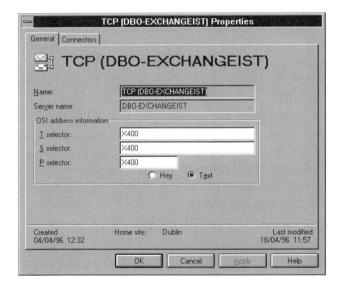

Figure 5.7
Configuring an MTA stack

Microsoft Exchange Server is able to communicate with other X.400-based systems that comply with either the 1984 or 1988 recommendations using a multithreaded Windows NT service called MSExchangeMTA. The first step in an X.400 implementation is to decide which transport stack is going to be used by the MTA to host the X.400 connector. Connections can be made simultaneously to a number of X.400 MTAs via three different transport stacks:

- TP0 (Transport class 0) over a TCP/IP connection via the RFC1006 specification.
- TP4/CNLP (Transport class 4/Connectionless Network Protocol) to provide a suitable OSI interface across a LAN.

▶ TP0 over a X.25 connection using an Eicon port adapter on a Windows NT computer.

Configuring a new transport stack for the MTA is done with the *File.New Other.MTA Transport Stack* option from the Administrator program. Once a stack is installed (such as the TCP/IP stack shown being configured in Figure 5.7) we can proceed to get a new connector up and running (see page 257). Before a connector can be created we need to know something about the capabilities of X.400-based messaging. We also need to understand the different terms used in the X.400 world.

The different X.400 recommendations

Most other X.400-compliant mail systems available today communicate using the 1984 or 1988 recommendations. In general, complying with a later recommendation implies that a greater degree of communication is possible with less effort, especially when dealing with multiple bodyparts, or attachments. The 1984 recommendations, for instance, only distinguish between text and binary body parts, whereas the 1988 recommendations allow each body part to be allocated its own tag, or indicator of which application should process the body part's content. We'll return to this point later on in this chapter.

Clearly it is best to pass as much explicit information as possible when communicating with other messaging systems, and the 1988 set of recommendations, at this point in time, represents the most complete and pragmatic guideline for intersystem message exchange available today. Before a connection is made to another messaging system it is important for you to know whether it supports the 1984 or 1988 recommendations.

The X.500 standard sets rules by which mail user agents and other applications are able to inquire for directory information no matter where the directory is located or how it is accessed. In terms of implementation the most common use of a mail directory is to look for the correct mail address to use for a particular person. Validating the addresses for a message doesn't need an X.500 service – the Global Address Book does an effective job for Microsoft Mail users. However, an X.500 directory is not restricted to just storing information about mail addresses; a directory can hold information about any type of data item that an application cares to store (and eventually retrieve). The value, of course, is that once the data is held in an X.500 directory the route to that data is well defined and the data is therefore available to any application that complies with the public X.500 programming interfaces.

The current version of the Exchange server does not comply with the X.500 recommendations. Instead, Microsoft has designed an 'X.500-like directory schema' to represent the directory entries for people and routing between servers. This distinction between different types of entries is important. Unlike the classic model of a mail directory, X.500 stores information about people who receive mail and how messages can be routed to other systems. The directory used by Exchange is very similar in many respects to a standard X.500 model, but it does not support interfaces such as LDAP (Lightweight Directory Access Protocol) or DAP (Directory Access Protocol) that can be used by external agents to interact with the directory. In addition, Exchange Server does not support the XDS (X.500 Directory Services) API. According to position papers published in April 1996,[1] Microsoft intend to support these standards in the next release of Exchange Server. At this time the directory service will be fully X.500-compliant. It is also likely that a future version of Windows NT will include some aspects of a directory service embedded as a standard part of the operating system. Details of this development are unclear at the time of writing.

Address synchronization between Exchange Server and other directory sources, such as those maintained by other messaging systems, would be facilitated if Exchange supported the full gambit of interfaces described in the X.500 recommendations, but until the time arrives when Microsoft upgrade Exchange to comply with the standard it is inevitable that hand crafted tools will be required to keep Exchange coordinated with other systems.

Microsoft Exchange Server is often represented as a strong supporter of the CCITT standards. This position is correct in relation to X.400, but the story is weaker for X.500. However, it is important to draw a clear line between the areas where Exchange Server fully complies with standards and the places where Microsoft has, for one reason or another, taken a stance that aligns a server component with the appropriate international standard but doesn't quite get there in terms of implementation or interfaces.

The X.400 messaging model

The X.400 standard is based on a store and forward messaging model. A store and forward model means that messages are transferred when links between servers and backbones are available, and when links are not present (for example, because of network failure) messages are held within the system ready to be released when the links are re-

---

1. 'Microsoft's position on LDAP', dated April 22, 1996.

established. After a message is sent it flows along the backbone from link to link, much like a telephone connection is made across a series of switches. In both cases the user who originated the transmission is unaware of all the work and links made on his or her behalf. The system takes care of the internal management and, as far as the user is concerned, nothing more needs to be done after the message enters the system. The store and forward model is robust, proven, and well suited to heavy traffic between multiple distributed sites.

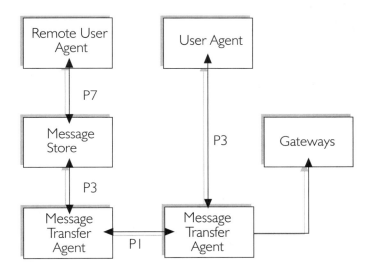

Figure 5.8
X.400 Reference Model

The X.400 recommendations describe a complete messaging system, referred to as a Message Handling System, or MHS. The components of a MHS include:

▶ *The Message Transfer Agent (MTA).* Literally, a method to route messages from their submission through user agents to the point of eventual delivery to recipients. A complete MTA is bundled in Exchange Server, so a single server can act as an MTA. However, a more practical view of an Exchange implementation would create a single MTA composed of a number of Exchange sites with a number of optional gateways for communication outside the MTA.

▶ *The Message Transfer System (MTS).* The set of one or more MTAs that communicate with each other to send and receive messages. Think of a number of Exchange servers located in a set of distributed sites that send messages to each other.

▶ *The Message Stores (MS).* In many electronic mail systems the message store is referred to as a 'file cabinet', a somewhat more human-friendly term to describe the location where messages are stored in transit between their creation and introduction to an MTA. In an Exchange environment the message store can be thought of as the set of folders used when people generate and send messages. Stores can hold messages and other objects, text or otherwise.

- *The User Agents (UA).* The client programs used to generate, send, and retrieve messages from an MTA. Think of the set of clients supported by Exchange Server and you'll know what user agents are. Some user agents operate in a remote manner over dial-up connections.

- *The Access Units (AU).* Gateways or methods used to communicate with other messaging systems that do not comply with the X.400 recommendations. For example, the Microsoft Mail X.400 gateway.

Figure 5.8 illustrates the components of the X.400 model and the protocols (Pn) used to communicate between the different components. We'll return to a variation of this picture shortly to map Exchange Server on top of the model.

The fundamental principles of an X.400 Message Handling System embody the concept of a global messaging network or global MHS. In other words, nothing is done while implementing an MHS to prevent its expansion to accommodate growth to a stage where the MHS is capable of serving a global audience. The global MHS, while obviously an X.400 messaging network itself at a macro level, is comprised of other, smaller X.400 messaging networks underneath.

X.400 is not a new standard that has suddenly descended onto the shoulders of electronic mail administrators. It is well known and understood and has formed part of the electronic mail strategy for many large corporations for the last ten years or so, especially in Europe. However, if you are moving from a PC LAN-based mail system you're probably not too familiar with X.400 as the standard didn't play a big part in LAN implementations, except when used as a connection from the PC mail system to other mail systems. The Microsoft Mail Gateway to X.400 is a good example of one such connection.

The first set of X.400 recommendations were defined in 1984, and a more functional set arrived in 1988. These dates are important when qualifying compliance. A system complying with the 1988 standard is capable of delivering more functionality than one that is 1984-compliant.

How can Exchange Server use X.400?

Microsoft Exchange server is able to use X.400 to interface with other mail systems in a number of different ways:

- *To communicate with other mail systems:* This is the most obvious use of X.400. Connections are made between Exchange servers and an X.400 backbone or MTA that acts as a message switch. The X.400 MTA might belong to a public carrier when communication is required with other organizations, or it might be an internal X.400 MTA used to provide a common messaging backbone for all of the mail systems used within an organization.

- *To connect two or more Exchange sites together via an X.400 network:* Each Exchange site is a separate MTA and the two connect on a peer to peer basis over an X.400 backbone. Messages are sent by each Exchange site to the X.400 MTA that forms the 'glue' in the middle. The X.400 MTA, probably provided by a public carrier such as a PTT, takes care of the routing and delivery of the messages to their destination where they are received by an Exchange server for eventual delivery to addressees. This type of set-up could be used to connect lots of different Exchange servers together in a single country without having to go to the trouble of establishing connections from each server to the other. The solution is flexible because a new server can be introduced without affecting other servers.

- *To link to Microsoft Mail systems via the Microsoft Mail Gateway to X.400:* In this scenario an Exchange server and the Microsoft Mail Gateway are two entry points to an X.400 MTA, again probably one provided by a public provider. Messages are sent by Exchange to the X.400 MTA and then fetched by the gateway for delivery to the Microsoft Mail users in the normal manner. This is an alternative to a direct connection from the Microsoft Mail clients to the Exchange server, possibly because the Microsoft Mail users are in a location that isn't served by a good or continuous network link.

As illustrated in Figure 5.9, from a purist's perspective Exchange Server does not implement the X.400 reference model, largely because of the use of MAPI as the internal protocol instead of the P3/P7 combination outlined in the model. Implementing the complete reference model would be an interesting exercise, but Exchange Server is designed to handle many more e-mail connections than X.400. The Exchange MTA and its X.400 connector form a practical and pragmatic real-world X.400 implementation which fully interoperates with other X.400 MTAs.

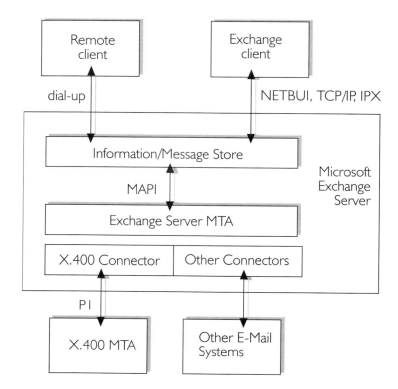

Figure 5.9
Exchange Server and X.400

X.400 body parts

Obviously because X.400 is all about standards, an X.400 message is built according to a carefully defined formula. That formula incorporates the concept of header data, including information about the message originator and the recipients the message will eventually be delivered to, and the component body parts, literally the pieces that collectively form the content.

Simple messages have a single body part, sometimes known as the cover memo. Depending on the user agent, cover memos can be created with a simple text editor or a more comprehensive editor. The Windows 95 Exchange client can create cover memos with Word for Windows, for instance, an editor that's slightly more complicated than the Windows Notepad, a good example of a simple text editor.

Compound messages have a set of one or more body parts, or attachments, which follow the cover memo. Each body part is tagged to tell receiving mail systems how to deal with the attachment. For example, if the attachment is an Excel worksheet an indication is given that this is the case, although the tag that's placed on the attachment is up to the originating user agent, and there is no general agreement between user agents from different vendors as to the tags that should be used for different types of attachments. Some of the more intelligent user agents available today are equipped with either format detection technology, which allows an attachment to be 'sniffed' and identified, often by comparing the first couple of bytes from the attachment with a set of known electronic 'signatures'. Once the attachment is identified it can be processed by launching the appropriate application or, if an application isn't available, the normal backup method is to call a specialized viewer program that is able to display the content of a file but not edit it.

Table 5.4 *X.400 file tagging mechanisms*

X.400 recommendations	Body part type	File format information passed as
1984	Body Part 14 (BP14)	None. Mail user agents must decide how to process binary body parts which could contain any format type (apart from text).
1988	Body Part 15 (BP15)	X.400 Object Identifier (OID)
1992	File Transfer Body Part (FTBP)	Original file name encapsulated and passed in the attachment attributes.

In addition to the body parts listed above Microsoft Exchange Server also supports body part 9 (BP9) to handle embedded or forwarded messages within an X.400 messaging system.

The difference in tagging behavior defined by the various sets of X.400 recommendations (see Table 5.4) is often a cause for confusion when the time comes to connect different systems together. The 1984 recommendations were defined at a stage when PC file formats were not generally used in electronic mail systems, so defining different types of attachments didn't receive much attention. All attachments in a 1984-compliant X.400 system are tagged as binary files, known as body part 14, or BP14. In this scenario it becomes the responsibility of a receiving user agent to interrogate the various binary attachments and decide what format they actually contain. An attachment could be a Word document, or an Excel worksheet, or even a simple text file but in all cases there is no external sign of what's inside.

The 1988 recommendations took note of the growing influence of PC systems and the wide variety of file formats in use and expanded the tagging scheme considerably to allow user agents to include format information to be sent along with each body part. 1988 X.400 systems use a tagging scheme referred to as body part 15, or BP15, where information about the file format of attachments is passed as an 'object identifier', or X.400 OID.

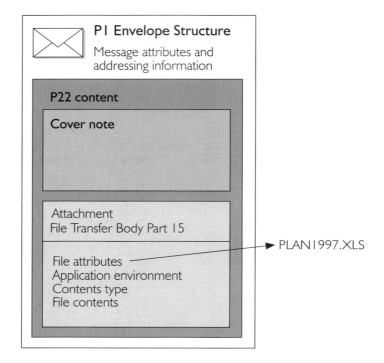

Figure 5.10 *Simplified X.400 message structure*

If a human being looks at an X.400 OID there is little information about file formats immediately obvious. Like many data structures associated with standards, an OID is carefully constructed to accommodate all possible circumstances. The eventual OID is therefore a string containing many different pieces of information, all useful in their own way, but the resulting combination is very unhuman friendly. Of more concern to application developers, if applications are to be able to deal with message attachments code must be written to extract the information about format types from the OID. The extraction code is, in itself, not particularly difficult to write nor will it take long to execute when the time comes, but sometimes incorporating a requirement to decipher encoded strings to extract a file format tag seems a bit of an overkill.

The latest version of the X.400 recommendations was established in 1992 at which time another attempt was made to provide format information. Body part 15 encoding was superseded by File Transfer Body Part, or FTBP15. Instead of holding format information in an

OID the original file name of an attachment is passed as an attribute. This scheme relies on user agents being able to use the file name to locate the correct application whenever the attachment's content needs to be processed and is by no means foolproof. For example, if I use Lotus Word Pro to create a document called FOO.DOC and attach it to a message, I rely on the mail user agents being used by recipients knowing that FOO.DOC should be processed by Word Pro. If, as in many cases, another application also creates documents with the .DOC file type much potential exists for confusion.

In defense of the FTBP scheme, creating associations between file types and applications is a well-known and understood method, and one that has been in use for many years by Windows clients. The most common example is perhaps the Windows File Manager, which creates associations between file types and applications to be able to launch the correct application when a user double-clicks on a file. The direct association between a file type and an application is very simple, a quick and dirty method to get the job done, and as we've seen above, is prone to error. Later versions of Windows, including Windows V3.1 and Windows 95, use a Windows API function called FindExecute to search the system registry to match files up with applications able to process their content. The use of the system registry in a Windows-dominant environment improves matters by largely ensuring that the correct application is located and then launched, provided of course an appropriate application is installed on the PC.

Microsoft Exchange Server is the first mainline messaging server to use FTBP15 as its baseline for communication with other 1988 X.400 MTAs, a fact that clearly causes some difficulty if any of the other MTAs you want to talk to don't support FTBP15. Encouraged by industry groups like the Electronic Mail Association (EMA), many X.400 vendors are retrofitting FTBP15 support into their 1988 X.400 implementations, but the majority of MTAs have not yet been upgraded. It seems ridiculous to make such a remark about a standard, but until the time arrives where all X.400 MTAs can agree on a common interchange format for multi-body part messages, probably FTBP15 in the long term, some degree of confusion and negotiation between MTAs will be required before seamless message exchange is possible. If possible, try and use FTBP15 as the basis for interpersonal message transmission between Microsoft Exchange Server and other X.400 systems.

X.400 encoding schemes

Before messages are introduced into an X.400 system they must be encoded. This is done to ensure that messages are sent in a common internal structure that can be processed globally. The internal structure of messages transmitted within an X.400 network differs according to the set of recommendations supported by the systems making up the network. The lowest common denominator for X.400 systems is a structure known as P2 established as part of the 1984 recommendations. X.400 1988 systems use a more developed internal structure referred to as P22.

The fact that encoding occurs at all and the differences between P2 and P22 are completely hidden from users so you don't normally have to worry about it, except to know that there is an overhead incurred by an Exchange server to encode messages for transmission via an X.400 link. The encoding translates messages from the internal MAPI structures (known as MBDEF, or Message Bodypart Encoding Format) used by Exchange into the format expected by other X.400-compliant systems. For instance, OLE objects inserted into Exchange messages are transformed into X.400-type body parts because there is no guarantee that the receiving system will be able to deal with an OLE object. If the translation wasn't done then objects would arrive as random collections of bytes that don't really make a lot of sense to recipients. Exchange Server knows which encoding should be done because the content type is defined when an X.400 connection is defined to the system. Clearly it's important to get this right because the two types of X.400 encoding are very different.

As well as the communication load, any Exchange server where an X.400 connector is active incurs all the processing overhead involved in translating messages from Exchange to X.400 structures and vice versa. A heavy load of messages being sent or received to or from an X.400 connection can slow an entire system. Evidence that this is happening can be gained from user feedback or the fact that queues of messages to be sent to X.400 build up, and in these circumstances it is best to move the X.400 connection to a more powerful system or to install a new server to take over the load. The same can be said of any Exchange connector, but due to the need to translate to and from X.400 content types, perhaps the X.400 connector needs to have most attention and monitoring, especially in circumstances such as where the connector is used to link Exchange Server to other legacy messaging systems together during the period where users are migrating from the older system to Exchange.

The work required to translate from MBDEF to the appropriate X.400 content type is only strictly necessary to communicate with other messaging systems. If you're in the situation where you want to use an X.400 network to link different Exchange servers you could instruct the connector to perform no conversion and send MBDEF content directly. This enables faster throughput and imposes lesser demands on the server, but you will run into problems if messages find their way to nonExchange systems, or if the X.400 network performs format integrity checks as messages are transported across the network. Several public X.400 systems will fail messages containing MBDEF content if they consider the messages to be 'invalid' because of their MBDEF content, so always perform some tests before making a final decision.

Interoperability with other X.400 messaging systems

Microsoft has validated the ability of Exchange Server to exchange messages with other X.400-based systems using a suite of interoperability tests defined by the OSINET (USA) and EUROSINET (Europe) organizations. Table 5.5 lists the most important X.400 systems that Exchange Server has been tested against.

Table 5.5   *Interoperability against other X.400 MTAs*

Manufacturer	X.400 MTA	X.400 standard
Retix	Open Server	1984
Microsoft	Microsoft Mail X.400 Gateway	1984
Lotus (IBM)	SoftSwitch Central	1984
Digital Equipment Corporation	Message Router X.400 Gateway (MRX)	1984
Isocor	Isoplex 800 MTA	1988
Hewlett-Packard	OpenMail	1988
Lotus/IBM	Message Switch	1988
Control Data Corporation	MailHub	1988
Digital Equipment Corporation	MAILbus 400 MTA	1988
Novell	MAWG X.400 Gateway	1988

The test suites cover points such as:

- P1 interoperability to test whether the information in message envelopes can be passed between Exchange and other MTAs. The most important information in this context is the MTA name, password (if required), and OSI addressing data.

- P2 and P22 interoperability. P2 defines the content of 1984-type messages and P22 defines the content for 1988-type messages. The test suites see whether Exchange server can successfully send and receive messages to and from other MTAs and that the content of the messages can be successfully viewed by recipients (user agents) after they arrive. The tests cover BP14, BP15, and FTBP15 as well as text-only body parts.

Further testing is performed to establish that communication can be achieved using TP0 over X.25 and TCP/IP connections, and TP4 over CLNP links. Finally, tests are performed to verify that Exchange Server can communicate with public administrative domains operated by PTTs and other public X.400 providers world-wide. Among the ADMDs tested are:

- AT&T X.400 and X.25 services (USA)
- MCI X.400 and X.25 services (USA)
- SPRINT X.400 and X.25 services (USA)
- Infonet X.400 services (USA)
- Northern Telecom X.400 services (Europe)
- British Telecom X.400 and X.25 services
- NTT X.400 services (Japan)
- Australia Telecom X.400 and X.25 services (Telstra)
- Swedish Telecom (Televerket) X.400 and X.25 services

OSTC (Open Systems Testing Consortium) act as a single point of contact for many other European PTTs including France, Germany, and Switzerland.

The existence of such a broad range of test suites and results means that there's a good chance that Exchange Server will be able to successfully interoperate with other X.400 MTAs which don't feature in the list above. After getting over the initial hurdle of getting the two systems to connect to each other the next most likely problem area is successful body part recognition as messages flow from one system to another. It's always likely that simple text messages will get through, but the fun only starts once multi-format attachments come into the picture. A process of trial and error is often required before a consistent and reliable message flow is established.

- **User Agent format handling**

All systems should be able to exchange simple text messages without real difficulty, but the true interoperability test is when compound messages with multiple body parts flow between systems without hindrance and all body parts can be read without difficulty by any user agent. Even after all the issues with body parts are resolved much of the responsibility for interpreting format tags correctly to make sure that the correct applications or viewers are called to process message contents is still devolved to user agents. Some intelligence or auto-format detection functionality is often built into the more feature-rich user agents. Auto-detection is usually carried out by reading a few bytes from the start of a file to see if it matches a known 'signature' attributed to a particular file format. Most user agents don't engage in this degree of sophistication and rely on the format tag itself to indicate which application should be called to process message content.

This isn't usually a problem when a single integrated messaging system is used because the same format tag can be used everywhere (for example, a format tag of 'XLS' always indicates an Excel attachment, while 'WK3' might mean a Lotus 1-2-3 spreadsheet), but it can often be a real issue when heterogeneous systems are operated.

How does the Exchange client handle format tags? The answer lies in the Windows system registry, the common repository on Windows-based systems where information is stored about applications. Details such as the OLE capabilities of an application, or the correct DDE commands to instruct an application to print a file are stored in the registration database, as well as a set of associations to link a format tag, such as XLS, with an application such as Excel. The majority of Windows applications capable of producing files in a specific format now provide details for the registration database and these details are loaded into the database during the installation procedure.

When the Exchange client encounters an attachment the format tag is compared against the registration database and if a match is found the associated application is launched to read or print the content. Problems can arise if the registration database is inaccurate or application details have not been loaded, but this is unlikely to occur.

Greater potential for problems arise when multiple applications share the same file extension. Selecting a common set of applications to use across an organization and ensuring that a consistent set of format tags are used everywhere normally eliminates the source of the problem.

Message encoding schemes used by Exchange Server

Several different message encoding schemes have been mentioned to this point. Some belong to X.400 and some do not. Before going any further this is an appropriate point at which to attempt to consolidate our knowledge of where and when Exchange uses the different encoding schemes available to it, outlined in Table 5.6.

Table 5.6 *Message encoding schemes*

Encoding scheme	Where used
MAPI (Microsoft Messaging Application Programming Interface)	Native coding scheme for Exchange message properties such as TO: or CC: recipient lists.
MBDEF (Message Bodypart Encoding Format)	Native coding scheme used to encapsulate body parts as they pass from Exchange Server to server.
MIME	Internet format used to encode binary body parts for transmission across an SMTP messaging network.
TNEF (Transport Neutral Encapsulation Format)	Used to package a message's MAPI properties into a binary attachment when a message passes across a non-MAPI backbone en route to another Exchange server.
P2	X.400 coding scheme used for transmission of message contents to 1984-compliant X.400 MTAs.
P22	X.400 coding scheme used for transmission of message contents to 1988-compliant X.400 MTAs.
P1	X.400 coding scheme used for transmission of message envelopes to foreign X.400 MTAs.

The meaning of TNEF

TNEF allows Exchange Server to preserve extended features such as rich text message content and information about attached or embedded (OLE) objects when messages are sent between Exchange servers across a messaging backbone that doesn't support the transmission of such data.

For example, X.400 envelopes do not normally support information about message formatting as this is usually left to the receiving mail user agent to sort out. The Exchange X.400 connector has a 'Remote clients support MAPI' check box on the General properties page. If checked, the X.400 connector will code the extended features into TNEF and include the data as part of the message envelope before a message is sent. This is OK as long as an Exchange client is at the receiving end, because it will be able to make sense of the extended features and it will allow a recipient to see the message content and format exactly as it appeared on the originator's PC. However, if the recipient uses a different user agent that doesn't know how to deal with the extended features it's likely to cause some problems. In these cases it's best to force the X.400 connector to strip off the extended features before sending the message by not checking the box. The most obvious effect of not using TNEF is that rich text memos will be translated into simple text, losing any formatting that may have been used.

Setting up an X.400 connector

We've spent a lot of time on X.400 concepts; let's proceed to use the X.400 connector to do some real work. A certain amount of information needs to be collected before the new X.400 connector can be created. Much of the necessary information can be gained by asking the questions listed in Table 5.7:

Table 5.7 *Questions to ask when setting up an X.400 connector*

Question/Area of investigation	When connecting is required to another Exchange site	When connecting to a foreign MTA
What is the name of the remote MTA? Does it have a password?	A password is seldom, if ever, required when two sites connect over X.400.	A password should be used when connecting to a foreign MTA.
What MTA transport stack is going to be used?	TP4, TCP/IP, or X.25	TP4, TCP/IP, or X.25
Do lines in messages have to be wrapped?	No.	It depends on whether the mail systems behind the X.400 connection are able to handle long lines of unwrapped text.
Will remote clients be able to support MAPI message contents?	Yes.	Unlikely.
When can messages be transferred?	Exchange servers should be able to transfer messages on a demand basis.	Scheduled transfer is often the most appropriate mechanism when connecting to foreign MTAs.
What OSI TSAP, SSAP, and PSAP[†] information is required?	Pass blank values or an agreed value up to 4 characters in each field.	You can decide what Exchange will pass, but have no control over what the incoming MTA will provide.
Will delivery restrictions be enforced?	Unlikely when using X.400 to connect two sites.	Possible to restrict the transfer of messages outside the company, or restrict whom you'll receive messages from.
Degree of X.400 compatibility?	Full 1988.	1984 or 1988.

Table 5.7 *Questions to ask when setting up an X.400 connector (continued)*

Question/Area of investigation	When connecting is required to another Exchange site	When connecting to a foreign MTA
Send MAPI-encoded messages?	Yes. It's best to use MAPI when connecting two sites together as this avoids any conversion overhead.	No. Foreign MTAs require messages to be presented in P2 or P22 format.
Allow two-way alternate communication?	Yes. Exchange servers are happy to send and receive messages alternatively during one connection.	Perhaps. Some MTAs prefer to send all messages and then receive any messages.
Limit on message size?	Unlikely when connecting two Exchange sites, unless the network link is very slow.	Many companies restrict the size of outgoing messages when sent to external agencies.
X.400 Global Domain Identifier OK?	The default GDI can be used.	May need to restate GDI for the remote MTA.
Connected sites?	Other sites may be reached through this connector.	Not applicable when connecting to a foreign MTA

† TSAP, SSAP, and PSAP are OSI Transport Service, Session Service, and Presentation Service Access Points representing the different layers in the OSI model that are used by the Exchange X.400 connector.

If you're unsure about the answers to any of these questions you should review the connection with the administrator who looks after the MTA you want to connect to. The Exchange administrator's guide also contains a lot of useful information, particularly in respect of the different settings that can be defined for a connector.

Two separate references to MAPI are made in Table 5.7. First, should MAPI contents be sent to remote clients? If the X.400 connector is configured to pass MAPI message contents for eventual delivery to clients it means that all of the rich text formatting in messages (bold, underline, different colors, and so on) will be retained. Attachments, and icons for those attachments, will be positioned where they were placed in the message. If the remote mail system can't handle MAPI contents the X.400 connector will convert rich text to plain text and convert embedded attachments into normal X.400 attachments. The rendering information, used to position an embedded attachment within a message, is also discarded. An extra attachment (the infamous WINMAIL.DAT) is added to the message. This file includes information about the rich text information that has been lost during conversion.

The second point relates to the internal format of the messages passed from one MTA to the other. If you're connecting Exchange sites together you can safely leave the messages in their native format (MDBEF). This avoids any need for the MTA to convert messages and attachments into P2 or P22 format and reduces the demand on system resources.

Connecting two sites with an X.400 connector

The most popular connection (and easiest to set up) is using the TCP/IP stack, so that's what we'll use as an example. The two sites we want to connect are Dublin and Denmark. The sites are in different European countries with a reasonable network link between them. It's a good idea to use an X.400 connector to link sites across wide geographical distances where it is costly or impractical to create the type of high-speed link required by the standard site connector. If there are a number of sites in each country the X.400 connector can be used as the glue in the middle, with site connectors used to link all the sites within each country.

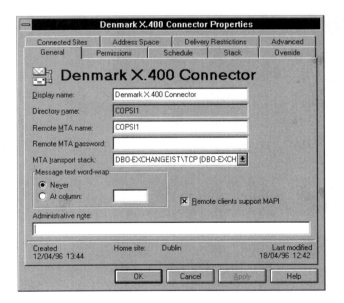

Figure 5.11
General properties for an X.400 site connector

The general properties for the connector are shown in Figure 5.11. Note that no password is required for the remote MTA. This is the normal course of events when connecting sites together. The stack defined is TCP/IP as installed on the DBO-EXCHANGEIST server. We can see more information about the stack by clicking on the Stack property page (Figure 5.12). Note the IP address entered for the server we want to talk to. If you refer back to the OSI settings for the TCP/IP stack configuration illustrated in Figure 5.7, you'll see how the outgoing OSI information is determined.

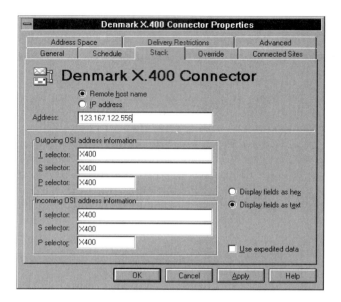

Figure 5.12
Stack properties

If you examine Figure 5.12 you'll see that a fixed TCP/IP address is specified for the remote server. This approach is a bad idea in production environments. Using a host name is preferable because it insulates you from any change in the underlying IP address for the remote server. IP addresses have been known to change in the past!

The Advanced property page contains all the settings to control the level of interoperability this connector will have with the remote MTA. In the case of two Exchange sites the interoperability, as expected, is extremely high, as shown in Figure 5.13. Refer to the earlier discussions regarding body part types or the Exchange Administrator's manual for the meanings of BP15 and BP14 (see page 248).

Many people have shied away from X.400 because it accumulated a reputation for unfriendliness in the past. It's certainly true that it's all too easy to lose your way if you are forced to resort to poking around under the hood and have to speak in the somewhat convoluted terminology the X.400 recommendations foster. The graphical interface presented by the Exchange administration utility eases the pain somewhat, even if there still are eight property pages to deal with, so the task of setting up an X.400 connector is easier in Exchange than most other messaging systems.

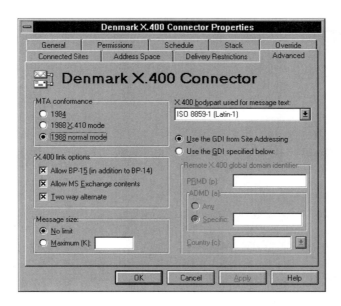

Figure 5.13
X.400 interoperability options

The Exchange Internet Mail Connector

The Internet Mail Connector (IMC) is a connector which enables messages to be sent and received using SMTP (simple mail transfer protocol), the predominant standard for electronic mail within the Internet.

Within the Internet world a set of standards for communication have been established through a series of generally agreed papers called Request for Comments, or RFCs, generated by the Internet Engineering Task Force (IETF), a volunteer group made up of representatives from major organizations and institutions. The Exchange IMC supports the RFC 821 and RFC 822 standards that define the SMTP server-to-server protocol and the format of messages sent between servers. As the name implies, SMTP began life as a very simple messaging format, basically marking the lowest common denominator for messages that could be sent between servers manufactured by different software vendors using different operating systems.

The original RFC 822 standard defined in 1982 considered messages that could only contain 7-bit ASCII text characters, had lines which could not contain more than 1,000 characters, and restricted overall message size. All these limitations appeared perfectly acceptable in a world where telex machines still generated the majority of electronic communications. These limitations have long been lifted.

SMTP and MIME

SMTP messages are always transmitted as text. Clearly the restrictions imposed by the original RFC 822 standard could not be maintained in a world where PC formats are now the norm. A new set of features were defined in RFC 1521 and RFC 1522 to allow for an agreed encoding standard for non-text attachments. These standards are referred to as MIME (Multipurpose Internet Mail Extensions) and are supported by the IMC. MIME allows users to send complex objects across an SMTP link up to and including multimedia files. The IMC also supports UUENCODE, an earlier encoding scheme for handling non-text attachments, defined in RFC 1154. Messages generated by Exchange are not simple ASCII text as the basic editor produces files in Rich Text Format. Lots of messages include embedded files. One of the functions of the IMC is to encode the Rich Text Format memos and any embedded files using MIME before the messages are sent out via SMTP. Upon receipt any foreign messaging system that understands MIME should be able to unpack the MIME-encoded parts and rebuild the message as it was originally sent.

Coding a message's body parts according to an established scheme is a great step towards being able to send complex files anywhere throughout the world via SMTP. But the world doesn't use an ASCII character set everywhere; different cultures use different character sets, so international mail servers must be able to support a range of character sets when messages are encoded or decoded. Exchange server supports US-ASCII, the Western European ISO 8859-1 set, Scandinavian IA5, and character sets support for Korea, Taiwan, and Japan.

The combination of SMTP and MIME have laid the foundation to allow companies to build messaging backbones comparable to those constructed with X.400 but at lower cost and with less technical effort. The combination has gone from the original proposals to world-wide deployment within the Internet in just a few years.

SMTP conversations

SMTP depends on TCP/IP networks to send and receive messages. The IMC uses TCP/IP to create the connection to the remote mail server, conduct a conversation with the remote server to transmit message header information and contents, and then break the connection. All SMTP communication generated by the IMC is channeled through TCP port 25, the port number defined in the SMTP standard.

The Exchange Internet Mail Connector

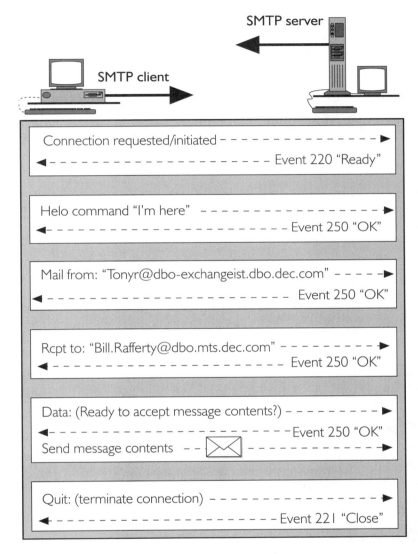

Figure 5.14
Steps in passing an SMTP message

A common set of steps forming a structured conversation are used to pass messages between SMTP mail servers. The conversation occurs between a system acting in the role of the client and one acting as a server. The client initiates and drives the conversation and the server responds to the demands from the client. These steps are illustrated in Figure 5.14 and proceed as follows:

1. The conversation is started by the client through a connection to port 25 on the server.

2. After the network connection is established the client sends an SMTP 'Helo' command to the server. The server responds with 'OK' to indicate that it is willing to accept an SMTP message.

3. The client proceeds to pass originator information in a 'Mail From' command. The server checks the information to ensure that it is willing to accept the message from the originator.

4. The client then sends a list of recipient information in the form of a set of 'Rcpt To' commands. Note that only SMTP recipient information is transmitted. Information about non SMTP recipients will be passed later in the general body of the message.

5. After all the header information is exchanged the client begins the process of sending content. A 'Data' command is sent to indicate that the client is ready to begin, followed by an acknowledgment from the server. The data is transmitted in 7-bit ASCII characters, which may include files encoded previously into MIME or UUENCODE format.

6. Once all the content has been sent the client signs off and terminates the connection by sending a 'Quit' command. However, if the client has another message to send it can start to send the next message by returning to step 3. This process continues until all messages have been sent.

You can trace a conversation between the IMC and another SMTP server by looking at the log files kept in the \EXCHANGE\IMC-DATA\LOG directory.

The Internet Mail Connector and SMTP

The IMC is a full-function SMTP service. Transport, message routing, translation, and delivery are all handled by the connector, giving this service a reasonable amount of work to do if a heavy volume of incoming or outgoing SMTP traffic is to be handled. If you expect a heavy volume of messages, perhaps based on the volume seen coming in or going out of a previous messaging system, or because you have decided to operate an SMTP-based corporate messaging backbone, then implementing specific servers to handle the SMTP traffic should be considered. Routing messages out of the system is not a very demanding activity; the majority of the potential system load is generated by the need to convert messages from the internal format used by Exchange Server into the appropriate SMTP format. Converting large attachments from PC file formats and the message's MAPI properties over to the appropriate MIME encoding is not a simple affair, especially when OLE objects are included.

The process of content conversion from Exchange's internal format can have some unforeseen side effects. One example is the rendering of rich text format content into simple ASCII for messages sent to SMTP recipients that aren't connected to an Exchange server. Any formatting effects inserted by users into messages such as bolding, underlining, italics, different colors, and typefaces are all reduced to simple nonproportional fonts. The advantage here is that the conversion creates content that can be read by almost any messaging system. The disadvantage is that the layout of messages may suffer greatly, leading to a situation where users become dissatisfied with the way the system treats 'their' messages.

Using the Internet Mail Connector

Exchange server is able to use the IMC in a number of different ways. These are the three most common options:

- Making a direct connection to another SMTP mail server in the Internet or within a corporate Intranet.
- Using an SMTP relay host for routing purposes.
- Using an internal SMTP backbone to link Exchange sites together. This option is slightly more complex than the preceding two because it usually involves directory replication in addition to interpersonal messaging. See page 291 for more information about directory synchronization and replication.

In all cases the IMC depends on Windows NT being correctly configured for TCP/IP. Use the Network option from the Windows NT Control Panel to allocate important TCP/IP parameters such as the IP address of the computer and a FQDN (Fully Qualified Domain Name).[2] In fact, the IMC will not start if you don't provide a FQDN. A test is made to see whether the computer's host name can be resolved during IMC initialization, and if a FQDN cannot be resolved the IMC will terminate. A Windows NT error is logged if this happens and you can see details of the error through the Windows NT event viewer (see page 364). The event viewer is the first place to look if you ever discover problems starting the IMC.

Making a direct connection to the Internet or an Intranet allows Exchange to send messages to any other SMTP server. The basic requirements for such a connection include TCP/IP and a static IP address for the server. The IP address is used in conjunction with your system's host name[3] by other SMTP mail servers to address messages

---

2. *An FQDN is basically the domain name containing all the pieces necessary to route data back to a particular computer.*

to Exchange users. If you use DHCP to allocate IP addresses you must take out a permanent lease for the IP address allocated to the server and not permit dynamic reallocation as this will prevent incoming messages finding the correct destination.

How messages flow through the Internet Mail Connector

We've already discussed how the Exchange MTA acts as a central point of contact for messages going out of and arriving into Exchange. The IMC plugs into the MTA in the same way as any other connector, but the way messages flow between the IMC, the MTA, and a user's mailbox deserves some discussion. The different components involved in sending and receiving messages via the IMC are illustrated in Figure 5.15.

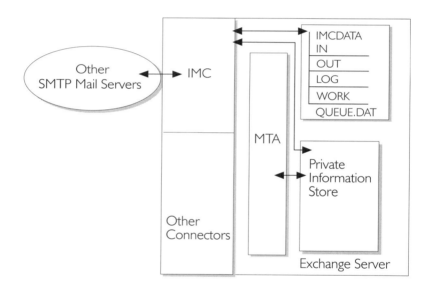

Figure 5.15
Message flow through the Internet Mail Connector

Messages originate in a user's mailbox when sent messages are placed into the OutBox folder. At this point the MTA looks at the address information and decides how the message should be routed to the recipients. If an SMTP address is found a copy of the message is transferred to a special hidden folder in the information store called MTS-OUT. This folder is used by the IMC as a temporary placeholder for messages in transit. Details of messages in transit are also written into \EXCHANGE\IMCDATA\QUEUE.DAT, a file used to track the

---

3. *If the name of the host for the IMC is not the same as the electronic mail domain an entry must be added to the local domain name server (DNS) to map the domain name to the IMC host name.*

status of messages in transit through the IMC. Once a copy of the message is moved into the special MTS-OUT folder the originator's copy is moved from the OutBox to the Sent Items folder.

The IMC processes messages in the MTS-OUT folder by converting them into STMP/MIME (or UUENCODE) format. Converted messages are placed into the \IMCDATA\OUT sub-directory. After they have been converted the messages can be transmitted to remote SMTP servers as described on page 262.

Incoming messages begin when remote SMTP clients initiate a TCP/IP connection to port 25. If the IMC has been configured to accept incoming messages they are copied into the \IMCDATA\WORK sub-directory. At this stage the messages can still fail to transfer (mostly due to communications problems), so they're retained in the \WORK sub-directory until the connection is closed and we're sure that the messages have been fully delivered. When the IMC has closed the connection it moves the messages into the \IMCDATA\IN sub-directory. The messages and attachments are still in SMTP/MIME (or UUENCODE) format and need to be converted before they can be delivered to Exchange recipients. The IMC proceeds to convert the messages and writes the converted content into another special folder in the information store, called MTS-IN. Once messages have been moved into the information store they are handed over to the MTA for onward delivery.

The path taken by messages to and from other SMTP servers sounds quite complex. Fortunately it's all hidden away from the eyes of users, or even system administrators. If problems occur users will be notified with Non Delivery Report messages. Don't attempt to clean up any files in any of the directories mentioned above, even in a fit of system spring cleaning, because the chances are that you'll delete something in transit or otherwise affect a message.

Notes about Internet Mail Connector operation

If a single IMC is established to handle all SMTP mail for the organization you should set the routing cost to be 1 in the Address Space properties. You also need to define the set of names that the IMC is able to process. For example, if you put '*.com' into the address space for a system's IMC it means that the connector is able to send messages to any SMTP address ending in '.com', such as my normal address:

Tony.Redmond@dbo.mts.dec.com

In the example where '*.com' is defined in its address space the IMC will reject any SMTP address ending in any other form. So in this instance if I were to attempt to send to:

```
Tony.Redmond@zyz.net
```
the message would be rejected and returned to me.

If the IMC address space is left blank it indicates that the IMC is able to handle any form of SMTP address, subject always to the ability of the local DNS to resolve the host's address and provide the appropriate TCP/IP address for onward routing.

When SMTP hosts (perhaps UNIX-based systems) are already active within an enterprise the IMC can connect to them for routing purposes. This is a variation on the theme above where the work is split between Exchange and the SMTP host. Exchange takes care of preparing messages for SMTP transmission (format conversion and so on), while the SMTP relay host actually sends the messages to other systems after they are delivered to the SMTP relay host by Exchange. The only difference between this option and the first is that the Message Delivery property for the connector is set to forward all messages to a single nominated host.

If lots of small messages are dispatched into the Internet this configuration offers a potential performance gain over letting Exchange do its own routing. But if the messages are large and complex then the additional routing cost incurred by Exchange to transmit messages to their final destination will largely be overshadowed by the work necessary to convert them from MAPI to SMTP/MIME.

Many enterprises, most commonly in the United States, already operate SMTP-based corporate messaging backbones to unify disparate electronic mail systems running on different platforms as well as to provide a single point of external contact (an SMTP 'smart' host) for the enterprise. To external recipients all the messages coming from the enterprise appear to be generated from a single domain. For example:

```
Tony.Redmond@xyz.com
```

rather than what might be the case where the full routing address required to reach my mailbox is:

```
Tony.Redmond@exchange.xyz.com
```

Proxies are used by the SMTP host to map the addresses on incoming messages to full routing addresses. The host is regarded to be 'smart' because it is able to reroute messages using proxies. You define the correct proxy for Exchange by creating an outbound proxy in the IMC Connections property page. The Message Delivery property for the connector is set to forward all messages to the 'smart' host.

The Exchange Internet Mail Connector

In all cases, external SMTP addressees can be created as custom recipients in the Exchange directory. This serves as a convenience for users, who then don't have to remember to add sometimes complex SMTP addresses to their personal address book (or type the addresses in directly from memory), but if you choose to put custom recipients into the directory a certain implied responsibility is assumed to ensure that the recipients' addresses are kept up to date. Keeping internal addresses updated is a task that can be approached with a certain air of confidence (assuming that directories of mail addresses are available from the other SMTP-compliant systems). Keeping external addresses updated is quite another matter because so much is out of your control. With this in mind it's probably best to devolve the responsibility onto users' shoulders and ask them to store any external SMTP addresses they need in their personal address book.

Using the Internet Mail Connector instead of a Site Connector

Within an internal TCP/IP network you have a choice as to the connector to use when linking sites together. Site connectors are the optimum choice and should be used whenever possible, but the IMC offers a viable alternative to the normal site connector when the link between sites is often interrupted and prone to failure.

Figure 5.16
Sites connected by the IMC

Site connectors use direct RPC communication to send and receive messages in real time. The data transmitted is in native Exchange format and requires no manipulation when it is received by the target system. Thus, site connectors provide the most efficient use of system resources but they depend on highly available bandwidth (>64 Kb).

While not as efficient as a site connector because of the requirement to translate messages into SMTP/MIME, the IMC permits store and forward messaging. Messages can be sent to a 'smart' host that collects messages from many different SMTP-based mail systems, and retrieved from the smart host when available. The SMTP version of a site connector still works even if part of the communications path to the other site(s) is unavailable for whatever reason. However, store and forward messaging via SMTP is bought at the price of the overhead required to translate messages into SMTP/MIME, an overhead which may be unacceptable on a heavily loaded system or one that must handle a high volume of messages.

Communicating with the Internet

The ease by which the Exchange IMC facilitates communication with recipients dotted around the Internet is a double-edged sword. On the one hand you get good interoperability and messages flow easily, but on the other, you possibly don't want all the information which might flow to escape outside your enterprise. The IMC includes a number of interesting features that allow system administrators to exercise some control over outbound and incoming connections. These include:

- Stopping out-of-office notifications going out to Internet users. People can use the Out of Office Assistant to create helpful messages for other users to know that they are unavailable and won't be able to process any messages they receive. It's not always a good idea for this information to be broadcast externally. Do you really want people to know when senior management are traveling? You should set up the IMC to prevent these notifications going outside. Use the interoperability dialog (see the IMC Internet Mail property page) for the connector to stop out of office notices and automatic replies going to Internet correspondents (Figure 5.17).

- The ability to accept or reject connections based on IP addresses. The Internet Mail Connector can be configured to only permit messages to be sent to particular hosts, or only accept messages arriving in from others. These restrictions can help you restrict communications to a set of hosts that are deemed essential to the business, or stop unwanted inflows of large quantities of messages from overactive Internet mailing lists, and so on. Stopping unwanted connections also helps to stop potential hackers probing your system for holes by which they can gain unauthorized and unwanted entry.

► You often don't want to give everyone the ability to access the Internet. Why should temporary staff or contractors have the chance and the tools to transmit confidential data (extracted, for instance, from an unguarded public folder) to people outside? Use the Delivery Restriction property page for the IMC to restrict any users you'd prefer not to have free and easy communications. Along the same line, you can restrict the size of messages that either go out to the Internet as well as those which come in. Restricting the size of outgoing messages can stop large chunks of data being transmitted (like strategy documents), and restricting the size of incoming messages can stop a 'denial of service' hacker strike, basically an attempt to send a system so much mail that disk space is exhausted and the system has to be taken off the air.

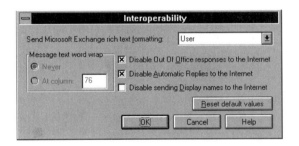

Figure 5.17
Internet interoperability options

These features should be operated in tandem with a well-configured and secure firewall. There is no situation when the IMC should be connected directly to other Internet hosts unless you want to create a truly open system (in terms of its ability to be attacked).

Interaction with the Domain Name Server

Another item to consider is how to enter records for Exchange servers into your organization's Domain Name Server. The basic function of DNS is to act as a distributed database that translates host names to and from IP addresses. The contents of the DNS database include entries for specific systems within your own network as well as the points of contact for other organizations. All organizations which connect to the Internet have 'bastion hosts', systems which connect to the Internet directly. Another term much used is a 'relay host', a system that is able to process or reroute messages for a domain, directing them from the time messages enter a domain down through the internal network to the correct server and recipient.

Digital, for instance, has a couple of systems acting as bastion hosts and relay hosts. Collectively these systems process all messages sent to 'dec.com' (the Digital domain). Addresses on arriving messages are examined by these systems, checked against the DNS database to see whether the addresses are valid, and then routed on their way to the eventual recipients. Large, distributed messaging networks incur a fundamental requirement to ensure that all mail servers are correctly entered into DNS as otherwise there will be no chance of messages ever being delivered.

A request to PING a named computer – `System1.xyz.digital.com` for example, results in a look-up against DNS to resolve the host name that's provided into its base IP address, unless of course the host name and IP address have been entered in the system's local 'hosts' file. Windows NT computers can also resolve host names using WINS or by looking up its local LMHOSTS file.

Apart from the straightforward host name to IP address mapping records DNS holds information specific to mail servers. These records are 'MX' (Mail Exchanger) records, and serve to identify which systems are able to accept mail, or act as 'relay hosts', systems that accept incoming messages for a domain and relay it onwards to their final destination.

MX records can also be used to give a different name to a computer being used for messaging, in effect an alias for a mail server. You might want to do this if you didn't want the FQDN of your computers published to the Internet. For example, a system called:

`Internet-gateway.xyz.com`

might have the following records in DNS:

`Internet-host.xyz.com IN A 16.240.111.111`

`Internet-host.xyz.com IN MX 10 Internet-host.xyz.com`

These DNS records associate the IP address 16.240.111.111 with the FQDN of a computer that we'll use to host an IMC. The second DNS record tells us that the system is able to accept mail messages.

The example host name I've chosen to use here may be very accurate in a purely technical sense but 'Internet-host@xyz.com' isn't going to win any prizes for brevity. Adding a different MX record to DNS allows us to substitute our long-winded name with a shorter version:

`Mail.xyz.com IN MX 10 Internet-host.xyz.com`

Now we've associated the alias `mail.xyz.com` with the system's FQDN, allowing external correspondents to address mail to people within our organization as:

```
username@mail.xyz.com
```

rather than

```
username@Internet-host.xyz.com
```

Putting both 'A' and 'MX' records into the DNS database speeds up message delivery by giving the system less work to do to figure out whether a computer is able to accept messages or not.

If an Exchange server is going to accept messages from external Internet systems you'll have to ensure that two records for the Exchange server are entered in your local DNS database. The first maps the host name for the Exchange server with its IP address, the second identifies the Exchange server as a mail system.

When you configure the IMC you can decide to provide it with the IP address for the DNS to query to resolve addresses for messages. This allows the IMC to resolve the IP address itself and send messages on their way without further intervention. However, you might not want to have every Exchange server in an organization generate messages in this manner, preferring instead to route all messages to one or more systems dedicated to the task of external mail connectivity. These systems might, for instance, be fully equipped with a range of gateways to enable messages to be exchanged with a wide range of other messaging systems. They might also serve as the point of connection with an Internet Service Provider (ISP): the company who provides the necessary link between your organization and the rest of the Internet. In this case you can configure the IMC to route all messages to a specific system.

There are many tips, tricks, and techniques that can be applied to DNS and the way external connections are handled, certainly far too much to be discussed in any comprehensive manner here. If you're in charge of Internet connectivity make sure you have a firm grasp of the techniques that can be applied. Messaging is a critical part of connectivity, but it's one that needs to be controlled, so make sure your implementation is well planned.

Sending rich text message contents

In an Exchange-pure environment all of the clients connected to the network are able to read rich text format messages. The same is true when an Exchange client sends a rich text message across an SMTP network to another Exchange client. Problems begin to occur once you begin to communicate with other mail systems.

The cover notes (initial body part) of rich text messages sent to external mail systems through the IMC will be translated into plain text. At the same time the IMC will attach a copy of the formatted text as an extra binary attachment. Depending on how the IMC is set up the extra attachment is provided as a UUENCODE file (called WIN-MAIL.DAT) or a MIME-encoded file with a MIME type of MS-TNEF (see the discussion about TNEF on page 256).

Recipients who expect a simple message can be quite confused when they see the extra attachment. There's no indication as to what the attachment might contain. It might be an exciting picture, a financial spreadsheet, a copy of their job plan, or details of an important project. All they see is the attachment. Naturally people are curious and won't just let the matter rest there, so they'll call the help desk and pester them with questions like 'what's in the file?', 'why have they sent me something I can't read?', or 'what application should I use to see inside the file?' All good questions, but something that the help desk can do without.

If you're in the situation where you expect a lot of mail to go out via the IMC to non-Exchange recipients you can configure whether rich text messages are sent to recipients on a per-domain basis. For instance, if you know that lots of messages go to a domain called xyz.com you can configure the IMC to never send rich text messages to a recipient in that domain. Recipients in users' personal address books[4] or custom recipients in the directory[5] can be configured to always receive messages in rich text format, but if you instruct the IMC to send plain text messages to specific domains the settings in personal address books or the directory are overridden. This step effectively stops Exchange adding the extra attachment and stops users worrying about the contents of the mysterious attachment. Note that if the IMC is used to connect sites together you should always allow rich text messages to flow unimpeded between the sites.

Rerouting SMTP addresses

A rerouted SMTP address is one that splits the address into two parts. The first part is the address for an intermediate router while the second is the address you'd use if a direct SMTP connection was possible. For example, the address:

xyz.com:Tony.Redmond@dbo.mts.dec.com

indicates that the message should first be routed to xyz.com, which will then take responsibility for onward delivery to:

---

4. *Via the SMTP Address property page for personal address book entries.*
5. *Via the Advanced properties for custom recipients.*

Tony.Redmond@dbo.mts.dec.com

By default, Exchange server V4.0 does not support rerouted SMTP addresses. An extension DLL is available to support rerouted SMTP addresses (in the Exchange Resource Kit) but you have to purchase the Resource Kit and then explicitly install the extension onto your system. The Exchange Resource Kit is discussed in Chapter 8 beginning on page 365.

Managing the message flow from the Internet

If you haven't been used to communicating via the Internet the amount of message traffic generated once a link is established may come as a shock. As soon as people realize they have been released from the boundaries imposed by the internal e-mail system and can send e-mail to friends, relatives, and other correspondents throughout the world they'll start doing it. Be prepared to see outgoing traffic volumes mount up at a fairly rapid rate.

Letting users subscribe to Internet list servers is a good way to generate lots of incoming messages. Many of the active lists handle well over a hundred messages per day, all of which will be sent to list subscribers unless they have opted to receive a daily digest (a concatenated set of all the submissions to the list server sent as a single message). If users do subscribe to Internet list servers make sure that you don't allow out of office notification messages being sent through the IMC (the default is to prohibit them). Apart from annoying the other people who subscribe to the list server, out of office messages can often convey business sensitive information to people you wouldn't really wish to share it with. It's OK to compose an out of office message to let fellow workers know that you're off to Australia for two weeks to work on an important deal, but do you really want this information going outside?

Having a single point of contact for Internet mail makes things easier to manage, but it also introduces a potential bottleneck into the messaging system. Any organization generating or receiving more than a thousand SMTP-type messages per day should consider spreading the load by implementing multiple IMCs. It is possible to configure multiple connectors so that each connector handles different domains. In other words, the IMC on one server deals with everything sent to '*.com' and '*.gov' whereas another handles messages sent to '*.edu'. Configuring connectors in this manner is really only possible if you have a good idea about the volume of traffic sent to different domains, so an easier solution is to let all connectors process messages to any domain and let the Exchange MTA balance the load across the available connectors.

Some of the heavier messaging sites have found it convenient to dedicate servers purely to Internet mail. In fact, some have gone so far as to dedicate one server to handle outgoing mail and another to handle incoming mail. Dedicated IMC servers don't need a high-end hardware configuration. A system equipped with a 100MHz Pentium, 64Mb of memory and 2Gb disk is a good starting point. Such a system is more than capable of handling the load for most organizations, and if you find that message queues build up you can divide the load across two servers or enhance the hardware configuration. Overall this is a convenient and practical solution for Internet messaging and avoids the need to run multiple connectors across an organization. Remember though that you need to license all servers to use the IMC.

Connecting to Microsoft Mail

The file-based architecture of Microsoft Mail (MS-Mail) is totally unlike the client–server approach taken by Exchange, but the replacement of Microsoft Mail post offices and clients represents one of the clearest initial markets for Exchange to grow and prosper in. Achieving good interoperability between MS-Mail and Exchange is therefore a critical success factor for the new server.

Two separate components are used to bridge the gap between MS-Mail and Exchange. These are:

1. The MS-Mail Connector: used to transport messages between MS-Mail and Exchange.

2. The Directory Synchronization Agent (DXA): used to enable directory information to be exchanged between MS-Mail and Exchange – see page 298.

Connections between Exchange and other MS-Mail post offices can be established over:

- LAN or WAN
- Asynchronous telephone dial-up
- X.25

Any protocol supported by Windows NT can be used to connect Exchange with other MS-Mail post offices over a LAN or WAN. These protocols include TCP/IP, NetBUI, and Novell's IPX/SPX.

Telephone dial-up connections require modems on the Exchange server and the computers hosting MS-Mail post offices. Dial-up connections are made by the MS-Mail Connector MTA (see section below) in exactly the same way as 'normal' MS-Mail MTAs.

X.25 connections can only be made if an X.25 card and X.25 software are installed and configured for Windows NT. As mentioned at the start of this chapter Eicon Technologies are the only vendor currently shipping X.25 cards and software for Windows NT. Windows NT RAS is not used for either asynchronous or X.25 connections between Exchange and MS-Mail post offices.

Components of the Microsoft Mail Connector

The MS-Mail Connector can be further broken down into three separate components:

1. MS-Mail Connector post office (sometimes called the 'shadow' post office). This is a specialized version of a normal MS-Mail post office used to manage messages in transit between other MS-Mail post offices and the Exchange environment. The Connector post office links the Interchange and MTA because both the other components read and write messages in the Connector post office. The Connector post office shares many of the files with a normal MS-Mail post office, but some important files are missing which means that the Connector post office can only be used in its specialized connectivity role.

2. MS-Mail Connector Interchange. This is a Windows NT service with two main functions. First, it accepts messages addressed to MS-Mail recipients from the Exchange MTA and writes them into the Connector post office. Second, the Interchange accepts messages from MS-Mail users addressed to Exchange recipients and dispatches them through the Exchange MTA to their final destination. Messages addressed to Exchange recipients are stored in the Connector post office until the Connector Interchange is able to deal with them. You'll find a queue for messages sent by Exchange users to MS-Mail recipients among all the others listed when you view MTA queues.

3. MS-Mail Connector MTA. Another Windows NT service that assumes responsibility for transferring messages between other MS-Mail post offices and the Connector post office. In essence, the Connector MTA provides the same functionality as a regular MS-Mail V3.2 MTA,[6] except that it is able to route messages to the Connector post office for eventual pick-up by the Connector Interchange. Several other differences exist in the Exchange version of the MS-Mail MTA, but these are enhancements rather than omissions. The bottom line is that it is possible to replace

---

6. *MS-Mail MTAs are available on the OS/2, Windows NT, and MS-DOS platforms.*

standard MS-Mail MTAs with Exchange MS-Mail Connector MTAs.

The route messages take between Exchange and Microsoft Mail users is illustrated in Figure 5.18.

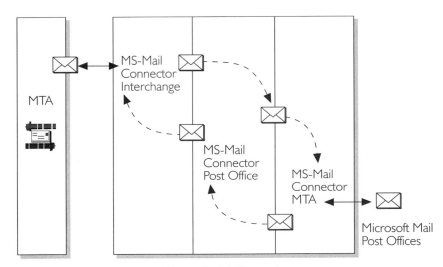

Figure 5.18
How the Microsoft Mail Connector transfers messages

The MS-Mail Connector post office acts as a temporary storage area for messages in transit between MS-Mail and Exchange. Messages vary greatly in size and it's important that enough space is available to allow messages to be processed correctly. The space taken up by messages rolls over as messages come in from the Connector Interchange (from or to Exchange) or the Connector MTA (from or to MS-Mail). Messages are deleted as soon as they've been passed on so the exact amount of space you'll need depends greatly on the volume of mail passing between Exchange and MS-Mail. Just like any other situation where disk space is required for temporary storage it is wiser to over allocate than end up in the position where everything grinds to a halt because the disk has filled up. The extra allocation will stand you in good stead during the times when users insist on sending messages with very large attachments, or during situations when (for one reason or another), problems exist in the link between Exchange and MS-Mail and a queue builds up.

Either an NTFS or FAT disk will do, but make sure that at least 200Mb is available after you install the connector and check progress on a regular basis. Danger signals should go up if less than 50Mb is available on the drive.

The MS-Mail Connector post office is a special version of the regular MS-Mail post office and uses the same directory structure on disk. Only one user (ADMIN) is known to the post office and many of the files you'd expect to find in an MS-Mail post office are missing. There are no folders, client message files, group membership files, or Schedule+ files, but none of these are necessary to route messages. The important configuration files – MASTER.GLB, CONTROL.GLB, and NETWORK.GLB – are all in place.

Configuring the Microsoft Mail Connector

Configuring the MS-Mail connector is relatively straightforward. Some of the more important points to consider are discussed below.

- Maximum message size (General properties). This property establishes the maximum size of messages (including the cover note and any attachments) that can be sent from Exchange to an MS-Mail recipient.

- Primary language for clients (Interchange properties – see Figure 5.19). Exchange is a truly international product, largely because of the UNICODE capability of Windows NT, but MS-Mail is not. Different language versions exist for MS-Mail. The default language chosen for this property is that of the Exchange server, but if you communicate with MS-Mail clients that use a different language you may want to change the language to that of the clients. A connector can only be configured to use one language.

- MS-Mail compatibility (Interchange properties). If not checked Exchange sends embedded OLE objects in messages to MS-Mail clients. The only problem is that MS-Mail won't be able to view or save these objects thus generating a fair amount of frustration among recipients! If checked Exchange will export embedded objects and add them as attachments which can be read by MS-Mail. The only problem is that this increases total message size, which may be an issue on servers that don't have a lot of disk space. In these situations you should get some more disk!

- Network and post office name (Local Post Office properties). By default this is the name of the Exchange organization (network) and site (post office). Unless really necessary it's best to leave these values alone as changing their values causes the MS-Mail for all the mailboxes to be regenerated, causing messages en route to Exchange to fail (because their destination address has changed since they started out).

Figure 5.19
Configuring the Microsoft Mail Connector

In addition MS-Mail connectors support the same concept of routing costs as the SMTP and X.400 connectors. You can have multiple paths to post offices through different connectors. The cost allocated to each connector tells Exchange which connector to use to send messages. If the MS-Mail connector with the lowest cost is unavailable Exchange will automatically route via the next-lowest connector, and so on.

Microsoft Mail supports the concept of 'downstream' post offices. This means that when the MS-Mail Connector joins an existing MS-Mail network via another MS-Mail post office (the point of contact between Exchange and MS-Mail) that post office may lead on to other post offices. Information about downstream post offices accessed through the point of contact is extracted from NETWORK.GLB data files held on the MS-Mail post office. NETWORK.GLB describes routing information between different MS-Mail post offices and its provision during the configuration process reveals the presence of those post offices to Exchange, thus making it possible for Exchange users to send messages to recipients hosted by all MS-Mail post offices in the network. If you like you can think of the information held in NETWORK.GLB as a primitive forerunner of the routing data for servers and connectors within an organization maintained by the Exchange directory.

It's always possible that you might have a requirement to link two separate MS-Mail networks together. Exchange allows you to create a logical backbone (in effect, to act as a message switch) between the two networks by configuring an MS-Mail Connector on one server to handle messages coming in from the first MS-Mail network and then configure another connector on another Exchange server to do the same thing for the second MS-Mail network. In this scenario messages flow into the Exchange organization from the two MS-Mail networks and are processed there in exactly the same way as any other messages. They are routed by Exchange from one server to another and can pass in this manner from the first MS-Mail network to the second. Apart from message switching Exchange can also use its directory synchronization capabilities to deliver a unified global address list to each MS-Mail network.

Using Microsoft Mail gateways with Exchange

Because of its popularity and market share there are many gateways available for MS-Mail. These gateways connect MS-Mail to backbones like X.400, SMTP, and e-mail systems like IBM PROFS. If you're migrating from MS-Mail and have some gateways in operation you have two choices:

1. Elect to channel messages from MS-Mail to Exchange and on to an Exchange connector. This option depends on a replacement connector being available and configured. It's easy to move in the case of the X.400 or IMC, but maybe not so easy if you have a more esoteric gateway in operation. In this situation you'll need to install the appropriate gateway access component in all the MS-Mail post offices that want to use the Exchange connector and then identify the MS-Mail Connector post office as the post office which provides the gateway to the rest of the MS-Mail network.

2. Continue to use the MS-Mail gateways. The gateways are left in place and operated as before. MS-Mail users continue to send messages via the gateway and you can also opt to make those gateways available to Exchange users. This is done by either installing an MS-Mail V3.*x* gateway access component in the MS-Mail Connector post office (to route messages via MS-Mail to the gateway), or to install a gateway against the MS-Mail Connector post office.

   The latter option allows the MS-Mail Connector post office to send mail directly via the gateway without having to route it via another MS-Mail post office. The list of supported gateway access components include PROFS, SNADS, FAX, AT&T Easylink, MHS, and M-Bridge (MCI).

Installing a gateway directly into the MS-Mail Connector post office seems a retrograde step. My preference is to opt for an Exchange-pure solution if at all possible. Installing another MS-Mail gateway, even under the guise of Exchange's MS-Mail Connector isn't a strategic step to take if Exchange represents the future cornerstone of your messaging infrastructure, so why take a short-term decision?

The advantages of moving from MS-Mail

Coming to Exchange from MS-Mail it may appear that the world has suddenly become much more complex. The client–server nature of Exchange and the replacement of the file sharing underpinnings of MS-Mail by a transactional database alone are enough reasons to consider that the level of complexity has greatly increased. But in return for the extra complexity Exchange delivers much more client and server-level functionality, integrates with and exploits Windows NT, provides a much nicer directory replication system, and has a highly capable MTA complete with many different connectors. More importantly everything is presented in an integrated and easy to use fashion instead of the somewhat scatter-gun or fragmented approach that's often all too visible in an MS-Mail environment composed of more than one post office.

Is the move worthwhile? Definitely. Should it happen as soon as you can swing Exchange into production to take over from MS-Mail post offices? Without a doubt. Will you gain any added value for the extra investment in time, energy, and money? You'll get a much more scaleable, reliable, and robust messaging system – one that's designed to operate as an integrated whole. The case to move from MS-Mail to Exchange is compelling. The good news is that the MS-Mail Connector will help you during the transition, but I wouldn't wait around to enjoy the connector in action for very long. If at all possible get to Exchange as soon as possible and leave MS-Mail to rest in peace.

The Microsoft Exchange Directory Service

The Exchange Directory Service is responsible for managing information held about an enterprise's messaging structure – user mailboxes, servers, distribution lists, and the configuration data used to route messages and map address types. All of this information is kept within a single directory.

Like other entities within Exchange server, all of the items held within the directory are treated and manipulated as objects. An object like a server has properties which define the specific characteristics of the object. Properties also specify the users who are able to manage objects. All management activities on the directory store are carried out through the Exchange administration program.

X.500 and the Exchange directory

As described earlier, X.500 is a set of ITU recommendations describing the interconnection of different information systems or directories. Two sets of X.500 recommendations have been issued to date, in 1988 and 1992. The central X.500 concept is the directory, an information system that holds data about a set of objects of interest. An object of interest is something that somebody might want to consult the directory to discover more information about. Recipients are practical examples of an object of interest. Clients consult the directory to discover information about recipients, such as correct address to use when sending messages to a particular recipient.

X.500 information is collectively stored in a DIB, or Directory Information Base. The DIB provides an interface between the users of the directory and the services which provide and maintain the information within the directory. You can think of objects, such as recipients, being stored as records within the DIB in much the same way as transactional information is written into an accounting database. The DIB imposes certain rules on the objects stored in the directory to ensure that a degree of consistency is maintained. The overall set of rules for the DIB is known as the directory schema. Objects are classified by type, known as object classes. The DIB imposes consistency by only allowing objects to be created according to the rules stated for a particular object class. For example, if you attempt to create a new custom recipient (a new directory object) and the Administration program is not currently positioned in a 'Recipients' container (an object class), Exchange signals an error and offers to move into a container that allows custom recipient objects to be created there.

The internal hierarchy and structure of an X.500 directory is determined by the Directory Information Tree (DIT). Beginning from the root, or top of the directory the DIT allows navigation through entries called containers and leaves. The basic difference between a container and a leaf is that a container acts as a repository for leaves and other containers whereas a leaf normally represents an object of interest. Think of the Exchange Administration program. You can see containers such as 'Configuration' and 'Recipients'. 'Configuration' holds other containers such as 'Monitors' and 'Servers', but the 'Recipients' container only holds objects of interest, actual recipients or mailboxes. In this example I am purposely ignoring distribution lists which are stored in 'Recipients' and can be regarded as containers, albeit not in the true meaning of the X.500 term.

The directory used within Exchange is based upon the X.500 recommendations, meaning that the directory schema used to represent an Exchange organization within the directory is very similar to the model defined in the X.500 recommendations. Microsoft decided not to implement a true, fully compliant X.500 directory because the Exchange Server directory is designed to store items not supported by X.500 such as titles, organizational information (manager and reports), and the customizable attributes that a system administrator can define for recipients. Product briefings delivered by Microsoft indicate that support of the X.500 protocols such as DAP and DSP will be forthcoming in future releases of Exchange Server. This advancement will be welcome as it should enable easier synchronization between Exchange and other X.500-compliant directories.

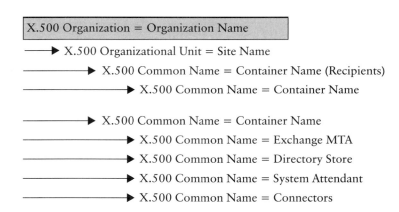

Figure 5.20
X.500 Object Classes used in the Exchange Directory

Figure 5.20 illustrates how the objects within the Exchange directory are mapped on top of X.500 object classes. Both directory schemes organize objects into a well-defined hierarchical structure, the DIT. The concept of the DIB is also supported as are container and leaf entries.

The full Exchange directory schema consists of:

- Object classes representing different types of objects such as mailboxes, servers, connectors, monitors, and so on.
- Sets of attributes for each object class. For example, a common name, the name of the object class itself, the distinguished name, the date and time when the object was created.
- Details of the hierarchical structure within the directory. For example, *Organization* ➡ *Site* ➡ *Recipients* ➡ *Mailbox*.
- The consistency rules governing which objects can be added to which containers.

Apart from recipients, the Exchange directory holds entries for the other objects that form Exchange including the System Attendant, the MTA, and the directory itself. Thus, all objects in Exchange are addressable, so you can see how this provides the basis for information to be transmitted between components in the form of specially formulated messages. Directory replication is an excellent example of this concept in action as messages containing the information to be replicated are exchanged between the directory store objects in all the sites within an organization.

The Exchange directory is physically represented by a database (DIR.EDB) which is subject to the same 16Gb restriction as the information stores. How many entries can be stored in the directory? Theoretically speaking, according to Microsoft sources, probably more than 5 million. Will a directory ever be constructed to hold such a number of entries? Probably not – and from a practical perspective it's fair to say that the Exchange directory is more than capable of handling the largest corporate directory in use today.

X.500 naming

Within an X.500 DIB each object is uniquely identified by a name called the X.500 Distinguished Name. A distinguished name is constructed from the ordered set of object names representing the path through the DIT that must be taken in order to arrive at a specific object. The set of names within a distinguished name are referred to as relative distinguished names, or RDNs. Each RDN provides the name of a container or leaf entry within the DIT. Within the Exchange directory Distinguished Names are made up from the name of the organization, the name of the site, the name of the recipient's container, and the name of the user's mailbox. Thus, based on the graphical representation of the Exchange DIT shown in Figure 5.21, the different RDNs necessary to form my X.500 distinguished name (and thus locate my mailbox within the directory) are:

Organization = Digital Equipment

Site = Dublin

Common Name = Recipients

Common Name = Tony Redmond

Amalgamated together in the format used by an X.500 directory the entry becomes:

o=*Digital Equipment*, ou=*Dublin*, cn=*recipients*, cn=*Tony Redmond*

Figure 5.21
Navigating through the Exchange Directory Information Tree

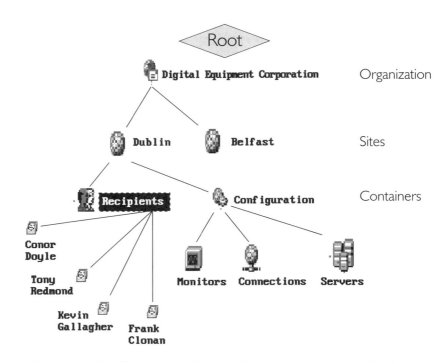

Obviously, the distinguished name is very important to Exchange – in some ways surprisingly so. Let me give you one example. Let's assume you have two sites – London and Chicago – with an Internet Mail Connector configured in each site. A user in London creates a message and addresses it by selecting an Internet recipient from the Global Address List, which just happens to come from a custom recipient entry made in Chicago. The message is duly sent. Instead of routing the message via the local Internet Mail Connector, Exchange examines the address, finds that the distinguished name (from the Global Address List) references the Chicago site, so the message is sent to Chicago for processing by the MTA there. Eventually the message is sent and will be delivered to the right place, but its route via Chicago is curious to say the least.

DUAs and DSAs

Having a directory stuffed full of information isn't very interesting if that information can't be easily and quickly retrieved. In the X.500 world retrieval is accomplished by Directory User Agents (DUAs) and Directory Service Agents (DSAs). A DUA is responsible for initiating a request for some information from the directory, while a DSA takes charge of responding to any requests that arrive into the directory. The DSA retrieves the information directly or corresponds with other

The Microsoft Exchange Directory Service

DSAs (if the directory is distributed throughout a network) to satisfy the request.

Figure 5.22 illustrates the Exchange implementation of X.500 DUAs and DSAs. Requests for directory information are initiated by Exchange clients, the Administrator program, or behind-the-scene components such as the MTA, Information Store, or System Attendant. A client might, for instance, request the directory to supply a mail address for a custom recipient. The Administrator program corresponds with the directory when information is added, amended, or deleted about mailboxes or custom recipients. The System Attendant uses the directory to store the certificates used by advanced security, among other things.

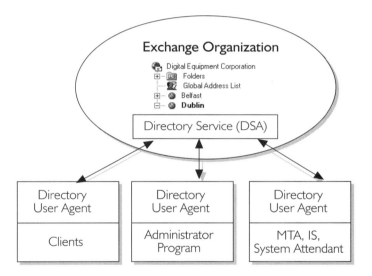

Figure 5.22
X.500 DSAs and DUAs in Exchange

In all instances requests for directory information are processed by the Exchange Directory service, which fulfills the role of an X.500 DSA. Because the Exchange Directory is distributed and replicated across all sites in an organization the chaining from one DSA to another to retrieve directory information when required is accomplished in a transparent manner.

Multiple address storage within the directory

Exchange server automatically creates a distinguished name within the directory when a new mailbox is created. At the same time a number of proxy addresses may be created, one for each connector that's available for sending messages. For example, if the MS-Mail, X.400, and SMTP connectors are operational, three separate proxy addresses will be created for a new mailbox. Each proxy address represents the address format used by another messaging system to reach an Exchange recipient (via a connector). So the proxy address for MS-Mail is therefore in MS-Mail format and looks and feels just like a regular MS-Mail address when viewed by an MS-Mail user. The same is true for an SMTP or X.400 address, and so on for all the various connectors. In fact, Microsoft require vendors who sell connectors for Exchange Server to create well-formed proxy addresses for recipients when connectors are plugged into an Exchange server. This is done by adding a template to the directory proxy table when the new connector is installed.

It's also possible for the directory to hold multiple addresses of the same type for mailboxes. This is a useful feature when you have modified an X.400 or SMTP addressing scheme, or when users have migrated to Exchange from another system. Let's look at an example to see if it clarifies things. Assume that you have migrated some users from a UNIX system to Exchange. The form of SMTP address used to direct messages to the Exchange IMC is user@imc.xyz.com. The SMTP address used for the UNIX system was user@mail.xyz.com. Default addresses for the IMC are generated automatically as mailboxes are created, and we can generate new Internet addresses for each mailbox afterwards.

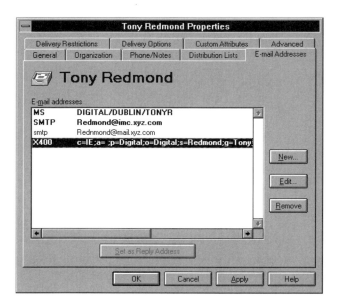

Figure 5.23
Multiple e-mail addresses

New addresses are added through the E-Mail Addresses property page for the mailbox. After you add a new address you'll see that some of the addresses are bolded and some aren't (see Figure 5.23). The bolded addresses are the primary address used by each connector type, in other words, the address that you expect the connector to use most often as well as the reply address that will be placed on ongoing messages.

Having a number of potential mail addresses seems confusing and wasteful, but it allows Exchange Server to meet a goal of the Universal Inbox concept. That is, to allow users to receive messages generated from many different mail systems into a single mailbox. This can only be done by providing a range of mail addresses for correspondents to send mail to. As it happens, all the different mail addresses actually end up in the same mailbox, but users are unaware of this fact.

X.400 addresses

Confusion often arises between X.400 addresses and X.500 directory entries. At first glance both can appear similar, but they are different. This is especially so within an Exchange environment where the X.500 distinguished name is used primarily to locate recipients or other objects within the directory and an X.400 address is just one of the proxy addresses that may exist for a recipient.

The X.400 recommendations set a standard whereby the electronic mail address for a recipient can be constructed in a perfectly unambiguous manner. This means that the address given to any one person should be built in such a way that it is guaranteed to be unique, and the quest to achieve the level of uniqueness necessary to achieve the goal has arrived at the somewhat strange and unwieldy address format used by X.400 systems today.

An X.400 e-mail address is built up in stages from the country where the MTA is located through the name of the organization responsible for the MTA and down eventually to the personal details of the user who actually composes and sends messages. The full address is referred to as an 'O/R address', or 'Originator/Recipient address', meaning, in effect, that the address of the originator (sender) can be taken from the message and used to address a response back without interfering with the address in any way. An O/R address is composed of a set of attributes. Each attribute has a value and the collective set of attributes and their values enables a messaging system to deliver messages to a person. Let's look at how an X.400 O/R address is built up using the following example:

C=IE; admd=EIRMAIL400; PRMD=XYZ Corporation; O=RETAIL; OU1=Sales; CN=Tony Redmond

Each of the component parts of an X.400 address has its own special meaning. The first term refers to the country where the recipient is located and each country has its own two-character code as defined in the ISO 3166 standard. In this case the code 'IE' refers to Ireland, so according to the standard this recipient must be located somewhere in Ireland. However, this isn't strictly true as some organizations group everyone under a single country code no matter where they are located in order to have a single common entry point into the organization.

The next component refers to the administrative domain (ADMD) while the third refers to the private management domain (PRMD), the two major types of X.400 management domains. An X.400 address must contain one or both domains.

A private administrative domain can be thought of as the collection of electronic mail systems within an organization. Within a single organization that never makes connections to the outside world you would only ever use the private administrative domain. The X.400 addresses created by Exchange Server use the Exchange organization name as the private administration domain, another good reason for getting the design of your organization, sites, and servers well thought out before you start an implementation.

On the other hand, administrative domains are typically managed by a PTT or other public telecommunications provider (such as those operated by MCI, Telecom Eireann, British Telecom, or AT&T) and serve the function of relaying messages between other management domains. A PTT is often used to connect together the administrative domains of organizations working within a single country, and then, on a somewhat higher level, to connect into the domains managed by other PTTs. The collection of administrative domains currently operated throughout the world forms an international message transfer backbone.

The 'O' attribute holds the organization name and in the case of the example it's XYZ Corporation. This should be the same top-level name used when Microsoft Exchange server is implemented for your organization. Up to four organizational units (the 'OU1' through 'OU4' attributes) can be specified to provide further definition. In most cases only a single organizational unit is ever used, and for our purposes we can equate the first organizational unit to a Microsoft Exchange site. The final attribute in the example (CN) defines the 'common name', literally the name used to identify a certain recipient within an organization. Many other attributes are available to help identify a recipient including initials and a generation qualifier. If all the attributes are spelled out it's certainly possible to create very long and complex X.400 addresses.

Directory synchronization and replication

Given that Exchange is a messaging system designed for distributed operation it's critical that the entries for user mailboxes which are stored and managed by the directory service can be quickly and easily synchronized between the different servers in an organization. Exchange automatically synchronizes address information within a site immediately changes are made to the directory from any server in the site. You don't have to do anything to initiate the process; it occurs automatically once a new server is added to the site.

Directory synchronization between sites is performed through a replication scheme similar to that used to distribute the contents of public folders. Because synchronization (or replication) between sites is accomplished by the exchange of specially formatted mail messages, everything depends on an operational mail connector being available between the sites. This is the reason why the directory service in each site is allocated a mail address. In itself the directory service takes no great interest in the underlying details of how its messages are transported between sites. The assumption is made that because a mail connection is available it can be used to transport messages containing directory information from the directory service on one site to its counterpart on another. The MTA, in its turn, regards these messages as any other and does not allocate any great importance to them. If you look at MTA queues you are quite likely to see messages originated from the directory service – notification messages to say that a change has occurred, or data messages containing directory information to be applied to a directory on a remote site.

Once a valid mail connection is available between sites you can configure a directory replication connector. Two approaches can be taken:

1. The connector can be configured on each site. In this case all you need is the ability to send messages to the remote site. This option is very useful when the systems in the remote site are not part of the same Windows NT domain and no trust relationship exists between your domain and the remote domain. The disadvantage is that a certain degree of cooperation and synchronization must take place between the system administrators in the two sites before directory replication works.

2. The connector can be configured in a single operation from either site. This option is only possible within the same domain or when trust relationships exist within the two domains. In addition, the account being used for configuration must possess administrative permissions for the remote site.

Figure 5.24 illustrates a directory replicator connector being configured. In this instance we have elected to configure each site separately.

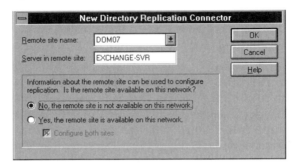

Figure 5.24 *Configuring a directory replication connector*

Transitive connections

Directory information never propagates more than one 'hop' (link between two servers) at a time. The connector can be direct or transitive. In other words, directory replication is possible when two sites are linked by a direct site connector or when two sites are linked indirectly, with another site in between. Take the example of three sites, Dublin, Belfast, and London. Dublin and Belfast are linked with a direct site connector, and Belfast and London are linked with an X.400 site connector. Dublin and London have no direct connection, but the intermediate link established via Belfast is enough to enable directory replication to proceed. In this instance the messages containing directory information are routed in two 'hops'; from Dublin to Belfast and hence to London, and vice versa in the other direction. The important point to understand is that as long as a path exists for messages to travel along, that same path can be used for directory replication. Note that transitive directory replication is configured automatically for standard site connectors, but not for X.400 or Dynamic RAS site connectors. In these instances the sites which 'hide' behind the directly connected site must be specified in the Connected Sites property page for the X.400 or Dynamic RAS connector.

Replication Bridgeheads

The Directory Replication Bridgehead is a term describing the server within a site that takes charge of managing the synchronization process for a connector between that site and another. There can be multiple replication bridgeheads active in a site, one for each operational site connector. However, a site cannot have two replication bridgeheads configured for any other particular site. This is logical – each site has a directory, and if multiple replication connects were made between one site and another there would be clear potential for synchronized chaos occurring within the directory. Preventing chaos or inconsistency within a distributed enterprise-wide directory is important because you want to encourage users to believe that the directory represents a definitive statement of user mail addresses for the organization. If erroneous or duplicated entries are registered users will lose faith in the directory, which is bad.

Figure 5.25
Directory Replication Connector

Figure 5.25 illustrates the general properties for a directory replication connector.

The local bridgehead server for the site is DBO-EXCHANGEIST server, whereas the bridgehead on the remote site is the TCHOUP1 server. Directory replication is accomplished through a request process. Bridgehead servers generate request messages to the remote site they service rather than pushing or force-feeding changes in directory information to remote sites.

Thus, the DBO-EXCHANGEIST server will issue requests to TCHOUP1 whenever it wants to be updated about the directory entries managed in the site where TCHOUP1 is located.

When a directory has changes (additions, deletions, or updates to existing entries) notification messages are generated and sent to all the other servers within a site and to all directory bridgehead servers in other sites, but the actual directory data is not transferred until remote sites request it. In addition to notification messages a scheme of Update Sequence Numbers (USNs) is used to track the status of directory updates between servers. USNs simply track the changes that have been made to a directory on a server, starting from 1. If a server queries another server to discover what its current USN is, and finds that the USN on the remote server is higher than its own, a request to transfer directory updates is immediately initiated.

The Knowledge Consistency Checker

With the possibility that servers, sites, and connectors constantly change within an organization it's easy to see how Exchange might lose track of the details of internal messaging structure, leading in turn to problems routing directory updates from site to site. To avoid this problem Exchange uses a component called the Knowledge Consistency Checker (KCC).

The role of the KCC is simple. It must make sense of all the configuration data exchanged between sites to determine what links have been set up between the different sites. Knowing which sites are connected prevents multiple directory replication bridgeheads being created between two sites, avoiding the problems discussed above. The KCC checks configuration information when it is first supplied (when a site is joined to an organization), and continues to review configuration information as it is replicated between sites at regular intervals. If new sites are discovered from configuration information the KCC attempts to figure out how the sites are connected into the organization and whether other sites are connected in via the newly discovered sites. Transitive directory replication, or propagation across multiple links, is enabled through knowledge of these indirectly connected sites.

How do you know that the KCC is active? The only real indicator is when new sites suddenly appear in the administration program. It is the KCC that discovers that the new site is available and then makes that information (about the site, configuration, and recipients containers from the new site) available for display to the administration program. Immediately after a new site is 'discovered' its containers appear to be empty, but fairly soon afterwards their contents will be populated via normal directory replication.

The process of populating directory information into newly discovered containers is known as backfill. If containers for a new site are displayed but their contents are not available three hours afterwards (given the standard directory replication schedule), it's a good indication that problems exist in the mail connection between the two sites.

For example, compare the two site views extracted from the administration program in Figure 5.26. The view of the Belfast site is complete, because we can see the different recipient containers within the Belfast configuration. However, the view of the Valbonne site is incomplete because only the configuration container can be seen. In this instance backfill has not occurred and we need to check whether the connector between the two sites is operational.

Figure 5.26
KCC is operational, but the mail connection isn't

Successful directory replication

Putting everything together we can see that successful directory replication across multiple sites depends on a number of steps:

1. Synchronization must be active between all servers within a site. This implies that all the servers within each site must be known to the nominated bridgehead server in each site. If a server is 'missed' the data exchanged with other sites will not be complete. Missing a server isn't important if that server does not have a connector to another site, but it's messy and worrying to have this situation occurring so it should be resolved as soon as possible.

2. Sites must be able to communicate together. In other words, a site connector (direct, X.400, or RAS) must be configured and operational to allow configuration data to be exchanged between the different sites.

3. The KCC in each site must be able to create the site and configuration containers for other sites to form an accurate picture of the complete replication environment.

4. Once the configuration containers have been established normal directory replication can proceed to request data from bridgehead replication connectors. The data is populated into the recipient containers for each site. Remember that there can be

several recipient containers active for each site. Replication will ensure that the appropriate recipient information is placed into the various recipient containers.

Understanding the replication schedule

Changes and new directory entries are normally replicated every three hours, unless overruled by the schedule property page for a directory replicator. Updating remote sites every three hours may not be satisfactory in the early stages of an Exchange implementation where the directory is likely to be in a state of flux as mailboxes and custom recipients are added at frequent intervals. Later on, when the system has stabilized, updates every three hours are more acceptable because there won't be so much traffic.

Figure 5.27
Directory Replication Schedule

You should remember that the directory replication schedule is a property which only applies to the connector it is configured for (see Figure 5.27). Take the example of the organization with sites in Dublin, Belfast, and London that we discussed earlier. Directory replication occurs every three hours between Dublin and Belfast and every three hours between Belfast and London. It doesn't follow that changes made in Dublin will turn up in London three hours afterwards, courtesy of the transitive connection through Belfast. It may well be the case that the replication schedule between Dublin and Belfast is not in line with the schedule between Belfast and London, meaning that it could take, at maximum, six hours to get a changed directory entry from Dublin to London. In one way this is pretty similar to making an airline connection through a hub airport. If you manage to time the connection just right you don't have to wait too long between getting off one plane to getting to your connection, but if anything goes wrong (weather, airport congestion, problems with the aircraft) then you end up waiting around looking at interesting items in an airport. The lesson here is not to assume anything: map how directory replication occurs on top of messaging links and chart out the likely time delays, and then adjust replication schedules as required. Users won't thank you if they send messages to outdated addresses just because the directory wasn't updated in time.

If required, you can force directory replication to occur, but only on a server by server basis. Forced updates are desirable in situations where you have applied many different updates to the directory and now want to have this information distributed throughout the organization. The 'Update Now' command button on the General property page for the Directory Service object sets off the process of forced directory updates. As directory propagation only happens one step at a time you may need to initiate several update processes, beginning at the bridgehead server furthest from the server you want to be updated. Think of this process as 'pulling' the updated directory information one step at a time, from server to server, through the organization until you reach the point you want the information to reach. The process isn't particularly graceful and it's easy to miss something along the way, so hopefully Microsoft will come up with a better way to start a forced directory update from every site in the organization, perhaps through the equivalent of an 'all points bulletin' message sent to all bridgehead servers requesting an immediate update in reply.

Synchronization with other Exchange organizations

Exchange V4.0 does not support automated directory replication between different organizations. This would be useful in an environment where a corporation is not able to form an Exchange organization for one reason or another but still wishes to share directory information. Microsoft is aware of a demand for such a feature and it may be supported in a future version.

There is a manual workaround to the problem. Exchange offers a feature to export and import directory entries in the form of CSV data files. Thus it is possible for organizations to export their directory to a file and arrange to swap their exported data with other organizations. Addresses in exported files are treated as custom X.400 or SMTP recipients by the importing organization, so an appropriate connector will also be required to send messages to the recipients after they've been imported. It is convenient to create a new recipients container for imported directory information. If you import data from multiple sources you may like to have separate recipients containers for each source.

Synchronization with foreign directories

Synchronization is also possible with non-Exchange sources through a Windows NT service called the Directory Synchronization Agent (DXA). The service operates in conjunction with the DXA database, built using the same database engine as the information and directory stores. The DXA database is used to track changes that have been made in the Exchange directory between the times when synchronization occurs with foreign directory sources. The database also maintains records of the synchronization operations it has recently performed. Unlike the information store no transactions logs are maintained.

The protocol used by DXA is the well-tried and tested mechanism implemented by Microsoft Mail V3.2 directory synchronization. This allows any system that performs directory synchronization with Microsoft Mail to also support Exchange server.

Microsoft Mail post offices synchronize the contents of their Global Address List (GAL) through a relatively complex series of events which, in outline:

- Generates directory information from individual post offices.
- Collects the directory information from the post offices to a central directory synchronizer.
- Merges the directory information into a new GAL.
- Distributes the new GAL to the different post offices.

Within this scheme Microsoft Mail post offices act as either a DirSync Server or a DirSync Requestor. The server acts as the central directory synchronizer while the requestors provide directory information and accept the merged GAL back afterwards. Through the DXA, Exchange is able to assume either role, but an individual server cannot be configured to act in both roles.

When the Exchange DXA assumes the role of the DirSync Server all the Microsoft Mail post offices must be reconfigured to identify the Exchange MS-Mail Connector post office as the DirSync Server. Only one DXA Server can be configured per site, and it takes charge of propagating the addresses for the MS-Mail users (attached to the post offices it synchronizes) to other Exchange sites via normal directory replication.

When DXA acts as a DirSync Requestor it means that DXA will receive copies of the MS-Mail GAL from another DirSync Server, and then propagate the addresses in the GAL to other Exchange sites. Multiple DirSync Requestors can be active within a site, but this configuration would only be used if there are multiple available sources of MS-Mail address information – for example, if there were two or more separate MS-Mail networks. In this case you could create a separate DirSync Requestor to receive the GAL from the DirSync Server acting in each MS-Mail network.

As Exchange Server becomes more and more established it's likely that a wide range of synchronization tools will be built by third parties. A good example of this is the 'Synchronizer 500' utility designed to connect the Exchange directory with Digital's Alta Vista Directory Services.

Synchronization with another directory raises a very important question. What is your strategy for an organization-wide directory? If you are moving to a homogeneous implementation of Exchange Server throughout the enterprise then the answer is easy – the strategy for directory synchronization should be based around the Exchange directory. But if you foresee a heterogeneous messaging environment composed of multiple e-mail systems you also have the option to select a common directory such as X.500 or a directory synchronization product such as LinkAge Software's Directory Exchange, a product capable of synchronizing the directories from Exchange, Microsoft Mail, Lotus Notes, Lotus cc:Mail, HP OpenMail, IBM PROFS, and Verimation MEMO among others.

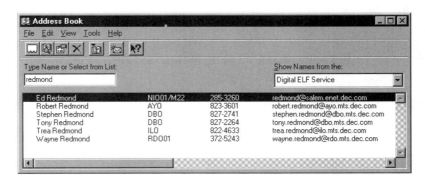

Figure 5.28
Digital's Employee Locator Facility accessed by an Exchange client

X.500 (or other corporate-level) directories don't have to remain hidden from Exchange users. MAPI extensions can be built to make a directory available as another source of address information, along the same lines as the Exchange directory or the Personal Address Book. Digital personnel have always enjoyed a facility called ELF (for

Employee Locator Facility) which can be consulted to find out details about other employees – their mail stop, electronic mail address, phone number, and so on. ELF data is stored in an X.500 database distributed across a set of UNIX servers, and the Exchange implementation within Digital uses a MAPI extension to map ELF as an additional address book for Exchange. Figure 5.28 shows the results gained by consulting ELF to discover the Digital employees with the surname 'Redmond'. Apart from anything else, making a corporate directory accessible to all users via their mail client helps the client to be accepted quickly. It also leverages the information in the corporate directory and prevents any requirement to rekey information or otherwise transfer entries into another directory.

To complete this discussion on corporate directories I'll take the opportunity to note that Digital offers a number of different synchronization tools that can help to keep Digital DDS (Message Router Distributed Directory Service) and X.500 directories in line with Exchange. If you're moving from a Digital system or simply trying to integrate Exchange into an existing Digital messaging environment you should check out DSU, XDSU, and X.500 synchronizer. DSU and XDSU enable synchronization between DDS and other directories, X.500 and other directories, while the X.500 Synchronizer product links Exchange and Digital's Alta Vista Directory Service. In the future, when Exchange offers direct support of external directory access products such as LDAP, it may be possible to build a more elegant directory synchronization scheme, possibly using features built into Exchange but more likely through third party add-ons.

In all cases the critical selection factor is which directory service supports the highest degree of automatic synchronization (once everything is set up – it's too much to expect totally automatic directory synchronization) across all potential directory sources. There's no point in performing manual synchronization if you can at all avoid it.

6

Conducting a Pilot for Exchange Server

Introduction

Conducting a pilot will be easier for some companies than others, and everyone will find that different aspects of the Exchange Server (or clients) and its interoperability with various components of already installed systems have to be covered.

The easiest pilots will be those for sites who already have a Microsoft Mail network up and running. Exchange Server is the natural and evolutionary path for Microsoft Mail installations and anyone who is operating this mail system should look at Exchange Server with a very serious eye on a quick introduction to production status. Exchange server addresses the majority if not all of the architectural weaknesses of the technology embodied in the Microsoft Mail post office and provides a great deal of new functionality at the same time. In addition, Exchange Server allows you to connect Microsoft Mail clients with the new server fairly easily so users don't have to be retrained when the new server is initially introduced. Finally, the migration wizards that are available for Microsoft Mail are much more developed and functional than the equivalents for any other mail system. The wizards enable Microsoft Mail users to migrate all their messages to Exchange private folders with ease. The fact that the migration wizards for Microsoft Mail are so good isn't altogether surprising but is welcome as it eliminates much of the pain otherwise felt at the user level during any migration process.

Longer and more complex pilots will have to be conducted if you currently operate a non-Microsoft mail system. The degree of complexity will vary considerably and no hard or fast rules can be given yet, but logic indicates that a pilot to assess the technical issues involved in the introduction of Exchange server into a Windows-based user community that's already running a LAN-based e-mail system, such as Novell GroupWise or Lotus cc:Mail, might well be easier than the altogether different issues that will come up during an analysis of a similar situation involving a system delivering 'more than just mail' already, such as Lotus Notes. In general in these circumstances you won't, for example, have to sort out basic problems like PC networking and connectivity. However, often other nontechnical issues like user unwillingness to move to a new system have to be addressed.

As discussed in an earlier chapter, all pilots must address the question of how Windows NT is to be operated within the organization. Where will the servers be located, how will they be connected, what security model will be used, how will traveling or mobile users be accommodated, and will the joint Windows NT and Exchange implementations be able to grow from initial implementation through a complete roll-out without undue disruption or redesign.

Approaching a pilot

In the world of monolithic, centralized computer applications specifying the boundaries of a pilot was pretty easy. The new mini- or mainframe computer was rolled in, the software was installed, and you connected a number of video terminals to run the application. Between ten and twenty-five terminals were enough to generate a realistic test load for the application's functionality, and you could confidently scale up the results gained from the test to get a good idea of the size of system required to support the eventual user community.

With client–server systems the situation isn't as clear-cut. It is easy to take client software out of the shrink-wrap and install it on individual PCs, then connect the clients to the server to check out the functionality. But this isn't really fulfilling the purpose of the pilot by generating a realistic load to check whether the application will function when it's scaled up. Consider the following questions:

- Are the client platforms used in the pilot representative of the PCs actually used by users? Are the systems covering the range of CPU types and speeds and is the memory configuration the same?

- Are all the client operating systems represented in the pilot? Do you, for example, want to use the Windows 95 Exchange client as well as the Windows NT Exchange client? In conjunction with this topic I would consider whether you intend to upgrade to a Windows 95 desktop environment in the near future and, if so, what impact this will have on the client configurations under test.

- What clients are you going to consider for deployment? Are all of these clients going to be adequately tested during the pilot so that a full and fair comparison of the different capabilities can be arrived at? Don't assume that Microsoft is the only client vendor in an Exchange environment. Many other vendors will support the MAPI interface over time, so a wide range of choice should be available, and there's more than a distinct possibility that a client from someone other than Microsoft might be most appropriate in your situation.

- What will you do to satisfy people who use systems like Apple Macintosh or UNIX workstations?
- Are the network connections between the clients and servers the same as will be used in production? For instance, do you need to check out remote access over an asynchronous telephone connection?
- Is the software installed in the same way as it will be if it is eventually deployed? For example, do you want to test the difference (if any) in start-up time for client software loaded from a network file service and local hard disks?
- Can the client software be deployed and managed easily? Microsoft's solution is System Management Server (SMS), another part of the Back Office suite, but you may already have another PC management tool in place. How will this work with Exchange?

Another point to consider is the type of personnel taking part in the pilot. To provide an accurate assessment of any application's value in real life it's important that a good cross-section of the user population is included in the pilot. If you have people who have never seen PCs in their lives before then clearly the pilot is going to take a long time before any worthwhile data becomes available. On the other hand, you don't want to staff the pilot with too many technical people because they tend to be either too forgiving or too critical of a product's performance depending on whether they 'like' the product. Liking a product often comes down to whether someone approves of the technical nature of the product, the vendor, or any associated reasons that come to hand during coffee room debates!

All of the above points could be made for any PC client–server product. Because Microsoft Exchange is a messaging system there are some other important points that must be considered during a pilot. These include:

- How will the entries for Exchange mailboxes and custom recipients be synchronized with other directory sources? This is only going to be really important if you already have a messaging system in production. If you do, you better make sure that it is possible to achieve an easy synchronization of addresses between Exchange and the other system, using an automated procedure if at all possible. Can the same synchronization procedure handle address information from all the potential sources within your organization? Is the synchronization bi-directional or only one-way?

- How will Exchange Server send and receive messages to and from any other messaging system that's in place internally or externally? What connectors (SMTP, X.400, etc.) are going to be operational and how will you test the connection between Exchange Server and other messaging systems? Do you have a full list of all the connections already used by people within your organization? How will you test that multi-body part messages are able to flow from one side to the other while preserving their essential attributes?

- Can the content of messages generated and sent by Exchange Server be read after they have been delivered to people using the other messaging systems in place within your organization? Exchange Server is able to generate messages in Word for Windows (V6 or V7), Rich Text Format (RTF), and ASCII, and it's wonderful to be able to send your thoughts out to the world in bold red 24-point Arial. There shouldn't be many problems with messages generated in ASCII, but will recipients throughout your organization (and beyond) be able to deal with RTF and Word?

Asking these questions, even if you think you're pretty sure of the answers, is a good way to make sure that all the essential issues are covered during the pilot. Possibly even more important it's a way to isolate potential costs so that you can factor them into a deployment budget. Software components like directory synchronizers, format converters, and mail gateways are expensive to buy or build. It's important that you uncover all the situations where additional costs might be incurred before Exchange can be put into full production, because if you don't you'll find that your deployment schedule and budget will be afflicted by complexities that arise and have to be dealt with when you should really be concentrating on delivery. Good preparation is half the battle in achieving good deployments.

Failure to ask the correct questions both when considering a migration and during a pilot implementation inevitably ends up in an exercise that's a waste of time, energy, and money, and one that will lead to a shoddy deployment that delivers a low level of service to the user community.

Training

I don't believe anyone can pick up the documentation set for Exchange Server and become a trained expert by close study of its contents. It's good to read the documentation, including the release notes, but some degree of formal training should be part of the project plan for any pilot.

Initially you'll want to cover training focused towards system management and administration. Programming, including the whiz-bang aspects of Exchange like electronic folders and MAPI, can be left until the next phase (formal deployment) begins. It's essential to master the basics of any subject, and the basics of Exchange include topics like planning the network, defining how servers are placed into sites, the relationship with the Windows NT security model, and other aspects of system management.

Your pilot shouldn't ignore user training. The people participating in the pilot will need some training, otherwise they won't be able to properly exercise the product's functionality, so make sure that at least one formal training session is made available to pilot users. It's likely that you won't have in-house skills to be able to run this course so you need to contact a local Microsoft qualified training center and get them involved.

Helping users form good habits

The opportunity to give people good e-mail habits is one major advantage gained through well-planned user training. If people learn how to do things properly right from the start they'll work with the system in an intelligent and constructive manner. Table 6.1 lists eight good user habits you may want to encourage. Use this table as a base to build on, adding your own ideas to the list.

Many installations print up 'cheat sheets' for users to publicize hints and tips. Users can keep the cheat sheets beside their PC and if you take the opportunity to inform people about good working habits among the other hints and tips there's a fair chance that users will actually follow the advice.

During the pilot it's a good idea to check with the people who received training and see whether the training was relevant and helpful. After reviewing feedback from users who have received training you can decide whether or not the same training can be used during the roll-out phase. Bear in mind that off-the-shelf training is often delivered at a lowest common denominator level so the content of the initial course will often need to be adjusted to reflect your organization's computing infrastructure as well as how you intend to use Exchange in day-to-day life. Some people are happy enough to go with standard training, perhaps supplementing the course material with a booklet covering site-specific details while others design and deliver their own tailored training. Cost, as always, has some bearing on the decision, but remember that good training will invariably repay its cost several times over by driving down the number of calls that support personnel have to deal with.

Table 6.1 *Good user habits to encourage*

	1	Make a decision to delete or keep a message as soon as you've read it. If you're keeping the message move it into an appropriate folder.
	2	Check the 'Empty Deleted Items folder upon exiting' option. This deletes unwanted mail and stops it accumulating in the Deleted Items folder.
	3	Don't include the text of original messages in replies as this increases the overall size of messages within the system.
	4	Don't include documents in messages unless you really need to. Send pointers to documents (the name of the file in a shared file service or a short-cut to the document) if at all possible.
	5	Don't use messaging as a way to broadcast information to people who may not want to receive it. In other words, try and keep the distribution list for messages as short as possible.
	6	Don't add graphics to Auto Signature files as this will drive up the overall size of messages and create a demand the network may not be able to handle.
	7	Compact personal folder files on a regular basis to reclaim space on your hard disk.
	8	Don't leave an unattended PC logged into your Exchange account. Protect your work with a password-protected screen saver or log-out of Exchange if you have to leave your PC alone.
	9	If you travel with your computer remember to download the off-line address book before you leave for a trip. This makes sure that any message you create while traveling will be addressed correctly.
	10	Use the Out of Office Assistant to notify people whenever you won't be able to respond to messages for any reason.

Programmer and administrator training

User training is a critical part of the pilot, but it's a mistake to concentrate totally on this aspect alone. Programmers and system administrators will also need training and this need should be factored into an overall training plan that begins in the pilot stage and continues on through implementation.

Consider the skills necessary in an Exchange Server environment. In your environment they might include:

- Windows NT server including Apple Macintosh client and networking support (if required)
- Exchange Server and clients
- TPC/IP utilities such as WINS, DHCP, and DNS
- SMTP, X.400, and the site connectors, plus knowledge of any other messaging systems you want to connect to
- Associated technologies such as Windows NT workstation
- Directory synchronization with external directories
- Migration tools and utilities
- Windows 95, Windows V3.11, DOS, UNIX utilities associated with SMTP-based messaging such as sendmail, and Internet firewalls
- Visual Basic, Visual C++, and other development tools used to build or enhance electronic forms applications
- General networking experience

Few people have the ability to master all of these skills, nor the time nor wide experience required to achieve a good understanding of them all. This means that you'll probably need to spread skills across a team of individuals engaged in the pilot or use expertise bought in externally.

Don't forget other associated developments which may be happening at the same time as they may affect your pilot or the implementation by introducing new skills that must be factored into a training plan. For instance, SMS might be used to manage the deployment of Exchange clients and other desktop applications. Or your company may well have decided to use the Microsoft Internet Explorer (client) and Microsoft Internet Information Server for World Wide Web access and home page management. Who's responsible for these issues?

Was the pilot successful?

At the end of the exercise all pilots have to come up with some results, the most fundamental of which is an assessment of whether the product under trial is suitable for widespread deployment. Attached to this assessment are many caveats that determine the degree of success the deployment is likely to have. You may find that network links between servers need to be upgraded, that new hardware needs to be installed, client systems need more memory, or even that the whole thing should be put off for six months or so to allow you to sort out some other aspect of the overall infrastructure. You'll definitely need to have determined a proposal for roll-out in order to gauge whether a roll-out is feasible, and this should include details of the Exchange sites and servers that are proposed together with details of how the Exchange structure is layered on top of the Windows NT security and network models. Finally, you should have a technical and end-user training plan laid out. All of these conclusions need to be documented and reviewed so that all possible issues are fully covered.

At the end of the day your management are likely to ask a number of basic questions that you'll need to have good answers for. Among the normal questions in this category are:

- How much will the deployment cost in total – software (server and clients), hardware (including upgrades), training, systems management, day-to-day operations, and consultancy?
- How long will the complete roll-out take from beginning to end?
- What benefits will the new messaging environment deliver to the organization (in general) as well as the end users?

The final question is whether or not it is worthwhile to move from an existing messaging infrastructure to a new one, albeit one as interesting as Microsoft Exchange. That question deserves far more attention than a brief paragraph or two here, so I'll cover it in detail in a separate chapter.

Summary

Running a pilot is always an interesting and important activity because it's the place where marketing hype is discarded and technical reality comes into focus. A good plan for the pilot which identifies all the important questions for your organization is an essential aid to producing accurate results and eventually a productive long-term implementation. Hopefully this chapter has managed to identify some of the challenges that you're likely to meet along the way if you make the decision to look at Microsoft Exchange Server and its clients.

7

Migrating from Other Messaging Systems

Introduction

Computer applications evolve in either of two ways. One route is to continually update, applying software and hardware upgrades as they become available. The other is to migrate from one system to another. The former is less painful than the latter, but sometimes a migration is deemed to be imperative and so it proceeds. In this chapter we'll look at some of the aspects of messaging systems that migrations bring to the fore, with particular reference to the tasks involved in planning for and then executing a migration of a messaging system to Microsoft Exchange Server.

An end, or a beginning?

I hate migrations. It's a fact of life that a large number of Microsoft Exchange Server installations will involve a migration in some form or other. Any migration I have ever been involved with has been painful, and many have left a bad taste in my mouth. No migration is or can be seamless and users always experience some impact. So it's important to be sure that a migration is justified, feasible, and the right thing to do. Asking yourself some questions and making sure you have answers, and then analyzing the content of the answers is an excellent way of verifying that a migration is the right thing to do. In my opinion, among the first questions that must be answered in relation to a migration from an existing electronic mail system to Microsoft Exchange Server are:

▶ Why are we considering a migration away from our existing system?

▶ What benefits are going to be delivered to the user community after the migration is accomplished?

- Can the benefits be quantified in terms of finance or extra functionality that can now be provided to users?
- When do we want the migration to be completed by?
- What data will be involved in the migration?
- How will the data be migrated?

Different organizations will place varying degrees of importance on the questions listed above, and no doubt everyone has their own specific questions that they'll want to add. I feel it's important to have absolute clarity about all the issues before plunging into a migration so that those involved can justify the time, expense, and other costs to both users and management.

Perhaps another question that should be asked at this time is whether a better and more effective job can be done with the messaging system that you're considering moving from? I have seen many situations where a messaging system is badly managed and doesn't deliver a good level of service to user communities. It may well be the case that replacing the current system with a new system, like Exchange Server, will draw a line underneath all of the ineffective management that has gone before, but it's more likely that the old bad habits will be transferred from one system to another. Clearly, if you're aware of the danger steps can be taken to ensure that current problems are addressed and eliminated as part of the migration project.

If a mail system is in operation today you should take advantage by extracting various operational statistics to help understand:

- The volume of messages being processed by the system.
- The amount of data (messages) being stored in shared system areas and user (or personal) areas.
- Details of any other application that depends in any way on the messaging system. Workflow systems are obvious examples of systems which often depend on electronic mail, but there can be applications that make sporadic use of electronic mail, possibly to generate warning or other status messages, and you need to know about these.
- The service levels being delivered to users. For example, how long does it take to transfer a message from one side of the organization to another? How long does it take for a message to arrive within the same physical site?

Migrations are unsuccessful if the new system cannot meet the same service levels as the existing system once the migration process is complete. If the hardware installed cannot cope with the volume of messages, if applications are disabled because they cannot communicate using the messaging system, if user data is lost or otherwise becomes inaccessible, or message delivery times are not improved then you really have to ask why you are even considering a migration in the first place.

Why migrate at all?

Are you migrating to Microsoft Exchange Server because:

- You think it's a good idea, and anyway, everyone else seems to want to do it.
- Windows NT is the strategic computing platform for your organization, or at least Windows NT is the strategic choice for distributed application servers.
- Microsoft is the preferred software vendor for desktop and other applications.
- Microsoft Exchange Server offers a significant increase in the functionality you already enjoy from your existing system.
- Microsoft Exchange Server is the natural upgrade path for your existing mail system.
- The operation of a Microsoft Exchange Server will help to achieve a return on the additional investment required to perform the migration.

Not many people will openly agree with the first response listed above. Thinking something is a good idea is not a rational argument to back up a major change in any technical or computing infrastructure. The old adage 'There goes the crowd; I must be with them' springs to mind here. Are you proposing to migrate because someone else says that it's a good idea.

I often wonder about the ideas and opinions expressed in the content of reviews written in computer magazines as well as the conclusions reached at the end of product reviews. There's no doubt that many journalists are very competent individuals with a broad range of expertise, but it's difficult to write knowledgeably about a mail system unless you've lived and breathed with the system in an operational environment over a period of time. Running a messaging system for ten or twenty users is easy, running the same software for hundreds of users exposes the weak points as well as the strengths. The lesson here is simple. Never take someone else's opinion as fact. You know your computing environment best so accept input from many sources and then make your own mind up.

Dealing with the existing investment

Many companies find themselves in a situation where they have a huge financial investment in their current mainframe or mini-computer based electronic mail system. The investment is represented by hardware, software licenses, knowledge (programming, administration, and user), data, any associated applications which may use the system in one form or another, the infrastructure put in place to enable the electronic mail system to operate, and whatever connections exist to other messaging systems. Quite a shopping list when the time comes to justify a migration!

If you find yourself in a situation where your company really must continue to leverage off its existing financial investment and can't afford to engage in a total migration the best tactic to adopt is to establish Exchange Server as the 'new' platform. If any opportunity arises to move users off the older system, perhaps as hardware maintenance contracts expire or systems reach their end of life, or new user communities request an electronic mail server they can be attached to an Exchange Server. This tactic establishes a situation where two 'islands' of electronic messaging exist within the company – the old established system and Exchange Server. Gradually, over time, the aim is to grow the Exchange island and diminish the other and get to a stage where a total cut-over can be justified.

An approach like this minimizes the additional investment required to introduce Exchange Server while it maximizes the investment represented by the existing system. It also allows the implementation of Exchange Server to progress at a comfortable, well-controlled pace. On the other hand, you will have to devote a lot of time and attention to ensuring that the best possible connectivity is maintained between the two messaging islands.

Electronic mail is a highly visible application because it affects almost every desktop in a company. Everyone from the Chief Executive Officer down to the newest entrant might well be using e-mail, so when something goes wrong its effects are felt everywhere, including in the job continuation prospects of system administrators. Accordingly it is essential that the migration is done right no matter what tactics need to be adopted in order to achieve eventual success.

Strategic computing platforms

The decision about the strategic computing platform for your organization is often not surrounded in clarity. The larger the organization and the more autonomous the divisions within the organization the harder it is to enforce strategic decisions. In these situations you'll often find tactical compromises being made to facilitate the requirements of specific applications or organizational entities.

Windows NT grows in capability and functionality all the time. The original version (V3.1) was slow, lacked applications, and needed lots of hardware. Even so, V3.1 created a clear differentiation between Windows, the user-oriented desktop operating system, and a much more robust and interesting high-end server specifically designed for applications. Each release since has added functionality to the point where Windows NT workstation is a more than viable option for deployment as a generalized desktop platform, and Windows NT server is probably the most flexible distributed application server available today. It's important not to engage in too much hype however. Windows NT is good, but there are lots of situations where it would be inappropriate or just plain foolish to even consider NT. The time when Windows NT takes over from mainframes for applications like airline reservation systems is probably not yet with us!

If your organization has determined that Windows NT is a strategic computing platform the decision to migrate towards Microsoft Exchange Server is easy. But what happens if the strategic platform is UNIX (any variant), or a proprietary operating system such as OpenVMS or IBM MVS? How then does Microsoft Exchange Server fit into the overall picture? Can the implementation of an electronic messaging system on Windows NT be represented (and agreed) as a tactical solution? And how will the Windows NT servers fit into other aspects of the computing infrastructure such as network security or integrated network management?

Even if Windows NT is the nominated choice for a strategic organization-wide computing platform you must ensure that the implementation of Exchange accommodates the Windows NT domain and network infrastructures that might already be in place. Or if you're only starting with Windows NT, as we've mentioned before, the initial implementation of Windows NT must take the requirements of Exchange Server into account. Remember that it is very difficult to change items such as server and site names once the implementation starts, so it's important to take these factors into account in your migration plan.

If Windows NT is new to your organization a migration is easier because you can plan the introduction of Exchange and Windows NT together as an integrated entity rather than having to retrofit Exchange on top of an existing NT infrastructure. However, the purely practical aspects involved in the introduction of any new computer platform such as physical security, data backups, and communications might well be impacted by the requirements of the Exchange Server. For instance, how will the Exchange data structures be backed up, when will this take place, and will it stop people using the messaging service while backups are taken?

The question of Microsoft as the preferred vendor for software applications is linked, in some respects, to the decision about Windows NT. If Windows NT is your strategic computing platform then there are strong and compelling reasons to select other Microsoft applications in the areas they are available. All of the products in the BackOffice and Microsoft Office sets fall into this category.

Will Exchange Server provide more functionality than my existing system?

Determining whether a move to Microsoft Exchange Server will provide more functionality than an existing system depends on:

- The functionality in Microsoft Exchange Server your users will actually use. For example, there's no value at all in replication of public folders if this type of information sharing is not going to be used.
- Whether any commonly used or otherwise desirable features available in the existing system are not available in Microsoft Exchange Server. Workflow is one example. The workflow in Microsoft Exchange Server is not as good as that available in Lotus Notes, for example, and if many workflow applications are used on a day-to-day basis to solve real business problems you'll have a challenge to move the people who depend on those applications if you can't come up with a replacement, not to mention a method to access old data represented by workflow items that have been processed in the past.

Knowledge of the features the user community deem to be important is essential when you compare one system against another. You might get excited about the prospect of the latest whiz-bang-wallop feature that's only available in a specific product. However, how many people actually use all of the features provided in the products they have today and will your users feel the same way about the features you now propose to introduce? Will the feature make them more productive, assuming they'll ever use it?

The AutoSignature and Inbox Assistant features offered by Exchange clients are two good examples of what I mean. AutoSignature allows users to add a piece of text to messages before they are sent to provide additional information about the originator. In the UNIX messaging world this text is known as a signature. Inbox Assistant can act as a filter against new mail messages as they arrive, taking action for messages that meet preset criteria. For instance, refile all new messages from my manager into the wastebasket, or send anything that references a particular project to another user because they've taken responsibility for that project now. These are features that are often demonstrated and attract a lot of interest, but I have a question in my own mind as to how many users actually go to the trouble to create a text library to use with the AutoText feature, or to create a set of rules for the Inbox Assistant.

Following the upgrade paths

Microsoft Mail is the only mail system for which Microsoft Exchange Server can reasonably be regarded as the natural or evolutionary upgrade path. Indeed, the primary market for the initial implementations of Exchange Server is the many thousands of Microsoft Mail post offices running around the world.

So if you're running Microsoft Mail now you have the easiest argument to make for a migration. Exchange servers can be installed to take the place of the Microsoft Mail post offices, and the Microsoft Mail clients can be replaced by Exchange clients. Because the two clients come from the same vendor they share many common features, at least on the surface and in terminology, so the visual and immediate impact on day to day use after a switch-over is reasonably limited. Exchange Server includes a 'Migration Wizard' to help users transfer the contents of their Microsoft Mail file cabinets into Exchange, so most of the important points in relation to a migration can be taken care of in an almost automatic manner.

If you're running another mail system the situation is different. No other vendor is going to be happy to see customers migrating away from their software (not to mention hardware), so you can hardly expect to see glowing recommendations for Microsoft Exchange Server as the upgrade option of choice. You can also expect to incur more costs during the migration because the movement of user information, messages, and documents is not going to be as automatic or straightforward.

Achieving a return on your investment

Messaging often becomes a mission-critical application. In other words, if messaging is not available to users business suffers. Even when this is the case you want to get good value for the investment made to build and operate the messaging environment, and if you now propose to migrate from one system to another then ideally the total value gained from the exercise should exceed the costs by a considerable margin.

Determining an accurate total for the costs of migration is not an exact science as there are many factors which will influence the outcome. Migrations tend to be difficult to cost to any exact degree. In fact, migrations are rather like household do-it-yourself exercises in that hidden costs reveal themselves after a start is made on a job. For instance, you decide to change the wallpaper in a room only to find that there are holes behind the existing wallpaper, so you need to fill them in. Once the paper is up it looks good, but the woodwork looks dull and blemished in comparison so you really need to apply a new coat of paint. And if the woodwork is done the ceilings should be done to match. All additional costs.

To avoid unpleasant surprises I think it's a good idea to set down a list of bullet points to cover the major cost headings. Here are some common areas of cost that might be met during a migration:

▶ Installation and configuration of all the necessary hardware, including upgrades to existing computers.

▶ Installation and configuration of Windows NT on the hardware according to the domain and security models you have chosen to use.

▶ Licensing and installation of Microsoft Exchange Server on all relevant Windows NT computers and clients on whatever PCs are required.

▶ Training people to use the client functionality (this is more expensive if you have to support a number of clients), including details about how to get to data that might remain on other systems.

▶ Migrating user messages and documents from the existing mail system.

▶ Running a pilot and then proceeding with a roll-out.

Apart from the financial aspects of a migration I think it is also wise to consider the question of the long term future for your current electronic mail system. Ask the vendor whether plans exist for new versions, when the new versions will be available and what features will be delivered in the new releases. If there is little future in the current mail system then the financial aspects of a proposal to migrate to Exchange may quickly become a moot point. If a migration is going to be required anyway at some point in the future it makes sense to take the pain now to establish a new messaging system and go forward so that maximum benefit can be gained from the new system. On the other hand, if detailed plans exist to develop and enhance your existing electronic mail system the question of how much it will cost to upgrade to new releases should be asked. If you don't have a maintenance or other type of support contract you may have to purchase server and client software again, albeit possibly at a discounted price, but even if the software upgrades are free what another possible costs might be incurred?

The points above list some of the areas where costs may arise. It's often a useful exercise to compare the costs of migration against the costs of staying with an existing mail system, as shown in Table 7.1 below. There are two ways to approach this exercise. First, you can assume that the existing system will stay in place in much the same shape as it is today. Or, more realistically if users are complaining about the features and service provided by the current system, you can factor in the costs to evolve the system so that it provides approximately the same level of functionality as you can expect from Exchange Server.

Table 7.1 *Comparing the cost of upgrading or migrating*

Potential area of cost	$ cost of migration to Microsoft Exchange	$ cost to evolve existing electronic mail system
Client software		
Server software		
Ongoing support costs for client software. For example, the cost to upgrade to new releases of the software or the right to report problems to a support center.		
Ongoing support costs for server software		
User training. Remember that moving to a new version of any software may impact users and require some degree of retraining.		
Programmer/system manager training.		
Any additional or new hardware costs (memory upgrades, disks, etc.) for user PCs.		
Any additional or new hardware costs for the servers involved in the electronic mail system.		
External consulting or other personnel costs.		
Messaging gateways. Some gateways may only be required during the migration period.		
File format converters or viewers either for PC clients or elsewhere in the network.		

Table 7.1 *Comparing the cost of upgrading or migrating (continued)*

Potential area of cost	$ cost of migration to Microsoft Exchange	$ cost to evolve existing electronic mail system
Associated applications (e.g., time management, workflow), both servers and clients. Costs might include rewriting or replacing applications.		
Directory synchronization, both initial costs to implement synchronization plus ongoing costs to ensure that synchronization occurs on a regular and predictable basis.		
Ongoing system management/system administration.		
Operating a user Help Desk.		
Remote access (telephone communications, RAS systems and whatever other infrastructure is required).		
LAN/WAN networks and other communications. For example, will you require new telecommunications links?		
Overall Total Costs	$	$

Listing the potential areas of cost is easy, but putting a real degree of exactitude on these costs is not. Costs are likely to occur over an extended period of time and the amounts involved will differ from site to site. The desired (or required) rate of return on investments will also vary from organization to organization. Technical people might sometimes wish that financial issues would go away but you have to be able to answer the question about how much the whole exercise will cost, and what additional value will be delivered to the organization once the migration is complete. Saying that everything will be better, more up to date, more robust and compliant with standards, messages will be transmitted more securely and faster or that the architecture of Microsoft Exchange Server is much more impressive than the current system will surely cut no ice with the financial wizards. It's better to come up with some realistic figures for the work, factor it into an operational budget, and seek to justify the expenditure through reasons like:

▶ Lower cost of ownership (based on deployment on Windows NT systems rather than mini- or mainframe computers) over a reasonable period, say three years.

- Enabling the organization to achieve higher levels of quality through the deployment of work-group applications rather than the purely interpersonal nature of simple electronic mail. Give some examples to illustrate the point such as the use of replicated public folders to automatically distribute up to date marketing information across the enterprise.
- Implementation of other valued-added applications enabled by Exchange Server that solve business problems. For instance, integrating a voice mail system with Exchange to replace an existing voice mail system that may be standalone and perhaps showing signs of age.

Whatever logic you come up with to justify the decision you must be realistic. Use figures intelligently to show costs benefits and illustrate your points with examples of how new functionality will enable people to work together more effectively. If your logic is not reasonable and cannot be backed up to other peoples' satisfaction the decision to progress with a migration is probably not a good one and you should take another hard look at your situation before going on.

When will the migration be over?

Migrations, like all other techniques, occupy a spectrum defining the different approaches that can be taken to the actual process. At one end you have the 'Big Bang' approach, moving all users as quickly as possible from the old system to the new. Right at the other end of the spectrum is the phased, gentle movement, generally involving the migration of groups of users over an extended period of time.

Few experienced system managers like the risk factor involved in one-shot migrations so the technique is only ever practiced when the number of users and data involved is small, certainly at levels where people are comfortable that the migration can be carried out in a single day or over a weekend. Extended migration periods can be difficult to manage, and more often than not involve the introduction of potential bottlenecks as messages pass through gateways. Directory synchronization for addressing information is also an issue to be managed during migrations. We'll discuss these points in more detail later on in this chapter.

Most organizations will conduct a pilot for Exchange Server before engaging in widespread deployment. Even if you have taken a strategic decision to use Windows NT and Exchange Server as your future messaging platform it's still a good idea to run a pilot. To reinforce the advice offered in a previous chapter, consider these good reasons for including a pilot implementation of Exchange Server and clients in your migration plan:

- A pilot allows technical staff to get to know the capabilities and weaknesses of the new server in a real-life environment. You can use this experience to plan for:
    - The hardware configuration for server deployment. Determine how many servers will be required to support the total user population and where those servers will be located, as well as how they will form sites within the Exchange organization. You should make a first pass at allocating users across the servers. You should consider the hardware and software required for client deployments too!
    - The operational rules to be followed by system administrators and operators. For example, when will backups be taken and how will the backups be secured?
    - The network links required to connect servers and clients. Do you need to reconfigure any parts of the network?
    - The way Exchange Server will be installed on top of the Windows NT domain and security models deployed within the organization. If problems are detected the models may need adjustment, work that must be carried out before general deployment of Exchange Server begins.
    - The order in which different groups within the organization will be moved to Exchange Server. In general it's best to plan to move groups that share a high degree of data commonality at one time in order to maximize the usefulness of functionality like public folders and to minimize the message flow outside the Exchange environment. This part of your plan will also help you identify when older systems can be switched off and hardware removed (and hardware and software maintenance contracts for the old systems terminated).
    - Which Exchange servers will act as messaging servers and which will fulfill special roles such as points of connection with foreign messaging systems or public folder servers.
    - Migration of documents and users. Perhaps some special tools are required to extract, manipulate, and then import data from the system you are migrating from? If so, can these tools be sourced from external agencies or will they have to be written internally?
- Users need to be trained as they move from the older system to an Exchange client. A training plan should be prepared so that users are ready to move. The pilot allows the plan to be developed and verified. The training plan should answer questions like:

- What training will they receive? Will you provide users with customized quick look-up guides or cheat sheets for items specific to your environment such as electronic forms applications? Are there any good habits (for example, how to effectively use disk space within the Private Information Store) that you want to enforce during training sessions?
- Do users need to be told how to deal with data migrated from the old system? For example, how to deal with distribution lists that contain a mixture of people using the old system as well as Exchange Server?
- Who will deliver the training? Do you have an internal training department that can do the work or will an external training provider come in to deliver courses? How much will the training cost? Do you have a proposal to charge departments for the training their personnel will receive or will the total cost of the training be rolled up into the overall migration plan?
- When is the training available? Make sure that training is synchronized with the movement of users to Exchange Server. Training people too early is nearly as bad as training them too late.

▶ Support must be put in place so it's important to involve those who deliver end-user support in the pilot. Support personnel need training too, and this requirement should be addressed in the overall training plan. Experience gained in the pilot will help you identify exactly what form and content that training should take.

A proper pilot cannot be rushed. There's always a temptation to take a short cut on the basis that the sooner the new system goes into production the better, but this is a short-term view that inevitably leads to tears. The old adage that fools rush in where angels fear to tread comes to mind here.

Several times during 1995 Bill Gates was widely quoted to say that Exchange Server would not ship until its customers told Microsoft that it was ready (the same was said about Windows 95). Customers in this sense are the technical community, not end-users, and the judgment as to when the software was ready was made in a technical context and not related in any sense to corporate deployments. Make sure you are ready on all fronts by conducting a comprehensive pilot before proceeding with the migration. How long will this take? That depends on your organization, but allow at least two months.

After a good pilot you should have much of the information necessary for the deployment. You won't have everything, and you can expect to encounter unforeseen problems as you proceed, but at least you should be confident enough to plan for a fairly aggressive roll-out schedule. Migrating 50 to 100 users a week is certainly a sustainable rate over a prolonged period of time. Going any faster will place strain on everyone – the implementation team, technical support, help desk, training department, and the users themselves. At 50–100 users per week you'll be able to migrate between 2,500 and 5,000 users in a year while maintaining service levels to users.

Migrating information

Messaging systems, or rather messaging systems that are not well managed, have a remarkable tendency to accumulate vast quantities of data. Even when systems are managed and the amount of messages users can keep are restricted there will still be a fair amount of data to deal with when migration time comes around.

All messaging systems have some degree of junk mail. By this I mean messages that have no relationship to any business activity. Invitations to lunch, to meet after hours, to engage in a social activity, or just people exchanging views on the major topics of the day all generate message traffic, tying up valuable disk space and possibly even preventing users sending business messages because some system limits are reached. Clearly junk mail should not be migrated and the first step before attempting to perform any migration is to strip any such message from the system.

The largest folder I ever saw in active use in a mail system held 14,000 messages, while the largest file cabinet held 225,000 objects. Migrating message containers holding such a large volume of documents is clearly a challenge, but maybe you don't have to migrate them at all? Can the older file cabinet system remain in situ for an agreed length of time after users begin to use Exchange Server as their default messaging system? Can the documents be accessed in a mode that allows users to perform read, fetch, and delete operations, perhaps from a customized version of the application that they were originally created with?

If you decide to leave the older system operational, albeit in a read-only mode, it's a good idea to clearly set a date in the future at which time the older system will be disconnected. Turning off a system, albeit it on a clearly advertised date is hard for users as it irrevocably removes their access to documents which may well contain valuable information, and this is the point when migration utilities need to be considered.

Migration wizards and other tools

Microsoft has provided a tool called the 'Migration Wizard' to move messages and other information created in foreign messaging systems to Exchange Server (Figure 7.1).

Figure 7.1 *The Migration Wizard*

The Migration Wizard always runs on a Windows NT workstation or server, so the information it processes must be made available to the Wizard. This is done in two ways:

- Direct access (perhaps via a networked drive) to PC files. This is the approach taken when migrating messages from Microsoft Mail and Lotus cc:Mail post offices.
- Stripping information from a messaging system and writing it out into files in a highly structured manner. These files are then moved to the Windows NT system and processed by the Migration Wizard. This is the approach used to migrate host-based electronic mail systems.

The Exchange Migration Wizard is able to migrate messages from the following messaging systems:

- Microsoft Mail
- Digital ALL-IN-1
- IBM PROFS
- Lotus cc:Mail
- Verimation MEMO

While all migrations eventually use the same Migration Wizard to import data there are fundamental differences between e-mail systems built around PC LAN file-sharing architectures and those which run on mini- or mainframe computers. When dealing with a PC LAN-based mail system, like Microsoft Mail or Lotus cc:Mail, the extract and load operations can sometimes be carried out on the same server, or at least the extract files can be created and immediately accessed by the Migration Wizard on a network file location that's accessible from the Windows NT computer where Exchange Server is running. This makes the whole process much easier as you don't have to copy files around the network during the transfer. Because data held in host-based systems (PROFS, MEMO, and ALL-IN-1) is not normally directly accessible from Windows NT the basic approach to the task of migration is evolved a little into three phases, illustrated in Figure 7.2.

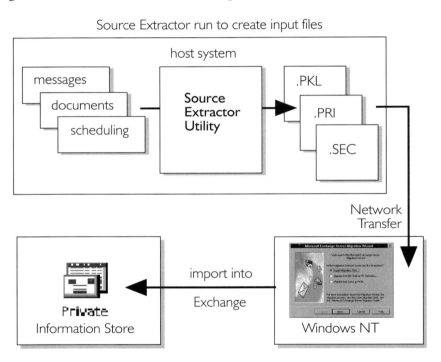

Figure 7.2 *Steps in migrating host-based messages*

1. Create the extract files on the host system. Procedures for the supported operating system are provided as part of the Exchange kit and can be used to create the extract files. The procedures are written in languages (interpreted or compiled) appropriate for the operating system. For example, some of the procedures to migrate information from Verimation MEMO systems are written in the JCL (Job Control Language) for IBM MVS mainframes while forms, scripts, and some VMS Macro code are provided for ALL-IN-1 systems.

2. Transfer the extract files to the target Exchange server. Some form of network connection can be used or the information can be transferred using magnetic media.

3. Run the Exchange Migration Wizard.

Apart from the ease of data access (for PC based migration utilities), the potential volume of data that may need to be migrated often marks another difference between host- and PC-based electronic mail systems. As I've mentioned before, there are known instances of single user accounts storing hundreds of thousands of messages. Of course, such accounts are unusual and the majority of system managers impose strict quotas based on the number of messages a user can store or the amount of disk space they can occupy on the server. Nevertheless, my own personal observation is that users on host-based systems are more prone to the accumulation of old or unwanted messages, what you might call 'file cabinet debris', especially if they've been using the host system for years. Clearly steps should be taken to eliminate as much of this debris before the migration process begins as otherwise the whole procedure will take much longer and will use more resources than necessary.

Extracting and importing

In simple terms, the Exchange Migration Wizard works by analyzing the contents of one or more files generated from a source messaging system. Typically three different types of files are extracted from a source system:

- *The packing list file.* This file contains some information about the data that is being migrated, such as the code page for the character set used to create the contents, plus the names of all the other files associated with the extract.

- *Primary intermediate files.* These files contain the data necessary to create new Exchange mailboxes or custom recipients. They also contain message headers, entries for the personal address book, and pointers to data used by secondary intermediate files.

- *Secondary intermediate files.* These files contain the bulk of the data to be imported into Exchange and include message bodies and attachments and any data that can be extracted from an older time management or scheduling system.

Packing list files are usually given a file extension of .PKL. For example, TREDMOND.PKL. Primary intermediate files use a file extension of .PRI while secondary intermediate files use .SEC. There are no hard and fast rules for naming the files and each source extractor is free to name files whatever way it wishes. The intermediate files must be located in the same directory as the packing list. The Exchange Migration Wizard is not able to search disks for intermediate files, so if they can't be found in the same directory the import operation will fail.

The source extract files are formatted according to a set of rules specified by the Exchange developers. Failure to follow the rules when extracting information from a source system will inevitably lead to problems when the time comes for the Exchange Migration Wizard to process the badly-formatted data. The old rule of 'rubbish in leads to rubbish out' is very true in this case.

The basic approach to the migration process for host-based messaging systems is:

- Extract files from the source messaging system
- Run the Migration Wizard

Figure 7.3
Selecting an extract file for the Migration Wizard

There can be a period of elapsed time between the two steps, but this is undesirable because the users involved cannot participate in messaging communications until their mailboxes have been transferred to Exchange. An important part of the planning for migration is establishing when mailboxes can be moved with the least impact on users. For best results the Migration Wizard should be run on the server where the Private Information Store for the new mailboxes is located. As the import operations require a fairly heavy level of processing it's wise to schedule some time when the server is relatively inactive. Attempting to import thousands of messages for newly migrated mailboxes in the morning when users are arriving and logging in to their mailboxes to read their new mail will not guarantee good system responsiveness.

How long will the wizard take?

Depending on the capacity of the server and its current workload the Migration Wizard can take some time to import files for a user who's been a prolific generator of messages and documents on their previous system. Rough measurements taken for a range of users migrated from a host-based system show that on a lightly loaded server powered by an Intel 120MHz Pentium CPU the Migration Wizard processes between 15 and 40 messages per minute. Messages range in size from small 2Kb files to 2Mb or more (including attachments), so clearly the throughput achieved in your environment greatly depends on the average size of message and the capacity of the server to unpack the messages from the source files. Farsighted system administrators include trial imports in the list of tasks for a pilot.

Apart from the length of time taken to import a user's files system administrators should be aware of two other side effects of the import process. First, importing a large quantity of information from a legacy system can quickly blow any limit that has been set on the space allocated in the private information store for a user's mailbox. The Migration Wizard ignores space limitations on user mailboxes, the logic apparently being that it's best to get the information into the mailbox and then let the user sort out what they should discard in order to get back under the limit. Second, importing large quantities of information gives the Exchange databases a lot of work to do and generates a significant load on the system, which may impact response times for other users. Before starting any import operation make sure that enough disk space is available to allow the Private Information Store to expand as files as imported. If you're about to import ten users, each of whom has generated source import files amounting to 30Mb or so (which isn't really a lot for many heavy mail users), make sure that the disk holding the Public Information Store has 300Mb (plus at least a 10% margin for error) available. This is basic system management, but it's amazing how many people forget to look after the simple things and are surprised when things go wrong.

The quality of the migration tools

The quality of the source extractors and their ability to deal with different items of data which may be stored in the repositories on the host systems varies greatly. I don't find this situation to be surprising at all because it is very difficult to build generic extract utilities capable of handling the situation at every installation. In general it seems that if you've restricted your use of the host system to pure messaging you shouldn't have any problems, but if you've built applications on top of the host messaging system then those application objects may not be processed correctly by the source extractors. And of course, even if the source extractor can process the application objects there is still the issue of what should be done with that object after it is imported into Exchange.

The evolution of a host-based system to incorporate PC clients can also cause problems. Host systems accessed through video terminals typically only store simple text messages and attachments, but PC clients introduce PC format objects as attachments to messages or electronic documents stored on the host in preference to a DOS device. PC clients such as TeamLinks (for Digital's ALL-IN-1 Mailworks servers) leverage the central storage capabilities of a host system and off-load processing to intelligent clients, and have become more and more popular over the last few years. The question that arises when PC clients join the equation is whether the source extractor is able to deal with PC format documents, messages, and attachments, and if they are, will the information written into the files for the Migration Wizard make any sense after it is imported into Exchange? I have certainly encountered some significant problems with the standard source extractors when they attempt to process PC format files, especially with ALL-IN-1. If you're interested in migrating from ALL-IN-1 be aware that the Macro code provided to populate the source extract files is only able to run on VAX processors.

These issues point to a general need to test the migration utilities in your own environment before making any assumption that just because the utilities come along with Exchange they're going to perform perfectly. My own experience with the migration utilities indicates that problem areas do exist and need to be worked around. Reducing the amount of data to be migrated helps. The less data there is to migrate, the less chance there will be that problems will be encountered.

Breaking up the migration

It is wise not to attempt to transfer too many users at one time, unless you know that the users have very few messages to move. Some of the migration tools impose a limit, but even if they don't you should think the whole operation through. Breaking up the user population into groups of 50 or 100 creates more extract and move operations, but it also creates a much more manageable situation. For instance, if you attempt to move 500 users at one time:

- Do you have enough disk space for all the temporary files required for extracted data?

- Will you be able to move the volume of data represented by the extract files over to the Exchange computer in a reasonable time?
- Will the Exchange Migration Wizard be able to import all the data in the extract files in a reasonable time?
- Will your training department be ready to train so many users in a short period of time?

It may be possible that everything can be accomplished in one weekend, but is it the case that everything can be done provided it all goes exactly to plan without any errors creeping in? In other words, do you have any redundancy built into the plan just in case something goes wrong?

Host systems that provide purely messaging functions are easier to migrate than those which take a broader view of office automation. MEMO and PROFS are both good electronic mail systems, and offer some degree of other functionality like scheduling. But neither takes the concept of an electronic file cabinet much further than the level necessary to store and access messages. Systems which enable distributed shared drawers or folders, such as Exchange Server, are more difficult to migrate because the shared elements of the file cabinet may not have an equivalent in Exchange, or the migration utilities may not be able to process the data stored in these repositories. Further complications arise if the file cabinet is used as a base for applications such as workflow or EDI, especially if users are allowed to mix and match application-specific objects with mail messages and documents within their mailboxes.

All messaging systems differ in one way or another, so it is more than possible that some of the information held about messages by your current mail system may not migrate across to Exchange Server. The Migration Wizard is easy to use and provides reasonable functionality, but it doesn't attempt to resolve conflicts between Exchange and the source system. The general rule is that if a reasonable match can be made between Exchange and the other system regarding message attributes the information will move across. Some message attributes are generic and shared across all systems, such as message subject. Others, such as the X.400 concept of a reply-to-list, are more esoteric and will not be migrated.

Getting help on migrations

Lots of people are going to migrate other messaging systems to Exchange. In turn this means that there should be plenty of experience recorded in public forums dedicated to Exchange like those maintained on CompuServe or the Microsoft Network (MSN). It would be unreasonable to expect that the migration utilities will be able to handle 100% of all the different types of messages and other objects held on messaging systems, so you can expect to encounter some problems or adventures along the way. In these situations it can be very profitable to browse through the contents of whatever forums are available to you, or to send a message to the Exchange mailing list maintained on the Internet.[1]

For example, the Migration Wizard uses the cc:Mail export program to extract information from cc:Mail post offices. There's a known problem with this export program in that it can't deal with any messages for users with account names containing quotes. For example, B O'Brien. When the export program comes to process such a name it notices the blank character between B and O and attempts to apply the export parsing rules which dictate that names containing blanks should be enclosed in quotes. Unfortunately the export program isn't able to handle quotes that already exist within names, and this forces the Migration Wizard to halt. The solution is to rename the cc:Mail user – easy if you know how. This is a good example of the type of information discussed in the Exchange mailing list, proving the usefulness of external or unofficial channels when problem-solving.

Migrating without a wizard

It's nice to have some automatic wizards available to migrate data to Exchange, but what happens if you have a mail system that Microsoft doesn't provide a Migration Wizard for? The wizards packaged in Exchange are carefully targeted to facilitate migration of the most popular electronic mail systems, but over the last decade almost every computer manufacturer has developed one or more electronic mail systems. For example, Digital's electronic mail systems include ALL-IN-1, MailWorks for OpenVMS and MailWorks for UNIX, not to mention the free VMSmail utility packaged with every OpenVMS computer. A Migration Wizard is only available for ALL-IN-1, so anyone migrating from one of the other systems is on their own.

What options exist for a do-it-yourself migration? The most obvious answer is to establish a connection via SMTP or X.400 and ask users to mail selected messages and other items of interest to their new account on the Exchange Server. This approach is practical and workable, but only when the quantity of messages involved are fairly limited. Most users rapidly lose patience if they are forced to mail more than a few dozen files, and no one will be happy to be faced with the

---

1. *The address of the Internet mailing list for Exchange is given on page 393.*

prospect of having to mail several hundred items before the connection is removed or their old account is deleted. Remember that mailing documents to Exchange is a two-part operation. First the messages have to be created and sent, and then they must be processed when they arrive into Exchange.

Some electronic mail systems have APIs or script languages and these can be used to develop automated procedures to export medium to large quantities of old messages and documents. One way to approach this task is to look at a sample load file generated from one of the source messaging systems supported by the Exchange Migration Wizard, and then proceed to work out how a similar load file can be created by extracting messages from your mail system. Make sure that all the necessary formatting information is included. There's no good rule to say what formatting information is mandatory and which is optional, so to avoid any messing around it's wise to create a load file that looks exactly the same as one prepared by an 'official' extractor. Be prepared to go through a certain amount of trial and error before everything works all the time. Depending on the richness of the source system's APIs and the availability of experienced programmers accustomed to the APIs, expect to devote three to four weeks of hard work to produce a robust source extractor.

If your current electronic mail system runs on a DOS platform it may be enough to just export the messages out to DOS and leave them there, letting users import the files into Exchange as they are required (or missed). Importing files is easy – a simple drag and drop operation from the Windows Explorer or File Manager direct to the folder where the files should go. It's so easy that users may be tempted to drag and drop a little too much information, thus clogging up the information store with data that isn't really valuable anymore.

Any do-it-yourself migration procedure will cost time and money. The question has to be asked whether all the energy devoted to migrating old messages could be used in a more productive manner elsewhere, and whether the cost involved in moving old information to Exchange can be justified by the content. Sites that have taken the radical approach to migration, that is to turn off the old system as the new system is turned on, often experience a period of confusion immediately after the change-over, but costs are lower and users quickly get used to the fact that the old messages are no longer available. As with many other aspects of a migration what users demand and how you react to the demands really depends on the situation pertaining within the installation. The golden rule is not to do any more work to migrate information than is strictly and absolutely necessary.

Migrating other data

An existing system may be used for more than just electronic mail or document management. Digital's ALL-IN-1 office system is a good example of a popular office system in use world-wide since 1982. One of the reasons for ALL-IN-1's popularity is its application development capabilities which have allowed many organizations to build reasonably complex data processing applications which can be totally integrated with the electronic mail subsystem. While a Migration Wizard exists to move documents and messages from ALL-IN-1 file cabinets into Exchange folders, the wizard's magic cannot cope with any application-specific data.

In cases where a messaging system has been used as the basis for applications arrangements will have to be made to migrate the application completely or move the data into a format that is understood by an application available for Windows NT. In the latter case the usual tactic is to try to output the data into a format that's understood by the target application. One instance of where I've been able to do this is with 20/20, a spreadsheet application sold by Access Technology and it was quite common in its day, due to its multi-platform nature. 20/20 is able to write information out in WK1 format, and most Windows spreadsheet programs such as Lotus 1-2-3 or Excel are quite happy to import WK1 data.

While it is often possible to output data from an older application in a compatible format the data may not be immediately reachable from Windows NT. This situation usually occurs when the source system is a mini- or mainframe computer. Moving data between computer systems is an area fraught with pitfalls, but there are at least three obvious methods to investigate:

1. Using a common network protocol to transfer data from source to target system. FTP (File Transfer Protocol) is the protocol that offers most potential because it is supported on a very wide range of computer systems, including Windows NT. Be careful to ensure that data originating on systems with different character sets (for example, mainframes running the IBM MVS operating system) is converted before or after the transfer is performed.

2. Moving the migration data to somewhere available to both source and target systems. For example, logical network-based disk drives that can be directly accessed by Windows NT. Novell NetWare or Digital PATHWORKS network drives are both good examples of network devices that can be mapped by Windows NT and other computer systems.

3. Using manual transfers via magnetic media. This method relies on a common type of media (disk or tape) being supported by both source and target systems as well as Windows NT having the ability to correctly interpret the data on the media once it is presented for reading.

In all cases don't assume that a method works just because you are able to transfer a small file, or even a selection of small files. Test all methods with real data and try and build an automated procedure to speed up the process. It's common to suddenly discover that the method you've chosen, or the procedure that's been carefully written, works quite happily with small amounts of data but falls over or takes an inordinate amount of time to complete when confronted with the data generated by more prolific users.

Cleaning up after the migration

It's obvious that disk space will be used during the migration process. You can't expect to extract information from the source messaging system to feed into Exchange without occupying some type of transient storage. Make sure that your preparations for the migration take transient disk space requirements into account. It's a good idea to thoroughly analyze the current disk space occupied by user messages and other files due to be moved before the migration process begins, and plan to make the total storage determined by the analysis plus an extra 20% margin for error available during the migration. The margin for error should also take care of the slight additional overhead imposed by the 'format wrapper' created around messages by the Exchange migration tools.

Calculating the disk space used by an individual user is pretty easy if the current messaging system delivers separate copies of messages to all users. All you have to do is see how much disk space is allocated to message files in any user's account to know what figure to use for planning purposes. Calculating the requirements when a shared server-based message model (like Exchange) is used is harder unless utilities exist to report how much space a user is responsible for within the shared message store. This figure isn't always easy to get, nor is it obvious as to how you might go about getting it, so you may even end up writing some utilities to analyze data structures and extract the relevant information.

Before the migration process gets under way it's important that you take whatever steps are feasible to reduce the amount of data to be moved. If the source system provides facilities to remove unwanted or obsolete messages and documents from user mailboxes they should be used before any extracts are created. There isn't much point in moving all the contents of users' wastebasket (deleted) folders across into their new Exchange mailboxes, for example.

Depending on the space available on the source system you even may have to install an additional drive to use during the migration period. Of course, if small groups of users are to be moved you'll only have to ensure that the total disk space occupied by these users (plus the safety margin) is available. The disk space used for this activity should be reclaimed as soon as possible after the extracted data has been loaded into Exchange.

Apart from space used for migration purposes, it's also important to recognize that disk space can be reclaimed by removing user-specific files from the system after a user has been successfully migrated to Exchange. You may want to leave a gap of a week or so after a user has been moved before taking the plunge and deleting their files, as you never know when problems might occur and the user has to be moved back to their original system. When the time comes to clean up you'll find that the task is purely manual as there is no functionality to do this included in the Migration Wizard.

Coexisting with other messaging systems

The vast majority of migrations do not happen overnight. In fact, if you are moving from another system supporting thousands of users the migration period is often extended over months or even years. During this time Exchange Server and its predecessor mail system will need to coexist and cooperate within a single, logical messaging environment.

It's obvious that the most basic need to coexist can be defined on the level of interpersonal message interchange between the two systems. One of the Exchange connectors or a link to an SMTP or X.400 backbone will probably solve this problem, albeit perhaps after a degree of testing to ensure that all message body parts can be successfully transmitted from one electronic mail system to the other.

After messages, what are the issues which may prove to be of concern during the period of coexistence? Here are a few of the issues I have encountered.

- *Directory Synchronization.* Exchange Server has its own directory which is no doubt different to the one used by the existing system. How will the address information contained in the two directories be synchronized so that users are able to address messages to anyone within the organization without having to remember complex address syntaxes?

- *Transferring users from Exchange back to the older electronic mail system.* During a migration phase the normal operation will be to transfer a user from the older system to Exchange, but there may be instances where someone is transferred from a department that uses Exchange to a department where they don't. In these cases there will be problems extracting user data from Exchange Server and transferring it to the 'old' mail system, mostly because no wizard or 'backward migration' tools are probably available (unless you build your own).
- *Interchange of scheduling information.* Schedule+ provides excellent scheduling functionality in an Exchange environment but it's difficult to schedule meetings and appointments with anyone else, even people using older versions of Schedule+!
- *Mail-enabled applications.* Workflow applications built on top of the electronic mail system are compromised if everyone who may be part of a document's routing cycle cannot be reached through the electronic mail system. Even if they can be reached with a message, the recipient may not be able to interact with the contents and participate in the workflow.
- *Guest users.* With a single consistent mail system throughout an organization it's normally possible to access your mail from any workstation, provided that your access can be authenticated from the workstation. If some parts of the organization are still using the old mail system will Exchange users be able to access their mail when they visit? Will users of the older mail system be able to read their mail when they visit a department that uses Exchange?
- *Distribution lists.* Maintaining the contents of distribution lists so that the addresses contained in the lists are up-to-date, accurate, and don't lead to undelivered messages can be a nightmare. How do you make sure that distribution lists are updated as users migrate from the older system to Exchange? Can the selected techniques cater for personal distribution lists as well as those shared between groups of users or system-wide? Can you apply the same technique to solve the problem posed by mail addresses held in nickname files or personal address books? While you can take some steps to enable local users to continue to use old addresses problems may still arise for external messages delivered from other organizations.

Human beings generally like a settled environment and often resist change. It's fair to assume that greater problems will be encountered at the beginning of the migration when users struggle to cope with new ways to address messages to colleagues, transfer documents from one system to the other, find equivalent options on client menus, or even just cope with the trauma of moving from a different style of computing and user interface to client–server Windows. Help desk and programming staff will experience the same transition pressures but their extra technical knowledge will assist their personal migration, so the overall impact on these people shouldn't be as great. Migrations proceed more smoothly (and usually quicker) when everyone recognizes that problems will occur, and steps are taken to lessen the impact of the problems before users meet them. This is one good reason why a thorough and extensive pilot is essential to pinpoint the specific areas of interoperability which may affect your users most. Knowledge gained through pilots is a great help in achieving nontraumatic migrations.

Operating mail gateways

Gateways have been a fact of electronic messaging life since the earliest days of e-mail. Following the same line as operating system development, no great efforts were initially made to ensure that messages could be sent to other systems. Everything was focused on optimizing the messaging design and architecture for the computer and operating system it ran on. Some of the IBM mainframe e-mail systems written in APL, a unique symbol-driven programming language in many respects, provide eloquent examples of the approach taken when developing e-mail.

With a wide range of e-mail systems in production, each having their own idea about how to create and send messages, gateways rapidly became a necessary evil of a messaging administrator's life. Gateways are a necessary evil because they delay messages en route to their final destination and so degrade some of the *raison d'être* for e-mail, the desire to send information quickly from one person to another. Gateways often impose restrictions on users, for instance limiting their ability to send anything but simple text messages to users contacted via the gateway. Attached or embedded documents are often stripped out as messages transit the gateways, and generally speaking the message that leaves an originator's desk arrives in a fairly bent shape at its final destination. Of course, it's a mistake to blame gateways for all the restrictions. Target e-mail systems might not be able to cope with embedded documents or rich text format cover memos, or many of the other advanced features of modern systems. In these cases gateways merely act as a negotiator between different e-mail systems, transforming messages arriving at the gateway into a form that's acceptable to the other systems.

Any medium to large-scale migration usually requires a gateway between the old system and the new, in this case Exchange. Smaller migrations that can be done in a 'big bang' or over a short period of time may remove any need to install and operate a gateway, but once you have to deal with more than a few hundred users the sheer logistics of migration determine that the period of migration extends to such an extent that a gateway is needed to facilitate communication between the two user communities.

Given that one or more gateway is necessary during an extended migration period it follows that it is sensible to take any necessary steps to ensure that the best possible interoperability for all types of messages is achieved. Important points to consider include:

- Can a common messaging standard be used by the gateway to transfer messages from the older system to Exchange? The two obvious options are SMTP/MIME and X.400.

- What features are supported by the gateway? Is it limited to simple (single-body part) messages or can attachments be sent through the gateway? Does the gateway preserve attachment information such as file formats and titles? Is the gateway able to handle attachments in a format that it doesn't recognize, for instance, a compressed file produced by the PKZIP application?

- What happens when a message generated by a mail-enabled application arrives at the gateway? Remember that this situation can arise from either direction. In other words, a message can be generated and sent from the older system or an electronic form can be generated and sent by Exchange Server. The important thing to consider is whether the fact that a message arrives at the gateway influences the immediate and future processing by the mail-enabled application? For example, if the message is part of a workflow cycle that consists of a number of serial steps, each of which involves a message being sent to the next person in the cycle, can the cycle be reestablished after the message is sent to a user via the gateway?

If the responses to these questions are largely negative it's time to consider whether another gateway should be used. There is no point in operating a gateway that enables a minimalist degree of interoperability between the two systems because this only leads to additional strain on the help desk staff and system administrators, all of whom have to explain to users the reasons why their messages sometimes don't get through. Buying a cheap gateway with a low level of functionality can be a case of engaging a low up-front cost while incurring higher costs over the lifetime of the gateway.

Sometimes the most demanding users, those who will place most strain on the gateway's capabilities, can be identified before the migration begins, or they become obvious quickly afterwards. If this is the case it's reasonable to concentrate on migrating these people first to avoid the problems they may encounter. For example, if you know that a specific group of people, perhaps spread across several departments, communicate on a regular basis via a workflow application it makes little sense to split them across different migration stages. Move them together instead. This is an example of where it's good to ignore organizational or corporate divisions when considering when users should be moved.

Hopefully a gateway is a transient component in your messaging environment, one that can be discarded once the migration is complete. Of course, larger migrations can take many years to arrive at the last user, so gateways can quickly become a semi-permanent fixture. Even if the gateway is temporary don't take short cuts. Pay attention to gateway details and avoid lots of problems in the future.

Maintaining addressing sources

After gateways, electronic directory services and other sources of address information are the most common problem areas that must be addressed during the migration period. People hate receiving nondelivery notifications, and the potential for 'bad' electronic mail addresses greatly increases as people are moved to any new messaging system. Exchange is no better or worse than any other mail system. It offers no panacea for misaddressed messages and during the course of the migration the chances are that you won't be able to avoid some undeliverable messages due to invalid addresses. Over the long term you can take steps to significantly reduce the number of invalid addresses within the system.

Most electronic mail systems in use today have some form of directory service. This may be a simple list of subscribers (mailboxes) or it might be something more complicated, such as an X.500 or similar distributed directory service. In all cases the repository holds information about other users' electronic mail addresses which people can consult when they wish to send messages. Some systems validate all addresses entered in message headers against the directory to ensure that a user cannot attempt to send a message to an undeliverable address. The personal address book is a form of directory service, in this case, a purely personal service totally under the control of an individual user.

When people are migrated from a system to Exchange server two basic courses of action in respect to the directory can be taken by a system administrator.

1. The directory entry for the user is removed. This can be frustrating for users who remain on the older system because they will no longer be able to 'see' the migrated user in the directory. Also, messages sent to the old address, perhaps those originating from another connected system, will be undeliverable unless they can be redirected.

2. The entry for the user is altered so that messages sent to the user are redirected to their new Exchange mailbox. Not all systems support message redirection, and this approach assumes that the system is capable of sending messages to Exchange, normally via a gateway. A further complication is that redirection may require that the user's old mailbox or account is retained. If this is the case you should disable access to the account so that no one can log into it.

Enabling directory synchronization between Exchange Server and the old system is a more sophisticated but costly answer. It requires the older system to support the MS-Mail directory synchronization facility or a utility program to provide directory information to Exchange and import directory information originating from Exchange. Despite the almost inevitable costs involved, maintaining a fully synchronized directory is the best solution and will stop users becoming unhappy during the migration process because they can't address messages to their friends, or their friends' messages don't arrive.

8

Keeping your Exchange Server Healthy

Performance Optimizer

To a certain degree Exchange Server can be said to be self-maintaining. You shouldn't have to continually perform system tuning to make everything run smoothly, but there are going to be times when things go wrong. In this chapter we'll look at some of the utilities that come with Exchange Server which help system administrators keep servers in shape.

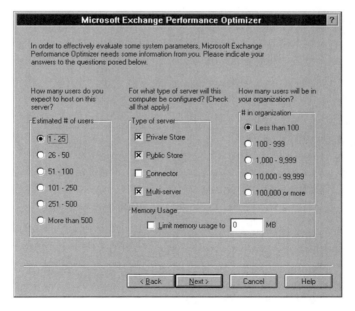

Figure 8.1
Setting parameters for the Performance Optimizer

The Exchange Performance Optimizer utility is a somewhat intelligent program designed to analyze the current status of an Exchange server and make changes based on:

- Information about the intended role for the server as input by a system administrator before the analysis begins (Figure 8.1). This allows the utility to consider what changes are required to enable the server to support an increase in the user community or the way the server is used. For example, a change in server workload from 'messaging only' to a situation where messaging and public folders are supported.
- The disk hardware available to the system.
- Internal parameters currently in operation and performance data gathered by Exchange as it runs.

Performance Optimizer cannot run with Exchange in an active state. All services must be halted before any analysis can begin. Run the utility early in the morning or late in the evening when the least impact will be felt by users.

By default Performance Optimizer reveals little of the internal calculations it makes and offers no opportunities for experienced system administrators to selectively tune one or more settings before new parameters are created. You can request (or force) Performance Optimizer to show you more options to change by running the program with the -v option enabled. To do this, select the desktop icon for the 'Microsoft Exchange Optimizer' and then change the properties to include the -v parameter. The resulting command line should look something like this:

C:\EXCHANGE\BIN\PERFWIZ.EXE -V

Figure 8.2
Log from Performance Optimizer run

```
------------------------------------------------------------
Microsoft Exchange Server Performance Optimizer log file
opened.: 2/29/96 - 2:21:34 PM
------------------------------------------------------------
Detected 1 processor(s)
Detected 134021120 bytes physical memory
Found fixed logical disk C:
Found fixed logical disk D:
Found fixed logical disk E:
Found fixed logical disk F:
Found fixed logical disk G:
Performance Results
(Smaller values better)
DiskRA(ms)Seq(ms)
------------------------------------------------------------
C: -- Not Analyzed --
```

```
D: 21789  15258
E: 21234  14969
F: 21101  14883
G: -- Not Analyzed --
Microsoft Exchange Server Information store log files was
moved from D:\exchsrvr\MDBDATA to E:\exchsrvr\MDBDATA
Microsoft Exchange Server Message Transfer Agent log files
was moved from D:\EXCHSRVR\mtadata to E:\EXCHSRVR\mtadata
Microsoft Exchange Server Public information store file was
moved from D:\exchsrvr\MDBDATA to F:\exchsrvr\MDBDATA
Microsoft Exchange Server Internet Mail Connector data files
was moved from D:\exchsrvr\imcdata to E:\exchsrvr\imcdata
Set # of information store buffers from 1000 to 12226
Set # of directory buffers from 1000 to 100
Set Minimum # of information store threads from 8 to 3
Set Maximum # of information store threads from 20 to 5
Set # of directory threads from 48 to 50
Set Maximum # of cached categorizations from 20 to 25
Set Maximum # of cached restrictions from 20 to 25
Set # of private information store send threads from 1 to 2
Set # of public information store send threads from 1 to 2
Set # of information store gateway in threads from 1 to 2
Set # of information store gateway out threads from 1 to 2
Set # of information store users from 500 to 25
Set # of XAPI MT threads from 1 to 2
Set # of XAPI MT queue threads from 1 to 2
Set # of dispatcher threads from 1 to 2
Set # of transfer threads from 1 to 2
Set # of kernel threads from 1 to 3
Set # of database data buffers per object from 3 to 6
Set # of RTS threads from 1 to 3
-------------------------------------------------------------
Microsoft Exchange Server Performance Optimizer log file
closed.: 2/29/96 - 2:26:08 PM
```

Each run of the Performance Analyzer creates a log called PERFOPT.LOG in the \WINNT35\SYSTEM32 directory. The log file can be reviewed at leisure after the analyzer has run, and any corrections that seem necessary can be made afterwards. If we look at the sample log illustrated in Figure 8.2 we can see that the Performance Optimizer took a number of steps to improve the configuration on the target server. These included:

▶ An analysis of all the logical disks found on the server. The analysis is performed to determine which are the fastest disks on the system. Some disks are discounted because they are FAT drives or don't have enough available space to be useful. Note that the Performance Optimizer cannot detect the difference between multiple partitions on a single physical drive. Each partition is analyzed separately, so this is one reason why you might want to adjust the results of the Performance Optimizer after it is complete. For example, it's always a good idea to separate the information store and its transaction logs by placing them on separate physical drives.

- After the analysis is completed the Performance Optimizer redistributes important Exchange data structures across all available disks. You will be given the option not to move the files according to the recommendations before anything happens.
- Performance Optimizer then proceeds to review internal counters and parameter settings maintained by Exchange Server to see whether any parameters need to be changed to accommodate the workload observed to date on the server.
- After the new parameter values are set all of the Microsoft Exchange services are restarted.

As a server's workload changes over time for many reasons including increases in user knowledge and the number of users supported by the server this is an important reason why Performance Optimizer should be run on a fairly regular basis.

Memory and RISC systems

Performance Optimizer allows you to limit the amount of memory that the system will allocate to Exchange Server. The value is used by the Optimizer to compute internal settings such as buffers, and if no value is set the Optimizer will assume that the total system memory is available for Exchange.

RISC systems such as the Digital Alpha or MIPS processors use executables which are larger than their Intel $x86$ equivalents. This fact means that the paging profile is different on RISC systems than x86 systems. The Performance Optimizer provided with Exchange Server V4.0 is tuned for $x86$ systems and you must take this into account when running the Optimizer for RISC systems. This issue may well be resolved in later releases of Exchange Server.

For example, because the Exchange executables are larger on RISC systems, it is better to have less memory allocated to buffers and more available for the executables as this results in less paging. Some tests performed by Digital for Alpha systems showed that instructing the Performance Optimizer to limit memory usage to 50% of the total available system memory produced good results in all cases. In other words, if your system has 128Mb available to it, the Performance Optimizer allocates 64Mb to Exchange; if 256Mb is available, Exchange gets 128Mb, and so on.

All of this goes to show that you can't completely depend on automated tuning devices. Knowledge of the system environment and observation of what's happening on an ongoing basis is essential when the time comes for a system tune-up.

Server monitors

Server monitors are used to determine whether specified Exchange services are operating correctly on target servers. All of the core services – System Attendant, Information Store, Directory, Message Transfer Agent as well as any optional connectors can be monitored.

Each server monitor operates on a set of servers that you select from any site in your organization. When you select a server you determine which of the Exchange services you wish to monitor. Each service is detected by sending an 'are you there' message over the link to the target service and seeing whether the message arrives.

Monitors can also check the system clock on servers to see whether any inconstancy exists between the expected and actual time. This is important because a server with an incorrect time can generate message time-stamps that cause concern to users. Receiving a message that appeared to be sent two days ago or a day in the future does not generate a great level of confidence in the messaging system.

Figure 8.3
Detecting an inoperative server with a monitor

The results of server monitors are recorded in two places – graphically and in a log file. The graphic display (see Figure 8.3) shows one line for each server being monitored. The beginning of each line displays an icon to flag the current server status. A red down-arrow means trouble. In Figure 8.3 you can see that the DPSW08 server in the Dublin site is flagged because the monitor cannot detect the System Attendant service. Graphical displays are great for indicating a problem, but only if someone is watching the display all the time. Not every installation can afford the luxury of having a system administrator engaged in nothing but monitoring all the time. To make sure that all problems are detected you should:

- Run one or more server monitors all the time to observe the most important servers in each site. The most important service to monitor is the System Attendant as without it Exchange Server has no chance of ever working correctly. Servers that host IMC or X.400 connectors on behalf of one or more sites should also be monitored to detect possible blocks in message transmission or reception.
- Review the server monitor log files on a regular basis, if possible once a day but at least once a week. A different log file is created for each monitor. You can find out the name of the server monitor log by viewing the general properties of the monitor.

Creating server monitors and making them active should be one of the first actions you take after deploying Exchange servers into an operational status. Server and link monitors form an important part of a proactive attitude to problem detection that can pay back great benefits from just a little effort put in at the start.

Link monitors

Link monitors operate by sending PING-like messages to all the servers configured in the monitor. Messages are dispatched at regular intervals and calculations are performed to determine the round-trip time between the server where the monitor is running and the servers being monitored. Administrators can configure the frequency and threshold times for messages and the notification list for any alarms generated as a result of a message not being returned or arriving outside the predetermined threshold. The results of the messages being sent to and from the servers are displayed in a separate window within the Exchange Administration utility, as illustrated in Figure 8.4. If a monitor is active when the Administration utility is closed it will be restarted the next time the Administration utility is initialized.

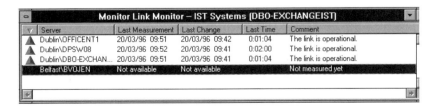

Figure 8.4 *A link monitor in operation*

It's a good idea to run a link monitor on all the important sites in your organization from a central server. No human intervention is required as automatic alarms are generated if anything goes wrong.

Alarms can be notified by standard Windows NT alerts, which flash a message up onto the server's screen, or by sending a mail message to a designated individual or distribution list. The latter is preferable in most cases, especially when a number of people share the task of managing the Exchange infrastructure.

Message tracking

Users send messages at the drop of a hat, but sometimes those messages don't get through and when this happens it falls on the head of the system administrator to try and find out just what happened to the message. Was it delivered to someone else? Did a gateway reject the message? Maybe the message is stuck somewhere waiting for a connection to be established to a remote system.

The majority of messaging systems allocate a unique identifier to messages as they are generated. Exchange Server is no different in this respect. Complete identifiers are built for Exchange messages as follows:

1. The country code for the server. For example, 'IE' means Ireland
2. The administrative X.400 domain for the server, if defined.
3. The private X.400 administrative domain – e.g., 'Digital'.
4. A unique identifier built from the name of the server, the date and time when the message was created, and a computer-generated suffix to ensure uniqueness.

The first three parts of the complete message identifier come from the X.400 site address. An example message identifier generated at 2.29 pm on 14 March 1996 on the server DBO-EXCHANGEIST is:

```
C=IE;A= ;P=Digital;L=DBO-EXCHANGE960314142937FA000101
```

You can view the message identifier generated for a message from any Exchange client as follows:

- Select the message
- Select the *File.Properties* menu option
- Select the Message Id page

A Message Id property page is only shown if the message originated on an Exchange server connected into the same organization. Messages generated by other messaging systems normally bear their own type of message identifiers.

Generating unique message identifiers provides the fundamental basis for message tracking but identifiers are of little use in themselves if they are not recorded somewhere as a message makes its way through the different links in the system. Exchange Server will record the necessary data, but only if it is instructed to do so. To turn message tracking on, select the MTA Site Configuration and tick the 'Enable Message Tracking' box.

Message tracking logs

After message tracking is enabled Exchange Server records details of messages as they are processed by the MTA. Details are held in a set of tracking log files stored in the \tracking.log directory on each server. A new tracking log is created at midnight, so each log holds details of all the messages processed in a single day. Tracking logs are named in a yyyymmdd.LOG format. For example, the tracking log created on 20th April 1996 is called 19960420.LOG.

```
/C=IE;A= ;P=Digital;L=DBO-EXCHANGE960314142937FA0001014       1996.3.14 14:29:36
/O=DIGITALEQUIPMENT CORPORATION/OU=DUBLIN/CN=CONFIGURATION/CN=SERVERS
/CN=DBO-EXCHANGEIST/CN=MICROSOFT PRIVATE MDB
/O=DIGITAL EQUIPMENT CORPORATION/OU=DUBLIN/CN=RECIPIENTS/CN=TONYR
/O=DIGITAL EQUIPMENT CORPORATION/OU=DUBLIN/CN=RECIPIENTS/CN=ExchangeIST
/C=IE;A= ;P=Digital;L=DBO-EXCHANGE960314142937FA00010126      1996.3.14 14:29:37
/o=DIGITAL EQUIPMENT CORPORATION/ou=DUBLIN/cn=RECIPIENTS/cn=ExchangeIST
/C=IE;A= ;P=Digital;L=DBO-EXCHANGE960314142937FA00010126      1996.3.14 14:29:39
/o=Digital Equipment Corporation/ou=Dublin/cn=Recipients/cn=IST-Management
/C=IE;A= ;P=Digital;L=DBO-EXCHANGE960314142937FA0001019       1996.3.14 14:29:40
/O=Digital Equipment Corporation/OU=Dublin/CN=Recipients/CN=JohnH
/C=IE;A= ;P=Digital;L=DBO-EXCHANGE960314142937FA0001019       1996.3.14 14:29:40
/O=Digital Equipment Corporation/OU=Dublin/CN=Recipients/CN=PeterM
/C=IE;A= ;P=Digital;L=DBO-EXCHANGE960314142937FA0001019       1996.3.14 14:29:40
/O=Digital Equipment Corporation/OU=Dublin/CN=Recipients/CN=EricP
/C=IE;A= ;P=Digital;L=DBO-EXCHANGE960314142937FA0001019       1996.3.14 14:29:40
/O=Digital Equipment Corporation/OU=Dublin/CN=Recipients/CN=JamesR
```

Figure 8.5 *Extract (above) from a message tracking log*

Tracking logs quickly grow to large sizes on even moderately busy Exchange servers. It is possible to edit or read the contents of tracking logs with a text editor and because the fields in the logs are tab delimited they can be loaded into a spreadsheet, such as Excel. Once in the editor or spreadsheet the contents of the log reveal the interaction between the MTA and messages, and how messages proceed as they are submitted by users, delivered to other mailboxes, or pass off the system via a site or other connector. Given experience and knowledge of the codes[1] and fields used in tracking logs it is feasible to use the raw logs as the basis for satisfying user requests to discover where messages went. Such an approach might be taken by masochists, but the more sanguine system administrator quickly learns to appreciate the standard 'Track Message' option featured on the Tools menu of the Exchange Administration utility.

Figure 8.5 illustrates a sample from a message tracking log. The sample has been edited slightly to clarify the information contained in the tracking log. In the extract a message is submitted (code 4) to the MTA. The message originates from a user whose local alias or distinguished name is 'TONYR' and is addressed to a distribution list called 'Exchange IST'. The first step the MTA takes is to expand the distribution list (code 26), where it is discovered that a nested distribution list called 'IST-Management' is part of the original list. The nested list is then expanded to complete the set of recipient mailboxes where the MTA must deliver the message.

Once all the recipients have been determined the MTA can begin to deliver the message. This occurs in a series of delivery operations (code 9), one for each recipient. The recipient is clearly indicated by recording their directory name in the log. If the message is transferred to another system via a connector the connector's name will be shown in the log. Apart from their obvious use in message tracking exercises there is no formal requirement to keep tracking logs for any length of time. If you find that tracking logs are occupying too much storage you can delete some or all of the logs to free up some space. However, if something with relatively low storage demands is causing disk storage problems perhaps it's time to buy another disk?

Using the Track Message command

Browsing through large amounts of tracking log data is an interesting once-off experience, but not something you want to do every day. The Track Message command provides an easy to use graphical interface to the data contained in message tracking logs and the steps necessary to interpret the data and follow the message from server to server. As an example we'll use the graphical interface to track the message described in the extract from the tracking log shown in Figure 8.5.

---

1. *Details of field and the data they store, and the meanings of the codes used in message tracking logs can be found in Chapter 17 of the 'Exchange Server administration guide'.*

Figure 8.6
Selecting a message to track

Tracking a message is a two stage process:

1. First, select the message to be tracked.
2. Track the selected message via the 'Message Tracking Center'

Selecting a message means that you provide Exchange with search criteria to filter the contents of message tracking logs in order to find messages that meet the stated criteria. You can elect to search the current tracking log (the default option) or search back through as many tracking logs as are available on a server. Searches can also be carried out against tracking logs stored on remote servers, an operation that can be quite slow if the network is occupied or the remote server is busy. Once a message is being tracked the logs on all the servers in the relevant site are automatically searched.

Clearly the better and more focused the search criteria the less messages will be discovered and the bigger chance that the messages found will actually be the ones you are interested in. The message we're interested in was sent by Tony Redmond to the Exchange IST distribution list. This information can be entered into the form (see Figure 8.6) as our initial criteria. We weren't quite sure when the message was sent, so the logs for the last seven days are to be scanned. After the search is executed we find that eight messages meet the criteria. Any of these messages can then be selected for tracking. Once a message is selected we return to the Message Tracking Center where the actual tracking process can begin.

Tracking begins after the 'Track' button is pressed and is accomplished by scanning the tracking log files to interpret the actions performed for the message. Each action is then displayed to the screen to allow the system administrator to see exactly how the message was processed. If you look at Figure 8.7 you'll see a graphical view of the conclusions we reached when the extract of the tracking log was analyzed earlier. As you can imagine, it's a lot easier to click a few buttons than it is to delve into the depths of a tracking log.

Figure 8.7
Tracking a message

At the bottom of Figure 8.7 you can just see that several attempts were made to reroute the message to a server called OFFICENT1, the site's bridgehead server for connections to sites where if you select one of the entries and then click on the Properties button, a little more information is revealed (Figure 8.8). The properties information doesn't tell us that anything has really gone wrong, but the fact that multiple attempts were made to transfer a message indicates that the connection between the server and OFFICENT1 was inoperative at the time. The fact that a number of attempts were made to transfer the message confirms that a problem existed.

Figure 8.8
Properties of a tracking entry

Eventually the OFFICENT1 server became available and the message was transferred. Viewing the properties of the transferred message tells us the names of the mailboxes on the remote site or system (Figure 8.9).

Figure 8.9
Properties for a transferred message

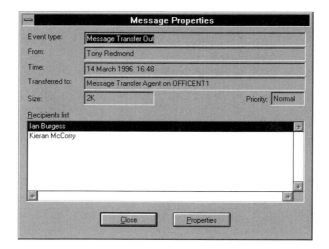

At this point in time we might think that all deliveries have been made, but the message tracking center now proceeds to consult the tracking logs on the remote system to see what happened after the message arrived. Details of events are displayed as they are uncovered, and we can see that an internal report was generated after the message was handed over to OFFICENT1 (Figure 8.10). Internal reports usually indicate that the message encountered a problem along its route. In this instance the recipient mailboxes in the remote site couldn't be found, so NDR (nondelivery receipt) messages had to be generated by the MTA to report this fact back to the originator.

Apart from the problem leading to generation of NDRs, the final set of information displayed by the Message Tracking Center shows that tracking could not be performed for recipients whose mailboxes are located on the local server DPSW08 because message tracking has not been enabled on that server.

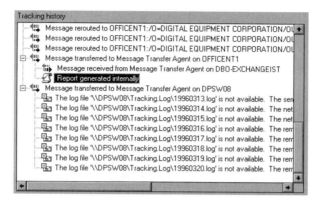

Figure 8.10
Problems with a message on a remote system

No message tracking system is ever perfect in the eyes of everyone who tries to use it. It's either too simple and doesn't display enough information or too complex and can't be used by normal human beings. The messaging tracking system in Exchange Server walks a line down the middle and as such will satisfy the vast majority of system administrators. If you're not happy with the out-of-the-box facilities you can always write your own tracking utility based on the data collected in the message tracking logs.

The Exchange Load Simulator

We've already discussed how you might approach the selection of hardware for Exchange servers, but how can you be sure that a particular configuration will perform to any given level? Do you depend on figures supplied by hardware vendors, or do you attempt to carry out your own tests, preferably in the same type of environment that you expect a production server to operate in?

Microsoft supplies a tool called LoadSim (Load Simulator) to help assess hardware configurations. You'll find the necessary files in the \SUPPORT\LOADSIM directory of the Exchange CD. Using LoadSim is easy – just double-click on LOADSIM.EXE and you'll be started, but before we do that let's consider what the tool is designed to do and the different steps you have to go through in order to use it properly.

In simple terms LoadSim allows you simulate the workload generated by multiple concurrently-connected clients. The workload is generated by multithreaded processes running on one or more computers (Windows NT servers or workstations); each of which has the

Exchange client software installed. Windows 95 clients can be used to place additional load on the server during the test but Windows 95 doesn't offer the operating system features necessary to support such a simulation. Up to several hundred clients can be simulated from a single computer, meaning that it's easy to conduct your own tests on different hardware configurations. You certainly don't have to create a hugely complex testing laboratory to test hardware with LoadSim.

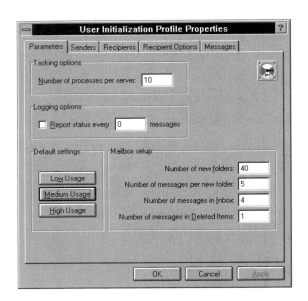

Figure 8.11
Defining parameters for LoadSim

LoadSim works by generating a number of processes, typically no more than 30. Each process represents a set of clients, each represented by a separate thread within the process. During the simulation the client threads generate MAPI calls to emulate common actions performed by real users. Commands are issued to create and send messages, to add recipients and distribution lists to messages, to read messages that have arrived in user mailboxes, to create appointments with Schedule+, and so on.

A LoadSim test is broken down into a number of phases:

1. *The topology for the test is defined.* In other words, what elements of an Exchange organization (specifically the servers) will be used to conduct the test. You can define how many accounts for simulated clients will be allocated to each server used for the test. You can also define the type of users profile to use during the test (see Figure 8.11), whether public folders are used, and if so, how many are stored on each server. If you want the test to include the extra processing required to expand distribution lists

you can specify that these should be configured into the test. Distribution list configuration means specifying parameters such as the minimum, maximum, and average number of recipients per list.

2. *Generation of user accounts.* LoadSim uses a specific naming convention for the user mailboxes employed during the simulation. Details of these mailboxes have to be generated into a file suitable for importing into the Exchange directory on the system under test. When the file is imported the mailboxes are created in a new 'LoadSim' recipients container. Note that you don't need to create separate Windows NT accounts for each mailbox because the import file grants access to all accounts to the Windows NT 'Domain Users' group, enabling any account in the local domain to access all LoadSim mailboxes. If you want to run a test across multiple domains or you have other reasons to force LoadSim to use specific accounts you can edit the import file to specify other account permissions. Three separate import files are created – the directory import (to set up the mailboxes) and separate import files to set X.400 and SMTP addresses for each mailbox. You only need to import the directory import file if you conduct tests within a single Exchange organization (the norm).

3. *User and public folder initialization.* LoadSim needs to place some messages into user mailboxes for use during the simulation. The user initialization (known as the 'UserInit' test) phase cycles through all the mailboxes and creates the necessary messages in each one. If you have included public folders in the simulation you should run the public folders initialization test. This step populates public folders with some test data. Before running these tests you can specify various parameters through property pages. For example, what recipients to use.

4. *Execute the load simulation test.* This can only be done properly after all the other steps are complete. You can give a name to each test scenario you create. The scenario defines how long the test should last (it can last forever, meaning that the test can be stopped at any time), the length of a typical user day, whether users should log off at night-time (a test can span several working days) and empty their deleted items folder, and whether clients log-off during the working day.

All of the information you enter to specify settings for a test (topology, number of users, parameters, etc.) is stored in a file with a .SIM extension. This allows you to repeat tests under the same conditions across multiple LoadSim sessions. The parameter file also allows you to run LoadSim from a command line prompt or from a batch file as follows:

`C:> LoadSim simulation_file_name test_name /q`

for example:

`C:> LoadSim LargeServer.SIM FullTest /q`

This command instructs LoadSim to recreate the simulation scenario described in the LargeServer.SIM file and then proceed to run the test called FullTest. If the name of a test is not specified LoadSim will open but won't attempt to run a test. The /q parameter instructs LoadSim to terminate after the specified test is complete.

During the test the actions being simulated for clients are echoed to the LoadSim window, allowing you to see exactly what's going on. Figure 8.12 illustrates results being echoed to the LoadSim window with a performance monitor also active (see later on in this chapter).

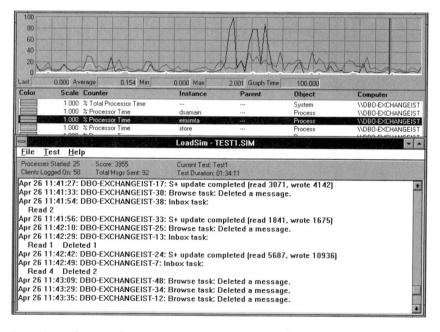

Figure 8.12
Load Simulation Test in progress

Running the performance monitor during the simulation allows you to see how different system components respond to the test load. Test results are logged to a file for later analysis. If multiple client computers are used each produces a log file. All of the log files from a test can be merged together at the end in order to create a single file for analysis.

You don't have to have a dedicated test system to run LoadSim. The utility will run happily on any Exchange server. If you decide to run a simulation on a production system be aware of several side-effects:

- The test recipients are created in the special LoadSim container.
- Details of the test recipients are automatically added to the global address list.
- The volume of messages created and sent during the test will impact the private and public information stores. PRIV.EDB and PUB.EDB will both expand as all the test messages are created and sent, and a large series of transaction logs are also written. It is possible to exhaust disk space if you're not careful, so make sure that the Performance Optimizer has been run before the test to distribute Exchange files across all available disk spindles, and also to check that there's at least 200Mb free on the disks where information stores and transaction logs are located.

It's a good idea to take a backup of the information stores before starting the test and compact them afterwards with the EDBUTIL utility. On test systems the ISWIPE utility (provided on the Exchange CD-ROM) can be used to completely erase the contents of the information store. It goes without saying that it's unwise to run ISWIPE without knowing what you're doing. A test can be stopped at any time or allowed to run through to its designated completion time. If you elect to stop a test the results are only indication of the events processed up to that time. Not all client processes may have connected, only a subset of message types might have been sent, and perhaps only some of the public folder manipulations may have been carried out. Stopping a test too early leads to unreliable results. You have to let the test run for long enough for the simulation to stabilize and have produced enough results to be meaningful when analyzed. Microsoft's Performance Testing Group run tests for between six and eight hours when they measure hardware configurations, a good indication of what they feel is an appropriate timespan.

Using the LSLOG utility

LsLog, the LoadSim Performance Log Parser, is a command line executable that can be found in the same directory as LoadSim. The major function of this utility is to analyze the log files recorded during a simulation test. The results or answer delivered by LsLog after it has analyzed the logs are 95th percentile[2] results for all of the actions tested

---

2. *In other words, 95% of all response times recorded were equal to or below the reported value. 95th percentile measurements are often found in statistical analyses.*

during the simulation as well as a weighted average 95th percentile for all actions. The results are reported in milliseconds, so lower values are better because the system has taken less time to respond to a client request to perform an action. If you compare two similar hardware configurations with the same test and one configuration delivers better results than the other it should be a fair indication of which one to use for production purposes. Don't accept results always without question. In a situation where you compare two similar configurations and find one performs significantly better than the other by a wide margin (more than 10%), ask the question whether the two configurations are really so similar. Are the network controllers identical? What disk controllers are used? Is there more memory cache in one system than the other? Because errors can arise during the set-up of test scenarios knowledge of Exchange Server and PC hardware is invaluable when conducting tests and then interpreting results afterwards.

The steps to use LsLog to analyze a performance log file are as follows:

- Merge the performance logs from each computer participating in the test. Ignore this step if only one computer is used.
- Extract a specific time window from the log. This is an optional step as the default is to analyze the entire log. Extracting a time window allows you to focus on a period after the test scenario has stabilized.

Figure 8.13
Sample results from a simulation run, as reported by LsLog

Category	Weight	Hits	95th Percentile
SEND	1	27	11084
Sub-weight	16	6	48640
Sub-weight	2	1	1863
Sub-weight	5	2	721
Sub-weight	60	15	2914
Sub-weight	4	3	991
READ	10	535	801
REPLY	1	6	1412
REPLY ALL	1	5	2103
FORWARD	1	56	1222
MOVE	1	104	490
DELETE	2	206	411
SUBMIT	0	94	942
RESOLVE NAME	0	83	560
LOAD IMSG	0	41	1712
DELIVER	0	236	660
Weighted Avg	17	1393	1479

▶ Use the LsLog 'answer' option to generate the 95th percentile results for the actions recorded in the performance log. The results are displayed to the screen, but can also be redirected to a file for inclusion in a report or distribution by mail. Figure 8.13 (above) illustrates results achieved from a simulation.

Some sample LsLog commands:

`C:> LsLog Merge System1.Log System2.Log > Systems.Log`

`C:> LsLog Truncate Systems.Log 2 4 > Test.Log`

`C:> LsLog Answer Test.Log > Results.Txt`

These commands merge `System1.Log` and `System2.Log` (performance log files from two client computers) to form `Systems.Log`, which is then stripped of data spanning four hours' testing (for 2 clients). The stripped test log is then analyzed and the test scores written into `Results.Txt`.

Putting results into context

Even after carrying out a successful test it's important to put the results into a realistic context. For example, you should realize that LoadSim is able to run everything on a single computer. That's fine, but in a production environment clients will connect to servers over the network, so the LoadSim results need to be adjusted because they don't account for any network latency or fallibility. It's important to ensure that the network bandwidth available to servers is sufficient to handle client connections in real life.

The type of messages used during the test is another item to bear in mind. Unless you customize the test by adding a set of messages you have determined to be typical, the set of default messages are quite simple. Some of the default messages contain Word and Excel attachments, and there's even one with an embedded bitmap image. Useful as these messages are they may not reflect the type of messages sent by your users, and they don't test the impact of users sending very large messages or messages with lots of complex attachments. They do, however, deliver a reasonably weighted average of the type of messages seen in general messaging, which is possibly the type of system you'll operate.

Finally, the server should run the same set of applications during the test that you expect to run in production. Executing a test for Exchange only is useful only if you want to compare one hardware configuration against another, as in the case when you might want to compare two Intel Pentium-powered systems from different vendors against each other. Depending on the other components wrapped around the CPU, two systems with apparently the same CPU type and clock speed can differ in real, delivered performance by 10% or more.

Using the Windows NT Performance Monitor

The Windows NT Performance Monitor provides a graphical interface to allow many different aspects of a Windows NT system to be monitored. The utility provides charting, alerting, and reporting capabilities to report live data as it is generated by applications or to capture performance data to log files for later analysis. Performance Monitor depends on applications having probes or points of measurement buried in the code, ready to provide information to the monitor should the need arise. Windows NT refers to the items being monitored as objects, and objects can be:

► aspects of the system itself such as memory usage
► an individual process
► a section of shared memory
► a physical device

In the case of Exchange Server you'll be interested in monitoring aspects of the many services that collectively deliver functionality to users. Important Exchange objects that can be monitored include:

Table 8.1 *Important Exchange Services for Performance Monitor*

Service Name	Meaning
MSExchangeDS	The Directory Store
MSExchangeISPriv	The Private Information Store
MSExchangeISPub	The Public Information Store
MSExchangeDX	Directory Synchronization
MSExchangeMTA	The MTA
MSExchangeIMC	The Internet Mail Connector

Each object is broken down into 'counters'. Monitoring tracks the counts of specific events and allows system administrators to report what it's found. Normally reporting is done graphically, as shown in Figure 8.14, perhaps on a dedicated workstation. Any counter supported by the Windows NT Performance Monitor can be exposed to and collected by an SNMP network-based monitoring service (such as HP's OpenView product). You can use the PERF2MIB utility (from the Windows NT V3.51 Resource Kit) to generate HP OpenView or IBM NetView compatible MIBs (Management Information Base) from any Performance Monitor counter. The MIBs allow the performance data collected about Exchange to be reported and monitored by these popular SNMP management tools.

When you start a Performance Monitor session you must tell it what objects and counters you're interested in. This process involves selecting from a list of available objects and counters and adding them to the 'workspace', a description of the current monitoring environment.

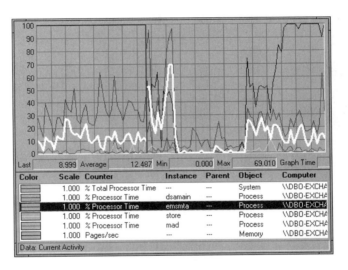

Figure 8.14
'Server Health' Performance Monitor

When you're happy with a set of parameters which record whatever data you need to log the whole scenario can be saved in the form of a workspace file. When you install Exchange Server onto a Windows NT computer a number of prepackaged performance monitor workspaces are installed into the \EXCHANGE\BIN directory. The set of workspaces are divided between five that are useful on all servers and three specifically for servers running the IMC.

Because they have been developed as Exchange Server evolved through the development process and therefore capture the most important statistics based on knowledge of server and system behavior these workspaces describe scenarios that are very usable and useful in their own right. The provided workspaces also serve as an excellent starting point for system administrators who wish to develop performance monitor workspaces tailored to fit their own server environment.

For example, EXHEALTH.PMW holds the parameters for the 'Server Health' workspace illustrated in Figure 8.14. To make things easier for system administrators, pointers to each workspace are created as icons in the Exchange Server program group. Table 8.2 shows a full list of the prepackaged workspaces.

Table 8.2 *Prepackaged Performance Monitor workspaces*

Packaged Performance Monitor workspace	Important statistics tracked in workspace
Server Health	Overall % processor time; % processor used by directory store; % processor used by MTA; % processor used by information store; system paging.
Server Load	Rate messages are delivered to recipients; rate messages are submitted by clients; number of connections to other MTAs; address book activity
Server History (since server was last stated)	Total messages delivered and submitted to users; total messages sent by MTA; total recipients for messages; number of users connected to the server; length of work queues (messages waiting to be processed by the MTA); system paging.
Server Users	Number of users currently connected to the information store.
Server Queues	Number of items in the MTA work queue; number of items in the send and receive queues for the private and public information stores.
IMC Traffic	Number of inbound and outbound connections to other SMTP hosts; number of messages awaiting conversion to and from SMTP/MIME format.
IMC Statistics (since server was last started)	Total number of messages delivered to the Internet Mail Connector and the total number of messages sent out to the Internet.
IMC Queues	Number of messages coming in from the Internet; number of messages going out to the Internet; number of messages waiting final delivery to recipients.

In cases where message submission and delivery activity is being tracked it is normal to collect separate figures for the private and public information store. Private information store activity relates to interpersonal messaging, that is, messages generated and sent between people. Public information store activity relates to messages and other documents posted to public folders. On most servers it would be safe to expect that the private information store gets more work to do than the public, the exception being those servers dedicated to public folder storage.

Which of the prepackaged workspaces are most useful? It all depends on the workload of your servers, but my favorites are:

- Server Health
- Server History
- IMC Traffic

All servers should have some indication that the system is running smoothly. I find the 'Server Health' workspace provides a good overall picture of what's going on at any particular point in time.

Figure 8.14 is a good example of the active workspace. You can see that there is a lot of activity in one of the counters because its line is at the top of the chart at the left-hand side (most recent figures). It's not obvious from the screen shot (because the different colors used for the counters are not reproduced), but the very active counter is system paging, expressed as paging operations per second. The other lines, including that for the MTA counter (shown as the white line), display a fair amount of activity, so clearly this computer is doing a reasonable amount of work. If system paging exhibited the same rate of activity during normal daily operations a system administrator would be worried because it's delivering a strong indication that the computer is overloaded, but in this instance there's a reasonable explanation: the screen shot was taken shortly after the computer was rebooted, and all the system services, including the Exchange services, had just been restarted. Just listen to the disk activity after a system is rebooted and you'll immediately realize that a great deal of work is done in this period, as reflected in the results charted by the counters in the 'System Health' workspace.

As to my other favorites, I like running 'Server History' from time to time just to see what workload the computer has processed since it was last restarted. The figures reported in this chart vary greatly and depend on the number of days since the last reboot. However, a browse through the different counters sometimes provokes questions which should be answered. For example, is there any reason why the computer has processed a larger number of messages than normal?

Systems running the Internet Mail Connector, especially those which connect internal messaging networks to the big (sometimes bad) world of the Internet, need careful monitoring if reliable message delivery times are to be guaranteed to users. The 'IMC Traffic' workspace captures and displays details of all the most important IMC counters.

Feel free to disagree with my opinions. Play around with the pre-packaged workspaces and make changes if you like, but don't add too many counters to any workspace as the chart will become very cluttered and difficult to interpret. The important thing is to ensure that monitoring is a part of day-to-day system administration and not just an activity that's engaged in whenever problems appear on the horizon.

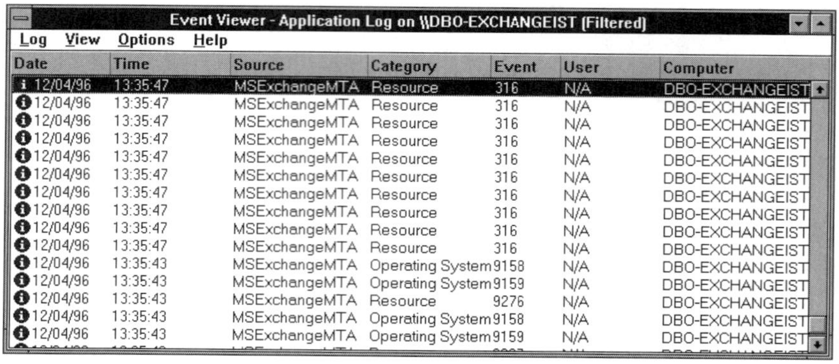

Figure 8.15
Windows NT Event Viewer

Logging and viewing Windows NT events

Windows NT logs a great deal of information about different events that occur during applications and system processing. Event information is initially logged internally, and can be written to a file if required for later analysis, or to be used as evidence relating to a problem. The Windows NT Event Viewer (Figure 8.15) allows you to view event logs on any server you have access to. On any moderately large server many events are generated each day, so filters can be applied if you know you're looking for a particular problem. For example, you could apply a filter to view only events relating to the MTA.

Exchange Server uses the Windows NT Event log to record information specific to the processing performed by Exchange components such as the MTA, Key Management Server, or Internet Mail Connector (to name but a few). All Exchange events are deemed to be 'application' events rather than system or other events. The Exchange Resource Kit contains a number of tools to help you filter and store event information related to Exchange Server.

You can influence the amount of information logged through the diagnostics property of these components, but be aware that it is all too easy to generate vast amounts of data if you enable maximum event logging. Few people have the patience and knowledge to be able to make very much sense of the huge quantity of events logged at full flow by the Exchange MTA. The quantity of data produced when full diagnostic logging is enabled will also exhaust the space reserved for the Event Log after a couple of minutes on any reasonably sized server, forcing you to clear the log and save existing data to a file if you want to continue to record information. For these reasons it's best to leave diagnostic logging at minimal levels in day-to-day operation and reserve full diagnostic levels for the times when it's justified, for instance, when requested by a support center to help track down the root cause of a problem.

Even when minimal diagnostics are enabled the Event log should be browsed on a daily basis to ensure that problems aren't being recorded and then missed. Any event associated with Exchange that is not information status (shown as an 'i' surrounded by a blue circle) must be investigated and the reason why the event was logged determined to your satisfaction. Failure to do this might lead to a situation where a small problem develops into something that's rather more serious.

Event logs should also be checked immediately after a system has been restarted. This step is to ensure that all the Exchange services have started correctly.

The Exchange Resource Kit

All large and complex applications generate spin-offs: small pieces of code (sometimes large pieces of code) that are useful add-ons to standard functionality, or documents which explain finer or less obvious parts of the product. Sometimes the spin-offs are written by engineers to help test functionality or find bugs during the development process, sometimes they're written by people who aren't part of the main development project but are knowledgeable about the product. The Exchange developers have made a collection of useful tools and documents available to you as the 'Exchange Resource Kit'. The Resource Kit can be found in the Exchange section on Microsoft's TechNet CD[3] (from May 1996 onwards) or it can be downloaded from Microsoft's World Wide Web site.[4]

Although I cannot confirm this feeling, I'm fairly confident that many of the tools in the Resource Kit were developed by Microsoft personnel to assist in the migration of their internal messaging system from Microsoft Mail to Exchange Server. The MIGSMTP tool is a classic example of what I mean. MIGSMTP allows old SMTP addresses that were used by the Microsoft Mail SMTP gateway to be imported into the Exchange directory as secondary proxy addresses for users.

---

3. *See the Technical Resource CD-ROM Components section.*
4. *See* **http://www.microsoft.com/Exchange/freesoft.htm** *for kit information. A table of contents for the Resource Kit can be found at* **http://www.microsoft.com/Exchange/techcd.htm** *Note that the Exchange Resource Kit is approx 30Mb (as at May 1996) and will therefore take a long time to download, even over a relatively fast connection. A TechNet subscription looks good value if you want access to 'free' software like this.*

Why is this important? Well, adding those secondary addresses to the directory allows Exchange Server to deliver messages to the right people when messages bearing the 'old' addresses arrive at the IMC. A nice technical feature, but also one that avoids any need for people to reprint business cards that might bear their SMTP address!

It's fair to assume that the code and documents provided in the Resource Kit haven't gone through the same quality assurance process imposed on the regular product. If you elect to follow the suggestions in nonapproved documents or use code that hasn't been through a full quality assurance process you have to live with any of the consequences arising from those actions. Any of the code from the kit I have used appears to be of high quality and is reluctant to fall over, but I can imagine situations where personnel in support centers might be less than happy to deal with installations using what they perceive to be 'nonstandard' code.

Table 8.3 lists the tools included in the Exchange Resource Kit. The listing reflects contents as of May 1996 and is quite likely to change over time. However, the listing will give you a good idea of the type and scope of the tools that can be found in the Resource Kit.

Table 8.3 *Tools in the Exchange Resource Kit*

Tool	Title
Cleanup	Process to clean up multiple client mailboxes
Crystal	Crystal Reports for Exchange. These allow administrators and end users to generate a variety of reports for traffic analysis, load balancing, and usage measurement.
Event log	Tools to analyze Exchange Server events extracted from the system event log. The tools can drive pop-up or e-mail alerts for specific events.
Headers	Tool to create header files for use in directory import and export operations.
IMC Extension	IMC Sample Extension DLL to reroute selective messages arriving at the IMC to other SMTP hosts before they can be processed by the IMC. This tool allows the IMC to serve as a single point of contact for all Internet mail.
IMC Save and Restore	Tools to save and restore IMC configuration data.

Table 8.3 *Tools in the Exchange Resource Kit (continued)*

Tool	Title
Microsoft Mail migration	Tools to facilitate directory import or export between Exchange and other systems – Microsoft Exchange Address Export to Microsoft Mail (EXIMWIZ5); Microsoft Mail proxy to Microsoft Exchange proxy conversion tool (PERL); Microsoft Mail SMTP Gateway Proxy Migration (MIGSMTP)
Preview Pane Extension (PPE)	Preview Pane Extension for Exchange 32-bit clients (see Figure 8.17).
RPC Counter	Count the RPCs passing between an Exchange client and the server.
Bulk Security Tool	Tool to encrypt or decrypt messages in bulk. Especially useful when moving users who have been enabled for advanced security.
Command Line Send Mail	Tool to allow messages to be composed and sent from a Windows 95 or Windows NT command line. This can be used to generate messages to notify when batch jobs are complete, or to notify that a particular condition exists on a server.
Storage Statistics	Extract and report statistics for user mailboxes.

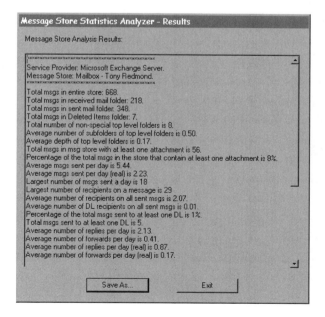

Figure 8.16
Reporting message store statistics

The Exchange modeling tool (see page 68) is also part of the Exchange Resource Kit. Currently, all tools are provided for Intel systems only but versions for other hardware platforms can be expected to be available by the end of 1996. The tools are only available in English, a fact that shouldn't cause too many problems because the majority of nonUS system administrators have been forced to learn English and work with system management utilities through English due to the volume of software originating from the US or UK.

The majority of the extensions packaged in the Resource Kit are directed at system administrators. The usefulness of these tools will depend on the situation in your own company. The Message store statistics analyzer (see Figure 8.16) is of interest if you want to know what's really contained in a user's mailboxes, but you're probably not likely to use the analyzer on a regular basis. On the other hand the mailbox cleanup agent is an automated version of the standard 'Clean Mailbox' administrator program option and is of interest to anyone who wants to keep a tight rein on the number of messages people keep in their mailboxes. Instead of having to manually select the user mailboxes to clean, the mailbox cleanup agent allows cleanups to occur in the background. You can determine which mailboxes are to be cleaned, the folders to be examined, the criteria on which to select messages for deletion and the frequency of clean up operations. Having such a tool at your disposal is a great help in the continuing battle to keep control of information store resources.

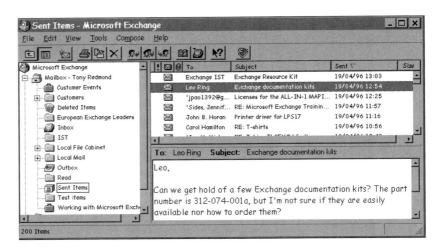

Figure 8.17
Exchange client for Windows 95 with the Preview Pane Extension

Anyone engaged in the often onerous task of setting up and maintaining directory synchronization between Exchange Server and other messaging systems will be glad of the tools that graphically aid to create directory header files or help convert Exchange source information to the format demanded by other systems. The best example in this respect is Exchange to Microsoft Mail.

Other items in the Resource Kit are of interest from a user perspective and can be used on a daily basis. The preview pane extension allows the first couple of lines from a message to be displayed in a separate pane within the client window, as illustrated in Figure 8.17. Unfortunately this useful tool is only available for 32-bit clients (Windows 95 and Windows NT).

Documentation included in the Exchange Resource Kit

Some interesting and worthwhile documentation is included along with the tools packaged in the Exchange Resource Kit. The most comprehensive documentation is provided for Crystal Reports for Exchange, a good indicative of the wide range of useful reporting features enabled by this tool.

The majority are provided as Word for Windows files (there is one Windows Help file). Each of the tools listed in Table 8.3 has a document containing notes and directions about its use, PPE.DOC, for instance, has installation directions and other information about the preview pane extension. Aside from documentation directly related to tools there are a number of other files that have been put together to document some of the lesser-known or darker corners of Exchange.

- Security procedures: How to set up security in different common Exchange Server situations. For example, how to delegate access to a mailbox, control permissions for a public folder, etc.
- A systems management checklist: things system administrators should do on a regular basis.
- Permissions: details of the different Windows NT and Exchange Server permissions used to control access to different objects stored in the Exchange structures.
- Procedures to rename a server.
- Details about system registry entries which control how the Internet Mail Connector functions.
- The Schedule+ Programmer's Reference manual.

As in the case of any documentation provided on an unsupported basis remember that the information presented must be verified as accurate within your own environment. Don't take anything as being 100% accurate unless you've checked it out.

9

Using Electronic Forms with Exchange Server

Introduction

Out of the box, Microsoft Exchange Server delivers great electronic mail functionality. The only problem is that very few people have been able to make a cogent case to show how electronic mail can provide a true return on the investment necessary for its implementation. Think of all the costs involved in installing servers, linking them together, connecting to other internal and external messaging systems, and the training necessary for system administrators, programmers, and users. Then factor in the costs for ongoing support and system maintenance. Now think about how you can satisfy accountants and prove that your electronic mail system really provides value to the enterprise. It's difficult to do in hard figures. Some intangible benefits can be achieved – better communications, a greater degree of staff engagement with the enterprise's business, and so on. But how can you put real values on such gains?

In my experience electronic mail systems become like the telephone, a necessary cost of doing business – something that you need because if you don't have it you'll be at a competitive disadvantage. This doesn't stop people trying to achieve a return on investment, or looking for software vendors to improve their offerings to enable real, measurable gains can be achieved.

Every copy of Microsoft Exchange Server includes an Application Design Environment (ADE). While the majority of Exchange deployments will initially concentrate on establishing a solid electronic mail infrastructure, there's no doubt that the potential to create applications on top of that infrastructure is a very attractive proposition to many enterprises. Using public folders to distribute data is a logical and progressive step forward from interpersonal electronic mail, and building electronic form-based applications to leverage off electronic mail and public folders completes the cycle. The ADE includes the components necessary to build those electronic form applications, or at least, to build simple to moderately complex applications and provide the basis for more complex applications to be finished off.

Many industry consultants predict that the ability to easily and quickly generate electronic forms applications is one of Exchange's major competitive advantages. We'll only know if this assertion is true in a couple of years when we'll be able to review just how many applications are in use in production environments. It would be a pity if electronic forms applications entered into a perpetual cycle of iterative rapid applications development, constantly changing as programmers think of new features to add, lured into this attitude by the ease of development and deployment. Avoiding this pitfall by entering into development projects with a clear end goal and exit criteria in mind is as important with electronic forms as it is with mainframe COBOL projects.

The remainder of this chapter reviews some of the major points about the Exchange ADE and how it can be used. It does not pretend to be an application developer's guide, nor is it a primer for electronic forms development. It will whet your appetite enough for you to know whether you're interested in building some electronic form applications. If you are you should consult the Exchange Application Designer's Guide.

Components of the Exchange Application Design application

The major components of the Exchange ADE are:

- The Electronic Forms Designer (Figure 9.1). As the name implies this tool allows programmers to design the shape and appearance of a new form, or generate custom help for a form. At the end of the design process code for the form can be generated. The generated code is in native Visual Basic (V4.0) format.

- Despite the fact that over four million copies of Visual Basic have been sold to date, not everyone has Visual Basic installed on their PC. To get around this issue a special run time version of the Visual Basic V4.0 programming language is included with the forms designer. Visual Basic is used to compile electronic form applications so that they can be distributed for execution. The special version of Visual Basic operates separately from the retail version, but can be called by clicking on VB.EXE in the \EFDFORMS\VB directory.

The Form Template Wizard helps programmers get going with the task of generating a new form application. Like the wizards in other applications the Template Wizard asks some questions about the type of application that you want to generate and then selects one of a set of template forms and uses that as the basis of the new form. When it's finished you'll find that the wizard has created a skeleton of the new form. All you have to do is complete the job by adding or amending fields and properties, and perhaps extending the Visual Basic code that's generated by the forms designer. Unfortunately whereas the wizard can do its job in a matter of minutes, the task of completion can take many iterations over a number of days. Automation is great, but human programming talent is still needed to complete the job.

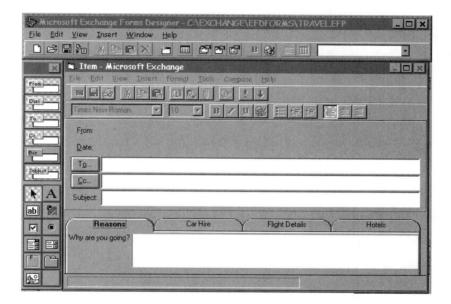

Figure 9.1
Electronic Forms Designer

The forms designer allows programmers to place different field types onto a form. It also allows you to determine whether your application can work with only one form or if it needs to use multiple forms. You might want to use one form to create an item and a different form to read or respond to it. As mentioned earlier, the contact tracking sample application comes complete with five different forms to allow users to enter different types of information.

Fields on e-forms are divided into header and body fields. Header fields are used to hold addressing and subject information for forms, basically the type of information you'd need to add whenever you create and send a normal message. Fields to hold TO: , CC: and BCC: addressing information are all supported, as are Subject, From (the person who sends the message), and Date (the date and time the message was sent). Quite logically each type of header field can only appear once in a form. It would be very confusing if you had multiple fields to enter TO: recipients into!

Where header information is fairly common across forms the data held in body fields differ from form to form because this is where application-specific information is held. The most important body field types are:

- Text labels (display-only)
- Text entry
- Check box and Option buttons
- ComboBox and ListBox
- Rich entry
- Picture Box

You can also use frame and tab fields in the format layout. Frames are used to create a visual container for a number of other fields. However, frames have largely been superseded by tab fields in the latest generation of Windows applications. Tabs also create visual containers for other fields, but unlike frames, tabs create additional panels for the form. Panels allow you to include many more fields in the form than would otherwise be possible.

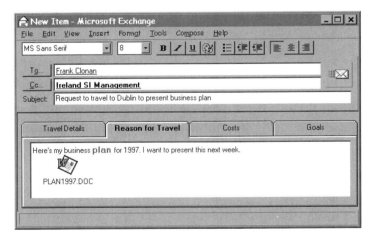

Figure 9.2
Embedding a file into an electronic form

Rich entry fields are especially interesting. In their basic form they allow users to enter text formatted with features such as different fonts, type sizes, colors, bullet points, italics, and bolding. A rich entry field can be extended to permit users to insert files (attachments) into the field, just like you can drag a file from the Windows Explorer and drop it into a regular Exchange message. This feature allows you to build applications that include Excel worksheets, Word documents, or files from many other Windows applications. Only one extended rich entry field can be defined per form.

Data storage

When someone uses an electronic form to generate a new item all of the data supplied by the user is written into the information store. Just like messages the data from electronic forms is stored as fields within the database. Each field defined on a form is allocated a reference name property, and together with the name of the form the reference name is used to locate the data for the field within the information store. Exchange uses the reference name to locate data for each field when a form is loaded. You can give a field whatever reference name you want, but it's important that the name for each field is unique if you want Exchange to be able to locate the right data when a form is loaded.

Figure 9.3
Setting properties for an e-form

Forms are identified internally within Exchange by an item type name. A number of standard items are used in every Exchange system – messages, posts, Schedule+ meeting notices, and so on. Exchange uses the item type to search a lookup table at run time to locate the correct form to activate. All items created from a form inherit that form's item type. Microsoft recommends that you follow a convention of *IPM.Vendor.Form* when creating a item type. IPM means 'Interpersonal Message' while vendor and form are the names of the person or company who created the form and a descriptive name for the form itself. Figure 9.3 illustrates the properties of a Travel Request form I created. If you don't specify an item type Exchange will do it for you, but the result is 'IPM' followed by a long series of numbers. Although such an item type is guaranteed to be unique and can easily be located by a computer, it isn't very human friendly.

Some reference names have special meanings. As discussed earlier (and illustrated in Figure 9.2) it's possible to allow rich entry fields to support embedded files. In this case users are able to include Word for Windows documents to help justify a business trip. The ability to support embedded files is controlled by the special `MAPI_Body_Custom` reference name which can be allocated to a single rich entry field per form. Rich entry fields given any other name won't allow users to insert files into the field.

Field names are supplemented with column names. A column name can be used in the criteria for creating customized views for folders containing e-forms. Column names appear in the dialog boxes used to create views, including Group By, Sort, and Filter.

What types of e-forms applications can I build?

Microsoft Exchange e-form applications can be divided into two categories. The first category can be thought of as electronic representations of paper forms. Instead of circulating written information via paper mail you complete an electronic form and circulate its contents in the same manner as electronic messages. The second category of applications allows users to enter structured data via forms and store that data in folders. Folder views can be used to organize the data in various ways, while public folder replication can be used to distribute the data to wherever it is required within the organization.

Because Exchange treats forms in the same way as any other object it might be called upon to store in a folder you can even write rules to check for new items that have been created through a form and added to a folder. For instance, if you write a help desk application to track the progress of support calls you might want to have a rule to forward a copy of each new item (the calls arriving at the help desk) to the help desk supervisor as users post items into the Help Desk folder.

Microsoft calls the first category 'form applications', and the second 'folder applications'. Sometimes they are referred to as 'send' and 'post', referring to the way that users send electronic forms or post data to a folder. Either term can be used in a discussion about e-forms.

Using the sample applications as a starting point

Microsoft has done a reasonable job in providing a range of sample electronic forms applications with Exchange. Sample applications are difficult to generate. They must be generic enough to make sense to a very wide audience, yet functional enough to be useful as a basis for a fully developed application. The sample applications must also demonstrate the possibilities and potential that can be realized through electronic forms. The sample applications include forms that have been generated entirely through the electronic forms designer utility as well as forms which have been extended with Visual Basic code added after the form has been generated by the forms designer.

Chess is the most famous, or at least the most demonstrated, of the extended applications. The Chess form is used to conduct a complete game of chess between users who communicate their moves to each other by entering moves (in chess notation) into an electronic form. A display section in the form allows the user to see how the game is progressing and the effect of their proposed move. When the player is happy the form can be sent to their opponent. This is an updated version of the old play-by-(paper)-mail form of chess. I don't think many people will have the patience to complete a full game but that isn't important. Like most sample applications the intention behind the Chess e-form is to get your creative juices flowing so that you can imagine the possibilities that open up through electronic forms.

Writing extensions to the code generated (almost automatically) by the forms designer allows programmers to add features to applications that aren't supported by the forms designer. You can write code to extract data from a form once it has been processed and write the data into a corporate database. You could use data from a database to populate fields in a newly created form. Extensions are easiest to write in Visual Basic because the code generated by the forms designer is Visual Basic. It's slightly more painful and convoluted to introduce bespoke code written in any other language but it's possible to do so, as we'll discuss later on. The majority of the sample applications are folder applications. The most interesting of these is the Contact Tracking application. This is an application built up of five forms to use when entering information about companies and contacts important to your business. The application includes some custom folder views to organize the forms into company name or contact name order. Apart from Chess, the most interesting of the form (or send) applications is Schedule Time Away. This form shows how to integrate Schedule+ into an application and includes features to allow users to apply for vacation time or report days off due to illness.

Developing a new e-form application

Figure 9.4 illustrates four major stages within the e-forms development cycle.

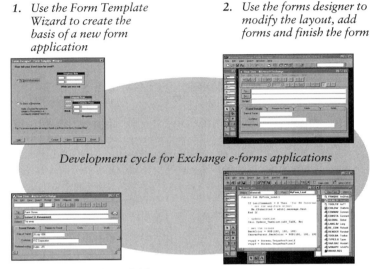

Figure 9.4 *The e-forms development cycle*

1. Use the Form Template Wizard to create the basis of a new form application
2. Use the forms designer to modify the layout, add forms and finish the form

Development cycle for Exchange e-forms applications

4. Store and send in a folder and let users create and send/post new forms
3. (Optionally) add some Visual Basic code to extend the application's functionality

Briefly, each stage involves:

1. Generation of a skeleton for the new e-form based on one of the form templates distributed with the Exchange forms designer. This activity is performed on your behalf by the template wizard.

2. The generated form contains the fields necessary to post or send an item. It doesn't contain the application-specific fields. For instance, a travel request form may need fields for users to enter information about where they want to travel, when they want to go, and so on. You use the forms designer to add new fields to the form, modify the properties of the form and the fields, and generally satisfy yourself as to the layout and appearance of the form.

3. Once you're happy with the form you can use the *File.Install* option to instruct the forms designer to generate Visual Basic source code for the form. After the Visual Basic code is created it

Developing a new e-form application

is compiled to form an executable. It is at this stage that you can intervene and insert some additional code. Of course you'll have to generate a new executable afterwards.

4. The compiled version of the form is now available for installation into a location where people can use it to create new items. During the (sometimes multiple) iterations of an e-form application's development phase it is usual to store the form in a personal folder, safe from any accidental usage before the form is fully ready. After the form is debugged and everyone is happy with it you can move the form into an organizational form library or public folder. At this stage anyone who has access to the organization form library or public folder will be able to use the form.

Figure 9.5 illustrates a location for an e-form being selected and how the new form is accessed by users afterwards. In this case I have elected to store the e-form in a personal folder, mostly because it was still being developed. The way forms are accessed is similar whether they are in personal or organizational form libraries. Once a folder containing a form is accessed Exchange automatically inserts an option to call the form into the Compose menu.

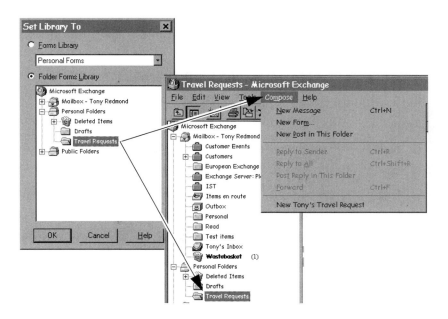

Figure 9.5
Selecting a location for an e-form

The whole process of generating a new e-form application doesn't take very long. Any reasonably skilled programmer who is used to the

Chapter 9

Visual Basic development environment can certainly have a form designed and installed within an hour. A lot of work is performed behind the scenes and without effort on your part, so the actual mechanics of the operation are largely taken care of for you. No amount of automatic code generation will design an application, so you need to know what purpose the form will serve and have an approximate idea of its contents and layout before you begin to create it. Because the design process is painless you can afford to go through a number of iterations before a satisfactory form is achieved, and all of this can be done quickly. Real effort is only required for complicated multi-page forms or applications that require you to create some add-on code by hand.

What skills are needed to create e-forms?

For simple forms the development of a new e-forms application is confined to the boundaries of the forms designer. No special programming skill is required to place fields on the form, allocate field and form properties, and install the form into a folder. All actions can be accomplished through menu options, including the generation of Visual Basic source code for your project. Even if you're never planning to write any code some familiarity with other Microsoft visual programming tools such as Access or Visual Basic is an advantage, if only because you'll recognize the icons for the different field types that are shown in the toolbox. You'll also be accustomed to the positioning and manipulation of fields and how to set properties.

Programming skills come into play when you want to extend the automatically generated source code to add some features that you want to include in the form. Perhaps you want to capture the data collected in the form and stuff it into a database somewhere, or take the data and merge it into a Word for Windows template to create a formatted document for printing. In these cases you'll need to amend the Visual Basic code. You can keep to Visual Basic and write your code in that language or you can use another language, such as Borland Delphi or Visual C++ to create functions in a Windows Dynamic Link Library (DLL). Those functions can then be called from Visual Basic.

Gauging the exact level of skills required to develop or extend an Exchange e-forms application is an impossible task without knowledge of the application. Suffice to say that you can never have too much programming experience when the time comes to create complex applications, but it's easy to find that you have too little and so end up having to read and re-read the programming documentation to discover how to do even the simplest of things.

Where are forms stored?

Once a form has been developed and fully debugged it becomes a candidate for general deployment. You now have to decide where its final storage location will be. The decision can be quite easy as it largely depends on the reason why you developed the form in the first place. Consider the scenarios outlined in Table 9.1.

Table 9.1 *Different e-form types and where they're stored*

Form application scenario	Stored in	Storage location
E-form intended for use throughout the organization; not tied to a specific folder	Organizational forms library	Exchange Server
E-form associated with a specific folder.	Public Folder	Exchange Server
E-form associated with a specific folder but also used off-line	Personal Folder	Client
E-form hidden from general view but used by applications	Local forms	File system

The forms cache

Have you ever wondered why Exchange sometimes loads an electronic form down from the server before a client can begin using the form? The reason why this happens is simple. A local cache, normally 1024Kb in size, is maintained on the client (in the \WINDOWS\FORMS directory). If the form is used regularly the chances are high that the form will be in the local cache and a call to download it from the server won't be necessary. Forms are always downloaded if a new version has been installed in a folder.

The size of forms vary greatly and if a client is using many different forms on a regular basis or the forms applications are complex (and large) then you'll either have to increase the local cache or put up with the minor inconvenience of the delay required for downloading.

The size of the local forms cache can be changed through the Exchange Server property page displayed through the *Tools.Option* menu option (see Figure 9.6). Clients achieve better performance with larger caches, primarily by avoiding the need to download commonly used forms. The setting is specific to each client.

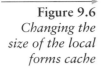
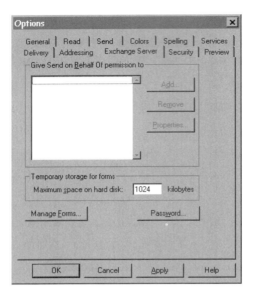

Figure 9.6
Changing the size of the local forms cache

Using the sample applications

The set of sample applications packaged with Exchange can be used to provide a solid base for your own applications. The code already exists. It's solidly written by people who knew what they were doing, and if you're able to create a new application through a process of cutting and pasting it's a great way to get the job done. Apart from anything else it's also going to reduce the elapsed time considerably.

The sample applications packaged with the Exchange kit are only one source of potential code. Even with the storage capacity available on CDs there will always be a limit on the amount of sample code that will be shipped with an application if only for the reason that once it's on a product CD that code needs to be supported in some respect. If you look at the TechNet CD you'll find an 'application farm'. This is a set of e-form applications written by various individuals within Microsoft. These applications may not have received the same type of testing as the 'official' sample code but they're still more than useful.

Creating a new e-forms application from one of the samples is easy. Start up the electronic forms designer, open the sample application you want to use, and begin to make changes. All you need to do afterwards is remember to save your changes under a different name so that you have the original (if you ever need to start over) as well as the new application.

Issues around Workflow and multiple platforms

It's important to note that real workflow is not currently part of the e-forms development environment. Microsoft is working on workflow capabilities for Exchange through their MAPI-WorkFlow FrameWork initiative, but in the interim if you need a true workflow application, one that supports serial and parallel routing, enables different roles for users to interact with the contents of the document, and is intelligent enough to know how to split a routing path and rejoin it after a parallel routing step has been executed, then you should consider a third party extension. Judging by the plans announced by a number of vendors I'm sure that there will be many of these available on the market as momentum builds behind Exchange.

Another issue is multi-platform coverage. Exchange e-form applications can only be used by clients that understand what an e-form is and how it can be processed. Exchange only runs on Windows NT so don't expect that people who use another operating system will be able to participate in electronic forms applications. This fact illustrates one of the eternal problems facing anyone who wants to begin the process of evolution towards the nirvana of the paperless office. Converting a paper form to an electronic version is all very well, but unless everyone who may want to use that form or who needs to participate in its processing are connected to the system you'll have to maintain both paper and electronic versions. Even worse, you may end up having to create some form of reconciliation between the two versions, especially if any data is collected via the form.

10

Bringing It All Together – How to Proceed

10 things you'll enjoy about Exchange Server

These are the best things I've enjoyed when working with Exchange Server. Selecting aspects of a product that are pleasing is a very personal activity so feel free to disagree… The points are not listed in any order of importance because they're all important.

1. *MAPI.* The power and flexibility of the Messaging Application Program Interface can be seen in Microsoft's own clients as well as the MAPI service providers appearing from other vendors.

2. *Exchange clients* are easy and powerful to use, even if they require fairly substantial hardware resources for truly satisfactory performance. Microsoft has followed its own user interface standards to good effect.

3. *Single point of administration.* Maybe it's missing some features that I'd like to see included, but the Exchange Administration program is the most integrated messaging administration utility I've encountered to date.

4. *The transactional nature of the information store* is a huge advance on Microsoft's previous file sharing architecture. It's also at the centre of Exchange's ability to scale up for corporate implementations.

5. *The Exchange MTA* almost manages to bring plug and play capabilities to the e-mail world. It also coordinates connectors for different messaging systems in a very nice manner.

6. *The Exchange Resource Kit* is a mine of useful information. It's backed up by TechNet. Together a lot of knowledge and useful tools on Exchange, Windows NT, and other products are available for those who care to search it out.

7. *Advanced security* delivers encryption and digital signatures for those who really need it. You have to invest time and energy to deploy advanced security, but once it's implemented advanced security delivers what it promises.

8. *Integration between a messaging system and its host operating system* has moved to a new level with Exchange. Account management, performance monitor, event logging, backup, and all the other points of integration make Windows NT and Exchange work together in a great combination act.

9. *Electronic forms* won't be at the top of everyone's list of things to do because getting the messaging infrastructure right is the must-do priority. But e-forms hold a lot of promise for the future, or even the present for some. Advanced workflow capabilities in future releases of Exchange will build on a solid base.

10. *The Load Simulation utility* is something every messaging system should provide. Being able to conduct your own automated benchmarks is great!

Some things that aren't so good

Nothing in life is ever perfect, and Exchange Server certainly doesn't attain that unreachable standard (despite the best efforts of Microsoft's undoubted marketing muscle). I have my own black list of pitfalls and imperfections. I imagine that Microsoft will address many of these as new versions of Exchange are rolled out over the next few years. At least, I hope they will. In the meantime you can avoid these areas of difficulty!

- *Directory synchronization* is the black hole of Exchange because lots of system administrators will spend many aimless hours wandering around unless they run a pure Exchange environment or only ever have to synchronize with Microsoft Mail. Moving away from the antiquated scheme used to synchronize the Microsoft Mail global address list to support a standard (and API) for directory synchronization is an essential step for the future. Directory synchronization should occupy many hours of Exchange administrators' time and be a happy hunting ground for third party tools.

- *The migration source extractors* vary in quality. I wonder how some managed to get through Microsoft's normally excellent QA cycle. They are certainly nowhere near the same level of quality achieved elsewhere in Exchange.

- *Intersite mailbox transfers* is not easy. Why can't it be as easy as moving a mailbox within a site?

- *Interorganization communications* (aside from messaging) doesn't appear to have been considered necessary. But people will move between operating companies within a group, or from an organizational unit in one country to another where each country wants to do its own thing. In short, it's not always going to be possible to go with a single organizational unit so it would be nice to be able to have items like advanced security, scheduling, user mailbox moves, and public folder replication supported on an interorganization basis.

- *Conflict handling* for updates applied to multiple copies of a document in a replicated public folder is not neat. Surely it should be possible to lock a document for exclusive write access without having to set permissions on the entire folder each time?

- *Backups are great, but restores aren't* Accidents will happen and restores will be necessary. Restoring a user mailbox without having to restore the entire information store would save a lot of time and money. In fact, needing to restore the entire information store when problems arise is going to cause a lot of system managers sleepness nights. Be sure you have a 'hot-box' server waiting to swap in to replace failed hardware, and practice restores, just in case.

- *The integration and dependency with Windows NT is a double-edged sword* because it's all too easy to mess up an Exchange implementation by not paying enough attention to the underlying Windows NT infrastructure. Microsoft can't do much about this point, but I make it yet again in the hope that a loud and clear message goes out – get Windows NT right first before trying to do anything with Exchange.

10 essential points to get right when implementing Exchange Server

Distilling the content of a complete book into a single page is not easy, but lots of people demand a road-map to follow when planning the implementation of Exchange Server. With this request in mind I have created my own 'Top-10' issues to consider and decide upon before an implementation begins. These issues are not presented in order of importance. However, it's obvious that the first three issues should be tackled before anything else. While I encourage you to conduct a pilot so that you gain valuable experience with Exchange, experience that will enable you to build a better plan afterwards, it is critical to have a clear and well thought-through plan before you commence a full implementation. Experience is a hard master, but it tells that taking shortcuts just to get a system into operation can have disastrous consequences afterwards!

Table 10.1 *10 essential points*

	Issue	*See chapter(s):*
1	Design the Windows NT infrastructure.	2
2	Plan how Windows NT will be layered onto the internal network.	2
3	Chart out the Exchange organization in terms of the sites and servers. Determine how the sites will communicate in terms of message flow, public folders, and all aspects of replication.	2
4	Determine what platforms are to be used for both servers and clients. Will you use Windows 95 or NT on the desktop? Also, what hardware configurations will be used for both clients and servers?	3
5	Design the naming conventions for use within the Exchange organization – sites, servers, and mailboxes.	2, 4
6	Determine where the points of external communications will lie and what connectors (SMTP, X.400, Microsoft Mail, others) will be used to connect Exchange Server with other mail systems.	2, 5
7	Look at how public folders can be used to address business needs and requirements within your enterprise. What folders are needed? Where will they be located? Who will control their content? Will electronic forms be required?	4
8	Consider how the Windows NT computers will be managed. What system administration policies will be implemented to cover important topics such as backups?	4
9	If you are migrating from another electronic mail system what plan are you going to follow to migrate users and their data to Exchange Server?	7
10	Create a training plan that accommodates the needs of users, programmers, and system administrators so that the true power of Microsoft Exchange Server can be unleashed.	6

Acronyms

Acronyms

The language of electronic messaging technology is full of acronyms. This section describes many of the acronyms used in a Microsoft Exchange environment.

BDC: *Backup domain controller.* A Windows NT server allocated the task of acting as a backup to the Primary Domain Controller (PDC) in case a problem arises with the PDC.

CA: *Certification Authority.* The Key Management Server is the Exchange component which acts as a certification authority to control X.509 security certificates.

CAST: A proprietary encryption algorithm developed by Northern Telecom.

CCITT: In English, the *International Consultative Committee on Telephony and Telegraphy*, a body concerned with the formulation and definition of standards for electronic communications. The CCITT is a sub-delegation of the International Telegraph Union (ITU).

DDA: *Domain Defined Attribute.* A DDA can be encapsulated in an X.400 O/R address to allow routing to occur through an X.400 network to a gateway which takes the DDA and uses it to deliver the message to its final recipient. In such cases the DDA holds the recipient's address in the format used by the mail system serviced by the gateway.

DES: *Data Encryption Standard.* An encryption algorithm developed by the US National Bureau of Standards.

DHCP: *Dynamic Host Control Program.*

DIB: *X.500 Directory Information Base.*

DIT: *X.500 Directory Information Tree.*

DMD: *Directory Management Domain.* The collection of DUAs and DSAs within an X500 directory. In an Exchange organization the DMD is represented by the set of directory services run in all sites.

DN: *X.500 Distinguished Name* composed of a set of RDNs.

DNS: *Domain Name Service.* The part of TCP/IP networks that contains and provides information about networked computer systems, basically by looking up computer names and providing the IP addresses for those that can be resolved.

DSA: *Directory Service Agent.* An X.500 concept of a computer process responsible for handling directory queries initiated by a DUA. The DSA will either satisfy the request itself or consult with another DSA.

DUA: *Directory User Agent.* An X.500 concept of a computer process that makes queries against an X.500 directory on behalf of a user.

DXA: *Directory Synchronization Agent.* The Exchange component responsible for synchronizing the contents of MS-Mail Global Address Lists and the Exchange directory.

FQDN: *Fully Qualified Domain Name.* An Internet (or Intranet) name for a computer which contains all the necessary pieces to allow data to be routed back to the computer.

GAL: *Global Address List.*

GWART: *Gateway Address Routing Table.* The internal routing table used by the Exchange MTA to determine how messages can be routed through all the connectors and gateways operating within an organization.

ISP: *Internet Service Provider.* A company which provides internet connectivity to other companies or individuals.

ISO: *International Organization for Standardization.*

ITU: *International Telegraph Union.*

KCC: *Knowledge Consistency Checker.* An Exchange component responsible for tracking the various links and connections that exist between different sites.

KMS: *Key Management Server.*

LDAP: *Lightweight Directory Access Protocol.* A protocol used by clients to access X.500-based directory services.

MAPI: Microsoft's *Messaging Application Programming Interface.*

MIB : *Management Information Base* for SNMP systems.

MTA: *Message Transfer Agent.*

Mail Exchanger: A type of record stored in DNS databases.

NDR: *Non Delivery Report.* A special form of message sent back to users if a message they send can't be delivered.

NNTP : *NetNews Transfer Protocol.*

PDC: *Primary Domain Controller.* The Windows NT server that validates all authentication and security requests within a domain. The PDC also maintains the definitive copy of the security database for the domain.

RAID: *Redundant Array of Inexpensive Disks.*

RAS: *Remote Access Server.* The component of Windows NT that permits dial-in or asynchronous connections to be made between a client and a Windows NT computer.

RDN: *Relative Distinguished Name.* A name used to navigate within the Exchange directory.

RFC: *Request for Comment.* An Internet standard.

RSA: A public key encryption standard developed by Ron Rivest, Adi Shamir, and Leonard Adleman at the Massachusetts Institute of Technology in 1977.

SMTP: *Simple Mail Transport Protocol.* SMTP is the de facto standard for electronic mail within the Internet.

SNMP: *Simple Network Management Protocol.* A protocol allowing applications and other components to be managed across a distributed network.

SPI: *Service Provider Interface.*

WINS: *Windows Internet Name Service.*

X.400: The international standard for electronic mail interchange.

X.500: The international standard for electronic directory services.

XAPI: X/Open Application Programming Interface.

XDS: X/Open Directory Services.

Useful Points of Reference

World Wide Web sites

Much useful information about Microsoft Exchange server or associated products is available from World Wide Web sites. These include:

http://www.microsoft.com/exchange/	General information about Microsoft Exchange Server
http://www.microsoft.com/backoffice/	General information about Microsoft BackOffice and Windows NT
http://www.microsoft.com/Exchange/freesoft.htm	Exchange Resource Kit
http://www.microsoft.com/TechNet	Microsoft TechNet information, including subscriptions
http://www.digital.com/	Home page for Digital Equipment Corporation
http://altavista.digital.com/	Alta Vista Search Engine
http://www.anjura.com/exchfaq/	Exchange Server Frequently Asked Questions (FAQ)
http://www.fenestrae.com	Fenestrae FAX connector for Exchange
http://www.facsys.com	FAXIS FAX connector for Exchange.
http://www.linkage.com	LinkAge connectivity products
http://www.integralis.co.uk	Integralis 'MIMEsweeper' virus checker

Internet Mailing List for Exchange

The Internet Mailing List for Microsoft Exchange is available by sending an electronic mail message to msexchange-request@insite.co.uk

The word SUBSCRIBE should appear in the body of the message. Do not include any other text. Leave the subject line blank.

Appendix

Client auto-upgrades

Auto-upgrade relies on:

- An entry in the client's system registry pointing to a local installation point. The entry is at:

HKEY_LOCAL_MACHINE\SOFTWARE\Microsoft\Exchange\Client\UpgradePath

and stores a UNC path like:

\\OFFICENT1\EXCHANGE\CLIENTS\WINDOWS95

- The version number for the client software. A comparison is made between the version number of the running client and the version stored in the EXCHNG.STF file at the location pointed to by the system registry. The version information is read from the 'App Version' string on the second line of the file.

The auto-upgrade mechanism is totally unsupported by Microsoft so no GUI utility is provided to control it. Everything must be done manually, either by making the necessary entry in the system registry on each client PC (very boring), or by editing the EXCHNG.STF file at the local installation point so that the necessary data is written into the system registry when Exchange client software is installed on PCs.

The contents of file EXCHNG.STF are used to drive SETUP.EXE, the standard Windows installation program, to drive the installation of Exchange client software. To enable the autoupgrade feature a line must be added to the end of EXCHNG.STF (any text editor can be used to do this) to instruct SETUP to either write a line into the system registry (for Windows NT and Windows 95 clients), or into EXCHNG.INI, the Exchange application initialization file used by Windows V3.1 clients. The relevant commands are:

▶ *Windows 95 and Windows NT*

```
nnnn AddRegData """LOCAL""","Software\Microsoft\Exchange\Client""", ""UpgradePath""",
"""\\OFFICENT1\EXCHANGE\CLIENTS\WINDOWS95""".
```

▶ *Windows V3.1*

```
nnnn AddIniLine """EXCHNG.INI""", ""Microsoft Exchange""", ""UpgradePath""",
"""\\OFFICENT1\EXCHANGE\CLIENTS\WINV31"""
```

nnnn indicates a line number within EXCHNG.STF. Add one to the value of the last line number shown in EXCHNG.STF and use this value for the new line. For example, if the last line is 1070, the correct line number to use is 1071. The instructions in STF files appear in groups and you must add a reference to the new line number in order to have SETUP process the instruction. Look back a couple of lines to find the last group statement, a line preceded by its own line number and containing the word 'Group' followed by references to a set of numbers. For example:

1067   Yes   Group 1068 1069 1070

Change the group statement by adding the line number containing the command to the end of the line as shown below.

1067 Group 1068 1069 1070 1071

After you have saved EXCHNG.STF and exited from the editor, perform a client installation to make sure that everything has worked as planned. After the client installation finishes, check the contents of the system registry (Windows NT or Windows 95) or EXCHNG.INI (for Windows V3.1) to make sure that the correct values have been written. For example, assuming that the AddIniFile command shown above is added to EXCHNG.STF, the relevant entry in EXCHNG.INI should appear like this:

[Microsoft Exchange]

Upgradepath=\\OFFICENT1\EXCHANGE\CLIENTS\WINV31

Because AutoUpgrade is not supported it's reasonable to expect that some limitations exist. Briefly, these are:

▶ Schedule+ is not supported. Only the Exchange client can be upgraded in this manner so separate arrangements need to be made for Schedule+. In addition, if Schedule+ is started before Exchange the user will never see an AutoUpgrade prompt even if newer client software is available.

- AutoUpgrade does not function properly in a shared application/local operating system environment. In other words, autoupgrade isn't good if users run local copies of Windows on their PCs.
- A considerable load is generated on the server if lots of clients discover the need to upgrade at one time. For example, if you install new client software overnight you can expect lots of demand for upgrade installations the next morning when users arrive and connect to the server. Depending on the number of clients involved and the configuration and capacity of the server this could slow down server responsiveness significantly. However, this is not an ongoing problem and only occurs after each upgrade of the client software.
- DOS clients are not supported.

AutoUpgrade is a convenient feature for hard-pressed system administrators, as long as the restrictions don't conflict with your system configurations. The preferred approach from a Microsoft perspective is to use SMS to upgrade client software. Using SMS has a major advantage in that the same method works for all applications, but installing and operating SMS costs time and money as it is most appropriately deployed on a separate Windows NT server. A further cost is incurred in the licensing of SQL Server, required by SMS. You could therefore view AutoUpgrade as a short-term tactical solution until you get the time and money to install and implement SMS.

While you may not think that you'll have to upgrade clients much in the future patches and new versions will appear over time, and users will want to upgrade. Putting the structure in place now to enable quick and easy upgrades seems like a proactive step to take, even if Microsoft doesn't formally support the feature.

Index

File name index

ADMIN.EXE 15,12
AUTOSIGN.SIG 114
CONTROL.GLB 279
DB000001.DAT 233
DIR.EDB 150, 285
DIR.PAT 192
EDB.CHK 154
EDB.LOG 151, 152
EDB00001.LOG 160
EXCHNG.INI 395
EXCHNG.STF 132, 395
EXSERVER.MDB 71
GWART0.MTA 224
KMSPWD.INI 207, 208
LOADSIM.EXE 353
MASTER.GLB 279
NETWORK.GLB 279, 280
NTBACKUP.EXE 186, 191, 194
PERFOPT.LOG 342, 343
PRIV.EDB 150, 155
PRIV.PAT 192
PUB.EDB 150, 155
PUB.PAT 192
REGEDIT.EXE 130
REGEDT32.EXE 158
RES1.LOG 154, 155
RES2.LOG 154, 155
SIMPORT.EXE 211
WINAT.EXE 190
WINMAIL.DAT 258, 274
yyyymmdd.LOG (message tracking) 348

File type index

.EPF 213
.OST 168, 169
.PKL 325
.PMW 361
.PRI 325
.PST 129–30, 166–7
.SEC 325
.SIM 355

Main index

A

ADMIN.EXE 12
  /R switch ('raw mode') 15
Administration (and management) – *see also Exchange Resource Kit*
  ADMIN.EXE
    NT workstation 12
    /R switch ('raw mode')
  automated tools 68
  connectors 228
  disk space – *see also Disk space*
    Exchange System Attendant 161
    freeing up 161
  Exchange Load Simulator (LoadSim–LOADSIM.EXE) 353–4
    analyzing results 359
    examples 356, 359
    LsLog utility 357–9
    message attachments 359
    test phases 354–5
    warnings 357
  Exchange Server Modeling Tool 69
  ISWIPE utility – a warning 357
  Key Management Server 198
  message tracking 347–53
  mailboxes
    'Clean Mailbox' 162–3
  permissions 87
  replication control – *see Directory replication*
  reports
    Crystal Reports for Exchange 162
  Setup Editor 132
  software installations and upgrades 16
  TechNet CD-ROM 68
  user mailboxes 118
    user mailbox reports 162
  message tracking 347
    message identifiers 347–8
    Message Tracking Center 351–3
    Track Message command 349–52
    tracking logs 348–9
  monitors
    link 346–7
    server 345–6
  Performance Optimizer 104, 341
    '-v' switch 342
    memory and RISC systems 344–5
    PERFOPT.LOG output log 342–3
    purpose of 342

settings 341
Windows NT – *see also Windows NT*
   Domain Planner 69
   events–viewing and logging 364–5
   Performance Monitor 360
   PERF2MIB utility 360
   workspace files 361–3
Alias Name 124
   auto-name generation 124
   %Last%1First 125
ALL-IN-1 – *see Digital Equipment Corporation*
APIs
   MAPI 16, 17 – *see also MAPI*
   VIM 17
Apple Macintosh 22
Application Design Environment (ADE) 41, 371–2
   Electronic Forms Designer 373
   Visual Basic 372
Arcada's Backup Exec 187
AT.EXE (command line scheduler) 191
Attachments
   and electronic forms 374
   and LoadSim testing 359
   OLE and X.400 252
   WINMAIL.DAT 258
Authors
   document-collaboration issues 181–3
AutoSignature 314
   AUTOSIGN.SIG file 114
   and bitmaps 113
   and network traffic 113
Automated software distribution 6

B

BackOffice 5, 314
   components
      Internet Information Server (IIS) 5
      SNA Server 5
      SQL Server 4
      Systems Management Server 5
      Windows NT Server 4
   Exchange and SMS 5
   license 5
   SNA server 5
   SQL server 5
Backups 186, 189
   Backup Domain Controller (BDC) 194
   circular logging, effect of 158, 187
   Exchange Performance Optimizer 194
   hardware failure 188
      server substitution 193–4
   Key Management 198
   LoadSim sessions 357
   log-file purging 154
   making 190
      NTBACKUP 190
   MTBF (Mean Time Between Failure) 188
   NTBACKUP.EXE 186, 194
      Exchange enhancements 186
   off-line 191
      and circular logging 187
      and Exchange databases 192
      vs. on-line 191
   patch files 192–3
      DIR.PAT 192
      PRIV.PAT 192
      PUB.PAT 192
   PST storage 167
   RAID-compliant disks 188
   recovery host 196
   restoring 189, 193
      a BDC – SAM (security database) implications 195
      an Exchange server 193
      a PDC – SAM (security database) implications 194–5
      public folders 197–8
      single documents 197
      single mailboxes 196–7
   strategy 188
   third party utilities 188
      Arcada's Backup Exec 187
   time reduction and EDBUTIL 200
Bastion hosts 271
BDC 61–2, 65–6
BLOBS 197
Bottlenecks
   avoiding message 235
   Internet list servers 275
Bridgehead
   Directory Replication Bridgehead 292–3
   server 236
      concept of 235
Briefcase
   icon 169

C

CCITT 241
Certification Authority 206
Character sets
   and data migration 332
   UNICODE 2

Circular logging 157
    effect on backups 158, 187
    enabling 157
    and REGEDT32.EXE 158
Client auto-upgrades 395
    using AutoUpgrade 397
        limitations 396
    and EXCHNG.INI 395
    and EXCHNG.STF 395
    using SMS 397
    warning 136
Client
    default settings 131–2
    disk space allocations 166
    international languages 2
    platform
        Macintosh 22
        selecting 33
        Windows-95 33
        Windows NT 33
        UNIX support 22
    Private Information Store 16Gb limit 166
    sample desktop configurations 37
    Setup Editor 132
    software upgrades 25
Clustering 107–9
    for messaging systems 107
    systems under development 108
Collaborative authoring (concurrent document editing) 180–1
    distributed updates (problems) 182–3
    techniques 182
Commonality (message sharing)
    effect on disk space 165
CompuServe
    installing the service provider 25
Conflict message 183–4
Connectors 11, 234
    availability
        included in 'standard' Exchange edition 219
        optional, list of 221–2
        purchasing extra 219
    bottlenecks (avoiding) 235–6
    configuring 223
        Address Space 224–5
        Connected Sites 224
    defined (as third-party gateways) 9
    FAX but no telex 223
    Internet mail – *see Internet Mail Connector*
    licensing 228–9
    linking sites 219, 237
    direct site connector 219
    domains and trust 239
    Dynamic Remote Access (RAS) connector 219
    four connector types 219
    Internet Mail – *see Internet Mail Connector*
    making the connection 239
    X.400 connector 219
    links to the MTA 219
    loading
        message-generation activities 230
        planning 234–5
    MHS 223
    Microsoft Mail 220
    multiple addresses 289
    multiple site-connectors
        cost–value scale 238–9
    proxy addresses 287–8
    RAS and X.25 links 220
    Remote Procedure Calls (RPCs) 219
    selecting 238
        types of 219
    site 236, 269 – *see also X.400*
        configuring 240
        standard site connector 237
    SMTP 221 – *see also SMTP*
    states 227
    X.400 221 – *see also X.400*
        loading 252
CONTROL.GLB 279
Crystal Reports for Exchange 162, 369
Custom recipients 118
    DDA – in the routing table 225

D

Data exchange
    inter-organization 59
Databases
    DBDATA directory 150
    BLOBS 197
    Directory Store – *see Directory Store*
    EDBUTIL (compacting) 155, 200
    Exchange 150
        'Database Paths' page 151
        locations and types 150
    fragmentation 198
        defragmenting databases with EDBUTIL 200
    Information Store – *see Information Store*
    technology
        Jet technology 147–8, 192
        used by Exchange 147–8
        SQL Server story 147

DB000001.DAT 233
Deleted Items folder 131, 160–1
Deleting
   messages 161
Desktop computing environments
   Microsoft-based desktop system 46–7
      cost of upgrading 35
      which one? 34–5
      sample configurations 36–7
Diagnostics Logging
   MSExchangeIS Private 120
Digital Equipment Corporation xi
   ALL-IN-1 323–4, 330, 332
      migrating from 324
         data types (and migration) 332
         macro code issue (and migration) 328
         Server – accessing 31
         Mailworks 328
   Alta Vista Directory Services 299
   bastion hosts and 'dec.com' 271–2
   clustering 108
   Digital Drivers for MAPI 31
   StorageWorks 111
   TeamLinks 328
   VAXclusters 107
   Web site 47
   MailWorks for UNIX 31
DIR.EDB 150, 285
DIR.PAT 192
Directory Development Kit 10
Directory Information Base
   and X.500 283
   directory schema 283–4
Directory Information Tree (DIT) 286
   X.500 283
Directory replication 58, 88, 294–5
   between organizations 58
   forcing 297
   Directory Replication Bridgehead 292–3
      Knowledge Consistency Checker 294
   Directory Replication Connector 291–3
   Directory Replication Schedule 296
      understanding 296
Directory Restrictions 116
Directory Service 282
   Directory Service Agents (DSAs) 286–7
   X.500 283–5
Directory Store 8, 94
   DIR.EDB 150
   and disk activity 150
   Patch File 192

Directory Synchronization 9, 114, 291, 334
   between organizations 297
      manual workaround 297
   Directory Development Kit 10
   'foreign' directories 298–9
   Knowledge Consistency Checker 294
   transitive connections 292
   Update Sequence Numbers (USNs) 294
Directory Synchronization Agent (DXA) 298
Directory User Agents (DUAs) 286–7
DirSync Requestor 298–9
DirSync Server 298–9
Disk Administrator (Windows NT) 111
Disk mirroring 110
Disk space
   calculating clients per server 166
   calculating space per client 166
   compressing PST files 167
   effect of Private Information Store 16Gb
   e-mail attachments 156
   exceeding alloted quota
      Exchange System Attendant 161
   exhausting 155–6
      common reasons 156
   freeing up 157, 161
      moving messages to PST files 167
   message storage 164
   monitoring with Windows NT Event Viewer 156
   RES1.LOG and RES2.LOG 155
   shared message model
      perceived storage 164–5
   and shutdowns 155
   system checks management
      of disk space 160
   and system migrations 327, 333–4
   usage and commonality (message sharing) 165
   user allocations 159–60
Display name 123
   auto-name generation 124
   example 123–4
Distinguished name 287
Distributed directory
   chaining and referral 8
Distributing information 137–8 – *see also Public folders*
Distribution lists 116, 118
   delivery restrictions 117
   expansion 226
   object limits 118
   and permissions 118
   storage 116

Index 403

Document management system
    Exchange Server as 185
    third-party products 185
Domain (defined) 60 – *see also Windows NT*
    Backup Domain Controllers (BDCs) 61
    boundaries
        joining sites across 84
    controllers 61
    domain models 63
        complete trust domain model 63, 66–7, 72
        multiple master domain model 63, 67–8
        single domain model 63–5
        single master domain model 63–6
    logical domain 95
    NT structure and Exchange installation 71
    Primary Domain Controller 61
    security database 61
    structure and installation 73
    trust relationships 62–3
    Windows NT Domain Planner 69
DNS (Domain Name Server) 271
    IP addresses 271
    Mail Exchanger records 272
    FQDNs and IP addresses 272–3
DOS clients 21

E

EDB.CHK 154
EDB.LOG 152
EDB00001.LOG 160
EDBUTIL 193, 199, 200
    database compacting 155
    locating 201
e-forms – *see Electronic forms*
Electronic Data Interchange (EDI) 78, 105
Electronic forms 42, 371–3
    building
        developing new applications 378
        development cycle 378–9
        electronic forms designer 42, 372
        'form' and 'folder' applications 376
        skills required 380
        using the sample applications 377
        Visual Basic, Borland Delphi, Visual C++ 380
    embedding a file 374
    fields 373
        body field types 374
        reference name property 375
        rich entry fields 374
    form storage 379, 381
    forms cache 381–2

    item type
        document inheritance 375
        multi-platform issues 383
        setting properties 375
        workflow 383
Electronic Mail Association (EMA) 251
Electronic signatures 206–7, 214
E-mail – *see also Messages*
    document viewers 29
        OutSide In 30
        Quick View Plus 30
    'green screen' variety 26
    growth of messaging activity 53
    huge file attachments 53–4
    Internets and Intranets 48
    legal actions 121
    privileged user access 120
E-mail addresses
    multiple 287–8
Enable Advanced Security 211
Encryption 201
    across the Internet 204
    basic concepts 204–5
    Entrust™ Security Technology 204
    and Internet Mail Connector 204
    keys
        .EPF files 205–6
        Certification Authority 206
        losing 205–6
        Key Management Server 206
        private/public key usage 205
        source of 209
    of PST files 167
    resources to decrypt 203
    RSA MD5 algorithm 204
    software
        french embargo 203
        US Defense Messaging System (DMS) 203
Exchange Administrator program 15, 122
Exchange clients
    client–server comunication (RPCs) 13
    functions of 26, 28–30
    non-Microsoft sources 30
    service providers for other mail servers 13
Exchange directory
    mailbox entries 116
    recipients container 116
Exchange Load Simulator 353–7
Exchange Modeling Tool 70
Exchange Resource Kit 365, 385
    Crystal Reports for Exchange 162, 369

documentation included 369
mailbox cleanup agent 163
MIGSMTP 365
SMTP message rerouting 275
STORSTAT utility 162
tools included 366–7
Web site URL 365
Exchange server (computer)
    constituent parts 8
        Directory Store 8
        Information Store 8
        Message Transfer Agent (MTA) 8
    enterprise edition – defined 10
    proliferation problems 73–4
Exchanger Server
    vs. Lotus Notes workflow 314
Exchange Server (software) instalation 83–4
    account used 72–3
    avoid the Primary Domain Controller 194
    defining organizations, sites and servers 55–6
    implementation 55
        10 essential points 387–8
        considering NT's domain model 60
        domain model 63
    instalation point – shared 132
    and NT infrastructure 71
    planning 55–6
        inter-organization issues 58–9
        messaging patterns 56
        network connections 57–8
        site designation 57
        user allocation 57
    piloting 302, 319, 321
        how long for? 321
        and Microsoft Mail 301
        plan 320–1
        questions to address 302–4
        review process 307–8
        training 305
        training for good user-habits 305–6
        training for programmers and administrators 306
        trial data imports 327
        and Windows NT 302
    privileged accounts 72
Exchange Setup Editor 162
Exchange System Attendant 161
EXCHANGE.PRO 131
EXCHNG.INI 395
EXCHNG.STF 132, 395
EXSERVER.MDB 71

F

Fault tolerance 109
    Disk Administrator 111
    disk duplexing 110
    disk mirroring 110
    disk striping 110
    hot-swapping 111
    RAID 110
Favorites
    public folder 172
Firewall 48–9
Folder Assistant 179
FQDN 272
FTBP15 (1992) 250–1

G

Gateway Address Routing Table (GWART) 224–6
Gateways 235–6, 336–8 – see also Connectors
Global address list 116, 286
    address validation 125
Groupware 40–1
    capabilities of Exchange 40–1
    cost of developing applications 45
    Exchange and electronic forms 42 – see also Electronic forms
    Exchange Server as? 39
    Exchange vs. Lotus notes 41
    Lotus Notes 41
GWART0.MTA 224
GWART1.MTA 224

H

Hardware requirements 91
    comparing processors 102
    disk drives
        FAT-formatted drives 103–4
        RAID 109–10
    disk space 12 – see also Disk space
        allocating to users 100
    Disk striping 103
    for Exchange clients 35–6
    Exchange Load Simulator 353–7
    Exchange vs. Microsoft Mail 36
    for Exchange Server 11
    load sources 93
        distribution 96
        Load Simulator program 104
        types of user 99, 100
    network 112
        adapter 112

Index

additional network demand 112
peak-time messaging 93
sample server configurations 103
selecting the hardware platform 100–101
system sizing 92–4, 96
    message activity 93
    sizing tables 92
typical hardware configurations 101–2
using a single server 95–6
Windows NT 100–101
for Windows NT V3.51 or V4.0 11
for Windows NT and Windows-95 34–5

Help desk
    call causes 6
    reducing calls 33
    requests to change directory data 126
Hot-swapping 111
HTML 49, 50
    dynamic generation 50

I

IBM 3270s
    no exchange support 26
IBM PROFS 222, 281, 323
IBM SNADS 222
Inbox Assistant 135, 314
Information Store 8, 94
    creating new 147
    data migrations and disk space 327
    and disk activity 150
    maintenance 198
        EDBUTIL 199, 200
        ISINTEG 199, 200
        off-line maintenance 199
        on-line 198–9
    PRIV.EDB and PUB.EDB 150
    and public folder replication 8
    size limit 145
    unique features of 8
Installation – *see Exchange Server (installation)*
Internet 47–8, 51, 103 – *see also Internet Mail Connector*
    bastion hosts 271
    blocking access to 271
    connecting to 270
        controlling connections 270
    corporate messaging solution? 48
    DHCP
        allocating IP addresses 266
        and the DNS 273
        and encrypted messages 204

Exchange mailing list 330, 393
Internet Assistant for Word for Windows 49
Internet Engineering Task Force (IETF) 261
Internet Information Server 49
for inter-organization data exchange 59
ISAPI Internet Programming Interface 51
list servers 275
    mail traffic 275
load, as an external source of 113–4
making a direct connection 265
message
    flow management 275
    list servers 275
    restricting size of 271
    traffic levels 275–6
messaging backbone 79
Microsoft Internet Information Server 51
and PGP (Pretty Good Privacy) 203
Request for Comments (RFCs) 261
security issues 49 – *see also Security*
    secure tunneling 48
support in Exchange Server 49, 50
    Exchange Internet News Connector 50
UUENCODE 262
Internet Mail Connector 76, 85, 103, 261
    Address Space
        '*.com' 267
        blocking IP addresses 270
        cost=1 267
        leaving blank 268
    blocking Internet access
        Delivery Restriction property page 271
    effect on system performance 105
    instead of site connector 269–70
    IP addresses 265, 272
        DNS records and FQDNs 272–3
        and the Domain Name Server 271
    list servers – managing messages 275
    message flow 266
        MTS-IN folder 267
        MTS-OUT hidden folder 266–7
        QUEUE.DAT message-tracking file 266
    and message encryption 204
    MIME support
        RFC 1522 and RFC 1521 262
    operation notes 267
    Out of Office Assistant
        preventing usage 270
    Rich Text Format and MIME 262
    setting Internet interoperability options 271
    SMTP

dedicated relay host 268
host – message proxies 268
and MIME 262
support for RFC-821 and RFC-822 261
UUENCODE support 262
viewing Windows NT events 364
Windows NT TCP/IP dependence 265
    FQDN (Fully Qualified Domain Name) 265
X.400 78
Internet Service Provider (ISP) 273
Intranet
    defined 48
ISINTEG 193, 200
    Information Store Integrity Checker 199
    locating 201
ISWIPE utility
    warning 357
ITU X.509 205

J

Jet Blue 147

K

Key Management Server 9, 204, 206, 208–9, 213, 217
    installing 207
    Master Encryption Key 207
        KMSPWD.INI 207–8
    viewing Windows NT events 364
Keys and certificates 205
KMSPWD.INI 207–8
Knowledge Consistency Checker (KCC) 294

L

Lawyers
    'discovery' actions 121–2
    and e-mail archives 121
    FAX vs. telex in legal disputes 223
Licenses
    for client access 11
Link monitors 346–7
LMHOSTS file 272
LoadSim (Exchange Load Simulator – LOADSIM.EXE) 106, 353–4
    and pre-run backups 357
Log files
    backups and EDB.LOG 154
    circular logging 157
    from message tracking 348–9
    from Performance Optimizer 342
    from server monitors 346
    generated by LoadSim 357–9
    locating, for performance 153
    and PRIV.EDB 155
    and PUB.EDB 155
    purging and backups 154
    RES1.LOG and RES2.LOG 154–5
    transaction log 151–2
        EDB.CHK 154
        EDB.LOG 151–2
        EDBxxxxx.LOG numbering 153
        forcing log-file creation 152
        forcing transactions 152
Lotus cc:Mail 323
Lotus Notes
    connecting to Exchange 44
    vs. Exchange Server 43–5
        Lotus and Microsoft debate papers 45
    migrating databases to Exchange 44
    Release-4 43, 45
        encryption algorithms 202
    and replication 136
    and Soft*Switch 222
LSLOG utility 357–9

M

Mail
    encryption 59
    remote mail 135
    folders
        Inbox, OutBox, Sent Items, Deleted Items 169
    systems
        and Exchange connectors 8
        MTAs and linking to 8
Mailbox 120
    accesses by privileged accounts 120
    account names and Exchange Server 123
    Alias Name 124
    analyzing users' 162
    Clean Mailbox 162–3
    creating 122
    delegation 126–8
    Display Name 123
    entries
        'Hide from Address Book' 116
        delivery restrictions 117
        Directory Restrictions 116
        interesting properties 116
        multiple containers 117–8
    Global Address List 116
    logging privileged access 120
    mailbox cleanup agent 163

Index

maintaining details 125
managing user mailboxes 118, 119
moving between servers 128–9
moving between sites 129–30
Private Information Store 120
setting restrictions 159–60
surrogacy 126
Windows NT accounts 119–20, 122
MAPI 13, 16, 32, 148, 256
    client limitations 32
    Common Mail Calls 18
    Digital Drivers for MAPI 31
    MAPI-Workflow Framework (MAPI-WF) 41
    MBDEF – Message Bodypart Encoding 252–3
    mixing clients and servers 32
    profile 30
    Simple MAPI 17
    structure 18
    and TAPI 17
    variations of 17
    and WOSA 17
    and X.400 258
MBDEF (Message Bodypart Encoding Format) 252–3, 256
MCI Mail 222
Messages
    address validation 125
    archiving, retrieval, and searching 121
    attachments
        auto detection of file formats 255
        file extensions 254
        file extensions – corporate standards 255
        file format confusion 254
        SMTP and RFC 1521/1522 262
        UUENCODE – RFC 1154 262
        vs. public folders 179
    bottlenecks, avoiding 235
    conflict 183–4
    character sets 262
    deletion 161
        Deleted Items folder 161
    encoding schemes 255
        MAPI, MBDEF, MIME, TNEF 256
    encryption 201
        nonsecure recipients 214
    format conversion
        unforeseen side effects 265
    growth of, planning 162
    integrity
        'hash' value 207
    Internet-generated traffic 275–6

keeping secret 201
moving to PST files 167
Non Delivery Report 267
nonrepudiation 206–7
queues
    internal ordering 232
    managing 229–31
    priority 231
    X.400 252
restoring deleted 197
returned 228
    MBDEF 253
Rich Text Messages, sending 273–4
signed
    icon for 215
storage 164
types exchanged between sites 237
using proxies 268
Message identifier
    viewing 347–8
Message model
    shared 149
        advantages 149
        commonality effects 165–6
        effect on perceived storage space 164–5
        message pointers 149
    single 149
Message routing 223
    algorithm 226–7
    default retry interval 228
    routing table
        DDA-type entries 225
        forcing a rebuild 224–5
        X400-type entries 226
Message tracking 347–53
    Message Tracking Center 351–2
Messaging backbone
    selecting 75–9
Metcalfe's Law 48
MHS 222–3
    and X.400 245–6
MIBs (Management Information Base)
    PERF2MIB conversion utility 360
Microsoft Certified Professional 7
Microsoft Internet Explorer 25, 42, 47
Microsoft Mail 17, 20, 24, 36, 52, 91, 168, 220, 301
    and BackOffice-2 5
    connector
        components of 277–8
        configuring 279–80

message routing 280
post office 277–9
connecting to 276
Directory Synchronization Agent (DXA) 276
DirSync Requestor 298
DirSync Server 298
Exchange and compatibility 15
gateways 281
and Macintosh 11,12, 23
migrating from 36, 315
  advantages 282
  using existing gateways 281
NETWORK.GLB 280
and piloting Exchange 301
synchronization tools 10
and the Universal Inbox 24
upgrading to Exchange 37
X.25 276
migration
  application-specific data
    20/20 spreadsheet utility (Access Technology) 332
    character sets 332
    possible export methods 332–3
  breaking-up the user population (phasing) 328–9
  determining cost 317
    existing investment 312
    justifying expenditure 318–9
    questions to address 316
    returns on your new investment 315–6
    upgrading vs. migrating 317–8
  extracting and importing data 325–6
    disk space implications 327, 333–4
    from host-based systems 326
    migration tools 327–8
    packing list file (.PKL filetype) 325
    primary intermediate files (.PRI filetype) 325
    problems with PC format files 328
    secondary intermediate files (.SEC filetype) 325
  from ALL-IN-1
    application-specific data 332
    data types 332
    macro code issue 328
  from host-based systems
    ALL-IN-1 324
    data volumes 325
    steps 324–5
    Verimation MEMO 324
  from Microsoft Mail 315
  from systems without a wizard
    do-it-yourself? 330–1

gaining functionality 314
getting help 329
  CompuServe or the Microsoft Network 330
Migration Wizard 315, 323–8
  cc:Mail export bug 330
  how long will it take? 327
phasing
  coexisting with other messaging systems 334–5
  maintaining addressing sources 338–9
  operating gateways 336–8
  users, transfering per week 322
plan 320–1
questions to address 309–10
  why migrate? 311
strategic computing platforms 312–3
  IBM MVS 313
  OpenVMS 313
  Windows NT 313–4
statistics, gathering operational 310–1
types of, and pilots 319
user community preferences 314
wizards and tools 323
  'Wizard'-supported messaging systems 323–4
MIME 221, 256, 270, 274
  converting OLE objects 264
  RFC-1521 and RFC-1522 262
  and SMTP 77–8, 262
MTA 221–2, 226, 236, 239 – *see also Connectors*
  data files 233
  'foreign' X.400 MTAs 8
  Gateway Address Routing Table (GWART) 224
  message queues 232
    viewing 229, 231
  message routing 223, 226, 228
  sliding window protocol 232
    adjusting settings 232–3
  the MTACHECK utility 233
    '/f' and '/v' switches 234
  X.400 221
    transport stacks 242
MTACHECK utility 233
  '/f' and '/v' switches 234

N

Naming contexts 87
Naming systems 79–81
  organization and sites 81–2
Netscape 47
NetWare V3.11
  upgrading from 3
NetWare V4

Index

vs. Windows NT 3
Network traffic
   caused by the World Wide Web 114
   and directory updates 126
   e-mail attachments 112
   public folder replication 141–2
   reducing messaging activity 179
   sources of load
      replication 137
      World Wide Web and Internet 114
NETWORK.GLB 279, 280
Nonrepudiation 207
NTBACKUP.EXE 186, 191, 194
   Exchange enhancements 186

O

OfficeVision 9, 222
Off-line storage folders 133, 168–9
   .OST files 168–9
   briefcase icon 169
   synchronizing 170
      synchronization log 170
   user profile settings 169
OLE 46
   and X.400 body parts 252
   MIME conversion 264
   properties, completed by users 46
   and TNEF 256
   to MS-Mail clients 279
OLPGDATA.MDB 71
Open Systems Interconnection (OSI) 241
OpenVMS 31, 108
   ALL-IN-1 31–2
OSTC (Open Systems Testing Consortium) 254
Out of Office Assistant 270
Outlook 37–8
   and Office-97 37

P

Password – *see Security*
Patch files 192
PDC 61–2, 65
PERF2MIB utility 360
PERFOPT.LOG 343
Performance
   disk striping 110
   spreading users across servers 106
Performance Optimizer – *see Administration*
Permissions 87–8
   and distribution lists 118
   naming contexts 87

and roles 89–90
Personal Address Book (PAB) 133
Personal Information Stores (PST files) 133, 166
   stored on floppy disk 133
PGP (Pretty Good Privacy) 203
PING 272
   and link monitors 346
Pre-installed software
   problems in a networked environment 6
Pretty name
   and display name 123–4
Primary Domain Controller 96, 194
   keeping separate from Exchange Server 194
PRIV.EDB 150, 155
   impact of LoadSim sessions 357
PRIV.PAT 192
Private Information Store 120, 145, 179, 237
   16Gb limit 145, 159, 165
   general properties 146
   how to delete 146
   Patch File 192
   viewing space used 162
Profile 30
   contents of 13
   Exchange profile 131, 134
   'hot' PC 134
   multiple-user profiles 13, 30
   for service providers 13
Profile Information 133
PROFS 9, 324
   connecting sites 222
Proxies 268
PST 168
   files 166–7
      encryption 167
   moving messages to 167
   using for mail delivery 167
PUB.EDB 150, 155
   impact of LoadSim sessions 357
PUB.PAT 192
Public Folder Resources 174–5
Public folders 42, 116, 118, 138
   access rights 177
   accessed from the Web 50
   affinity 140
   age limits 174
   collaborative authoring 180–1
      distributed updates (problems) 182–3
      techniques 182
   dedicated server 146
   roles 177–8

setting 178
distributing 114
favorites 172
hiding 144–5
moving 144
    between servers 179
object types stored 141
off-line 169
permissions and deletions 143
planning issues 171–2
reducing messaging activity 179
replacing attachments 180
replicas and affinities 137–8
replication 137–8
    and affinity 139
    and the Information Store 8
    traffic 141–2
restoring 197–8
settings
    Folder Assistant 179
sharing across organizations 58–9
side effect of deletions 143
space allocated
    Public Folder Resources 174–5
time expiration limits 173–4
to minimize network traffic 113
used with the Web 50
and USENET 50
Public Information Store 142, 146, 171, 174
    16Gb limit per server 171
    Instances 144
    managing 171
    Patch File 192
    transactions for 155

R

RAID 109–10
    'hot-swapping' 111
    levels of 110
    RAID-1 and disk mirroring 110–11
    RAID-5 and disk striping 111
RAS (remote access services) 227
    and Inbox Assistant 135
    Windows 95 Dial-Up Networking 135
Recipient types 115
    custom recipients 116
    distribution lists 116
    mailboxes 116
    public folders 116
Recovery host 196
REGEDT32.EXE

and circular logging 158
Registry editor
    REGEDIT.EXE 130
    system registry 131
        REGEDIT32.EXE 158
    changing settings 158
    REGEDT32.EXE 158
Relay host 271
Removing a system 845
Replication 136, 183
    control 140
    defined 136
    defining rules 142
    network load 137
    philosophy 143
    public folder 137–8
    scheduling and transaction logs 153
    and SETUP \R 194
    status 142–3
    with Exchange Server 136, 137
Replication Bridgeheads 292
RES1.LOG 154–5
RES2.LOG 154–5
Restores – *see Backups*
RFC 1154 262
RFC 1521 262
RFC 1522 262
RFC 821 and RFC 822 261
Rich Text Format (RTF) 46, 262
    and AUTOSIGN.SIG 114
Rights 89
Roaming users 133–5
    .EPF file implications 213
    and PST storage 167
Roles 177
    Exchange 88
    and permissions 89–90
    public folders 177–8
    and rights 89
RSA security 201

S

SAM 65
    and user numbers 64
Schedule+ 38, 46, 335
    Exchange version 39
    Free/Busy connector 9
    the Office 95 version 39
Security 59, 208
    .EPF files 212–13
    .EPF files and CAST-64 213

Index

Advanced Security 201
  advantages and disadvantages 216–17
  enabling 210–12
  installing 208–9
  using 214
certificates 213
database 61–2
domain controllers 61
encryption 201
  algorithms differ between countries 202
  CAST encryption 201
  CAST-64 in the USA 202
  DES (Data Encryption Standard) 202
  DES encryption 201
  PGP (Pretty Good Privacy) 203
Exchange's reliance on Windows NT 59, 60
installing advanced security 207
keeping messages secret 201
Key Management Server 198, 204
keys
  and certificates 205
  recovering lost 214
  source of 209
location of security objects 215
model 63
Out of Office Assistant
  preventing usage 270
password 127
  and advanced security 207–8
  encrypted password files 134
  file, moving between computers 134
  of security administrator 208
  PAB 134
  and PST files 167
  users, swapping – Exchange solutions 127
and PST 167
RSA security 201
Security Account Manager (SAM) 60
security workload 61–2
swapping passwords
  Exchange solutions 127
system components 210
temporary credentials 212
  SIMPORT.EXE 211
user authentication 60, 61
Windows NT NetLogon 60
X.400 76
X.509 213
  certificate 215
Server monitor 345–6
Service packs 11, 85
  for NT 86
  number 4 for Windows NT V3.51 11
Service providers 25
  client-centric 13
  defined 12
  profiles for users 13
SETUP
  '\R' switch 194
Setup Editor 132, 133
  EXCHNG.STF 132
  steps to use 132
Shutdown
  and disk space 155
Simple MAPI 18
SIMPORT.EXE 211
Site
  defined 56
  connector – *see Connectors*
  discrete 57
  how many? 82–3
  joining across domains 84
  moving users between 129
SMS 5
  automated software distribution 6
  creating a software inventory 5
  the need for 5, 6
SMTP 76–9, 104, 116, 220–1, 229, 270
  address
    example 77
    rerouting 274–5
  compared to X.400 76–8
    factors involved 78–9
  compound messages 77
  conversations 262
  dedicated server 264
  defined 76
  external addressees 269
  Internet Mail Connector 261, 264
  message
    encryption 204
    processing steps 263–4
    routing 268
  and MIME 77–8, 262
  OLE objects and MIME 264
  or X.400, the choice 75
  relay hosts 268
SNADS 9
Server software upgrades
  service packs 85–6
Software inventory
  creating with SMS 5

SQL Server 4
    and Exchange databases 147
    do you need it? 5
Standalone systems
    integrating 73, 74
STORSTAT utility 162
System Attendant 9

T

TAPI 17
TCP/IP 3, 47, 76, 269
    connection to port-25 267
    Exchange and Intranets 14
    SMTP 262
    Windows NT 12
    Windows Sockets 13
    X.400 example 259
TechNet CD 7, 68, 382
Telex 223
Text retrieval
    third-party products 185
TNEF (Transport Neutral Encapsulation Format) 256, 274
    and X.400 256–7
Training 305
Transactions
    forcing 152
Travel
    and off-line folders 170
Trust relationships 62, 84 – *see also Domains*

U

Underscores
    avoid in addresses 123
UNICODE 2, 279
Unified organization
    creating 73
Universal Inbox 25, 51
    confusion with the 'full' Exchange client 23–4
    focus for developing Exchange extensions 42
    renamed as 'Windows Messaging' 24
    replacing Microsoft Mail clients 24
UNIX 22
    Insignia Software 22
    Sun Solaris 22
Update Sequence Numbers (USNs) 294
URL (defined) 47
    Exchange support for 49, 180
US National Bureau of Standards
    and encryption standards 202
USENET
    and Exchange Server 50
User
    allocating to servers 106–7, 128, 145
    categories 98–100
    disk space 159
        setting limits 159–60
    habits and network traffic 113–4
    mailboxes
        analysis – *see STORSTAT*
        cleaning 163
        per server 106
        setting mailbox limits 159–60
    moving between servers 179
    names 118
        naming principles 119
        and 'pretty name' 122
    profile 130
        off-line storage folders 169
    registration 115
UUENCODE 267, 274

V

VB.EXE 372
Verimation MEMO 323
    migration from 324
Video Terminals (VTs)
    no support for 26
Virus checking 175
    document viruses 176–7
        Microsoft Word 'prank' macro 176
Visual Basic V4.0
    and Application Design Environment (ADE) 372
    and electronic forms 380

W

White papers (Microsoft)
    where to get them 7
WINAT.EXE 190
Windows-95
    16- and 32-bit hybrid 33
    as a client platform 33
    'free' Exchange client 23
    Plus pack 25
    Universal Inbox 13, 23–4
        connecting to a fax, CompuServe etc. 25
    vs. Windows NT 34
Windows NT 59, 63, 87
    account naming 122
        20-character limit 123
        surname-based 122–3
        underscore problems 123

accounts and messaging 119–20
backup utility 187
client platform 33–4
clustering 108–9
common platform for Exchange 4
Disk Administrator utility 111
domain
    defined 60
    Domain Planner 69, 70
    domain controllers 61
    models 63
    Primary Domain Controller (PDC) 60
    trust model 60
duplexed disks 110
Event Viewer and disk space 156
growing influence 3
Lotus Notes (integration) 43
machine accounts 65
migrating to 34
mirrored disks 110
naming systems 79–81
    organization and sites 81–2
Performance Monitor 360
platform independence 100
privileged accounts 72
RAID 110
reasons to choose NT 3
    NetWare4 4
Remote Access Server 135
Resource Kit 7, 360
'Server' and 'Workstation' 12, 56
Services for Macintosh 12
supported X.25 card (Eicon Technologies) 220
TCP/IP for Windows NT 12
trust relationships 62
user accounts 122
utilities
    'Services' option and Exchanger Server management 9
    vs. NetWare4 3
    vs. Windows-95 34
WINAT.EXE 190
X.25 277
Windows NT V4.0 34, 51
    relationship to Exchanger Server 56
Windows registry 130
Windows Sockets 13, 14
Windows-95
    briefcase 134
    Universal Inbox 23
WINMAIL.DAT 258, 274

WordMail 46
Workflow capabilities 41
World Wide Web 47, 50
    Exchange Web Connector 51
    Front Page software 49
    Microsoft Exchange Web Connector 50
    sites
        http://www.digital.com 47
        http://www.microsoft.com/exchange 85
    source of network load 114
    URLs 47
    useful sources 393
WOSA 17

X

X.25 277
    and MS-Mail 276
    and RAS connectors 220
    and Windows NT 277
    Windows NT card (Eicon Technology) 220
X.400 75, 77–9, 104, 116, 220–1, 227, 229, 237, 240–1, 292
    address – *see X.400 address*
    advantages as a site connector 241–2
    attachments
        file format information 250
    body parts 248–9
        and OLE objects 252
        body-part-9, 249
    compared to SMTP 76–8
        factors involved 78–9
    connector
        connecting 2 sites 259
        loading and traffic 252
        'Remote clients support MAPI' check box 256
        setting up (questions to ask) 257–8
        site connector properties 259
        stack properties 260
    effect on performance 105
    encoding schemes 251–2
        P1 253, 256
        P2 (1984) 252–3, 256
        P22 (1988) 252–3, 256
    Exchange and interoperability 253, 260
        ADMDs tested 254
        BP14, BP15 254
        EUROSINET (Europe) 253
        OSINET (USA) 253
        PTTs 254
        setting X.400 interoperability options 261
        TCP/IP connections 254

TP0 over X.25 254
TP4 over CLNP links 254
and Exchange naming 124
file tagging 249
   confusing system connections 249
MAPI 258
MBDEF message failures 253
Message Handling System 246
messaging model 244–5
and MHS 245–6
MTA
   configuring 243
   transport stacks 242
O/R address example 289
OID (object identifier) 250
reference model 245
server monitors 346
and TNEF 256–7
using with Exchange 241, 248
the various recommendations 243–4
vs. SMTP, the choice 75
and WINMAIL.DAT 258
X.400 address 288–9, 291
   administrative domain (ADMD) 290
   common name 290
   example 290
   ISO 3166 standard 290

'O/R address', or 'Originator/Recipient address' 289
   organizational units 290
   private management domain (PRMD) 290
   vs. X.500 directory entries 289
X.400 body parts
   body-part-15 249
   FTBP15 (1992) 250–1
X.500 240–4, 284, 299
   DAP (Directory Access Protocol) 244
   Directory Information Base 283
   Directory Information Tree (DIT) 283
   Directory Service Agents (DSAs) 286–7
   Directory User Agents (DUAs) 286–7
   and Exchange directory 283–5
      DIR.EDB 285
   Lightweight Directory Access Protocol 244
   naming 285
      X.500 Distinguished Name 285–6
   Object Classes
      Exchange Directory 284
   XDS (X.500 Directory Services) API 244
X.500 directory entries
   and X.400 addresses 289
X.509 213

Y

yyyymmdd.LOG (message tracking) 348